Scribe Publications
HELL-BENT

Douglas Newton was born in Sydney in 1952 and is a retired academic, having taught European history at the Victoria University of Wellington, New Zealand, in 1986–90, and at the University of Western Sydney for the following eighteen years. His special interests are peace and war in the period 1890–1919. He has published academic studies of the peace movement before 1914, the peacemaking of 1918–1919, and Germany in the period of Weimar and Nazism, and is currently preparing a history of the struggle for a negotiated peace during the Great War. He lives in Sydney.

By the same author

British Labour, European Socialism, and the Struggle for Peace,
1889–1914

Germany 1918–1945: from days of hope to years of horror

British Policy and the Weimar Republic, 1918–1919

The Darkest Days: the truth behind Britain's rush to war, 1914

HELL-BENT

Australia's leap into
the Great War

DOUGLAS NEWTON

SCRIBE

Melbourne • London

Scribe Publications Pty Ltd
18–20 Edward St, Brunswick, Victoria 3056, Australia
50A Kingsway Place, Sans Walk, London, EC1R 0LU, United Kingdom

First published by Scribe 2014

Typeset in 11.5/15.25 pt Minion Pro by the publishers
Printed and bound in Australia by Griffin Press

 The paper this book is printed on is certified against the Forest Stewardship Council® Standards. Griffin Press holds FSC chain of custody certification SGS-COC-005088. FSC promotes environmentally responsible, socially beneficial and economically viable management of the world's forests.

National Library of Australia
Cataloguing-in-Publication data

Newton, Douglas J., author.

Hell-Bent: Australia's leap into the Great War / Douglas Newton.

9781925106060 (paperback)
9781925113365 (e-book)

1. World War, 1914-1918–Participation, Australian. 2. World War, 1914-1918–Participation, British. 3. War, Declaration of–Great Britain. 4. Great Britain–Politics and government–1901-1936. 5. Australia–Politics and government–1901-1914.

940.32241

This project has been assisted by the Australian government through the Australia Council for the Arts, its arts funding and advisory body.

 **Australian Government**

 Australia Council for the Arts

scribepublications.com.au
scribepublications.co.uk

For David Keir and Juliette Kim

'Utterly incredible … The long expected European war has come. A dozen or so diplomats, a score of ministers, and two or three monarchs have been offending one another, so to make things straight they have ordered out millions of peaceful citizens to go and get massacred. The Government have been telling us lies and we believed them. We were committed and we did not know it, so without being attacked or our own interests in any way threatened we joined in. It is an end of Liberalism, of social reform, of progress itself for the moment. And no one can see what the future has in store.'

– *Arthur Ponsonby, Diary, 13 August 1914*

Contents

Introduction

AUSTRALIA WAS BOUND to fight in 1914 — end of story. Australia was constitutionally, politically, and emotionally incapable of any other response than absolute loyalty to the British Empire in 1914 — end of story. That is the proposition advanced in many histories of Australia's Great War. And it is essentially correct, at least in terms of ultimate outcomes. If the British Empire plunged into war in 1914, Australia was indeed bound to fight. No doubt about it.

But should this be the end of the story? Is there really nothing more to investigate in the *manner* of Australia's leap into the Great War?

What if Australia leapt *before* the British themselves? What if Australia publicly offered troops to any destination, entirely at Australia's expense, under the control of the imperial authorities, *before* the British had decided upon war at all? What if Australia offered to transfer her entire newly christened Royal Australian Navy to the British Admiralty *before* the British asked for it?

Then, conceding that the decision for war was always going to be London's, we might ask questions about the interleaving of events in Britain and Australia in the countdown to war. What if the choice for war in London was a very close-run thing, while Australia threw caution to the winds and gave the impression of being eager for action? What if Australia's offer of troops and ships was made at a moment when the British cabinet of Liberal prime minister Herbert Asquith was locked in a dispute between neutralists and interventionists over the need for Britain to intervene at all in a continental war? What if Australia's politicians, competing with each other in the middle of a federal election campaign, made their open-ended offers of assistance to Britain for war at a moment when that British cabinet was tottering on the brink of collapse over the issue of intervention? What if Australia — in a spirit of competition with New Zealand and Canada — made these offers at the very moment prime minister Asquith faced four resignations from his cabinet — in real time, on Monday morning 3 August 1914?

Then the issue of the impact of Australia's offers at the centre of the empire becomes important. What if Australia's apparent champing at the bit had an effect in London? What if Australia's politicians, in a spirit of political competition, gave the impression that the nation was desperate to contribute to an imperial war? What if the Australian politicians' rhetorical boasts of their readiness to throw the last stripling and the last penny into Armageddon were flaunted in the British press? What if they were trumpeted by the British Tory politicians, in a frantic political campaign to steer the Liberal government into war for the sake of Russia and France?

We may search deeper into the detail. What if Australia's eagerness to offer her new navy came at a time when the neutralist British cabinet ministers were furious that Winston Churchill, First Lord of the Admiralty, was ordering naval movements early in the crisis, without cabinet sanction — movements that incited the hard-liners in Russia and France? What if the neutralist faction in Asquith's cabinet, which had long struggled against the idea of throwing a British expeditionary force (BEF) into war in Europe, were hobbled in their efforts by the dominions' public offers of expeditionary forces, to go anywhere, for any objective, defensive or offensive?

As we shall see, all the things suggested in these questions *did* happen on the swift path to the cataclysm of world war in July–August 1914. Therefore, a bland 'end of story' — a fatalistic acceptance that no better outcome was ever possible — undersells the drama, the tragedy, and the infinite possibilities for something better in this story. There is a story here — a new story. New perspectives are possible if we interleave the story of Australia's leap into the Great War and the story of the choice for war in Britain. That is the aim of this book.

This book takes its place in a long parade of works on Australia's Great War. It also appears as the centenary of the Great War occurs, and at a moment when a debate is underway over the proper memorialising of that war. A reader might reasonably ask where this book stands in the tradition, and what it has to contribute to the memorialisation of Australia's Great War.

Let me begin by noting that Australia's first revered historian of the war, Charles Bean, was alive to the dangers of history descending into mere celebration. At Gallipoli in September 1915, he jotted down in his diary instances of Australian gallantry — and instances of men running away. He wrote:

> Well, this is the true side of war – but I wonder if anyone would believe me outside of the army. I've never written higher praise of Australians than is on this page, but the probability is that if I were to put it into print tomorrow the tender Australian public, which only tolerates flattery, and that in its cheapest form, would howl me out of existence. One has some satisfaction in sticking to the truth in spite of the prejudice against it — the satisfaction of putting up a sort of a fight.[1]

Here was a good conviction for the man who would go on to write six volumes, and edit six others, in the twelve-volume *Official History of Australia in the War of 1914–1918*.

Sadly, in telling the story of Australia's 1914 in the *Official History*, Bean did not resist the opportunity to offer flattering history. Australia's small role in the outbreak of war became a tale of democratic audacity in action, at London's expense. In Bean's pages, the young Commonwealth of Australia acted with greater virility than the Mother Country itself in the crisis of July–August 1914. Readers were invited to scorn the prospect of Britain's neutrality, and to take pride in Australia having pushed Britain to face up to her duty. Britain had wobbled — and Australia had put steel into the British wobblers. Moreover, according to Bean, the Australian people endorsed the rush to war. They were enthusiastic about their government's prompt offers of assistance to Britain, and absolutely unanimous that war was the only choice. It was a stand-tall moment for Australia.

Bean's *The Story of Anzac* (1921) included some extraordinary claims. In the last days of peace, he wrote, 'the mass of Australians became possessed of one anxiety alone — the fear that Britain might hold aloof from the war'. Australia was more determined than Britain, explained Bean, because the 'general sense of a democracy seems to point curiously straight in large questions of national honour'. Fortunately, Australia was well prepared for war. Bean praised two men in particular, George Pearce, the Labor defence minister, and Major Brudenell White, the director of military operations, for having made plans for an expeditionary force, and for hiding them — so that they 'officially had no existence'. With these plans in her back pocket, Australia had been able to leap confidently into war. Britain almost shirked 'the test' — but Australians were of different clay. The reaction of the Australian people to the crisis in Europe, according to Bean, was 'from the first perfectly definite and united'. Bean cited the war whoop in the city streets outside newspaper offices as if this were proof of a universal public endorsement. He laid it on thick: 'When on the night of the 4th of August 1914, Britain declared war upon Germany, the whole of the Australian people was behind its Government in offering unreserved help.'[2] Not a single dissenter, apparently, could be detected.

In 1936, Bean's collaborator, Ernest Scott, embellished this tale in his volume *Australia During the War* for the *Official History*. Revisiting the outbreak of war, Scott preened the national character. He dwelt upon Britain's 'hesitation' in going to war. The British had not instantly accepted Australia's offer of troops and ships because the colonial secretary, Lewis Harcourt, had cherished a lingering hope for peace. Scott interpreted this as a shameful failure of nerve. It revealed, he wrote, the 'quivering condition of uncertainty and apprehension which prevailed in London during the afternoon of August 4th'.[3] Again, Australia was heroically free of any such hesitation. 'It was certain,' wrote Scott, 'that the people of the country would give their enthusiastic support to a policy of military co-operation'. Scott claimed there was universal support for the Australian government's offer of an expeditionary force on Monday 3 August. As Scott eulogised, the Cook government 'never had come to a decision in which there was less doubt as to a correct interpretation of the resolve of Australia'.[4]

When Bean published his popular *Anzac to Amiens* in 1946, in the aftermath of the Second World War, he polished up this story once again. Australia in 1914 stood taller and shone brighter. Her politicians and her people, apparently, never put a foot wrong. Australia publicly offered 20,000 troops and her entire navy to Britain on Monday 3 August simply to reassure the Mother Country and strengthen her hands as peace disintegrated. There was nothing remotely problematic in the offer, its timing, or its impact.

But Bean's narrative of the July–August crisis was defective. Of course, he asserted British innocence and German wickedness. For example, the two controversial British provocations early in the crisis, the decision to keep the fleet concentrated on Sunday 26 July in a state approaching mobilisation, and the movement of the fleet to its war stations in the early hours of Wednesday 29 July, were accepted with the remark: 'For the first time since Trafalgar, 109 years before, the British Fleet was at sea on a mission of life and death for all British nations.'[5] However, simple errors marred Bean's tale of the unfolding crisis. He played fast and loose with the dates.[6] Quite wrongly, he told his readers that Germany had invaded Belgium on Sunday 2 August — in fact, the invasion did not come until two days later, on the morning of Tuesday 4 August.[7] This error was fundamental. By advancing by two days the date of the German invasion, Bean portrayed Australia's offer of an expeditionary force to Britain on Monday 3 August as a *response* to a war of aggression already under way. It was not.

In fact, Australia's offer of Monday 3 August was sent to London some forty hours in real time *before* Britain herself announced her declaration of war upon Germany. It thrilled those in London pushing for Britain's instant intervention. Most importantly, in offering an expeditionary force to Britain, Australia was not answering any call for assistance from the heart of the Empire — she was anticipating it. She was not responding to a British decision for war — she was pre-empting it. In popular memory, the idea that Australia 'answered the call' still persists.[8] It is not true.

The epic tradition — and the tragic school

Where does this book stand in the pattern of histories of Australia's Great War? To begin, let me survey the landscape in the historical literature. Speaking very broadly, there are two venerable traditions in the great mountain of works on Australia's Great War.

On the one hand, there is what can be conveniently labelled the 'epic tradition'. Works in this tradition respectfully explore Australia's military achievement in the First World War. They stress the gritty resolve, mateship, and jack's-as-good-as-his-master egalitarianism that Australians displayed in the war — characteristics, they say, that helped define the national character. Books in this tradition emphatically repudiate any notion of Australia fighting 'other people's wars'. Imperial defence, they assert, was Australian defence. They turn a blind eye to the embarrassing excesses of the ultra-patriots, who fawned before the imperial idol. Some of these works are simply celebratory, but some are not — they contain trenchant criticism of aspects of Australia's military history. Yet always the suffering and loss in war is accepted as necessary.[9]

In this tradition, many authors are sympathetically leagued with the contemporary British school of 'dire necessity' military historians. Prolonged and bloody as it was, these historians argue, the war must be accepted as a 'dire necessity'. They crusade against any notion of 'futility'.[10] Victory must be venerated, and people must find their solace in it. Some Australian popular works crusade in the same spirit. Some promote a 'greatest-pluckiest-little-nation-in-the-whole-wide-world' message — self-love coming so easily. Some are almost devotional. One book ends by assuring us that, following the death of the last Anzac, they 'are all together again, marching on as an immortal army'.[11]

On the other hand, there is a 'tragic' school of Australian historians of the Great War. These historians write critically of the Australian experience of war. They are conscious of the cost in corpses, and of the broken bodies and the battered minds. They generally concede that Australia's participation in the war was irresistible, given that most Australians considered themselves transplanted Britons. But regret overshadows pride. They remind readers that Britain made the key decisions in this war for Australia, that Britain managed the diplomacy of the war, and that Britain fashioned the ever-enlarging war aims to which Australia was committed. In focusing upon the domestic front, they tell the story of dissent and its repression. They see the deep sectarian divisions and political extremism that scarred Australian politics. They highlight neglected aspects of Australia's war, such as the suffering of returned soldiers, the impact of the war upon women and families, the experience of conscientious objectors, and the slide to authoritarianism on the home front.[12]

This book sides with the tragic tradition. It does not suggest that Australia could have escaped the war, or should have stood aside from it. That was simply impossible. But it does argue that Australia's leaders, the trustees of the nation's life and treasure, could have done better in 1914 than to leap so rapidly and recklessly, without any conditions or limits, into the all-consuming conflict.

Most Australian historians of 1914 show little interest in the details of Australia's passage to war. They skip over the 'political stuff' — and dash into the trenches. But there are two exceptional historians, Neville Meaney and John Mordike, who examine the road to war over the long term.

Meaney's major works, *The Search for Security in the Pacific, 1901–1914* (1976) and *Australia and World Crisis 1914–1923* (2010) are indispensable.[13] He highlights the extraordinary fear of Asia that drove Australian defence planning after 1905. He also traces the emergence of a more independent streak in policy from 1907 — as the Protectionist prime minister, Alfred Deakin, promoted his plan for a separate Australian naval fleet unit, and stronger land forces based on compulsory military training. This was adopted by Labor and realised by Andrew Fisher's Labor government from 1910 to 1913. Meaney explores the many tensions between imperial priorities and local anxieties, especially over naval forces. But Meaney's conclusions are consoling. He asserts that, while loyal to the British Empire, the new Commonwealth did develop 'the rudiments of a distinctive Australian foreign and defence policy, a policy which was directed towards attaining security in the Pacific'. Meaney's tone is one of acceptance. Australia did what she had to do, in preparing for war, and in fighting it — because she faced 'implacable geo-politics'.[14]

Exploring the events of July–August 1914, Meaney describes the 'outpouring of national emotion' in the face of war. Enthusiasm for the imperial cause, he writes, 'embraced all sections of society'. Only after this sketch does he review the steps taken by the politicians as they prepared Australia for war in the last days of July, culminating in the offer of an expeditionary force to Britain on Monday 3 August.[15] Arranged in this way, there is no problem in the narrative: the people appear to endorse the politicians' choices for war at every point, both before and after the British declaration of war. It appears to have been a people's war.

While Meaney decries a narrow nationalism, in his narrative Australia does well. The politicians spent more and more on defence before 1914, and kept their focus on 'Pacific perils'. It was all prescient preparedness. He is seldom critical — right up to Gallipoli. 'The Dardanelles offensive was ill-conceived and poorly executed,' he writes, 'and Melbourne was neither consulted nor informed about the British plans.'[16] But the fact that Australia was left in the dark appears in the story as unremarkable. It is just the culmination of the endless 'search for security' — which Australia never finds, short of war. The war came, and Australia was prepared for it.

The military historian John Mordike is more critical. In his two studies, *An Army for a Nation* (1992) and *'We Should Do This Thing Quietly'* (2002), he focusses on military planning.[17] Before 1914, he argues, significant tensions developed within the small group of Australian staff officers over defence priorities. Some favoured the creation of an Australian mobile force to serve on imperial expeditions, while others were reluctant. Some Australian politicians shared that reluctance, and accordingly Australia's first *Defence Act* of 1903 specified that no soldier could be directed to serve outside Australia unless he volunteered. However, in Mordike's narrative, over the following decade, those politicians and staff officers favouring an imperial commitment eventually prevailed over those favouring home defence. In this period, he argues, the British deliberately played up the Japanese threat in order to sustain Australia's commitment to the imperial cause. Looking for British support for Australia's security into the future, Australia's politicians between 1911 and 1914 authorised planning for expeditionary warfare to assist Britain in any war. They did so, Mordike argues, rather underhandedly, to avoid being rolled in the political surf.

Mordike — an ex-army officer, writing originally from within the Department of Defence — defied expectations. He clearly irritates the confraternity of military historians by putting expeditionary warfare in a negative light. He attracts criticism. First, his critics suggest he overplays the tension between imperial and national defence priorities. They insist that in the Australian mindset of 1914 there was little such tension — because for the Austral–Britons, imperial defence and the defence of Australia were inextricable.[18] Second, his critics reject his stress on the secrecy of planning for expeditionary warfare. They take exception to his choice of words — 'conspiracy', 'cover-up', and 'deception'.[19] Some dismiss his interpretation as 'conspiratorial'.[20] But Mordike was, in fact, building on Bean. Bean's *Story of Anzac* noted that planning for the expeditionary force before 1914 took place behind the scenes — and Bean lauded the secrecy.[21] Mordike probes the record, and establishes that the British and Australian politicians and military planners who promoted expeditionary warfare in the decade before 1914 were often secretive and manipulative in their approach.[22]

There is no need to resolve this complex debate here; it concerns decades of Australia's military history, whereas this book is focussed principally on the last days of peace in 1914. But Mordike's combative interpretation certainly suggests that Australia's passage to war in July–August 1914 is in need of a close critical analysis.

Whose war was Australia fighting?

Critical historians are often accused of disparaging Australia's Great War as a case of the country fighting 'other people's wars'. This catch-cry is certainly part of political debate, but it is difficult to find a historian who makes the claim that Australia should have stayed neutral in 1914, steering clear of 'other people's wars'. Almost all accept that neutrality was impossible. The attack on critical historians for supposedly deploying such a jibe is very much a case of kicking the stuffing out of a straw man.[23]

This book does *not* claim that Australia's contribution to the First World War was a case of Australia fighting 'other people's wars'. War, chosen by London, was inevitably 'Australia's war'. In addition, it is obvious that Australia faced threats if Britain's vast and weary *Imperium Britannica* came into collision with Germany's ambitious new *Weltpolitik* (World Policy) over the division of the world. Australia had an economic interest in a British victory.[24] Clearly, both Britain and Germany planned measures of economic warfare against each other to begin at the outbreak of war. Recent research on Germany's naval plans before 1914 has shown that Berlin planned to pursue her *Handelskrieg* (commercial war) in the Pacific, against Britain's trade. The German East Asian squadron, based in Tsingtao in China, was slated to undertake cruiser warfare upon the outbreak of war, interdicting Anglo–Australian trade and doing all it could to tie up naval forces and troops in Australia while the great conflict was resolved in Europe.[25]

The German navy's plans reflected the wishes of the imperial fantasists in Berlin, who pushed the nation toward *Weltpolitik* and urged the expenditure of huge sums on a new navy after 1899, supposedly essential to protect German trade and expand her colonies, but largely driven by right-wing domestic political calculations.[26] The propaganda of lobbies and leagues promoting navalism, of course, was by no means unique to Germany.[27] But in light of German naval planning, some historians argue that Australian and British military steps were all about prescient preparedness. It should be remembered that Britain also planned before 1914 to sweep all German trade from the oceans, to arrest all German merchant ships in port, to crush Germany's export-led economy, to starve the German nation, and to seize all her colonies — and Britain succeeded in her plans.[28] Australia's own naval 'War Orders' not only planned action against German cruisers to protect Australian trade, but also a period of 'swabbing up the seas of enemy merchantmen'.[29] In that light, it might be argued that German naval preparation before 1914 was also all about prescient preparedness.

In this world of rival wolf packs so presciently prepared, therefore, the Great War was, of necessity, Australia's war. But the reaction against the catch-cry 'other people's wars' can be easily overdone. It would be very misleading to leap to the conviction that it was 'Australia's very own war' — hers by choice, hers by interest, or hers in action. It was not. Britain's high diplomatic decisions on the road to war were never genuinely shared with Australia.[30] Australia's politicians were not aware of Britain's negotiations with Japan that resulted in the Anglo–Japanese Alliance of January 1902.[31] When the Anglo–French Entente Cordiale was signed in April 1904, Australian ministers first read about it in the newspapers.[32] When Britain aligned her empire with Russia under the terms of the Anglo–Russian Convention of August 1907, Australia was not consulted. When Sir Edward Grey, as foreign secretary, authorised secret Anglo–French military conversations between 1906 and 1911, Australia was not consulted. When the Anglo–Japanese alliance was renewed in July

1911, the Australian ministers were for the first time consulted —
but only because they happened to be in London.[33] When the British
leaders almost went to war in order to back-up French imperialism
in Morocco in August 1911, Australia was not consulted. Neither was
Australia consulted over the Anglo–French naval agreement of July
1912, with its enormous consequences for 1914, nor over the Anglo–
Russian naval conversations of 1914.

When war broke out, Australians fought in campaigns planned
by others, in places belonging to others, in battles underpinned by
diplomatic deals done by others, for war aims decided upon and
endlessly enlarged by others, and in coalitions of nations assembled
by others. In this sense, Australia's Great War was never wholly its
own — not in origin, objectives, diplomacy, or command. It was
scarcely 'Australia's very own war'. Rather, it was simply 'Australia's
war' — inescapably, like death. This hard reality scarcely justifies all
that Australia's leaders did in the descent into war in 1914.

We have now marked the centenary of the outbreak of what
became a huge, common European tragedy — a descent into a
hideous episode of industrialised slaughter. Estimates of the total
killed in the First World War vary wildly, but one respected authority
puts it at more than 17,867,000 persons.[34] On average, therefore,
more than 11,448 people perished, each and every day of that war
— more than four times the 2,750 persons killed at the World Trade
Centre on 11 September 2001. That simple comparison helps us see
the appalling disfiguring scar on European civilisation that was the
Great War.

This book, which reviews the intersecting of events in Australia
and Britain in July–August 1914, attempts to add to our understanding
of Australia's small role at the advent of that vast imperial war. It is
for Australians to decide how we shall memorialise such a calamity.
Shall it be in an inward-looking spirit, seeking national vindication,
adding to the store of national self-approval, soaking up pride in our
eagerness to send military aid to Britain as if it were a chest-swelling
moment? Or is it more fitting that the moment is approached in a
mood of simple respect, mourning, and infinite regret?

CHAPTER ONE

Cabinet crisis

Melbourne and London, Monday 3 August 1914

Further prepared to despatch expeditionary force [of] 20,000 men of any suggested composition to any destination desired by the Home Government. Force to be at complete disposal of the Home Government. Cost of despatch and maintenance would be borne by this Government.[1]

– Munro Ferguson to Colonial Office, Monday 3 August 1914

IN THE CROWDED last days of peace leading up to the outbreak of the First World War in early August 1914, two now half-forgotten events occurred almost simultaneously at opposite ends of the earth.

The first event took place in Melbourne, at that time the home of the Australian parliament and the nerve-centre of the federal administration. At about 6.00 p.m. Melbourne time in the evening of Monday 3 August 1914, a cablegram was despatched to London via the imperial 'All-Red Route'.[2] It was an official cablegram. In common with all such Australian communications on high diplomatic matters, it was signed by the governor-general, Sir Ronald Munro Ferguson, and was sent to the Colonial Office in Whitehall, the heart of decision-making for all Britain's colonies and dominions. The contents of this cable were historic. The Australian cablegram offered to Britain, in the event of war breaking out, an expeditionary force of 20,000 Australian troops 'to any destination desired'. The cablegram specified that the force would be 'at [the] complete disposal of the Home Government,' and that Australia would meet all costs associated with it. In addition, the cablegram promised the immediate transfer to the British Admiralty of the entire fleet of the Royal Australian Navy — Australia's pride, and a relatively new creation, having gained that title only three years before.[3]

This was the most open-ended of offers. No conditions were set. The cablegram had been authorised by Australian prime minister Joseph Cook, the leader of the Commonwealth Liberal Party (not to be confused with the modern Liberal Party of Australia, founded in 1944). He was an anxious man at that moment. The crisis in Europe had blown up just as he was leading his party in a federal election campaign for both houses of parliament. Moreover, it was an unprecedented election, prompted by Cook's request for a double dissolution to end a year of political instability. Polling day was only a little over a month away. A mere rump of Cook's hastily assembled cabinet endorsed the offer of an expeditionary force to London — in fact, only four of Cook's ten ministers made it to Melbourne in time to attend an emergency meeting of the cabinet on the Monday afternoon.

The timing of the Australian offer is important, and the time in London matters most. Because London was the source of almost all news, and London's view of the unfolding European crisis was the only view that really mattered across the Empire, it is vital to place the Australian offer of Monday evening in the order of events taking place in London. As eastern Australia was ten hours ahead of London, from London's perspective this Australian cablegram was sent at about 8.00 a.m. London time on the morning of that same Monday.[4]

The second event took place just two hours afterwards, in London, on that same Monday morning of 3 August. A serious internal crisis imperilling the life of the British government reached its climax in the historic cabinet room at 10 Downing Street. There, a cabinet meeting began at 10.00 a.m. This climactic cabinet meeting took place *before* the outbreak of war — for Britain would not declare war upon Germany until very late on the evening of Tuesday 4 August.

Presiding over the meeting at the cabinet table was Herbert Henry Asquith, the leader of Britain's last great reforming Liberal government. Around the table was arrayed a famous cabinet. It included such giants in British political life as the Welsh Radical David Lloyd George, the bumptious hero of the 'People's Budget' of 1909 and the scourge of the House of Lords; Sir Edward Grey, the sad-eyed and sensitive foreign secretary, a passionate believer in Britain's close diplomatic alignments with Russia and France; Richard Haldane, founder of the Territorial Army and the most senior of the 'Liberal Imperialists', as those ministers in Asquith's faction proudly called themselves; and Winston Churchill, the youthful party-hopper, former Tory, and former Radical who had become a Liberal Imperialist when promoted to the post of First Lord of the Admiralty in 1911.

Prime minister Asquith was much distracted as he took counsel from this assembly. The European crisis had erupted at the very moment when his attempts to pass a Home Rule Bill for Ireland were being derailed by the threat of civil war in that troubled island. At a personal level, too, he was under tremendous stress. Asquith, aged sixty-one, had fallen deeply in love with the beautiful twenty-six-year-old Venetia Stanley, his daughter Violet's best friend. The relationship was at its most intense in the summer of 1914. Over critical days, when the prime minister's fixed focus on the international crisis was required, Asquith's private life was fantastical. He was pouring out his heart to a young woman in a great stream of letters crammed with endearments, expressing dependency and a desire for counsel, and sometimes penned on the front bench of the House of Commons or even in cabinet meetings.[5]

At this Monday morning cabinet meeting, Asquith reviewed the latest diplomatic information on the danger of a general war erupting in Europe. Then he turned gravely to the state of the cabinet itself. He reported that, overnight, two cabinet ministers had sent in their resignation letters to Downing Street, as they had threatened to do on Sunday, and that this very morning a third minister had sent in his. Then, when the prime minister paused, a fourth minister passed his resignation letter across the cabinet table to him. Now four had confirmed their intention to walk away — from a cabinet of nineteen men.[6] By any measure, the government was tottering.

One minister recalled that, at this moment, Asquith's eyes 'filled with tears'. He explained that such serious dissent was unprecedented in the life of his prime ministership. Moreover, he told his careworn colleagues, it was not just the cabinet but also the wider Liberal Party that was 'still hesitating' with regard to the impending war.[7] Another minister recalled Asquith staring down the cabinet table over his glasses and saying, in a tone close to gallows humour, 'Seems as if I shall have to go on alone'.[8]

Lewis Harcourt, the colonial secretary, and leader of the faction of Radical ministers desperate to preserve Britain's neutrality, sat at the cabinet table by the prime minister's side. He recorded more of Asquith's words in his private journal. According to Harcourt, Asquith observed that, beyond the four resigning ministers, he was aware of 'many others' who were 'uneasy'. The prime minister signalled that more resignations were possible — and no doubt he was alluding here to the resignation of Harcourt himself. If the cabinet decided to press on, Asquith observed sombrely, it would face the 'great stress' of the current European crisis with 'much shattered authority'. The prime minister remarked that he might well choose to resign in such circumstances — but he could not face it. Harcourt jotted down Asquith's explanation for sticking to his post: 'Dislikes and abhors a Coalition'. Asquith told his colleagues that his clinging to power at this moment was 'in the best interests of the country', even though it might prove to be a 'most thankless task to go on'.[9] It was all 'very moving', wrote Herbert Samuel, another prominent cabinet minister, to his wife Beatrice afterwards. 'Most of us could hardly speak at all for emotion'.[10]

There had been cabinet revolts before, but nothing on this scale. This time, the four resignation letters had come from both the humble half and the mighty half of the cabinet pecking order.

But the resigning ministers were all significant figures in their own right. Beginning with the most junior, John Burns, the famous hero of the London dock strike of 1889, was a charismatic agitator who had evolved into an independent-minded moderate Liberal who was steadfastly opposed to 'entangling alliances'. Sir John Simon, the immensely talented and ambitious attorney-general, was an ornament of the cabinet, regarded by many as a future leader of the Liberal Party. Earl Beauchamp was a dogmatic free trader, a long-standing critic of the arms race, and a high-ranking Liberal in the House of Lords. (He had a connection with Australia; in 1899–1900, while still single and in his twenties, he had been a governor of New South Wales, sometimes controversial for being by turns insensitive, superior, or progressive.) John Morley, Viscount Morley, was the venerable lord president of the Privy Council, and the most senior man in the government. He was a vigilant guardian of the Liberal Party's anti-war traditions, a role easily claimed by the man who had written weighty biographies of the nineteenth-century Liberal Party's heroes, Richard Cobden and William Gladstone.[11] A fifth resignation, from the wider ministry, would come in the afternoon of Monday 3 August, from the young Charles Trevelyan, a well-connected man from a famous Liberal family, but only a junior minister at the Board of Education.[12] The loss of the four ministers from the cabinet on the Monday morning was far more serious for Asquith.

These cabinet ministers' resignation letters were frank and final in tone. John Burns' resignation letter, the first to be sent, on Sunday 2 August, had complained simply that 'The decision of the Cabinet to intervene in a European war is an act with which I profoundly disagree'.[13] John Simon explained in his letter that foreign secretary Sir Edward Grey's promise of naval support to the French ambassador that afternoon was 'tantamount to a declaration that we take part in this quarrel with France and against Germany. I think we should not take part, and so I must resign my post'.[14]

For John Morley, the chief consideration, as he explained in his letter of Monday 3 August, was his fundamental disagreement with the entire direction of the government's foreign policy. Britain had been cringingly loyal to France and Russia for too long. Britain had not acted in this crisis as the neutral power that she still was, in formal terms, and Morley wished her to be. Morley knew that the Liberal Imperialist faction of the cabinet would never agree with him on Britain's neutrality. He explained that he could not be in a cabinet where he inclined one way and 'three or four of my leading colleagues incline the other way' — a reference, of course, to the strong desire to intervene in any European war that appeared to animate Asquith, Grey, Churchill, and Haldane, the four leading Liberal Imperialists in the cabinet. 'This being so, I could contribute nothing to your deliberations, and my presence could only hamper the concentrated energy, the zealous and convinced accord, that are indispensable,' Morley explained.[15] Earl Beauchamp's letter of Monday argued that Sunday's decision to promise assistance to France was too much. 'By successive acts the cabinet has passed to a position at wh[ich] war seems to me inevitable. That is not a responsibility wh[ich] in present circumstances I c[oul]d share,' he wrote.[16] In a private memorandum, Beauchamp was even more blunt. 'The decision which was taken at yesterday's Cabinet — in the morning — to promise France [the] defence of her coast and shipping against Germany was so momentous that I wish to fix it'.[17]

In this way, each minister's resignation letter protested vehemently against the foreign-policy decisions of the government over the long term, and especially during the latest Balkan crisis — the crisis that threatened imminently to explode into a continental war. Each dissident minister complained that the Asquith government had been supine in its relations with Russia and France during this crisis, as it had been for years past. Each objected, in particular, to the British promise of naval support given to France on the previous day, Sunday 2 August. It was a reckless promise, the rebels complained; it was tantamount to a declaration of war on Britain's part, and might even provoke Germany into a declaration of war upon Britain. After all, by the time the promise of naval support had been given to France on Sunday afternoon, Germany had declared war upon one power only, Russia, in the evening of Saturday 1 August.

It is important to recall also that when these resignations were lined up on Asquith's table on that Monday morning, there was as yet no news in London of any German ultimatum to Belgium. War in the west had not yet exploded, and yet Britain was threatening to close off the Channel to the German navy. In this way, Britain was acting as if she had a formal defence alliance with France — which, as the dissenting Radicals correctly insisted, she did not.

This cabinet revolt was an event laden with dramatic power. Moreover, it had no parallel among the other nations that plunged into war during those first days of August 1914. Nowhere else in Europe did ministers resign with the hot breath of war on their faces. Nowhere else did ministers with troubled consciences denounce the decisions of their own government, renounce their salaries, and abandon their careers in the course of the crisis. Nowhere else did they protest at the eleventh hour by walking out of cabinets, councils, or ministries — not in Berlin, Vienna, Budapest, St Petersburg, Paris, Brussels, Belgrade, or indeed in any of the dominions of the British Empire. Only in London did this happen.

Australia leaps ahead of Britain's choice

At the very moment that the British cabinet was weighing the choice for the Empire between strict neutrality and rapid intervention in a continental war on the side of Russia and France, Australia despatched her sweeping offer of military assistance. Australia's cablegram had proposed an expeditionary force that would be 'at [the] complete disposal of the Home Government'. The men would fight anywhere, for any objective, under British command, and Australia's treasury would pick up the tab. The question suggests itself: what was the significance of this offer in the larger story?

Australian historians have rarely linked these two events in London and Melbourne on Monday 3 August, when the declaration of war was still a day-and-a-half away. They generally tell the story of the prompt Australian offer of an expeditionary force with pride, or it appears in the historical narrative as an unremarkable development.

They seldom take account of its timing or its deep, pathetic significance — that it came *before* the British themselves had decided finally upon war, and indeed at a moment when the British cabinet was sharply divided on the issue. In popular memory, Australia simply answered Britain's call for assistance. Behind the received narrative is acceptance of the *realpolitik* that neutrality was impossible for Australia, and that she had a clear economic interest in the victory of the British Empire. Moreover, large numbers of Australians did quickly volunteer for the fight. Therefore, the consensus has developed that it matters little whether Australia's politicians may have fallen over themselves in a rush to throw Australian manhood into the looming conflagration.

So, too, the crisis in the British cabinet is often neglected in narratives of the coming of the war. The German aggression in Belgium from Tuesday 4 August has made it easy to pass off the resignations of four British ministers as a mere gesture on the part of the faint-hearted. It is often overlooked that these resignations preceded the German attack on Belgium. In some histories, if the cabinet resignations are mentioned at all, they are treated as forgettable embarrassments of little significance.[18] After all, the great majority of Asquith's ministers did swiftly rally behind the government's decision to go to war late on Tuesday 4 August, and only two of the four resigning cabinet ministers in the end actually stuck to their decision. Therefore, it has been easy also for British historians to ignore the British cabinet crisis on the eve of the war.

But, as this initial exploration of just two neglected events on Monday 3 August 1914 demonstrates, to paint Australia or Britain's plunge into war as simply inevitable is to misjudge the situation. Moreover, it would be to miss the elements of tragedy, confusion, and low political calculation in the tale. Most importantly, to insist that the war was irresistible would be to miss the alternatives along the path to war. For London's choice for war on behalf of the vast British Empire was a very close-run thing. War was resisted, vigorously, even within the British cabinet. The Australian ministers were leaping ahead of events. A study of events in Melbourne and London over the last days of peace can shed a critical light on the whole story of the Empire's descent into the cataclysm of war. All is not simple and straightforward, nor is everything vindicated by the outcome — victory. It is a confronting tale, a tale of a reckless descent into an incalculable ocean of bereavement and misery.

CHAPTER TWO

Premonitions

Australia and Britain, 1900–1911

Because we are part of the Empire, and have created a precedent,
are we to be considered forever as liable to take up any quarrel into
which Great Britain may have entered, whether we have had a voice
in bringing about that quarrel or not?[1]
– Labor Senator Gregor McGregor, 22 January 1902

How was it that in 1914 Australia's politicians seemed ready to
charge pell-mell into war? Of course, Australia had no power to
choose neutrality.[2] But a decade before 1914, especially in the years
immediately following the Boer War (1899–1902), the instinct for
greater autonomy in Australia's foreign and defence policy had been
strong. What had happened to it?

Essentially, it had been overshadowed by an intense premonition
— of invasion. In the aftermath of the spectacular Japanese naval
victory over Russia at Tsushima Strait in May 1905, fear of Japan
intensified. Australians began to weigh the danger of Australia
being swept into a war of Britain's choosing against the perceived
advantages of being securely sheltered by the Royal Navy. Both
sides of Australian politics depicted the White Ensign, the flag of
the British Admiralty, as the ultimate shield in the defence of White
Australia.[3]

Those with long memories knew it had not always been so obvious. In the second half of the nineteenth century there had been 'troublemakers' urging decisive steps toward autonomy for Australia.[4] This sentiment appealed to that important minority of Australians, the Catholic and the Irish-born — almost one quarter of the population — for whom faith in British imperialism was overshadowed by greater loyalties.[5]

In 1900, many Australians could still recall the nineteenth-century British imperial conflicts that had peppered the globe. The century had ended in a spectacular bloodletting in South Africa — the prolonged Boer War.[6] Some 20,000 Australians served there voluntarily, and almost six hundred perished.[7] As the Boer War dragged on, some Australians wondered whether their government might somehow stand back from a grubby imperial war in the future. In January 1902, in the new Commonwealth parliament, Chris Watson, the Labor Party leader, a critic of the war, was hounded into conceding that, 'if the Empire asks for troops, I am prepared to assist her'.[8] But other Labor speakers stood firm. Charlie McDonald from Queensland declared that the Boer War was 'the most unjust war England has ever taken part in'.[9] The Labor senator Gregor McGregor argued that it was absurd for Australia to enter into all of Britain's quarrels, when she was scarcely likely to be given any voice in the quarrel or in the decision for war.[10] The radically minded MP Henry Bournes Higgins shared this sentiment. He warned the parliament of the consequences of 'the extreme step' of sending troops to any war: 'Are we, without going into the causes of the wars of Great Britain, to adopt the principle that we should actively side with Great Britain, no matter what is done?'[11]

The divisive Boer War was the backdrop to the creation of the new 'Australian Commonwealth Military Forces' in 1901. Historians have disagreed sharply over developments in its early years. Some argue that the Australian defence staff was divided between 'nationalists' and 'imperialists'. Others insist that most officers accepted that the defence of Australia was achieved within the defence of the Empire.[12] Politicians certainly quarrelled along these lines as they debated the nation's first Defence Bill between 1901 and 1903. Higgins led a majority of MPs advocating a 'volunteers only' clause to apply to military service outside Australia. Higgins spoke boldly. 'So long as we are not a sovereign state, in the sense of being able to dictate peace or war,' he warned, 'we shall not be consulted as to peace or war'.[13] Therefore, he argued, no Australian soldier should be forced to serve on imperial missions abroad.

Major-General Edward Hutton, the British officer serving as the first General Officer Commanding of the new Australian forces from 1902 to 1904, a fervent 'imperialist', choked on this.[14] In Hutton's view, Australia was secured by the Empire's might; therefore, Australia must prepare to fight anywhere, to keep the Empire strong. Upon his appointment to Australia, Hutton sought to create a mobile force of 9,000 men for imperial missions — an 'Imperial Australian Force'.[15] In advancing his case, he dressed up this force as vital for White Australia, and vital for Australia's colonial destiny, but he 'was undoubtedly being duplicitous'.[16]

Hutton lost the debate. The Boer War's poison lingered in the well of public opinion. Critics insisted that rapacious mining interests had provoked the war. In this altered political atmosphere, Australia's original *Defence Act* was passed in August 1903. It specified that soldiers could not be directed to serve in operations beyond Australia and its territories 'unless they voluntarily agree to do so'. This was clearly fired by a reluctance to be dragooned into a British imperial war.[17]

Hutton sought to dissolve this reluctance. During 1904, he prepared a strategic analysis under the title 'Defence Scheme for the Commonwealth of Australia'.[18] The scheme advanced ideas that were to be influential for the next decade.[19] It began by conceding that Australia was scarcely likely to be invaded. On the other hand, 'Australian interests outside Australia', her trade and imperial connections, were 'peculiarly open to foreign interference'. Moreover, Hutton argued that invasion could not be altogether ruled out. The continent was clotted with enviable resources. Even more darkly, his document noted a common belief — no source was given — that

Australia was 'looked upon by China and Japan as a possible outlet in the future for their surplus population'. If the Royal Navy's supremacy was even temporarily interrupted, he warned, an enemy of 20,000 men could invade. Accordingly, Australia had to build an equal force to repel it. How? Hutton spruiked for expeditions. Defence of 'a purely passive kind' was contemptible. 'History has shown that the surest and best defence is by a vigorous offence'. Offering a dig at his critics, Hutton wrote that it was 'hardly consistent' for 'a young and vigorous nation' to shun wider responsibilities.

Finally, Hutton was defiantly political. Australia's *Defence Act* 'confines her forces to action upon Australian soil,' he wrote. He boldly 'assumed' that a revision had to come, so he recommended a 'Field Force', 'mobile' and 'ready for active operations in the field at the shortest notice'. But where? It was 'obvious,' he wrote, that Britain's domination of the oceans 'will enable the Field Force to be utilized hereafter for the larger defence of Australian interests *elsewhere than in Australia*'.[20] Think big, think imperially, and think heroically — this was Hutton's firm advice.

This kind of imperial faith — ever ready to contemplate expeditionary warfare — was not easily reconciled with the Australian instinct for greater autonomy in defence. But Australia's politicians did assert it, spasmodically.

At the Colonial Conference in London in April-May 1907, prime minister Alfred Deakin represented Australia. Deakin faced an uphill battle. Looking for a share in foreign policy-making in London, he called for the creation of an 'Imperial Council'. He was rebuffed. He then urged dominion representation on the crucial Committee of Imperial Defence (CID), the centre of defence policy-making. He was rebuffed again. Instead, the British proposed an Imperial General Staff (IGS), to guide military 'co-operation' with the dominions. But Deakin did succeed on another front. He pressed the case for the creation of a separate fleet — Australia's own navy. London grumbled, and specified that it had to be ultimately under Admiralty command.[21]

On his return, Deakin advanced the project, announcing a 'new departure' in the spirit of greater self-reliance in December 1907.[22] Deakin told parliament that Australia needed her own fleet. He proposed new destroyers and submarines, which 'must remain under the control of the Government'. He acknowledged that 'in a time of danger' Australia would place the flotilla temporarily under the British Admiralty. Deakin also outlined proposals for larger land forces. These included far-reaching plans for 'Compulsory Military Training' for boys and young men, to form a 'National Guard of Defence'.[23]

He played down the possibility of expeditions. The government was 'not preparing for any expeditionary adventures outside Australia'. But, he explained, 'while we remain a mere handful of people, clustered around practically in one segment of the continent, any invasion attempted would probably be at a remote part'. Therefore, a mobile force would be required to guard 'the great unoccupied parts of this immense continent'.[24] Here was the enduring compromise: an expeditionary force to secure remote Australia. 'Our ideal is a defence of the people for the people and by the people,' Deakin concluded. Replying for Labor, Andrew Fisher endorsed Deakin's defence statement.[25]

When Labor returned briefly to power in late 1908, Labor prime minister Fisher and his defence minister, George Pearce, showed some reluctance to accept the IGS scheme, and both were privately wary that it might imply Australia's automatic commitment to expeditionary warfare.[26] But they moved forward on naval defence. Taking up Deakin's plans, Fisher placed orders for three destroyers in February 1909. The Australian Fleet was being assembled.[27] Then came the hysterical episode in March 1909 known to history as the great 'Naval Scare'.[28] This began in London, where agitators for Britain's 'big Navy' policy sparked a panic by alleging a secret acceleration in Germany's construction of battleships — later disproven. The scare was taken up by the Tory press to hound the Liberals into building eight Dreadnoughts ('We want eight and we won't wait!'). Soon the panic spread to the dominions. In Australia, imperial enthusiasts mounted a crusade to 'donate' a Dreadnought to

Britain. Fisher resisted the agitation, and for his pains was monstered as disloyal by the 'union jackals' — as the *Bulletin* dubbed his critics.[29]

Deakin chose this moment to corral the anti-Labor political forces, under the banner of the scramble for Dreadnoughts.[30] Thus, Deakin returned as prime minister to lead the 'Fusion' on 2 June 1909. Two days later he offered a Dreadnought to Britain, cannily offering as an alternative to spend an equivalent sum on Australia's own navy. His first test came almost immediately: an Imperial Defence Conference.

Deakin's appointee to that conference, Colonel Justin Foxton, was pliable. In London in July and August 1909 he quickly capitulated. The Australian plan to build ships essentially for coastal defence 'fell to pieces'. Foxton agreed to the Admiralty's prescriptions — a battle-cruiser, three light cruisers, six destroyers and three submarines.[31] Britain, in its turn, made a major commitment: to help fund a strong 'Pacific Fleet' over four years. Australia was going to have its own fleet — or so it seemed. Britain saw gains in this for herself. The Australians would pay up happily for *their* navy. As Admiral Sir John Fisher wrote, 'We manage it ... as occasion requires out there!'[32] Most significantly, Foxton also gave two pledges. He formally agreed to the transfer of Australian naval ships to the British Admiralty in wartime. Even more importantly, he agreed that Australia would 'take its share in the general defence of the Empire'.[33] As Asquith told the Commons, if the dominions wished 'their forces could be rapidly combined into one homogeneous Imperial Army'.[34]

More decisive steps followed at home. Joseph Cook, Deakin's defence minister, introduced a new Defence Bill in September 1909. It incorporated compulsory training: cadet training for boys aged 12 to 18, and more intensive training for young men aged 18 to 20 — all voteless. He conceded that 'one aim of this organization will be to provide an expeditionary force for immediate despatch overseas or elsewhere whenever the Government of the day feel themselves under an obligation to send a force'.[35] On this aspect of the Bill, he was challenged by Andrew Fisher, Labor's leader, showing that the matter was still politically sensitive. But Cook clung to his plan.[36]

Having unveiled the training schemes, the government then

summoned imperial expertise. Field Marshal Viscount Kitchener of Khartoum visited Australia in December 1909.[37] Ostensibly, he came to advise on defending the Australian continent. He completed his 'Memorandum on the Defence of Australia' in February 1910. Kitchener echoed Hutton: Australia's vulnerability followed from her small population and 'isolated position'. Kitchener also flattered the Australians by expressing confidence in their 'excellent fighting material'. He recommended extending the compulsory training. The annual cost, he estimated at £1.88 million — just a little more than already budgeted.[38]

Kitchener's attached 'Strategical Considerations' were revealing. Taking up Hutton's mantra, Kitchener bound together imperial and home defence. The foundation was clear: Britain's 'ultimate superiority at sea'. But again, Australia had to be ready to repel invasion if Britannia's rule was interrupted. Therefore, Australia needed a large army to make invasion too risky. Kitchener recommended '80,000 fighting troops'.[39] There was one hint about expeditions. Half the army had to 'be free to operate as a mobile striking force anywhere in Australia'. Moreover, Kitchener added, 'the best defence is generally by taking the offensive, and there should therefore be no difference in the enrolment, organization, and equipment of any unit'.[40] All, therefore, had to be capable of 'offensive' action. Kitchener privately stressed the importance of the enlarged Australian forces being trained and structured in a manner to facilitate their being combined with British forces. Their divisional organisation down to battalion level was designed with a view to their transport by sea, and when on active service abroad they would be subject to the British Army Act. Clearly, imperial missions still beckoned.[41]

When Labor returned to power in April 1910, Andrew Fisher's new government quickly accepted the Kitchener memorandum. There was nothing unexpected in this. Labor had embraced military training at its party conference of 1908.[42] Thus, it was Labor that introduced the Compulsory Military Training scheme in January 1911, and sharply increased defence spending.[43]

But, in truth, much more was accepted. Labor crabwalked away from any suggestion of Australia 'standing aloof' from an imperial war, such as Watson, Higgins, McGregor, and McDonald had envisaged a decade before. Instead, Labor embraced the dogma of the essential unity between imperial and national defence. Pearce, in particular, urged unquestioning allegiance to Britain. For example, in August 1910, Pearce argued that Australia owed its security to 'the unassailable supremacy of the British Navy, and to nothing else'. He accepted the risk of war:

> we may at any time be involved in a war in the causing of which we had no voice, and in which we have no desire to take part. But, nevertheless, by reason of the fact that we are part of the Empire, we may be called upon, willy nilly, to bear the consequences of our Imperial connexion.[44]

Introducing the Naval Defence Bill in the Senate in October 1910, Pearce repeated this line: 'Whatever wars the Empire may become involved in, we shall be involved in also. If those wars are of a naval character, we shall be concerned in them, even though they should be wars in which we may have done nothing to bring about'.[45] Revising his earlier wariness regarding expeditionary warfare, he suggested, too, that overseas service was inevitable. 'I would remind the Senate that, as Australia is an island, it can be reached by no foe except by sea, and that if war has to take place, it is far better that it should be conducted on some other land than ours. If we can prevent a landing, a war can never take place on our shores'.[46]

The 'technical fiction' of dominion autonomy

Meanwhile, Australia's fleet unit was forming. Deakin had ordered a battle-cruiser in December 1909, the ship that would become HMAS *Australia*.[47] The first destroyers ordered by Labor had arrived from Britain in late 1910, amid public celebrations.[48] By 1911, Australia's politicians were enjoying talking about the coming fleet, as symbolic of the country's greater autonomy.

But Britain's politicians were scarcely bothered. For example, early in 1911, preparing for the coming Imperial Conference, the British authorities debated the theoretical possibility of a dominion remaining neutral upon the outbreak of war. Such a decision might disable British plans to capture enemy merchant ships across the globe. Reginald McKenna, First Lord of the Admiralty, advised letting sleeping dogs snore. He prevailed, and the CID decided — the words are worth emphasising — 'to accept *the technical "fiction"* implied in the idea that the Dominions acted of their own free will in waging war'.[49]

In May 1911, the Australian delegates to the Imperial Conference, led by Fisher and Pearce, arrived in London. During his three months in Britain, Fisher skilfully combined statesmanlike conformity and egalitarian gestures.[50] On the one hand, he attended the coronation of George V at Westminster Abbey, and the Spithead Naval Review. He also wandered the lawns at a garden party at Nuneham Park, the grand home of the colonial secretary, Lewis Harcourt. 'He [Harcourt] did not understand Fisher and Fisher did not understand him,' as Malcolm Shepherd, Fisher's secretary, unhappily recorded.[51] On the other hand, he defied conventions — he bristled at having to wear court dress, declined an honorary degree at Oxford, and dodged a court ceremony to be sworn as a privy councillor. Fisher also travelled with British Labour legend Keir Hardie to Scotland, and supped with miners in Ayrshire. Challenged there on Australian Labor's 'militarism', Fisher replied that his critics should 'take up a map, see a great Continent lying in the South Pacific, and see how it was surrounded, and then think, and think, and think'.[52]

At the Imperial Conference of May–June 1911, tensions between the statesmen soon surfaced. On the second day of discussions, Joseph Ward, the New Zealand prime minister, again suggested an 'Imperial Council' so that the dominions might contribute to policy at the centre of Empire. Fisher backed away. He trusted Britain's 'wisdom' and leadership in defence. In the event, Asquith rejected the 'Imperial Council'. War, peace, and foreign policy were quite rightly 'in the hands of the Imperial Government'. 'That authority cannot be shared,' he declared.[53] In later discussions, the Canadian prime minister, Sir Wilfrid Laurier, sensationally observed that 'we do not think we are bound to take part in every war, and that our fleet may not be called upon in all cases'.[54] Briefly, the wraith of 'neutrality' had surfaced.[55] But it existed only as a rhetorical phantom. Fisher did not touch it.

The dominion delegates to London were invited to attend meetings of the famous Committee of Imperial Defence in late May. Later, Fisher would praise Britain for taking the dominions 'into the inner family circle and unreservedly laying before them its international policy'.[56] However, the Australian delegates' commitments at these meetings were to become intensely controversial.[57]

At the CID meetings, the star lecturer was Sir Edward Grey. He gave the dominion representatives a tour of the global hazards that faced the British Empire. He warned of the danger of Germany seeking domination of the Continent. In that event, Britain could not stand aloof. Britain might lose her sea supremacy. Nightmarish consequences would follow for Australia. Britain's Pacific colonies, and Australia's trade, would be hostage to 'the will of the Power which held the sea'. Grey warned that 'all the Dominions would be separated from us, never to be rejoined'. After this, bizarrely, Fisher and Pearce pressed Grey on the Anglo–Japanese alliance, which Grey wanted renewed to 1921. The Australians insisted it must not imperil their 'whites-only' immigration barrier — against Japan. In response, Japan 'bent over backwards to give assurances which would meet the anxieties of the Dominions'.[58]

The new Australian fleet was also debated. Symbolic concessions were easily won. Australia's ships could fly the Australian flag from the jackstaff, and the White Ensign from the stern. More importantly, Fisher and Pearce reassured their British hosts that Australia would transfer the fleet to the Admiralty in war. Anything else was 'inconceivable,' declared Pearce, promising that 'you can always count the fleets in'. But, shy of publicity, Pearce also pleaded it would be 'far wiser to leave it unwritten'. Striking a similar note, Fisher assured all that Australia's navy would take on wider imperial tasks:

'Do not depreciate us. We shall do things, and not talk about them'.[59] Australia wished to 'co-operate' against a common enemy, but she preferred to have the 'freedom and liberty' to choose. 'I say the tie of affection will be stronger the more loosely you allow it to remain'. Asquith responded that he, too, preferred 'spontaneous co-operation' rather than 'talk of bargains and conditions'.[60]

At the CID meeting, Richard Haldane, the war secretary, also addressed the dominions' leaders, on 'mutual assistance'. Britain's army was 'an overseas army', 'an expeditionary army' — six divisions and a cavalry division — a force that could go to the dominions, 'to your assistance as you may need'. He stressed that Britain had developed smaller military units, easily transportable by sea — and clearly he recommended that the dominions should do likewise. Turning to Australia, Haldane described Kitchener's scheme as strengthening 'home defence'. But he stressed also that there were 'possibilities in it of a section to volunteer for overseas work and to be sent by the Government for the purpose of co-operating in the mutual defence of whatever part of the Empire might most need assistance'.[61] Haldane spoke in the same spirit that evening at a dinner, in a speech reported in Australia.[62]

A real breakthrough came at two more meetings at the War Office, on 14 and 17 June, to discuss military co-operation.[63] Here, General William Nicholson ('Old Nick'), the chief of the IGS, addressed the dominion defence ministers. At the table for Australia were Pearce, Sam Pethebridge, his departmental secretary, and Captain Brudenell White, a young Australian officer attached to the War Office — who would play a key role in Australia's mobilisation in 1914.[64] The objective of the War Office for Australia was quite plain. As General Henry Wilson explained, upon the outbreak of war, Australian troops 'should be placed under the orders of the War Office (C. I. G. S.) and made available for service in any part of the world'.[65] Therefore, to steer the Australians, the War Office had produced a series of papers upgrading the threat from Japan. The message was simple: assurances of British action to secure Australia would require a *quid pro quo* — a wide Australian commitment to imperial defence.[66]

At these meetings, General Nicholson introduced a paper seeking 'harmonious co-operation in war'. All easily agreed on standardisation in organisation and equipment, but Pearce then proposed more. He called for 'the preparation of schemes of mobilisation by the local sections of the Imperial General Staff in order to enable that uniformity to be availed of'. Pearce wanted 'a general understanding — there does not need to be any resolution — that the local section of the Imperial General Staff are to work along these lines'. This included schemes of mobilisation for expeditionary forces. Nicholson clarified this point. Pearce's military staff should 'work out a scheme so that, if the Government of Australia so desires, they will have preparations made for mobilising a certain proportion of their force to proceed to certain ports for oversea [*sic*] action'. All agreed that such preparations should be kept secret, and the War Office paper 'suppressed or withdrawn'. The dominions wanted no domestic troubles. Nicholson summed up: 'I think it much better we should do this thing quietly without any paper on the subject, because I am sure in some of the Dominions it might be better not to say anything about preparations'.[67]

Pearce had been thinking along these lines for some time. Interviewed on his way to London, he had told C. Brunsdon Fletcher, a conservative journalist, that Australia's forces 'should be capable of offence': 'Our Imperial responsibilities may require expeditionary forces, and we must be ready at any moment to get well forward into a fighting line beyond the territorial limits of Australia'.[68]

There was a controversial aftermath to the Imperial Conference, when Fisher gave an interview to W. T. Stead, a famous sensationalist journalist. According to Stead, on the crucial question of future Australian action in war, Fisher said: 'If we were threatened we should have to decide whether to defend ourselves, or, if we thought the war unjust and that England's enemy was in the right, to haul down the Union Jack and hoist our own flag and start on our own'.[69]

The Australian newspapers got wind of these breathtaking remarks in late July, while Fisher was on his way home on RMS *Osterley*.[70] Ever watchful for disloyalty, the ardently imperial Australian press crucified Fisher.[71] Labor newspapers, however, rushed to his defence. *Labor Call* commented that 'Andy' obviously had the infamous Boer War in mind.[72] When his ship called at Colombo, Fisher issued an emphatic denial. But Shepherd found him cantankerous, and ready to debate 'what our *powers* are'. Shepherd urged an unqualified repudiation, but Fisher was 'very timid of expressing any opinions in favour of imperialism and such like topics'.[73] The tensions give real insights into Fisher's inner turmoil on defence policy.

In parliament on 6 September, Fisher faced his accusers, all fret and foam. He acknowledged that, as a matter of law, Britain chose war for Australia. But Australia would decide upon the military aid. Fisher declared that 'the safest way to preserve the Empire, and every part and every citizen of it, is to leave the self-governing Dominions the right and power to say what they shall do in all circumstances'.[74] Of course, if it came to war, Fisher declared, no one should think Australia would 'allow the Old Land to be attacked with impunity'.[75]

Behind Labor's shifting rhetoric stood a settled conviction: only British naval power secured Australia from Japan. It also reflected the victory of the 'preparedness' crusaders over the internationalist minority in Labor. It testified in particular to the influence of Billy Hughes, who had been a founding secretary in 1905 of the New South Wales (NSW) division of the Australian National Defence League (ANDL) — a pressure group that went on to campaign zealously for compulsory military training. Hughes had brought other Labor personalities into the ANDL.[76]

The ANDL reflected similar lobbies and leagues in Britain and the USA. Rich men — corporate lawyers, mining tycoons, bankers, and reactionary publicists — dominated these movements. There were parallels in ideology, financing, and even personnel among them.[77] Men of the Rhodes Trust and the pro-imperialist Round Table movement were prominent. The flutter of money from the banking firm of J. P. Morgan & Co. was to be heard, too. For example, one of the founders of the National Service League in Britain in 1902 was Clinton Dawkins, chief bankroller for Lord Milner and his Round Table activists, and resident senior partner at J. S. Morgan & Co.

in London from 1900. He had negotiated Britain's Boer War loans from J. P. Morgan & Co. in New York.[78] The British Round Table men permeated the political leadership in Australia, and had a foothold in Labor.[79]

These 'preparedness' crusaders argued that a great struggle for the division of the world was under way. Protection ('tariff reform') for economically self-sufficient imperial units was the wave of the future, everywhere. Some argued, too, that war was inevitable and beneficial for the race. They preached economic nationalism, and the need to 'capture' markets and resources. In short, they urged that a militarised state should enforce the right of its own producers to buy in the cheapest market and sell in the dearest, while denying the foreign competitor that same right. When Hughes helped create the ANDL back in 1905, leading Labor figures began to rub shoulders with men hurrying the world to a dangerous place.

Hughes crusaded with passion. In dozens of speeches and news-paper columns, he pounded away. War was an ever-present threat; preparation for it was an ever-present duty. In light of that threat, imperial loyalty was indispensable. 'We stand now in what security we do stand in by virtue only of the power of Great Britain,' he wrote in May 1911.[80] Asia was at the gate. Five million white Australians were claiming 'a continent capable of containing one hundred millions, and which we took and held by the bayonet and the rum-bottle'. Dread and peril pervaded. In October 1911, he wrote that Australia was 'the natural prey of the teeming, sweating millions of the East'. It was only 'fear of the mighty British Navy that keeps them penned up in their overcrowded native lands'.[81]

CHAPTER THREE

Nightmares

Australia and Britain, 1911–1914

I approve of: Preparation of plans for despatch of forces over sea by Commonwealth Government.[1]

– Senator George Pearce, 30 December 1912

BETWEEN 1912 AND 1914, planning began in earnest in Australia for an expeditionary force to wage war beyond the country's shores. What drove the decision was the persistence of a nightmare — the nightmare of a samurai-wielding Japanese warrior advancing up the stairs of the family home. Not all Australians experienced this, but many did. Australia's politicians scarcely moved to investigate or resolve the sources of unease. Few sought to understand Japan, to find the good in the forces of Japanese commercialism to balance against the evil of Japanese militarism, or to assess coolly the real likelihood of such a distant threat from Japan.[2] Few took account of the reality — namely, that between 1905 and 1914 Japanese foreign policy-makers were utterly absorbed by events in China and Manchuria.[3] Few Australians took comfort from the very successful operation of the Anglo–Japanese alliance, in spite of Britain's reassurances about its benefits.[4] Fewer still sought to soften Australian racial prejudice or encourage Japanese economic ties, as Britain did.[5]

Because Australian politicians did so little to challenge the ghost stories, the nightmare simply took hold. Therefore, ever hopeful that Britain would shield Australia from Japan, Australia's politicians never risked alienating the imperial authorities, even as they delighted in showing off the new ships of Australia's navy as tokens of Australia's greater 'autonomy' in defence. For the same reason, they decided that if London wanted expeditionary forces to be prepared, then, so be it — but better, as we have seen, if it were done on the quiet.

The subject of planning for an expeditionary force is still intensely controversial among historians. Some insist that there is no problem to be explored. They acknowledge that Australia did indeed plan for such a force, quietly. But it was rudimentary, and those involved in the planning respected the voluntary clauses of the *Defence Act* of 1903. They prepared only for a flood of volunteers in wartime. Nothing remotely underhand took place to commit Australia to participating in an imperial war. Everyone simply faced up to hard facts — what we would today call geo-political realities.[6]

This is to put a beaming face on everything, for things were *not* all above board. The politicians involved were sometimes secretive, misleading, and manipulative. They gave every indication of being bothered by their having authorised the planning. Moreover, much more than the defence of Australia's island home was planned by 1914. Colonial conquest in the region was planned, too.

Two European war scares sparked the planning. The first came in the southern winter of 1911. After their return to Australia from the Imperial Conference in August, Fisher and Pearce confronted the 'Agadir Crisis', which had begun in June when the French increased their military intervention in Morocco and Germany responded. On 1 July 1911, the small German gunboat *Panther*, returning from South-West Africa, arrived at the Moroccan port of Agadir on the Atlantic coast.[7] With Paris and Berlin locked in dispute over the future of Morocco, a European war seemed very close. Tension increased on 21 July when David Lloyd George, the British chancellor of the exchequer, made a belligerent speech at the Mansion House in London that was widely interpreted as the Asquith government waving its spears at Germany. But there was no rush to war. Instead, the crisis bubbled away for months. This gave the British and European labour movements time to get into the streets. French and German socialists organised a series of monster demonstrations against war in August and September. British Labour also held rallies for peace.[8]

Australian Labor reacted very differently. When Admiral George King-Hall, the British admiral in command of the Australia Station, received his orders to get ready for war, he and the governor-general, Lord Denman, immediately contacted prime minister Fisher. The nation's leader did not resist the agreed plan that the newly built Australian naval ships would be immediately transferred to the British Admiralty if war came — and even before that. 'I got Fisher to agree to hoisting the white ensign on the two Australian destroyers, though the new Admiralty agreement had not come into force,' Denman told Harcourt. Fisher ordered Pearce 'to have his mobilization schemes in readiness'. The Australian ministers immediately offered 'a plan for re-enlisting men who had served in South Africa'. Denman was buoyant. 'I found Fisher and Pearce ready and willing to help in every way, and everything was kept quite secret'.[9]

Eventually, the crisis over Morocco was resolved by a diplomatic compromise in early November. But the events of 1911 stimulated defence preparation in Australia. In August 1912, Denman reported to Harcourt that Australia's own Council of Defence had considered CID documents dwelling upon the threat from Japan. As a result, explained Denman, the Australian government had commissioned a new 'Commonwealth Defence Scheme'. It would be comprehensive, and it would include a plan for 'the concentration of a mobile expeditionary force'.[10]

A second serious international crisis, the outbreak of the First Balkan War in October 1912, produced more scurrying in Australia. Again, both Fisher and Pearce displayed their readiness to fall in with London's requirements. When the crisis began, the newly launched cruiser HMAS *Melbourne* was still in England, waiting for her commissioning, and two other Australian cruisers were being finished. Fisher and Pearce promptly offered all three to the

Admiralty. Writing from the Adelaide Club, Denman reported the offer to London, and singled out Fisher for special applause as a man who 'would be difficult to replace'.[11]

Much to Denman's joy, the existence of the new Royal Australian Navy (RAN), so named in July 1911, proved to be no obstacle during the Balkan crisis. Labor had been scrupulously loyal.[12] Fisher was 'a reliable man,' wrote Denman, 'strong enough to deal with some awkward extremists in his own party'.[13] Denman felt vindicated. On the eve of the crisis, he had been pressing Churchill to soften his stance against dominion navies as 'thoroughly vicious'. Without Australia's sense of its own fleet, Denman had pleaded, 'public opinion here would never have come round to enable Parliament to vote money for this purpose'. With the Australian fleet as the badge of nationhood, Australia was spending almost £5 million a year — 'not bad for a population of under five million people,' crowed Denman.[14] An Australian flag on the jackstaff of the new ships was a small sacrifice for Britain to make to get such a boon in spending.

The number-one priority, of course, was a smooth transfer to the Admiralty of the ships at the outbreak of war. Accordingly, during 1912 and 1913, the Admiralty negotiated with Australia, when drawing up 'War Orders' for the Australian fleet, on procedures for the transfer of the Australian fleet. Australia rejected the idea of a five-year 'agreement' to hand over command of the fleet instantly in wartime. Instead, both sides simply acknowledged the firm expectation that the RAN would be immediately transferred 'in time of emergency or war' to the command of the British Admiralty, via the China Station headquarters at Hong Kong.[15] On this basis, the Admiralty's 'War Orders' were issued for the ships of the RAN in May 1913 — and Australia was consulted about them. To strengthen the expectation of transfer, Denman worked his London connections. He wrote again to Churchill in June 1913 urging him to encourage naval co-operation between Australia and New Zealand. The well-behaved Kiwis could work wonders on the Australians, he predicted. For even if the New Zealanders eventually had their own fleet, their undoubted eagerness to transfer it 'without conditions in time of war' would serve to nudge the Australians, and thus 'it would strengthen the hands of those who are working for the same object in this country'.[16]

The Balkan crisis of October 1912 had an impact on the army also. It sparked planning for an expeditionary force — a matter that Pearce had not moved quickly on since returning from London.[17] The Australian chief of the general staff (CGS), Brigadier-General Joseph Maria Gordon, saw a chance to jockey Pearce on the subject. He decided to champion the expeditionary force, under the banner of 'mutual assistance' between Australia and New Zealand.

Therefore, from his headquarters in Melbourne on 4 October, on the eve of war in the Balkans, Gordon wrote to Pearce a frankly alarmist letter: 'The situation in Europe is of the gravest'. War was possible 'at any moment' with 'complications' for Britain. Looking for maximum impact, he declared that 'Australia and New Zealand stand alone in the Southern Pacific'. Therefore, negotiations between them were imperative. They should start 'at the earliest moment convenient'.[18] Fisher cabled William Massey, the New Zealand prime minister, asking him to instruct his military chief, General Alexander Godley, to meet his Australian counterpart in Melbourne to discuss a 'proposed scheme of mutual assistance'.[19] Massey swiftly complied.[20] Notably, nobody mentioned an expeditionary force in these exchanges.

A three-day conference of the top military brass began in the historic bluestone buildings of Victoria Barracks on St Kilda Road in Melbourne on 18 November 1912, with Gordon and Godley at the head of the table.[21] Significantly, too, the conference secretary was Major Brudenell White, recently appointed Australia's director of military operations. It was a spectacular moment for White, always a zealous Empire-first man.[22] Both he and Gordon were keen to create a force 'for service anywhere in the Empire or out of it if required'.[23] Earlier that year, White had returned from England, full of a passion for expeditionary warfare.[24]

Pearce gave the opening address, during which he put the issue of an expeditionary force on the table. There was an obstacle that stood in the way of 'co-operation in Imperial military undertakings,' announced Pearce. Both nations faced 'the difficulty that statutorily there is no power to employ the respective forces oversea unless they voluntarily agree to serve'.[25] Therefore, Pearce asked the officers to suggest ways to get around 'the disorganisation resultant from present restrictions', while specifying that they should 'not do violence to the feelings of the people which had originated the restrictive clauses'. Pearce hinted heavily that the clauses had to go. These might soon be abandoned, he observed, and fortunately the navy was exempt. Godley replied that New Zealand was managing to plan around the voluntary clauses in its own *Defence Act*. If New Zealand could plan ahead, so could Australia. Pearce stressed again how 'difficult' it was for Australia and New Zealand 'to promise a definite quota to augment an Imperial expeditionary force'.[26]

Gordon took the hint. The solution was simple. As he put it, 'so long as plans were prepared beforehand he thought that it might be left to the Government of the day, when the crisis arose, to say whether the plans should be put in operation; the rest might safely be left to the spirit of the British people'. The flood of volunteers would come. Remarkably, Pearce declared the conference 'unanimous on broad principles', and he left the officers to it. He had pointed the way. The officers were being asked to focus upon an expeditionary force, and to regard Australia's *Defence Act* as an antiquated and temporary obstacle to be side-stepped with the minister's blessing.[27]

Over the next three days, the officers sketched out their plans. They easily agreed on the nuts and bolts: the two nations should assist in intelligence sharing, and Australia should become an arsenal for manufacturing war materiel.[28] Then the officers turned to the expeditionary force. Gordon calculated that Australia would supply 'contingents totalling some 10,000 men'. General Godley chipped in with a 'probable contribution from New Zealand of some 6,000–7,000 men'. The men would form 'an Australasian division'. The two nations, not London, should pay for the lot. The conference admitted that the plan was 'complicated' by voluntary enlistment. There could be 'no committal', and 'the Government of the day' had to be left free to decide. But advanced planning would 'in the end prove to be an economy'. Thus, the conference agreed to ask the two governments 'for approval that authority be given to proceed with plans for the despatch of the force', and agreed also that 'the Imperial authorities should be informed that such plans are being prepared'.[29]

But how was such a force to be assembled? The conference listed two methods. A register could be composed, listing men 'who would express their willingness to serve overseas'. But this force would lack 'homogeneity'. Alternatively, an earmarked 'extra-territorial force' of volunteers could be formed — clearly the officers' choice. Turning to structure, the conference again provided two alternative models. The first suggested one composite division, 'an Australasian division', with Australia supplying 11,623 men and New Zealand 6,043 men. The second suggested 'an Australasian mounted force', with fewer men.[30]

What would this expeditionary force do? The conference anticipated 'operations in either the East Indian Archipelago or the Pacific'. This was shorthand for the seizure of the colonies of Germany, Holland, Portugal, and France in these regions. The conference even sought to discern the different 'spheres' of conquest for Australia and New Zealand. Like the medieval papacy, the officers divided this portion of the globe, according to a convenient degree of longitude — 170 degrees west. Australia would take colonies to the east; New Zealand, to the west.[31]

The officers listed their final recommendations. Notwithstanding the 'restrictive clauses' of each nation's *Defence Act*, the key was: 'To have plans prepared beforehand for the despatch of such a force in order that all may be in readiness at any time it is desired to take action'. Similarly, to accomplish the seizures of colonies, 'the necessary plans should be prepared beforehand'.[32] On the basis of the longitudinal split, Australia was slated to capture the lion's share of colonies.[33]

To their report, Gordon, Godley, and White also appended an important document entitled 'Scheme of Defence — Mobile forces of Australia — Strategical Considerations'. London had already seen it.[34] This put the familiar case for expeditionary forces. If British naval forces were concentrated for a great sea battle far away, Australia might be under threat for a brief time from 'an Eastern Power' — a euphemism, of course, for Japan. Raids might come. The bulk of an Australian army of 100,000 men would hold ports and cities. 'The remainder must be left to form a field army capable of acting as a mobile expeditionary force.' Then came the familiar hymn of praise for offensive action. 'A defensive attitude of a purely passive nature' was 'ineffectual'. The military forces of Australia must be ready 'to assume the offensive'. Expeditions must be prepared. The familiar justification for this — quoted in many documents — was Australia's acceptance in 1909 of its duty 'to take its share in the general defence of the Empire'.[35] So, too, declared the paper, at the birth of the new RAN in 1911 the navy had been 'imbued with the same spirit of active offence as the Royal Navy', and stood ready to accept 'an increase in the responsibilities of Australia'.

The strategic assessment put the case for planning the seizure of French, German, Dutch, and Portuguese possessions in New Caledonia, the Bismarck Archipelago, New Guinea, and the Java and Flores Seas (present-day Indonesia and Timor). It was vital 'that war preparations must include plans for the occupation, if necessary of hostile bases in these localities'. To achieve these conquests, 'plans of operation should contemplate the employment overseas of such portion of Australian forces as may from time to time be deemed necessary and is voluntarily agreeable so to serve'. The strategic document then listed a series of ports that might be used by 'a hostile squadron'. All or any might have to be seized in the future.[36]

Thus, a proposal for precise planning for both an expeditionary force and colonial conquest was for the first time squarely before the government. Pearce responded on 30 December 1912. In a handwritten minute to Pethebridge, he recorded the key decision: he gave formal approval to the defence mandarins to draw up plans for an Australian expeditionary force that would serve overseas.[37] He also authorised 'direct correspondence' between the Trans-Tasman general staffs. But, notably, Pearce did *not* give permission for the officers to inform London about the plans, ignoring their advice.

On display here were indications of Pearce's reluctance and

secretiveness. Driving this, no doubt, was his sensitivity to the politics of expeditionary warfare. He was also careful to record Australia's ultimate right to decide for itself if such a force should depart at all:

> This decision in no way commits the Commonwealth to send any force oversea. It is not considered advisable to take any action in respect, to;
> (a) earmarking any particular portion of the Defence Forces for such duty, (b) notify the British authorities of any such action.[38]

The caveat was expected, but the two bans were startling. 'Earmarking' of some kind was implicit in the officers' suggestions for either a 'register' or a designated extra-territorial force. The idea that Australia should plan colonial conquests and not inform London was breathtaking. Both bans betrayed Pearce's lurking wariness about the project — or his fear of its exposure.

Trans-Tasman contacts followed. James Allen, the New Zealand defence minister, visited Melbourne in December 1912 on his way to London. He supported 'mutual assistance', while always outdoing Australia in loyalty by promising London that he stood for 'single Imperial control' of all local navies.[39] In January 1913, Fisher sent Massey the final decisions on 'mutual assistance'.[40] Pearce composed the key passages in this letter. Again, he sought to bottle up knowledge of the planning for expeditions. In an undated draft, he eventually deleted his advice that it was 'inadvisable to notify the Imperial Authorities that such plans are in course of preparation'.[41] Shorn of this astounding provision, the letter from Fisher to Massey recorded the key decision:

> That the Commonwealth Government approves of the preparation of plans for the despatch of portions of the Commonwealth Military Forces oversea on the lines suggested by the Conference, provided they agree so to serve ...[42]

The letter preserved Pearce's other 'reservations'. The planning 'in no way commits the Commonwealth Government to sending any force over-sea'. He noted also that it was 'not at present advisable to designate any particular portion of the forces for such duty'. New Zealand was not asked to keep the planning from London. Behind the scenes, however, Pearce did try to stop Australian officers from contacting London. At least one, Kirkpatrick, did so anyway.[43] New Zealand soon signalled its acceptance of all the key decisions.[44]

Politics then intervened in Australia. Labor lost office at the end of May 1913, and Liberal Senator Edward Millen became the new defence minister. Was there to be continuity in policy with regard to an expeditionary force? Brigadier-General Gordon immediately put some pressure on Millen to act. He was aided by the fact that New Zealand had moved first. On 21 June 1913, the cabinet in Wellington agreed to supply 7,500 men to an expeditionary force, comprising an infantry brigade and a mounted rifles brigade.[45] On 2 July 1913, Gordon wrote to Millen asking for permission to plan for the Australian contribution.[46] Millen temporised. In November 1913, Gordon was still pressing him. In putting his argument for Australia to move forward, Gordon now supplied the details of New Zealand's expeditionary force.[47] He soon got his permission.[48]

Planning for an expeditionary force was quickly combined with the work already underway on the new 'General Scheme of Defence'. This was clearly modelled on the key document 'Scheme of Defence — Mobile forces of Australia — Strategical Considerations' that had a pedigree stretching back to Hutton, and had been refined at the Gordon–Godley–White conference of November 1912.

Progress was rapid. As early as March 1913, the governor-general, Lord Denman, sent to Harcourt a bundle of 'Defence Schemes' for the CID. Even at this early date, the 'Expeditionary Force' got a special mention: 'This scheme provides for the chief command and central administration of the whole of the Commonwealth Forces in time of war and contemplates in addition to the complete protection of districts, the formation of a mobile Field Army which has advisedly been termed an Expeditionary Force.'[49]

The 'imperial authorities' gave their encouragement. In April 1913, the CID prepared a paper entitled 'Australia — Preparation of Defence Schemes'.[50] This commended the project. It suggested that a War Book be incorporated, showing the sequence of civil and military actions on the outbreak of war. Significantly, the CID also gave its blessings to the attached document entitled 'Strategical Considerations' — including the contemplated colonial conquests. The CID underlined the Japanese danger again, and warned Australia against overconfidence.[51]

Most importantly, the CID paper endorsed the expeditionary force. It cheered the Australians' willingness to move beyond 'the primary duty' of 'local defence' and to embrace as well 'mutual assistance in time of emergency'. As usual, 'passive defence' was dismissed, and praise lavished upon a capability 'to assume the offensive'. Accordingly, it blessed plans 'to despatch oversea without delay after the outbreak of war such parts of the forces as may volunteer to serve outside their home territories'. The paper also endorsed Australian plans for 'the occupation of hostile bases in the Western Pacific'. 'In a great war,' the paper argued, victory would depend not on local operations, but on 'the main struggle at the decisive point'. Concentration of the empire's manpower must come 'in the case of a prolonged struggle'. Britain, therefore, wanted Australia to prepare for both duties: first, to seize colonies in her 'offensive against foreign territory in Australasian waters'; and, second, to join the concentrated forces at the seat of the war to safeguard 'the ultimate fate of the British Empire'.

When the CID itself discussed this paper in April 1913, General Sir John French, the CIGS, pointed to the nugget in the document: 'that to attain the best results in war, it was essential to concentrate all our available naval and military forces at the decisive point'.[52] Assured of this single fact, the CID approved the paper.

The Australian files associated with the defence scheme show that, in planning 'offensive action', the military officers were opening their mouths wide. A list of eleven 'Plans of Overseas Operations' was added to the file on 'Defence Schemes'. Under the heading 'Plan for seizure of ...' was a long list of proposed conquests, including New Caledonia, the New Hebrides, the 'Bismark [sic] Archipelago, and Simpson's Haven', German New Guinea, Dutch New Guinea, Timor, and 'Batavia and other parts of Java'. In addition, plans were listed 'for the relief of Papua'. The list of Australian operations included 'Co-operation with India in Sumatra, Borneo, and Dutch East Indies generally', 'Co-operation with India in the Phillipines [*sic*]', and, finally, 'Despatch of a force to co-operate in India'.[53] There were few places within four thousand miles of Australia, it seemed, for which a case for conquest could not be made.

But how to make war? Brigadier-General Gordon circulated the finished 'General Scheme of Defence' in August 1913.[54] Streamlining mobilisation, it included a famous 'Preface' — the equivalent of Australia's own 'War Book'. This listed the precise signals that London would cable to Australia, and a step-by-step mobilisation schedule.

Once again, the new scheme revealed Australia's staff officers as boosters of expeditionary warfare — and of the 'cult of the offensive'. Of course, the Ark of the Covenant, Britain's supremacy at sea, was there. The new scheme's 'Strategic Considerations' paid homage to that. The usual argument for a large army in Australia was restated; while waiting for British might to prevail at sea, Australia would be vulnerable to attack from 'an Eastern Power' — Japan, not Germany. Therefore, Australia needed land forces of 'no less than 100,000' to repel invasion.[55]

The new defence scheme was even more overtly political than the last. It emphatically rejected the voluntary clauses of the *Defence Act* of 1903. Indeed, 'the time has now arrived,' announced the document, 'when provision must be made for giving effect to the policy of active offence'. This policy necessitated 'plans of operation for the mobile forces of Australia'. To justify this, Australia's commitment in 1909 'to take its share in the General Defence of the Empire' was wheeled out, again. The Naval Agreement of June 1911, under which Australia drank deep of the Royal Navy's spirit of 'active offence', was wheeled out, again. So, too, Australia's greatly enlarged 'responsibilities'.[56] The familiar shopping list of colonial conquests followed — the French, German, and Dutch possessions to Australia's north, from New Caledonia to the Java Seas. But it would not end there. At the 'War Stage', the document listed the two Australian duties. The first was the despatch of 'small expeditionary forces against foreign possessions'. The second glimpsed the big future: 'the despatch of a voluntarily enlisted force for co-operation in Imperial military operations'. Australian troops could go anywhere.[57]

The planners still described the expeditionary force as a 'voluntarily enlisted force'. But they obviously chafed under the restriction. The scheme explained that 'the Field Army has been advisedly designated the Expeditionary Force' for two reasons. First, the document posited 'that in the defence of Australian soil it may be necessary to transport [a] portion of the Field Army by sea' — Deakin's force, bound for remote Australia. The second reason got to the heart of the matter. The document adventurously explained that the name 'expeditionary force' was appropriate because the defence planners were 'in contemplation' that 'at some time in the future the present statutory restriction upon employment of portion of the Australian forces overseas may be removed'. This was a curious political prophecy for a sober-minded defence plan — but it revealed the imperial spirit at its core.[58]

The defence scheme then described the stages of mobilisation. Only at stages four and five did the document list the 'despatch of a voluntarily enlisted force for employment overseas', including action by 'a small expeditionary force against foreign possessions in the East Indian Archipelago'.[59] Actual blueprints for the operations were not included in the defence scheme documents.[60] But they existed. The first, a plan for the seizure of Rabaul, had been sketched in October 1911.[61] Expeditionary warfare was now integral to Australia's 'defence' planning and its mobilisation schedule.

There is a famous passage in Charles Bean's *Official History* of the war in which he downplayed such plans. 'The Defence Scheme of Australia provided only for the chance of an enemy raiding or invading her shores,' wrote Bean. 'A plan for meeting the enemy in the enemy's own country — or, indeed, anywhere except within Australia — officially had no existence'.[62] That scarcely matches the evidence. Before 1914, Australia did plan for expeditionary warfare, and for colonial conquest, and she did so officially — it was all there in the Defence Scheme of 1913 and its supporting documents.

Why were Australians so willing to contemplate wider imperial 'responsibilities'? A strategic argument that exploded inside the Commonwealth Naval Board during 1913 illustrates the thinking.[63] The Japanese menace backlit planning at the board; the German complication was secondary. But because it hypnotised London, it eroded Australian faith in British sea power as the counter to Japan. In July 1913, Eldon Manisty, secretary of the board, put it this way:

> The possibility of war with Japan and the probable effect of such [a] war on Australia are no new factors. They have been in the mind of leading Australians ever since the Russo-Japanese War and possibly even before that date ... The pressure of the German menace upon the British Isles had emphasised the need for Australia to take stock of her whole position in the Pacific. The former position of Britannia ruling the waves has for the moment ceased to have a world-wide application.[64]

The immediate background to the quarrel in the Naval Board in 1913 was doubt over the age and firepower of British ships allocated to the Pacific.[65] Apprehensions were sincerely held, and again Japan was assumed to be the enemy. Lieutenant-Colonel Gordon Legge, for example, writing from the War Office in London, sent an estimate in July 1913 that the Japanese army could land three divisions in Australia inside one month.[66]

In this atmosphere, two naval officers, Captain C. H. Hughes-Onslow and Commander Walter Thring, had prepared several strategic assessments in early 1913. They favoured a line of new naval bases in the north. The reports envisaged a coming racial war. If Britain faced war in Europe, they argued, Japan might seek to resolve the problem of her people's racial exclusion from Australia by direct coercion.[67] Rival naval strategists went to war over the 'Thring Line'.[68] In September, Manisty wrote a critique. The 'Thring Line' was a costly distraction. If attacked by Japan, Manisty advised, Australia would do better to abandon the north. There was danger in trying to 'defend an advanced line'. Australia should defend only her 'vital points', and wait for British assistance to turn out the invader.[69]

Admiral William Creswell, the 'First Naval Member' of the Naval Board and 'father of the Australian Navy', decided the debate.[70] In his initial response, he conceded the reality and the racial character of the Japanese threat to 'force the free entry of her people into Australia'.[71] But he rejected the 'Thring Line'. Creswell stuck to the plans of Admiral Reginald Henderson, the visiting British expert, whose report of 1911 had advised the government to strengthen existing ports in the south. Northern bases, in the coming age of long-range oil-fired ships, wrote Creswell, were 'as futile as building a wall to catch a bird'.[72] Most significantly, Creswell grew impatient with the uppity tone of his officers' criticism of the admiralty. This 'general tone', he warned, 'seems scarcely to recognise that Australia is a portion of the Empire and that *all questions of peace and war as well as the conduct of the forces of the Empire in war are directed by the Home Government*'.[73] It was a timely restatement of the essential reality.

The war plans and the politicians

Of course, in planning for expeditionary war, secrecy prevailed. But it was not just a military requirement. The politicians sought to escape scrutiny. Major White's specific plans were 'not tabled'.[74] Pearce urged White to keep such plans 'most strictly to himself'.[75] Furtiveness prevailed.

The New Zealand military planners, by way of contrast, were embarrassingly candid. In January 1913, James Allen boasted to English journalists of New Zealand's readiness to supply a force of 8,000 men for imperial service — provoking complaints from the New Zealand Labour Party.[76] General Godley also bragged of his plans publicly. This inspired the *Sydney Morning Herald* to urge that Australia should openly embrace an expeditionary force.[77] New Zealand's boasts were repeated in late 1913.[78] But Australia's leaders were silent.

Pearce had it both ways. Sometimes, he fatalistically accepted the need for overseas service, as in the Senate in 1910. But on other occasions he misleadingly paraded his hostility to the idea. For example, in December 1913 the Senate debated proposals (emanating from Major-General George Kirkpatrick) that certain 'national regiments' (designated as English, Scottish, and Irish) should be preserved ready for service overseas. Pearce had rejected Kirkpatrick's original proposals in 1911. In the Senate, Pearce attacked the proposals, and left the impression that he, a true Australian nationalist, was opposed to the old national regiments — and to service overseas.[79] He urged Millen to repudiate 'the proposal for foreign service'. Millen replied that he had never endorsed any plan for that.[80] Six months later, the brawl erupted again. Pearce attacked the national regiments as costly and backward-looking.[81] This time, Millen explained that 'what General Kirkpatrick was aiming at was the formation of a brigade that could be mobilised instantly for foreign service'.[82] His explanation was to no avail. Pearce carried the Senate, and the national regiments merged into the army. But planning for an expeditionary force — clearly supported by both Millen and Pearce — survived.

It was political shadowboxing. The truth on the Labor side was that both Fisher and Pearce had absorbed a new pro-imperial ethic. This struck Lord Emmott, Harcourt's under-secretary at the Colonial Office, when he toured New Zealand and Australia in September 1913. Emmott reported proudly to London that Fisher had made 'loyal and patriotic speeches of an Imperialist kind'.[83] Fisher and his colleagues had been converted, wrote Emmott, to 'sane Imperialism'. Why? Emmott speculated that, 'I am inclined to think that the fear of Japan has brought a lot home to them.' As a result, the Labor politicians realised 'that they have an obligation to assist us & others in the defence of our world-wide possessions'.[84]

Fear of Japan could achieve great things. But it could also fortify Australia's determination to keep control of its fleet. For example, in April 1914, Henry Stead, editor of the *Review of Reviews for Australasia* and a personal friend of Harcourt, wrote to him that

Australia was devoted to its new fleet and 'determined not to let it out of her sight'. Why? Stead explained that the Australians, 'on whom the Asiatic danger has been worked for all it is worth,' were still most anxious about Japan, in spite of Britain's alliance with her.[85]

General Sir Ian Hamilton, who made a visit to Australia beginning in February 1914 as inspector-general of overseas services, preferred to see the benefits for Britain in exploiting that fear. The tour of inspection by the future commander at Gallipoli, undertaken as an assessment of the Kitchener scheme of compulsory military training, was memorable — in part for his willingness to confess to a trusted few his happy duplicity when it came to dealing with Australians. He advised prime minister Asquith in April 1914 that the training scheme was costing much more than Kitchener had estimated. On the gush of money spent on defence, Hamilton speculated that perhaps Kitchener had underestimated expenses, or perhaps he had simply sought to 'lure the Australians on'.[86] It mattered not — a huge increase had been achieved.[87] On the same trip, Hamilton told a friend of Henry Stead in confidence that he really thought 'that the whole scheme here was "damned rot"'. Stead confessed to Harcourt that, in British circles in Australia in touch with Hamilton, it was the universal conviction that land forces were too expensive and that the big money should be expended on Britain's 'command of the sea'.[88]

Hamilton freely admitted to his manipulative tactics in his letter to Asquith in April 1914. He explained that in coming to Australia he had intended 'to urge upon the Commonwealth the importance of having some small section of their Army earmarked, in peace, for expeditionary Imperial service'. But it was better not to push this openly. Better to be tactical; better to stress the Japanese danger. 'Play the tune, an Australian army for Australia, and they dance to any extent. Not otherwise. Australia — not Empire — is then the string we must harp on.' Then, he predicted, the Australians would make preparations 'willing and lavishly' for 'safeguarding a White Australia from the cursed Jap'. They definitely did not wish to fight, he conceded, 'outside the areas washed by the Pacific'. But if Britain manipulated Australian pride and anxieties, then 'when the time comes, and when we are fighting for our lives in India or elsewhere, I for one am confident that the whole military force of Australia will be freely at our disposal'.[89] How right he was — and there would soon be many Australian graves 'outside the areas washed by the Pacific'.

By the eve of the Great War, therefore, Australian plans for war were well advanced. The dogma of 'active offence' was in the ascendant. Moreover, the long-cherished British aim of preparations for an expeditionary force to serve imperial objectives had been conceded by Australians. It is absolutely clear that in 1914 there were plans being developed for Australia's forces, on sea and land, to fight well beyond Australian territory. There was a clutch of plans for colonial conquest. Australia had decided to stick to Britain — like a pilot fish to a shark.

Australia was no victim here. She was willingly pledged to Britain, from fear of Asia, and in the hope of future deliverance from Asia. As a result, it was a practical certainty that the men and the shillings would flow — whatever the cause, wherever the fighting — as soon as Britain was engulfed in war.

CHAPTER FOUR

Double Dissolution

Australia, July 1914

You can hardly believe what solidarity of national life there is between
G[reat] B[ritain] and Australia, and how all natural expression of
loyalty to the Crown is more apparent even than at home. Australia
seems closer to us than any part of the Empire that I know. It is
certainly British, and is so by itself.[1]
– Ronald Munro Ferguson, 10 July 1914

ON THE EVE of the Great War, Australia's political warriors were
locked in combat. Another episode in what was already an endless
political contest — over social and industrial issues still painfully
familiar in Australia — was underway. Overseeing the domestic
struggle was a newly minted governor-general, a knighted Scot with
a double-barrelled and sometimes hyphenated name, Sir Ronald
Munro Ferguson. He was the King-Emperor George V's man in
Australia — and immensely powerful.

On the great issues of international politics before 1914, newly
federated Australia was like a toddler in leading strings, always steered
by the Mother Country. The key men in the relationship were the
governor-general and the colonial secretary. In 1914, Lewis Harcourt,
son of the famous Liberal chancellor Sir William Harcourt, and like
him a Radical from the left of the Liberal Party, had been colonial

secretary for four years. He was the choice of Margot Asquith, wife of the prime minister Herbert Asquith. In 1910, Margot explained to 'Loulou' why she had recommended him to her husband, whom she always called 'Henry':

> You were my choice for as I said to Henry 'apart from his cleverness Loulou has perfect manners and genuine kindness'. I think Colonials want *all* one's kindness. They bore me *to death*! & are so conceited I feel my manners vanish when I am with them.[2]

This typifies the 'general disdain' among those in authority in Whitehall toward the colonial people.[3] A natural sense of superiority, and a habitual sense of deference on the part of some Australians, bedevilled the relationship. That Britain's commanders of empire assumed dominance in this relationship was plain. For example, in December 1912, Arthur Jose, the Australian correspondent of *The Times*, and a man in touch with the main players, explained to prime minister Andrew Fisher that when a British politician spoke of consultation, 'he pictures to himself a good little boy admitted for the first time to hear his father discuss politics and sitting there ready to say "Yes, papa" and "No, papa" in the proper place'.[4] Similarly, when the British admiral George King-Hall finished his three years' service in Australia in December 1913, he wrote to Harcourt that his task had been 'to educate and form public opinion in the Commonwealth and to shepherd them into our fold'.[5]

Of course, the Australian leaders, especially Alfred Deakin, could be assertive. The creation of the Anglo–French Condominium in the New Hebrides in 1906, in spite of Australia's objections, had led to loud complaints.[6] Australians were proud of their status in the British Empire, so near the top of the racial and constitutional pyramid. They were citizens of a white-skinned 'self-governing' dominion. The status flowing from the white skin was everywhere asserted, but, in truth, Britain effectively controlled all the significant diplomatic and defence matters affecting Australia. By 1914, most Australian politicians had made their peace with this. Frequently, they preached that there was no distinction between imperial and national defence priorities. They professed to believe that Australians would defend their continent best by defending the empire. Some put it the other way round — but the effect was the same. Both duties would be fulfilled.

Australia's 'foreign policy', if it existed at all, was very largely in the hands of others. Australia had established its own small 'Department of External Affairs' in 1901, but it was busily absorbed in such matters as immigration, fisheries, and the administration of Papua and (from 1911) the Northern Territory.[7] The Australian governor-general was acknowledged as the chief manager of Australia's relations with the imperial government — and the world. Of course, he acted on the advice of the prime minister, but did not inform him of all his contacts with London. Australia also maintained a high commissioner in London to act on Australia's behalf. George Reid filled the post in 1914, but he was hardly ever consulted on important diplomatic matters. Reid's appointment to London by the Deakin government in 1910 had been seen as an early example of political patronage in diplomatic appointments — the post was a prize for former ministers who 'deserved well of their party, had outlived their usefulness or had become an embarrassment or threat if left idle on the back benches'.[8]

All communications of substance from Australia to London had to pass through the hands of the governor-general. He directed them not to the British prime minister, but to the secretary of state for the colonies. His letters and cables flowed to the great Colonial Office, and he jealously guarded this official channel. Naturally, the governor-general, a political appointee, also had close personal friendships among the political elites in London. Thus, in addition to his official letters to London, he also sent private correspondence to his friends, and specially marked 'secret' and 'private' letters to the colonial secretary.[9]

In 1914, the Australian prime minister did not even possess the right to communicate directly with the British prime minister. Certainly, no personal letters could be exchanged. Asquith insisted that Harcourt should handle all correspondence with the dominion prime ministers.[10] So, too, the Australian prime minister did not write directly to the colonial secretary, but only through the governor-general; the vice-regal channel was the only channel. In this sense, Australia's governor-general in 1914 served in practice not only as commander-in-chief of the military forces, but also as a kind of Australian foreign minister. Certainly, he wielded much greater power in this field than either the Australian minister of external affairs or the high commissioner in London.

A glance briefly forward beyond 1914 serves to confirm these imperial realities. When Lloyd George announced an 'Imperial War Cabinet' in March 1917, it was hoped that the dominions would settle for this promised periodic consultation in London. However, the British elite's private letters told the real story. 'There is undoubtedly a good deal of eyewash about it all,' wrote Lord Hardinge. Lloyd George's invitation to the dominion prime ministers was 'to flatter their vanity'.[11] Similarly, when the dominion prime ministers at last gained the right to send correspondence directly to the British prime minister in 1918, again the reaction of the imperial elite was telling. Lord Liverpool, the governor of New Zealand, wrote to Harcourt privately that 'I am personally convinced that no Prime Minister of the United Kingdom would have time to deal with such correspondence.'[12]

Because Sir Ronald Munro Ferguson was a significant player in the events that took place in Australia on the eve of the war, he requires some introduction. The governor-general was a Scottish aristocrat, a graduate of the military college Sandhurst, and a Liberal Imperialist politician with a seat in the House of Commons until 1914. His life-long passion for things imperial placed him on the right of the Liberal Party. He had been an officer in the Grenadier Guards as a young man, and his wife, Lady Helen Munro Ferguson, was the daughter of the viceroy of India, Lord Dufferin. In the early 1890s, Munro Ferguson had been private secretary to Lord Rosebery, the much-loved mentor of the leading figures in the emerging Liberal Imperialist faction inside the Liberal Party. As a good Liberal Imperialist, Munro Ferguson had supported the Boer War when his party was bitterly divided on the issue. After the Liberal victory at the elections of 1906, no cabinet post had come his way. The key men at the helm of Britain's government after 1908 — Asquith, Haldane, and Grey — were Liberal Imperialists, but Munro Ferguson's career had stalled. So the announcement in February 1914 of his appointment as governor-general to Australia meant that his beloved empire was re-launching his career. He seized the opportunity.[13]

Munro Ferguson landed in Melbourne as the plumed and starred representative of George V on 18 May 1914. He spent that morning on the new Australian cruiser HMAS *Melbourne*, where he met prime minister Joseph Cook and his ministers. Then followed a procession and a ceremony of welcome. Imperial loyalists were effusive and courteous in their welcome. Naturally, Munro Ferguson relayed home an uplifting report of his warm reception. He confessed himself to be 'astonished at the cordiality'. 'The Crown is certainly a great asset in Australia,' he wrote to Harcourt.[14] Ten days later, he was still full of enthusiasm. After attending an Empire Day ceremony at the Melbourne Town Hall, taking lunch with ministers at the parliament, and then being sandwiched between Labor politicians at a football match in the afternoon, he told Harcourt that 'H. M. in person could not have been treated with greater respect'. He came to favourable conclusions very quickly: 'Australia is certainly very English, extremely loyal in a quiet undemonstrative way.'[15]

During his first weeks in Australia, he thoroughly enjoyed the elaborate shows of fealty and affection, especially in country districts. It appealed to the aristocrat in Munro Ferguson, and he could not quite hide his condescension. He explained to Harcourt, a fellow landowner, that 'a lifetime largely given over to visiting tenants is a useful preparation for the role of a rural Governor-General'.[16] The Australians were apparently as loyal as tenant farmers could be to their powerful laird.

But he was not entirely impressed. 'Mere Society people are very British,' he told Harcourt. After meeting a great many such people in his first weeks in the wide brown land of supposed equality, at such places as the Melbourne Club and at the odd 'levée' in various town talls, as he described his receptions, he confessed that 'Society's exclusiveness is unmitigated.' Diverting as were the Society women, he was disappointed to find that the 'Ladies do not know the difference between State and Federal Governments'.[17] Such were the truths sent home in private letters.

It was not all sweetness and light. Soon, Munro Ferguson's private letters to Harcourt revealed the vehement quarrels dividing Australia's politicians. One concerned his own accommodation in Sydney — for, at that moment, there was no official residence available for the governor-general in Sydney. Therefore, as Munro Ferguson explained to Harcourt, he was planning to stay in a private house when he visited Sydney for the first time in July 1914. Various suggestions were being considered. For example, prominent citizens of Scottish descent at the 'Highland Society' were suggesting that one of their number, Colonel James Burns, was willing to help. Burns, a wealthy entrepreneur at the head of the famous Burns, Philp and Company, a very profitable trading company with extensive interests and ambitions in the Pacific islands, had proudly offered his own grand house and garden, 'Gowan Brae' (now incorporated in The King's School), near Parramatta.[18]

This lack of an official 'home' for the governor-general in Sydney was to complicate the crisis of 1914. The quarrel dated back to 1912, when the NSW Labor government of premier J. S. T. McGowen had adventurously terminated the lease to the federal government of the capacious old Government House, blessed with to-die-for views over the Botanic Gardens and Farm Cove in Sydney Harbour. This had deprived the governor-general at that time, Lord Denman, of a designated residence when visiting the glorious harbour city.

Naturally, the 'eviction' of the King's representative provoked a bitter dispute. Denman made no secret of his simmering resentment against NSW Labor politicians. He saw big issues at play. He told Harcourt that 'my eviction is a rude shock to the cause of Imperialism in this country'.[19] He reported Sir Edmund Barton's haughty explanation that the state politicians were 'the spoilt children of the Empire'. Denman agreed they were 'insignificant people', and he observed that 'an assertion of imperial authority would do them a lot of good'.[20] He blamed in particular William Holman, a rising star in the Labor ministry and a 'plausible scoundrel'.[21] Holman rose to the premiership in June 1913, whereupon he stoutly persisted in his case that maintaining two vice-regal properties in Sydney was extravagant — old Government House for the governor-general's use on his very occasional visits to Sydney, as well as a mansion named 'Cranbrook' in Rose Bay (now incorporated in a private school), for the NSW governor. Labor proceeded with plans to return the old Government House and its gardens to public use.[22]

Monarchists and imperial loyalists, who had formed a NSW Citizens' Committee, rallied in Denman's support. Fearing political ramifications, Harcourt advised Denman to have nothing to do with it.[23] When Cook formed a new federal Liberal government in June 1913, he offered a compromise: a federal rental of the British Admiral's residence, Admiralty House at Kirribilli, with fine harbour views, for the governor-general. But Denman declined.[24] So the quarrel rumbled on. The issue even disrupted vice-regal relations. Sir Gerald Strickland, the NSW governor, and a Catholic, fell out with Denman and then with Munro Ferguson.[25] The scandal of the governor-general's 'homelessness' in Sydney was still festering in July 1914.

Munro Ferguson, a Protestant, was soon uncomfortably aware of another, much more serious, irritant in Australian politics: sectarian tension. The passions unleashed by the 'Home Rule' crisis in Britain followed the governor-general to the new land. As the Asquith government launched its plans to achieve Home Rule for Ireland in 1914, and then faced the threat of violent resistance to it in Ulster, each twist and turn in the crisis was big news in Australia, too. The crisis naturally stirred Australian emotions — for the outwardly homogeneous British 'stock' was actually deeply divided according to the people's varying religious allegiances. Australian Ulstermen and Australian Catholics sniped at each other, and the familiar charges — Irish terrorist, Ulster mutineer — were flung back and forth.

On the very eve of the First World War in Australia, this issue was suddenly poisonous. There were large public meetings in favour of Home Rule in Melbourne in May, and then in Sydney in June. At these 'Green' meetings, Labor political leaders were prominent in their attendance. Naturally, these gatherings soon inspired noisy counter-demonstrations and public rallies from organised Orangemen. There were local incidents suggesting a depth of feeling, especially in military circles; for instance, a quarrel over Home Rule saw one pro-Home Rule officer expelled from the Naval and Military Club in Melbourne. The accusation of disloyalty lay ready to hand to be deployed against Catholics in politics. This could be very much overdone as, in reality, the leading spirits of the Australian Catholic community from the mid-1890s onward had been generally moderate on the subject of Irish Home Rule. While critical of Westminster, they did not denounce the British Empire. Nor did they call upon Australia to break her ties with the empire. In 1914, their argument, and that of many Labor politicians, was that, just as Australia's dominion status had given her a form of Home Rule within the empire, so too Ireland should have it.[26]

In his initial meetings with the new governor-general, prime minister Cook, while exceedingly cordial, had kept his cards close. 'The P. M. said nothing about politics — except that the Home Rule question s[houl]d never be mentioned,' Munro Ferguson wrote home. The reason was plain. The 'Catholic Irish' were 'nearly a fourth of the population,' as Munro Ferguson explained. The sectarian issue popped up in many of the governor-general's 'Personal' letters. He carefully recorded those Australians he encountered in positions of authority who happened to be Catholic, such as the lord mayor of Melbourne, as if a future potential for disloyalty should be noted. Home Rule was exciting 'great interest' in Australia, he wrote. 'Resolutions favourable to Home Rule may come up at any time in Parliament.'[27] The forces favouring Irish Home Rule were clearly in the ascendant in Australia.

On a happier subject always close to the vice-regal heart, Munro Ferguson reported that Australia was advancing rapidly in its military preparedness. Munro Ferguson knew he was in the shadow of Lord

Denman, who had actively stimulated the expansion of Australia's military forces. He clearly wished to emulate Denman. In his first letters to London, he included up-beat reports on the swelling military spirit in Australia. There was 'no slackening in zeal for compulsory training'. The bearing and morale of troops and cadets in Australia, he added, was enviable, and this could be exploited in Britain. He recommended to Harcourt that the films of smartly parading young cadets that had been taken during General Sir Ian Hamilton's tour of Australia in early 1914 should be shown in Britain, in order to drum up enthusiasm for Britain's own Territorial Army and so 'boost our 2nd line of defence'. Munro Ferguson received every encouragement from Cook and his ministers to march proudly in Denman's boot prints. Senator Millen, the minister of defence, told him at an early meeting that Lord Denman had been deeply interested in the military. Millen explained, as Munro Ferguson put it, that 'my predecessor had taken his C[ommander] in Chiefship rather seriously'. Millen advised Munro Ferguson that he should plunge in, too, with both hands.[28]

On one aspect of Australia's military preparedness, however, the governor-general offered a qualification. He conceded that on naval matters there were still nationalist impulses at work. The Australians, he told Harcourt, were sensitive about maintaining the separate status of their naval fleet. There was 'but one opinion' on that subject, he wrote. The new Royal Australian Navy had been conceded by London in 1911 — but there was a silver lining. Munro Ferguson speculated hopefully that perhaps the rising expense of the separate fleet unit might soon persuade the Australians of the good sense in maintaining the closest co-operation with the Royal Navy.[29]

Double Dissolution — and international crisis

Just two weeks after his arrival in Australia, Munro Ferguson was thrust into an unprecedented federal political crisis. On 2 June, prime minister Joseph Cook, leader of the anti-Labor 'Fusion' forces that had been formed under the banner of the Commonwealth Liberal Party, made a request for a double dissolution of the federal parliament —

that is, a dissolution of both the House of Representatives and the Senate.

Cook had struggled since his Liberal Party's one-seat victory in the election of 31 May 1913 over the Labor Party, led by Andrew Fisher. In the House of Representatives, Cook had been reliant upon his Speaker's casting vote. But in the Senate, Cook's Liberals were heavily outnumbered — twenty-nine seats to seven — by the Labor Senators. Cook had lost an important piece of legislation in the Senate in May 1914, his Government Preference Prohibition Bill, which sought to eliminate preference for trade unionists in government employment. As this Bill had been twice passed by the House of Representatives and then twice rejected by the Senate, in early June Cook requested a double dissolution under Section 57 of the Constitution to resolve the political deadlock. He had been in office for just a year.[30]

Cook pressed the democratic case. According to Cook, the governor-general's duty was plain: he should act promptly upon his advice, dissolve both the House and Senate, and call for new elections. However, Munro Ferguson, revealing his preference for a more active role, was reluctant to comply instantly. He indicated to Cook that he should like to consult with Fisher, the leader of the opposition, before deciding. Offended, Cook opposed this. Munro Ferguson wrote to Harcourt, rather understating the tension, 'Mr Cook was evidently much against my seeing Mr Fisher'. Much bothered, Munro Ferguson was careful to record that 'the onus of my not having the view of the Opposition is on Mr Cook'.[31] After consulting instead with Sir Samuel Griffith, the chief justice, Munro Ferguson eventually decided to grant Cook's request.[32]

On 5 June came the announcement of a double dissolution and a fresh federal election. Fisher was shut out of the process. Again revealing his instinct for authoritarianism, the governor-general then controversially denied formal requests from Labor for the release of all the correspondence that had guided his decision. The formalities followed. The federal parliament was prorogued on 29 June, and then formally dissolved on 30 July. New elections were fixed for Saturday 5 September.[33]

'How topsy turvey [*sic*] everything appears in Australia to the newcomer,' Munro Ferguson reported to Harcourt in mid-June. In Britain, the reforming Liberals in their struggle with Conservatives had battled to limit the powers of the upper chamber, the House of Lords; in Australia, the reforming Labor men battled to preserve the powers of the upper chamber, the Senate, as their 'idol', because they had a majority there. In Britain, the Labour Party steadfastly opposed militarism and conscription; in Australia, the Labor Party had 'initiated conscription for land and sea to enforce its exclusion policy against men and goods'. The governor-general's analysis was accurate enough: Labor had indeed embraced militarisation in order to defend White Australia and protectionism, believing that both safeguarded working conditions. In the vanguard of this policy of militarisation, wrote Munro Ferguson, was William Morris Hughes, 'the soul of the Labor Party'. Labor was utterly 'self-centred', he complained, and in clinging to 'exclusion' it showed only 'indifference' to Australia's real problem — its under-development and lack of population.[34]

Therefore, the political situation in Australia was unique in its short history just when the danger of a European war was suddenly apprehended: Australia was in the throes of a federal election campaign arising from its very first double dissolution. Across the nation from early July, the politicians locked horns over old and new Australian political quarrels: 'White Australia', protection, monopolies, the former Labor government's new Commonwealth Bank, electoral reforms, railway gauges, experiments in social insurance, maternity allowances, pensions for widows and orphans, industrial arbitration, and, the most contentious issue of all, preference to trade unionists in employment.

Significantly, the parties had their differences on defence policy. Both were prepared to spend more, but Fisher announced that the upgrading of the navy should be accomplished in time of peace from the annual revenue. He denounced the Cook government's readiness to resort to borrowing. Cook, on the other hand, pledged to build 'without delay' the naval establishments for the fleet, as recommended in Admiral Henderson's report of 1911.[35] Such were the issues being debated across Australia in July 1914.

It is important to be aware of how closely political events inside Australia pressed upon international events — and thus squeezed them from the consciousness of many. The Archduke Franz Ferdinand and his wife were assassinated in Sarajevo on 28 June. Andrew Fisher, the federal Labor Party leader, delivered his policy speech at Bundaberg just over a week later, on 6 July. At Parramatta on 15 July, Joseph Cook delivered his policy speech for the Liberal Party. The sudden sharpening in European tension coincided with a quickening pace in the march toward Australia's federal election. The politicians had embarked upon their speaking tours when news broke that Austria–Hungary had delivered its ultimatum to Serbia, on the evening of Thursday 23 July. Austria–Hungary declared war on Serbia on the following Tuesday, 28 July, and the shelling of Belgrade was reported on Thursday 30 July. In Australia, Thursday 30 July was also the day that the proclamation dissolving the federal parliament was announced, and that the writs were issued. It was also the last day for enrolment on the electoral rolls. By that date, as the Balkan crisis threatened to escalate into a clash involving the great powers, Australia's politicians were on tour, selling their policies in public halls across the nation. Prime minister Cook was campaigning in rural Victoria; opposition leader Fisher was speaking to election meetings in Tasmania and Adelaide, before returning to Victoria also on Friday 31 July.

The 'caretaker conventions' commonly invoked in Australia today were quite unknown in 1914. Accordingly, the members of the government gave no indication that they considered themselves under any restraint from making vital decisions that would bind their successors.[36] Neither Cook nor his ministers ever conceded for a moment that, because their government was waiting upon an election, they should act with great caution at this moment of international crisis. As everyone recognised, on the ultimate issue, London would decide — and Australia would be loyal. But, meanwhile, the executive clearly considered itself perfectly entitled to make far-reaching decisions. The nation's safety was sacred — and under the spell of that idol, the Cook government would indeed bind its successor.

And yet, some vital questions about Australia's deployment of military forces were theoretically still open in 1914. Certainly, if Britain fought, Australia would fight, too. But what type of military aid would Australia offer? *When* would Australia make an offer of military assistance — in the wake of a declaration of war, or before? Was she bound to follow any military plans designed before 1914? Would Australia offer *both* naval and military assistance? Would her politicians exercise caution in offering that assistance? Would they put forward the defence of Australian territory as the first priority? Or would they make sweeping offers to assist the empire anywhere? All these questions would soon be answered — and, all along the line, the impulse toward effusive loyalty would trump more moderate impulses.

CHAPTER FIVE

Slip-sliding to war

London, Friday 24 July to Wednesday 29 July

I told him that under no circ[umstance]s could I be a party to our participation in a European War.[1]
– Lewis Harcourt to Asquith, Sunday 26 July 1914

IN LATE-JULY 1914, twelve thousand miles away from Australia, in London, the diplomatic circuits began to hum. Statesmen and diplomats whose names were utterly unfamiliar to ninety-nine out of a hundred Australians began to discuss remote places, ancient rivalries, obscure treaties, and mysterious military commitments that would soon decide the fate of Europe — and with it the fate of tens of thousands of Australians.

Things began to move quickly from Friday 24 July. On that day, Count Albert Mensdorff, the Austro–Hungarian ambassador to Britain, drove the short distance from his embassy at fashionable Belgrave Square to the Foreign Office in Whitehall. His duty was to pass on to Sir Edward Grey a copy of the ultimatum his government had delivered to Serbia on the previous day. Grey greeted Mensdorff in the handsome foreign secretary's office in the magnificent Foreign Office building overlooking St James' Park. It was a very tense meeting. Grey declined to discuss 'the merits of the dispute', but remonstrated with Mensdorff over the harsh terms of the ultimatum.

The rights and wrongs of the Austrian case were 'not our concern,' Grey told Mensdorff. 'It was solely from the point of view of the peace of Europe that I should concern myself with the matter, and I felt great apprehension.'[2]

How would Britain react? Nineteen Liberal ministers, an uneasy grouping of immoveable Entente loyalists and firm neutralists, sat in the Asquith cabinet in the last week of July 1914. Historians differ in their counting of heads — as did the ministers themselves. However, most historians agree that, at the beginning of the crisis, a clear majority of ministers, probably eleven of the nineteen, were leaning decisively against Britain's intervention in a European war.[3]

Who was likely to favour intervention? Eight ministers looked to Britain to show solidarity with her diplomatic partners, France and Russia — especially if their innocence was clear. These eight included some of the most powerful men in the cabinet. First, the group included three long-standing Liberal Imperialists from the right of the party: Herbert Asquith (prime minister and, since March 1914, secretary of state for war); Sir Edward Grey (foreign secretary); and Viscount Haldane (the lord chancellor, a former secretary of state for war). Second, within the circle of interventionists had to be added two more recent converts to the 'policy of the Entente': Winston Churchill (Admiralty), and Charles Masterman (Chancellor of the Duchy of Lancaster). Finally, inside this group there were three 'doubtfuls' — but men whose loyalty to Grey and Asquith weighed heavily in their minds. In this moderate camp were Augustine Birrell (Ireland), Lord Crewe (India Office), and perhaps Reginald McKenna (Home Office).

Who were the convinced neutralists? How many Radicals were there? Churchill thought they made up at least 'three quarters' of the cabinet in 1914.[4] Grey conceded that the Radicals were 'sufficient in number and influence to have broken up the cabinet'.[5] The man most familiar with mustering the neutralist faction was Lewis Harcourt. Harcourt's private memoranda show that, at various points in the crisis, he tallied up his men. On Monday 27 July, he listed eleven names as pledged disciples in the 'Peace party', in this order: Lewis Harcourt (Colonial Office); John Morley (Privy Council); Walter Runciman (Agriculture); T. McKinnon Wood (Scotland); 'Jack' Pease (Education); Reginald McKenna (Home Office); Lord Beauchamp (Works); John Burns (Trade); John Simon (Attorney-General's Office); Charles Hobhouse (Post Office); and Augustine Birrell (Ireland). He added two more names as 'probably' inside his camp: Herbert Samuel (Local Government), and Charles Masterman, because they were aligned with the Radicals in domestic policy. That made a total of thirteen.[6] But, as can be seen, there was some unpredictability. For instance, both camps counted Birrell and Masterman as being on their side. Most notably, Lloyd George did not appear on any list. He was suspected by both camps. He had opposed a big increase in naval spending in January 1914.[7] But most Radicals believed that his belligerent 'Mansion House speech' at the time of the Moroccan Crisis in July 1911 had revealed him to be a believer in the 'continental commitment' — with just a gambler's eye on the main chance.[8]

This highly factionalised cabinet first learned of what one minister recalled as 'a little cloud in the east, appearing out of a blue sky' at a cabinet meeting at 10 Downing Street in the late afternoon of the same day, Friday 24 July.[9] It came at the end of a long cabinet meeting considering the Irish problem. The Buckingham Palace Conference — a controversial effort by King George V to broker a deal between the politicians on Irish Home Rule — had just broken up without any significant gain. Asquith reported at length on the unhappy experiment of monarchical mediation. Naturally, all ministers at the Friday cabinet were utterly absorbed in the Irish crisis. When that was finished with, they were impatient to leave. Grey detained his colleagues, however, just long enough to review the problem in the Balkans that had been created by the Austro–Hungarian ultimatum. He pronounced the situation to be 'very critical'.[10]

Grey's presentation certainly got Asquith's attention. Already, in his imagination, he surveyed the potential for ruinous complications. In his now almost daily letter to his young lover Venetia Stanley, Asquith borrowed Grey's most telling phrase: he told her that he foresaw the danger of the Austro–German and Franco–Russian alliance systems leading to 'a real Armageddon' that would instantly eclipse the noisy Ulstermen with their threats of civil war in Ireland. But then, immediately, Asquith reassured Venetia. 'Happily there seems to be no reason why we should be anything more than spectators. But it is a blood-curdling prospect — is it not?'[11]

Grey's most well known initiative at the beginning of the crisis was to recommend a four-power mediation of the Austro–Serbian quarrel. On Sunday 26 July, the Foreign Office invited the London-based ambassadors of those powers judged *not* to be directly involved in the Austro–Serbian quarrel — that is, Italy, Germany, and France — to meet with Grey in a conference of ambassadors in London. This was an attempt to revive the ambassadorial conference that Grey believed had prevented any escalation of war in Europe at the time of the Balkan Wars of 1912–13. At the same time, Grey urged Vienna, Belgrade, and St Petersburg to suspend all military operations until diplomatic mediation had time to work.[12]

Various British cabinet ministers sought refuge from their worries over Ireland in the countryside over the weekend of Saturday and Sunday 25 and 26 July. It was to his own weekend retreat, 'The Wharf', tucked away in the village of Sutton Courtenay near Oxford, that the prime minister found respite with a few close friends. On the Saturday, walking by the river near Sutton Courtenay with Lady Ottoline Morrell, wife of the leading Radical Philip Morrell, Asquith displayed a certain calm, especially with regard to the Balkans. He told Lady Ottoline that the dispute between Austria and Serbia was not serious. Morrell preserved her impression that Asquith 'did not seem worried'. 'This will take the attention away from Ulster, which is a good thing,' he told her, 'with a laugh'.[13]

But others at 'The Wharf' were worried. Among the few guests that weekend was Edwin Montagu, one of Asquith's junior ministers, and, importantly, his rival for the affections of Venetia Stanley over the previous two years. Montagu speculated on the potential for trouble flowing from the Balkan dispute. He 'feared it would lead to a world war'. Thinking aloud, Montagu allowed his mind to race on as he paced the room: 'Of course, I suppose we shall have to go to war sooner or later with Germany about the Navy, and this may be a good time as any other — they are probably not so well prepared now as they would be later.' Morrell recorded the conversation that followed, with Asquith declaring that Britain was 'under no obligation' to assist the Belgians. His companions apparently agreed among themselves that the prime minister was correct with respect to the Belgians: 'We have made no pledge to help them,' was the common theme.[14]

What did the Radical faction of Asquith's cabinet make of the Balkan quarrel? At a meeting of the party faithful in Manchester on Saturday 25 July, the Radicals' expectations were publicly voiced. Before the requirements of cabinet confidentiality descended on the subject of the crisis, Sir John Simon could be quite open as he addressed a meeting of Altrincham Liberals. He told them that 'in times of anxiety' such as the Balkan crisis, everyone had 'reason to be glad that our foreign administration is in the calm, cool hands of Sir Edward Grey (Cheers.)' Simon asked his audience to resolve, with him, that 'whatever may be the difficulties and dangers which threaten peaceful relations in Europe, the part which this country plays shall from beginning to end be the part of a mediator simply desirous of promoting better and more peaceful relations'.[15]

Another blunt assertion of the Radical view came the next morning, on Sunday 26 July. Lewis Harcourt, the leader of the Radical neutralist faction in the cabinet, motored over to 'The Wharf' from his nearby grand residence, Nuneham Park, south of Oxford. He wanted to discuss with Asquith the government's tactics on Ireland. Harcourt was wary of royal influence on the matter. He pressed Asquith to resist any conditions that the King might seek to impose before granting his assent to any Home Rule Bill, such as a requirement for an immediate dissolution. Asquith responded that if the King made such an offer, and he resisted and was dismissed, then 'the King would win at the Election'. Ireland was still *the* issue, in Asquith's judgement.

Next, Harcourt turned the discussion to, as he put it, 'the probable Austro–Serbian War'. This immediately underlined for Asquith the possibility of significant political divisions arising in his cabinet over that far-off dispute. Speaking as a leading Radical, Harcourt warned the prime minister in blunt terms. He told him he was rigidly opposed to Britain entering a European war. He also cautioned him against entrusting anything to Churchill's judgement in this crisis. Harcourt depicted Churchill, a former Radical and recent convert to Liberal Imperialism, as subject to a dyspeptic impatience. He might slip his collar at any time. Harcourt wanted Asquith to resist Churchill's impulsiveness:

> I warned him that he ought to order Churchill to move no ship anywhere without instructions from the cabinet. I have a profound distrust of Winston's judgment and loyalty and I believe that if the German fleet moved out into the Channel (against France — not us) he would be capable of launching our fleet at them without reference to the cabinet. The PM pooh poohed the idea — but I think he is wrong not to take this precaution.[16]

Thus, right from the outset, Harcourt — as the leading Radical, and as colonial secretary, the minister in closest touch with Australia — made plain his implacable opposition to British intervention in a European war.

Churchill readies the fleet

On the same day, just as Harcourt had feared, Churchill did indeed initiate a most significant naval development. Some background is vital here. That summer, rather than perform ordinary manoeuvres, the British fleets underwent a test mobilisation. This had been announced in parliament in March. Under Admiral Callaghan, some 460 ships took part, which were assembled at Portland Harbour on the Dorset coast by 16 July. The exercise was concluded on 23 July, and the fleets were then scheduled to disperse. This was to have been completed by Monday 27 July.[17]

Churchill, as First Lord of the Admiralty, was ultimately

responsible for a change in this schedule. Enjoying a brief 'paddling' holiday at the seaside in Cromer on the Norfolk coast with his young family over the weekend, Churchill granted a general permission over the telephone at noon on the Sunday to his First Sea Lord, Prince Louis of Battenberg, to take 'whatever steps' he thought necessary in light of the developing Balkan crisis.

When Churchill returned to London at 10.00 p.m., he found that at 4.05 p.m. on the Sunday afternoon Battenberg had indeed acted. Citing Austrian–Serbian tension, Battenberg had ordered that no ships of the First Fleet or its attached flotillas were to disperse from Portland, and that the ships of the Second Fleet 'were to remain at their home ports in proximity to their balance crews'. The order came 'at the eleventh hour' for Callaghan, but the dispersal of the fleets was effectively halted, and naval forces were being held in an advanced state of readiness — close to mobilisation. The Second and Third Fleets 'were to complete with coal, stores and ammunition but all was to be done as quietly as possible'.[18]

That same evening, Churchill walked around to his former house in Eccleston Square, which Grey at that time was renting. There he found Grey with his assistant, Sir William Tyrrell. Churchill sought Grey's support for the naval initiative, and very significantly, for his own idea: an announcement of the naval moves. According to Churchill, both Grey and Tyrrell agreed to his proposal for a newspaper announcement on the Monday that 'might have the effect of sobering the Central Powers and steadying Europe'.[19] Supposedly, the measure would deter Germany and Austria without encouraging Russia and France to be reckless — or so its promoters argued. Britain was flaunting her fealty to the Ententes.

The Times carried the report on Monday 27 July: 'Orders have been given to the First Fleet which is concentrated at Portland, not to disperse for manoeuvre leave for the present. All vessels of the Second Fleet are remaining at their home ports.'[20] All of the world could read it, and it was reported, of course, even in faraway Australia. The British cabinet could scarcely challenge it — after the event.

For good measure, Grey told Alexander Benckendorff, the

Russian ambassador in London, this fortifying news on the Monday
— in one of his few interviews with Benckendorff during the crisis.
As Grey put it, the Germans were wrong if they thought that Britain
'shall stand aside in any event'. Next day, Grey spoke to Cambon on
the same subject. Cambon also 'expressed great satisfaction' at this
indication that Britain was interested in the Balkan crisis. Grey told
his ambassadors in St Petersburg and Paris to relay the news.[21] In
this way, Britain was sending mixed signals: she was attempting to
mediate, certainly, *and* she was ready for war. *The Times* — stridently
pro-interventionist — hailed the naval move as exactly the 'earnest'
signal required.[22]

What was its effect? Did it incite the wilder men to risk more?
The biggest risk, of course, was that too much confidence in British
support would serve as an incitement of Russia, inspiring her to act
boldly in support of Serbia — her protégé in the Balkan imbroglio.
So it proved to be, although the incitement came via France.

On that same Monday, the French president, Raymond Poincaré,
and his freshly elected prime minister, René Viviani, were on board
the battleship *France*, returning from a crucially important trip to
St Petersburg where they had consulted with Tsar Nicholas on a
common stand to be taken by the two allies on the Balkan crisis.
As *France* steamed through the Baltic, the latest diplomatic cables
on the crisis reached the French leaders. Poincaré took heart from
reports from the French embassy in London, and decided that he had
to embolden the Russians. He highlighted one telegram in particular
showing that, in response to German pleas for the localisation of any
war, 'Sir Edw[ard] Grey gave a firm reply that if war breaks out in
the east, no nation could avoid being implicated'.[23] This was a tonic.
'I point to this firmness as an example to Viviani', Poincaré wrote in
his diary. He pleaded with his prime minister to authorise a telegram
promising the Russians that 'France will second her action'.[24] So the
telegram was sent. It assured the Russians that France saw the need
for the two allies to 'affirm their perfect *entente*' and that France was
'prepared, in the interests of general peace, to back fully the action of
the imperial government'.[25]

On Monday 27 July, Grey spoke in the House of Commons about his plans for ambassadorial mediation of the crisis.[26] Then the cabinet ministers gathered in Asquith's room at the House of Commons at 5.30 pm for a short pre-dinner cabinet meeting. It lasted just an hour.[27] Naturally, the situation in Ireland took precedence over the Balkans. For in Dublin the day before, British soldiers had fired upon a nationalist crowd, and the House was in uproar. In order to give time for parliamentary tempers to settle, the cabinet decided that it should postpone consideration of the Amending Bill to the Home Rule Bill from the coming Tuesday to the Thursday.[28]

Only when this was settled did the cabinet turn to consider the Serbian crisis once again. As Grey recalled, at this stage both sides of the cabinet preferred to agree 'to work together for the one object on which both were heartily agreed, to prevent a European war'.[29] His plan for mediation via an ambassadors' conference in London had only just been launched, so Grey explained the details to the cabinet. Another minister, Jack Pease, in his account, noted that Grey did allow himself to vent some criticism of the 'most uncompromising and unreasonable' Austrian attitudes, which showed which way his mind was leading. Then Grey explained the essence of his policy: he was 'anxious not to disclose that as [a] Gov[ernme]nt we intended if possible to keep out of all war, lest his influence as mediator might be thereby diminished'.[30] In this way, Grey suggested that he and the neutralists were close in spirit — keeping out of the war seemed to be the default position. He implied that his position, 'apparent indecision', was very close to the Radicals' position of 'neutrality'. But, while the Radicals might prefer an unequivocal disavowal of war, Grey insisted that doubt about the likelihood of British intervention helped him as a mediator.

This was Grey's first advocacy of the case for an enigmatic stance on Britain's part with respect to the Balkan crisis. It was clever, and expedient. The politically safer course at home, in terms of preserving cabinet unity, matched the diplomatically safer course abroad, in terms of preventing war — at least according to Grey. Inscrutability in Britain's stance was the best tactic for dissuading both sides in the

European crisis from risky action, he had explained. As Hobhouse recorded, Grey had argued that 'our influence for peace depended on our apparent indecision'.[31]

But even on that same day, Grey's plan for a conference of ambassadors began to fall apart. Both Russia and Germany found fault with the plan. In the afternoon of Monday 27 July, George Buchanan, British ambassador to Russia, reported that Sergei Sazonov, the Russian foreign minister, had changed his mind yet again and was now proposing direct negotiations instead between Vienna and St Petersburg. At this, even Arthur Nicolson, the permanent under-secretary and an indefatigable pro-Russian, was moved to complain over the Russian response, minuting that, 'One really does not know where one is with Mr Sazonov'.[32] In the evening, the Germans famously replied to Grey's proposal with the observation that they could not accept what would amount to a 'court of arbitration' in London for Austria, unless it was called together at the request of Austria and Russia.[33] By the afternoon of Tuesday 28 July, Grey himself backed away from the proposal. He expressed the view that a direct exchange of views between Austria and Russia was 'the most preferable method of all'. If the talks could be brought off, he wrote, he would 'suspend every other suggestion'. Clearly, both German reluctance *and* the Russian initiatives at Vienna and St Petersburg had their effect upon Grey.[34]

At the same time, within the Admiralty, naval preparations under Churchill's guidance gathered pace and served to undermine the stance of inscrutability endorsed by the cabinet. After Monday's cabinet meeting, Churchill sent to all his commanders — including those on the Australia station — a secret telegram. It began with the observation that the 'European political situation makes war between the Triple Entente and Triple Alliance Powers by no means impossible.' Tellingly, he employed the controversial expression 'Triple Entente' — disliked by Radicals, because it falsely suggested that Britain was tied to both Russia and France with bonds comparable to those binding Russia and France. Churchill's telegram was careful to specify that 'this is not the warning telegram'. Rather, commanders were ordered to 'be prepared to shadow hostile men-of-war' and to consider the disposition of their ships with that shadowing task in mind. 'Measure is purely precautionary,' explained the telegram.[35]

At 10.00 a.m. on Tuesday morning 28 July, Churchill and his advisers decided on another important step: the fleet, now concentrated, was to be ordered to journey north to its various war stations in the north and at Scapa Flow. 'I feared to bring this matter before the cabinet,' Churchill explained brazenly in his memoirs 'lest it should mistakenly be considered a provocative action likely to damage the chances of peace.' Thus, as Churchill told the story, he informed only Asquith, 'who at once gave his approval.'[36] When the decision was made, there had still been no declaration of war, even in the Balkans. Orders were sent at 5.00 p.m. on the Tuesday evening for the rapid movement of the First Fleet under cover of darkness.[37]

Very early on Wednesday morning 29 July, the First Fleet steamed out at speed, without lights, from Portland. The warships passed through the Straits of Dover and then turned north, toward the fleet's war stations. Meanwhile the Second Fleet assembled at Portland.[38] Why did the First Fleet take the eastern route to the north? In the official history, Julian Corbett explained that, under war plans, the fleet would normally have taken the safer western route. It would only 'face the risk of going east-about up the North Sea' if there were a 'sudden crisis' and 'a chance of bringing on a fleet action'. Corbett claimed that the eastern route was chosen because 'that chance was clearly in view'. He explained that navy Intelligence believed that the German High Seas Fleet was 'concentrated off the coast of Norway' and, therefore, that action was possible.[39]

There was no action. But there was a poignant encounter for Vice-Admiral Sir George Warrender, who commanded the fleet temporarily while Admiral Callaghan attended conferences at the Admiralty. Steaming up the Channel, Warrender on HMS *Iron Duke*, exchanged salutes with the French battleship that was returning to Dunkirk with Poincaré and Viviani at the end of their shortened trip in the Baltic.[40] The encouragement given directly to France by the British naval movements could not have been more dramatically signalled.

In his memoirs, Churchill conjured up the vision of 'eighteen miles of ships running at high speed and in absolute blackness through the narrow straits'.[41] The ships, therefore, were well on their way before the British cabinet met again, on the morning of Wednesday 29 July. For a second time in three days, crucial military preparations, which could not help but have an influence on the diplomatic stance of Britain, as perceived both by friends and enemies, had been undertaken without the authority of cabinet. Britain was edging closer to war.

So, too, was the Continent. Direct talks between Russia and Austria–Hungary were proceeding. But news of the Russian response to the Austrian ultimatum — Russia's partial mobilisation — followed by the Austrian declaration of war against Serbia late on Tuesday 28 July, had severely disabled any prospect of the Austro–Russian talks bearing fruit.[42] Nevertheless, it was still early in the crisis. No escalation of the war had taken place.

Britain's two pre-emptive naval initiatives — the retention of the fleets in a near-to-mobilised state at Portland on Sunday 26 July, and then the dramatic move to war stations overnight on Tuesday 28– Wednesday 29 July — were extremely significant moves. They made the final move, full naval mobilisation, just a small, swift step away. The mood in Churchill's Admiralty was reflected in Julian Corbett's official history, where he described the move to war stations as having been driven by loyalty to France: 'Seeing what our engagements were to France, no less could be done.' This flew in the face of the many assurances given when the redistributions of the fleets of the two powers had taken place in 1912 — namely, that no moral obligations flowed from them.[43] Even more importantly, Britain's two naval initiatives made it much easier to argue that Britain's own expeditionary force — six divisions, the great bulk of her army in the United Kingdom — could be despatched abroad as soon as war was declared, just as enthusiasts for the 'continental commitment' had planned. Because Britain had moved ahead of events to secure her own seas, fear of German invasion receded. As Corbett argued, the consequence was clear: 'So far, then, as naval readiness could secure the country against invasion, there was now no reason why part at least of the Expeditionary Force should not now leave.'[44]

On the morning of Wednesday 29 July, a long meeting of the Asquith cabinet ended with another vital decision: the decision to 'open the War Book' and institute what was called the 'precautionary stage'. Maurice Hankey, secretary of the Committee of Imperial Defence, had pressed this upon Asquith and Grey the previous day, only to be put off. Then Churchill had organised for Hankey to deliver a copy of the 'War Book' to Downing Street on the Wednesday. By a slender margin, the Liberal Imperialists' argument for prudent 'precautions' overcame Radical reluctance — even though war was still confined to the Balkans.[45] The relevant ministers were requested to despatch the official 'Warning' Telegram to all parts of the empire, including Australia.[46]

One of those ministers deeply disturbed by this drift of events was Lewis Harcourt. In his usual private notes on the cabinet, he wrote: 'I am determined not to remain in the Cab[inet] if they decide to join in a war — but they cannot so decide as I am certain now that I can take at least 9 colleagues out with me on resignation, viz Morley, Burns, Beauchamp, McK[innon] Wood, Samuel, Hobhouse, Runciman, Simon.'[47] The balance in the cabinet was still very close, and the Radicals' determination was still strong.

Nevertheless, on that day Harcourt acted as the cabinet majority had decided, of course. After lunch at Downing Street, he walked across to his Colonial Office rooms in the Foreign Office building and instructed his staff to prepare the 'Warning Telegram' to be sent to all the dominions and colonies of the Empire.[48] The message to Australia left London in cipher at 6.35 p.m. GMT on the evening of Wednesday 29 July. It read:

> See preface defence scheme adopt precautionary stage. Names of Powers will be communicated later if necessary.[49]

CHAPTER SIX

The 'Warning Telegram'

Melbourne and Sydney,
Tuesday 28 July to Saturday 1 August

I don't know why we are doing it, because there is nothing moving
in Germany.[1]
– General Henry Wilson, British director of military operations, on
the despatch of the 'Warning Telegram', Diary, 29 July 1914

WHEN THE BRITISH 'Warning Telegram' arrived in Australia, the
pace of events sped up a notch. But it sputtered at first. In fact, in
political circles the Australian response to the arrival of the telegram
was a stumbling affair. Astonishingly, the leading politicians did not
immediately comprehend what London required them to do, under
the terms of the latest Defence Scheme. In part, this resulted from
the fact that key decision-makers in the inner core of prime minister
Cook's cabinet were scattered about the country electioneering. By
chance, too, the necessary ciphers to understand mysterious cables
from London were not immediately available to the travelling
politicians.

In this setting, it was Australia's naval officers who exercised
a decisive influence. Indeed, some among the top brass of the
Royal Australian Navy had been actively pushing to initiate naval
preparation even before the arrival of the telegram. They soon steered

their political masters toward hasty actions, beyond the measures suggested by London as necessary. In that sense, after initially faltering, Australia by her actions began to assist those in London who wanted to rush ahead of events.

As an imperial communication, the warning telegram from London was naturally addressed to the governor-general. Therefore, Major George Steward, the governor-general's official secretary, received it at 3.00 p.m. on Thursday 30 July. At that time, the 'All-Red Route' for cablegrams terminated in Sydney, and so it was delivered to a temporary office that Steward was maintaining for the governor-general among the medical consulting rooms at a prestigious building called 'Craignish' on Macquarie Street, Sydney. The governor-general himself had eventually decided not to stay at Colonel Burns's 'Gowan Brae', but instead at a large private home called 'Yaralla', at Concord West, some nine miles from the city. He was being driven in to Sydney for formal events, while using Steward's office at 'Craignish' as a base. Steward had some small difficulty deciphering the telegram. Initially, he rendered the word 'adopt' as 'adoption (adopt?)' — which weakened the force of the message.[2] Was it a mere request for information about procedures for the adoption of the precautionary stage? Or was it a request that Australia should act, and adopt the precautionary stage?

In this ambiguous form, Steward then delivered the message to Munro Ferguson, who was at 'Craignish' that day. Indeed, he had presided at a meeting of the federal Executive Council in Steward's small office in the morning. Later, the governor-general 'handed' a copy of the telegram to Senator Edward Millen, the minister of defence. Millen was in Sydney, too, scheduled to speak at a political rally at Mosman on the coming Friday evening. Millen had also attended the federal Executive Council in the morning. He had an office close by, at the grand sandstone building, the Customs House, at Circular Quay, only a short distance downhill from 'Craignish'.[3] Steward also sent a copy of the cable from London to Malcolm Shepherd, now the head of the Prime Minister's Department, at his home in Melbourne.[4]

The meaning of the warning telegram ought to have been immediately clear. For it followed almost exactly the form given in the formal 'Preface' to Australia's 'General Scheme of Defence' (1913), as co-ordinated with Britain. Presumably, this document was familiar at least to the prime minister and minister of defence. In this preface, the warning telegram was listed as the *first* of seven possible telegrams that would be sent to Australia in the event of a danger of war — each telegram requesting certain actions from Australia, ranging from the defence of ports to the mobilisation of the military, the search and detention of ships, and the imposition of censorship. According to the signal agreed upon in 1913, the warning telegram would read: 'See Preface, Defence Scheme: Adopt Precautionary Stage against (Power(s))'.[5] Significantly, in the actual warning telegram sent from London on Wednesday 29 July, the power against which precautions were to be taken was not named. That detail would be 'communicated later if necessary'. This added to the provisional character of the warning — no enemy was named. In any case, in the 'General Scheme of Defence', the meaning of the warning telegram was spelt out:

> Meaning of 'Warning' Telegram is:
> Relations with (Power(s)) have become so strained that, in the opinion of His Majesty's Government, it is expedient to adopt such precautions against possible surprise attack, and such limited preparations in anticipation of war as are laid down for the precautionary stage of Defence Schemes.[6]

The defence plan then listed the actions required of Australia at this 'precautionary stage'. In essence, these were the measures outlined under various local 'Defended Ports Defence Schemes', aimed at securing Australia's major port facilities.[7]

However, when the telegram was sent on from Macquarie Street on the afternoon of Thursday 30 July, there followed some confusion — confusion in Cook's circle that lasted until Saturday. This sprang partly from the fact that the prime minister was campaigning in various small towns in rural Victoria and using a hotel in Ballarat as a base to which he returned only in the evenings. Cook's staff could not decipher the various messages they received there. So, too, the minister of defence did not understand immediately the meaning of the telegram when the deciphered version was passed to him. Steward's initial error in the deciphering, with the word 'adopt' rendered as 'adoption (adopt?)', puzzled everyone. Not until the Saturday afternoon of 1 August in Sydney was Millen entirely clear about Britain's request.[8]

Things had already moved much more quickly in the navy. Indeed, Australia's chief naval officers were well ahead of their politicians; it might even be said that they jumped the gun. Leading members of the naval administration at the Navy Department in Lonsdale Street in Melbourne, and naval officers aboard Australian warships cruising off the Queensland coast, pushed for preparatory moves even *before* any request came from London. The Melbourne-based officers were somewhat perturbed that Millen was in Sydney, so far from his advisers. Millen did have George Macandie, the recently appointed secretary of the Naval Board, by his side. Both men were staying at the Athenaeum Club, in Castlereagh Street, one of Sydney's most prestigious clubs — indeed, Munro Ferguson was to dine there on Thursday 30 July. The Athenaeum Chambers, incorporating the club, were only a short walk from Millen's room at the Customs House.

On Tuesday 28 July, Admiral Creswell sought to press the button, ahead of the schedule of measures given in the Defence Scheme. It is worth emphasising how very early this was in the course of the crisis: at about noon on Tuesday 28 July the Austro–Hungarian government declared war upon Serbia, but no news about this had yet arrived in Australia. So far as was known in Australia, no war, even in the Balkans, had yet been declared nor a shot fired. Nevertheless, on that day Creswell wrote a letter marked 'Secret' to George Macandie, recommending certain preliminary steps to the Naval Board. Offering an overall justification for these, he noted that the British Admiralty's special 'War Orders' for the Australian fleet issued in May 1913 had included a suggestion that the Australian authorities 'should secretly move the vessels as near as possible to their war stations when relations with a foreign Power are strained'.[9] The Admiralty in London, claimed Creswell, would 'give no warning when such action is desirable'.[10]

So perhaps there was no need to wait for London? In fact, the board had asked the Admiralty in April 1914 to clarify this very point, and to send a warning message 'whenever a situation rendering precautionary naval movements desirable has arisen'.[11] The Admiralty had acknowledged this request in July.[12] But at this stage of the Balkan crisis, no formal message had yet come from London, so the situation was unclear. Why was action necessary at this early point? Remarkably, in his letter to Macandie, Creswell simply cited reports in newspapers as a justification for Australia embarking upon her own first steps in preparation for war. 'According to the papers the Admiralty have taken some preliminary steps; Germany also,' he wrote.[13] This was, of course, a reference to Churchill's well-publicised first naval initiative — his decision of Sunday 26 July to keep the First Fleet assembled in Portland. The decision now had its effect, even in faraway Australia.

It is, of course, astonishing that the newspapers could be credited with such a role. However, Arthur Jose, correspondent of *The Times* in Australia, later confirmed this. According to Jose, press cables were already unsettling men of the military class in Melbourne as early as Tuesday 28 July. In Jose's words, 'the messages cabled from London to the Australian press were in themselves a warning, and the two members of the [Naval] Board present in Melbourne decided to recommend that certain precautions should be taken'.[14] It is telling that initial requests for action, fuelled probably by Jose, who was both an early member of the Australian National Defence League and a loyal servant of *The Times*, were bubbling up in Australia ahead of any request from London for action.

In his letter to Macandie, Creswell suggested to the Naval Board 'that we should prepare to take certain preliminary steps now'. First, he urged that Rear-Admiral Sir George Patey, the British officer in command of the Australian squadron, who was at that point on board HMAS *Australia* cruising south from Palm Island and bound for Bundaberg, should be contacted. Creswell wanted Patey informed 'that International relations are strained and it may soon be desirable that vessels should be moved towards their war stations'. In addition, Creswell recommended that Patey should be asked to suggest whatever arrangements he wanted in place so that he could 'act on his War Orders in case of necessity'. Second, Creswell urged that all leave should be restricted to six hours, and that all ships be made ready to put to sea at six hours' notice. Next, he advised that the 'Captain-in-Charge' should prepare store ships ready to be sent to both Thursday Island and Fremantle, from where they could supply ships at their war stations. Finally, he recommended that postal authorities and resident magistrates be contacted in order to prepare for the imposition of censorship on wireless-telegraphy stations.[15] All of this was proposed before Australia knew that war had been declared even between Vienna and Belgrade.

The Naval Board sent a telegram to Sydney on the same day asking Senator Millen for permission to set in train all the preliminary steps listed by Creswell, in view of 'the present situation in Europe'. In particular, the board sought permission to ask Patey to make his own suggestions.[16] Millen replied the next day, Wednesday 29 July, agreeing to all these proposals. Most importantly, he agreed that Patey himself should be invited to put forward his own list of essential suggestions. Millen agreed also that the initial preparations for censorship should be made 'irrespective of the present International Outlook'. Finally, Millen pressed the Navy Office to consider immediately measures for a large emergency order of coal supplies for the navy to facilitate their movements for war.[17]

On Wednesday 29 July, Patey seized the opportunity extended by the Naval Board to suggest his own preparatory measures. On that date, Patey's flagship, the battle-cruiser HMAS *Australia*, reached Hervey Bay, north of Brisbane, in company with the two light cruisers HMAS *Melbourne* and HMAS *Encounter*, plus the two destroyers HMAS *Warrego* and HMAS *Yarra*. The cruiser HMAS *Sydney* was at

Townsville on its way to join the fleet. In response to the board's open invitation to suggest any immediate actions, Patey telegraphed from Hervey Bay to Melbourne recommending that the whole fleet should steam south to take on fuel and stores in preparation for a move to war stations. At first, according to Patey's account, Millen in Sydney was unwilling to concede to all of Patey's requests. He needed more facts, he said. Millen indicated also that the next federal Executive Council was scheduled to meet in Sydney on the morning of Thursday 30 July, when it would wish to consider Patey's proposals in more detail.[18] In the interim, Millen offered a compromise, suggesting that perhaps one light cruiser from the fleet might be redirected south.[19]

On Thursday, the arrival of the famous warning telegram from London then lit a fire under events in Sydney. As mentioned, on the morning of that day the governor-general had presided over a very thinly attended federal Executive Council in his cramped office at 'Craignish'. In fact, only two ministers had attended, Edward Millen and William Kelly. Most members of the Cook cabinet were still travelling inter-state on campaign duties. The main business of the federal executive meeting was clearly formal: the endorsing of a proclamation dissolving the parliament, and the issuing of writs for the election on Saturday 5 September.[20] Apparently, the meeting did discuss Patey's request. But before sending any formal response to Patey, during the afternoon Munro Ferguson received from Major Steward his copy of the deciphered warning telegram from London. Millen, too, was given his copy. This served to hurry them both to make their decisions.

At the same time, the British senior naval officers commanding the China Station (which included New Zealand) and the East Indies Station had begun to circulate copies of London's warning telegram to their naval colleagues. For, at the Admiralty in London on the afternoon of Wednesday 29 July, Churchill had directed the despatch of the telegram to naval authorities throughout the empire. The senior naval officer in New Zealand relayed copies to Patey himself and to the Naval Board in Melbourne at 5.00 p.m. on Thursday 30 July. With London's formal telegram now providing some tangible proof of danger, so the naval officers believed, Admiral Creswell and the other board members eagerly pressed all Patey's plans upon Millen. They urged that he should authorise the Australian navy to distribute its ships according to the pre-arranged 'war position tables'. That same Thursday evening, Millen agreed, and the requisite orders were issued. The firepower of the Australian fleet was directed to move south — just as Patey had requested before London's warning telegram had won the debate for him. Millen and Macandie also moved to authorise other preparations on that day. Macandie placed a phone call to the Navy Department in Melbourne, asking for 'a responsible officer' to travel to Sydney overnight with a copy of Australia's 'war orders' and the 'war book', to be delivered to the Athenaeum Club as soon as he arrived.[21]

In this way, the Royal Australian Navy was the first of the Australian forces to move closer to a war footing. On Thursday 30 July, at 10.30 p.m. all the ships under Patey's command within Hervey Bay weighed anchor. HMAS *Melbourne* was directed to call in at Moreton Bay to be oiled, before proceeding to Sydney. HMAS *Sydney* continued to load coal at Townsville, and awaited orders. HMAS *Encounter* and HMAS *Australia* set off for Sydney at top speed. Later, Munro Ferguson would assure Harcourt how mightily impressed he was by all this: the Australian navy's steps to prepare for war at the outset of the crisis had been not just speedy but 'instantaneous.'[22]

Not everyone was happy. Some tensions between the naval staff and the minister had developed over the previous year. Since coming to office in 1913, Millen had engaged in some prickly exchanges with his staff about the fleet's War Orders. In early 1914, Millen had reminded the officers in the Naval Department that he, and only he, could authorise naval movements.[23] Now Patey, in his record of these latest events, was careful to note embarrassing details of diffidence on the part of Millen. To be precise, he noted that HMAS *Australia* was initially 'ordered to Sydney at 20 knots', but then she reduced speed to 13 knots 'about midnight in consequence of orders from the Minister of Defence'. According to Patey, 'these orders were cancelled shortly afterwards and speed was again increased to 20 knots'.[24] Thus, HMAS *Australia* arrived in Sydney at eleven o'clock on the morning of Saturday 1 August, and immediately began to load coal and ammunition — attracting the attention of photographers. The prickliness between Millen and Patey served to indicate an important reality in political-military relations on the eve of the war: namely, that any hesitation on the part of Australia's politicians in preparation for war was bound to be met with solid opposition from the officer corps. The navy's success in pressing for early preparations, just ahead of those nominated by London, no doubt also encouraged the military officers to believe that any political caution could be overcome by the plea of military necessity.

There was some unhappiness, too, in contacts between the Naval Board and Millen. On Saturday 1 August, the board telegraphed Millen in Sydney, pleading with him to return to Melbourne, the headquarters of Australia's defence administration. This was desirable, argued the board, 'to avoid duplication of control and issues of contradictory orders'. In addition, the board complained of 'the great difficulties that are being experienced' and 'the uncertainty existing owing to change [in] War plans'.[25] All week Millen had been on a busy election schedule, travelling and speaking every day.[26] On Saturday, he did not set off for Melbourne immediately, as we shall see, but waited until the Sunday evening, when he was to make use of the governor-general's express train to Melbourne.

The active role of the governor-general in this story of Australia's hasty naval preparations was clear. He appears to have grown anxious that Australia was not reacting swiftly enough to indications of the danger of war during Thursday 30 July. On that day, only two cabinet ministers had been available to discuss Admiral Patey's suggestion for the redirection of the fleet. Probably later that same afternoon, after both Munro Ferguson and Millen had received their copies of the warning telegram, the governor-general decided to confront the minister. He pressed Millen for a private assurance on the key matter that had begun to weigh most heavily in his assessment of the situation: would the Australian fleet be transferred immediately to the British Admiralty's control upon the outbreak of war, as had been agreed at the Imperial Conferences? Millen instantly gave the assurance.

Munro Ferguson, undoubtedly relieved, sent a telegram to Harcourt at the Colonial Office, acknowledging receipt of the warning telegram. Most importantly, he conveyed the joyful news that Millen had privately promised that the Australian fleet would promptly be handed over to London's control. The telegram read:

> Your telegram of 29 July received. Shall have cipher by Saturday from Melbourne.
>
> I understood from Minister of Defence unofficially that Australian ships would be placed at Admiralty's disposal *at once*.

FERGUSON[27]

This was quite a coup for the governor-general. For Australians had betrayed their sensitivity regarding the separate status of their 'Royal Australian Navy' on many occasions over recent years. Munro Ferguson himself had written to Harcourt as recently as June stressing the devotion of Australians to the notion of their 'own' navy. 'Nothing could be more disturbing in naval circles in the Pacific,' he had observed, 'than to cast doubt on the value of separate Fleet units'.[28] Similarly, Henry Stead had written to Harcourt that, when the new Australian fleet paraded in Sydney Harbour in October 1913 for the first time, attracting big crowds, he found Australians resentful of anyone voicing the real facts — namely, that their new fleet 'must always be regarded as part of the Imperial Fleet not purely an Australian one, which means that in some time of grave crisis it might have to leave our waters to help Imperial ships elsewhere'.[29] Of course, Australian politicians had acknowledged in 1909 and 1911 that the fleet would be transferred to the British Admiralty in wartime, simply insisting that Australia must make the decision to hand it over. Now, at the outset of the Balkan crisis, Munro Ferguson had secured by means of private pressure behind the scenes a significant prize: an unofficial promise that Australian naval power would be instantly available to add to British naval forces if war broke out.

Resisting the march to war

Munro Ferguson's telegram from Sydney conveying the promised transfer chimed in with developments in London quite dramatically — and unfortunately. For the telegram from the outskirts of the empire helped those hoping to overcome the efforts that Liberal ministers, led by Harcourt, were making to keep Britain's own activity in this crisis fixed upon neutral diplomacy, which they hoped might dissuade Russia and France from any premature action.

Already there were indications during these first few days of the crisis that the rivalries being played out in London between neutralists and interventionists in the Asquith cabinet were affecting the various instructions reaching Australia. For instance, cabinet's decision on Wednesday 29 July to send the warning telegram had been a victory for the interventionists in Asquith's cabinet — that is, Asquith, Grey, Haldane, and Churchill. At this point, Harcourt was still desperate to avoid any incidents that might suddenly inflame international tensions. He was intensely suspicious that Churchill might provoke something. 'No "search" of ships in ports to be made at present,' wrote Harcourt in his usual notes on the cabinet of 29 July.[30] Thus, the day after the warning telegram was sent, Thursday 30 July, it was Harcourt who despatched a second telegram cautioning the Australian authorities *not* to institute searches of presumed enemy ships within their harbours, but rather only to prepare for future searches.[31] On the same day in London, Harcourt was angered at reports that some ships *had* been searched at Gibraltar overnight. Harcourt instantly blamed Churchill. 'I think he has gone mad,' he wrote. Churchill, Harcourt complained, was 'getting prematurely in the war stage'.[32]

Therefore, during Thursday 30 July in London, Harcourt agonised over the next step. He was anxious not to be seen to be pushing

Australia into premature action. Clearly, he preferred to leave Australia herself with some room for her own decision-making. For some hours, Harcourt sat on a proposed telegram composed by the Admiralty that he was asked to send to Australia — a telegram urging the transfer of the fleet. He explained his dilemma in his cabinet journal, and described how this was quickly resolved by the arrival of the telegram from Munro Ferguson quoted above:

> My prescribed duty in 'precautionary stage' [is] to ask Australia to place her entire fleet at our disposal and to put [it] under command of Admiralty. I declined to send this tel[egram] this morn[ing] on [the] ground [that it is] premature, unnecessary, and that I wanted [the] initiative taken by Australia — if initiative failed I w[oul]d tel[egram] (priv[ate] and pers[onal]) to R. M. Ferguson to try to produce it. At 5 p.m. [I] received acknowledgement fr[om] Australia of my 'Warning' tel[egram] with [the] unofficial offer of their fleet for our purposes.[33]

This may have resolved Harcourt's dilemma, but it was scarcely a pleasing outcome. Those forcing the pace of preparation were beginning to dominate in both London and the dominions.

By no means was it the end of Harcourt's rivalry with Churchill. For on the evening of the same day, Thursday 30 July, Harcourt received another request to ramp up Australia's naval preparations. The Admiralty, which had also received a copy of Munro Ferguson's unofficial assurance about the transfer of the Australian fleet, pressed Harcourt to follow this up with a further request. It was 'urgent', pleaded the Admiralty, that the Australian ships should be requested to take up their war stations immediately. The Admiralty supplied a draft telegram, which asked Munro Ferguson to 'arrange with the Minister of Defence' for 'the Australian ships to take up their preliminary stations in accordance with their war orders'. Australia's major defence asset, the battle-cruiser HMAS *Australia*, should 'proceed to West Australia, ready to proceed to Hong Kong' — that is, to the China station, under British command. A consoling sentence was added, possibly to help Harcourt swallow the task: 'These movements are purely precautionary, but in view of the great distances to be traversed they should not be delayed.'[34]

The parallel in Britain at this point is worth recalling. As noted above, the First Fleet of the Royal Navy had been moved dramatically from Portland to its war stations at Scapa Flow and in the north during the very early morning of Wednesday 29 July.[35] Asquith and Churchill had arranged this, before the cabinet had considered the matter. It had infuriated the cabinet Radicals. They alleged it was just another example of Churchill frog-marching military preparations and pre-empting the cabinet. Naturally, Harcourt was wary of conveying orders to Australia for a similar movement of her warships. However, he eventually complied, sending the telegram at 8.00 p.m. on Thursday 30 July. But he recorded his anxiety and reluctance about yet another 'premature' move in these terms:

> Admiralty asked me to tel[egram] to Australia for fleet to go to 'War Stations'. I did so with regret (c[oul]d not take responsibil[ity] of refusing) — think premature, but possibly justified on ground of great distances for their fleet. e. g. The *Australia* has got to go to the coast of West Australia.[36]

This emphatic and direct request to Australia for her ships to be moved to their war stations — as solicited by Munro Ferguson and urged by Churchill — arrived in Sydney on the morning of Friday 31 July. At 2.00 p.m., Munro Ferguson was able to reply with the good news. He told Harcourt that he had wired the request to Cook and had handed a copy to Millen. In response, Millen had told him that HMAS *Australia* was already steaming toward Sydney to take on coal before heading to Albany in Western Australia.[37]

At the Admiralty, Churchill did not miss an obvious opportunity to encourage the dominions in their eager co-operation with the imperial authorities, by showering them with praise. An effusive message was procured for Australia, underpinned by the formal support of 'the Lords Commissioners of the Admiralty'. This was despatched to Munro Ferguson on Friday 31 July: 'Admiralty desire [to] convey warmest appreciation of Commonwealth action at present critical time.' Harcourt sent a very similar message to Melbourne, expressing the British government's 'warm appreciation' of Australia's offer of her fleet.[38] The next day, he sent a different inquiry. Did Australia, he asked, want this correspondence regarding the transfer of its fleet published? 'If so, please telegraph what should be published,' he instructed. There was just a hint here that Harcourt had no desire to publicise the Australian offer at this point, and in fact nothing appeared in the London press about the offer over the weekend.[39]

Indeed, Harcourt's real feelings must have been very different from the 'warm appreciation' he conveyed so politely. From his perspective, twice in two days he had reluctantly despatched requests to Australia for naval actions that he privately considered 'premature' and even 'unnecessary'. Harcourt's reluctance to send these messages no doubt arose from his conviction that Churchill and others were seeking to steamroll resistance. Such naval preparations, Harcourt feared, might invite incidents that could draw Britain into Russia's war. As he fought in London against men he believed to be acting recklessly, he was not aware of any principled reluctance in Australia that might have helped his cause. The Australian politicians — so far as he could perceive them through the communications of Munro Ferguson — seemed to be on the side of those ready to ratchet up preparations for war, even before any major power in Europe was involved. On the evening of Thursday 30 July, as related earlier, Harcourt was despondent: 'War situation I fear much worse tonight. Pray God I can still smash our cabinet before they can commit the crime.'[40]

CHAPTER SEVEN

Champing at the bit

Wellington, Ottawa, Melbourne,
Friday 31 July to Sunday 2 August

... if the occasion arises — and it may — the Government will ask
Parliament and the people of New Zealand to do their duty by offering
the services of an expeditionary force to the Imperial government.
(Hear, hear.)[1]
– New Zealand prime minister William Massey, in parliament, 31 July
1914

AUSTRALIA WAS NOT ALONE in sending messages to London that
seemed to say *If there is to be a war, can we please be involved?* On
receipt of London's warning telegram, the three leading dominions
— New Zealand, Canada, and Australia — displayed a zealous
impulsiveness in putting forward public offers of military aid to
Britain. The 'daughter nations' bawled their readiness to help the
'mother country'. But it is important to stress that these offers were
not simply generalised assurances of support in case of war. Such
offers might have been redeemed merely by active preparation for
self-defence if war broke out. More than that, much more, was
offered. Public promises of *expeditionary* forces were made — and
proclaimed to the world.

According to the official documents, the dominion of New

Zealand was the first to make an offer of an expeditionary force. Early on Friday 31 July, the Colonial Office received an enquiry from Arthur Foljambe, Lord Liverpool, the governor of New Zealand and a former Liberal politician. Liverpool asked Harcourt to inform him 'at the earliest possible moment when we should bring into operation Section 19 of the New Zealand Naval Defence Act'. This was the provision under the Act providing that, whenever war was declared between Britain and another country, all of New Zealand's naval forces 'shall pass and remainder under the control and be at the disposition of the Government of Great Britain'.[2]

Some hours later, Liverpool sent much more exciting news. On the evening of Friday 31 July, New Zealand time, there had been emotional scenes in the parliament in Wellington. William Massey, leader of the Reform Party and the prime minister of New Zealand, had made an offer of support to Britain. Liverpool telegraphed to London on the same night, reporting that Massey had declared solemnly to the parliament 'that, if necessity unfortunately arose, New Zealand was prepared to send her utmost quota of help in support of the Empire'. Liverpool stressed the 'great enthusiasm' and 'the acclamation of all parties in Parliament' that had greeted this announcement. He noted that he had been asked to convey the New Zealand parliament's declaration of readiness to help Britain to both the King and the Imperial government.[3]

The Admiralty, of course, was instantly advised of this offer. Here Winston Churchill immediately saw a chance to hearten New Zealand in her eagerness to advertise her fealty. He requested that a formal reply be sent, again citing the support of the lords commissioners, and expressing the Admiralty's 'profound appreciation' of the 'patriotic action [of] New Zealand at this most critical time'. He added, for the benefit of expectant naval enthusiasts in New Zealand, that 'H. M. S. *New Zealand* is with the First Battle Cruiser Squadron' — that is, that the Dreadnought paid for by New Zealand was already at its war station and ready for action.[4] Harcourt replied more simply to Liverpool on behalf of the King on the Saturday afternoon. He telegraphed that the King had asked him to pass on assurances of his 'high appreciation' of the 'staunch loyalty of the Dominion'.[5] There was no allusion to the 'utmost quota' mentioned in the New Zealand offer.

The next day, Saturday 1 August, Lord Liverpool followed up his news of the parliament's patriotic declaration with a long cable giving more thrilling details. This revealed that New Zealand's political leaders had actually foreshadowed a precise offer: an expeditionary force. Liverpool reproduced the relevant passages from the speeches in parliament on the Friday night from both Massey and Sir Joseph Ward, the leader of the opposition Liberal Party. Reacting to a question without notice from a member of his Reform Party, regarding the possibility of an expeditionary force, Massey had announced that 'there is no occasion for serious alarm'. But, Massey had added, in the event of war, he would indeed ask the parliament and people to heed the call of 'duty' and send an expeditionary force to assist the Empire wherever required. He had proudly explained how well prepared New Zealand was to send such an expeditionary force. He told MPs that 'an understanding has been arrived at with regard to the numbers and constitution of a Force which will fit in with Imperial requirements'. The prospect of New Zealand being the first dominion in the field to help Britain danced before the eyes of every needy MP. Then, alluding to the news in the evening papers in New Zealand that Canada had already offered an expeditionary force, Massey summed up his response in three words, 'Well done, Canada!' There was loud applause, and all members of the chamber then rose and sang the National Anthem.

Sir Joseph Ward spoke next for the opposition, remarking that he had heard Massey's statement with the 'utmost satisfaction'. Ward did express the hope that, through the 'wise counsels of the leading men', the danger of war in Europe might yet pass and, therefore, that there would be no need 'to co-operate with the Old Country'. But the opposition, he announced, would heartily support the government. Indeed, he announced his enthusiastic backing for the government in sweeping terms, promising to get behind 'whatever may be necessary in the way of sending an expeditionary force'.[6] Both politicians, therefore, had endorsed the public offer of an expeditionary force.

Liverpool kept up a flow of telegrams reaffirming that the speechmakers' offer of an expeditionary force was not merely rhetorical but very real. On Sunday 2 August, he advised Harcourt that prime minister Massey was 'anxious to ascertain whether the circumstances warrant [the] New Zealand government in calling immediately for the names of the volunteers to compose an expeditionary force'. To be sure, Massey noted that mobilisation would not take place until the imperial authorities directed it. But Massey wanted a reply as soon as possible, Liverpool explained, 'so as to enable [the] sanction of Parliament to be obtained immediately'.[7] The tone of urgency rang clear and proud. The Colonial Office naturally shared this latest urgent offer from New Zealand with the Admiralty, the War Office and the Foreign Office.[8]

The effect upon Harcourt, who was meeting on a daily basis with other cabinet Radicals determined to avert a British commitment to war and expeditionary force, can be easily imagined. No doubt he felt increasingly under siege at the Colonial Office when such cables — prompting visions of the imperial pups slavering to join a dogfight — were delivered to him. When Lord Liverpool's urgent enquiry about 'calling immediately' for the men to make up the proposed expeditionary force in New Zealand arrived at the Colonial Office on the afternoon of Sunday 2 August, Harcourt replied politely, but stiffly. He sent a cable in the evening, naturally expressing 'deep gratitude' for New Zealand's offer to summon volunteers immediately for an expeditionary force, but concluding bluntly: 'No condition, however, has yet arisen which would make this step necessary.'[9]

By contrast, these offers from New Zealand emboldened those officers in the Admiralty pressing for Britain to display greater loyalty to the Entente, and to contemplate immediate offensive action against Germany at the same time. Imperial spoils beckoned. The effect can be traced in the documents exchanged by Admiralty staff. For example, New Zealand's offers of an expeditionary force, when relayed to the Admiralty on Sunday 2 August, prompted Rear-Admiral Arthur Leveson, director of operations on the Admiralty war staff, to advise Vice-Admiral Doveton Sturdee, the chief of war staff, that the Admiralty should signal its support for the immediate preparation of such a New Zealand force in order to capture German Samoa. It would 'protect trade in the South Pacific,' he wrote. Moreover, such offensive action could draw the German warship SMS *Leipzig* from the coast of South America, and then British warships could eliminate it, Leveson argued.[10] 'This seems desirable,' Prince Louis of Battenberg, First Sea Lord, noted on the document.

Similarly, Sturdee lined up behind the proposal. He saw immediately that such offers from the dominions could be utilised to capture German colonies. The reason he adduced for immediately accepting the offers was revealing, too. He advised Battenberg that, 'If hostilities break out, it would be well to accept all offers from Dominions to attack German colonies. Besides being a powerful threat *it will stimulate the imperial idea.*' With colonies under threat, German forces might be distracted from disturbing the empire's trade, Sturdee added. At such a time, when the issue of war and peace stood in the balance, it is depressingly instructive that such a senior British naval official could mention the stimulation of 'the imperial idea' as a reason for advancing plans for the seizure of German colonies.[11]

The dominion of Canada — as Massey had advertised in the New Zealand parliament — had also been very early in signalling its readiness to help Britain. The theatrical and impulsive Canadian minister of defence, Colonel Sam Hughes, had set the ball rolling. He spoke to journalists in Ottawa about the possibility of raising an expeditionary force as early as Thursday 30 July.[12] A proposed figure of 30,000 troops was widely reported in the Canadian press and then swiftly in newspapers throughout the empire. In Ottawa, Prince Arthur, Duke of Connaught, and uncle of King George V, who had served as the Canadian governor-general since 1911, did his best to encourage the Conservative government of prime minister Robert Borden to follow up this speculative talk with a formal offer of assistance.

This was realised on Sunday morning, 2 August. It came in the shape of an enquiry that simultaneously sought to prompt the desired answer. On that day, a telegram in cipher from the Duke of Connaught arrived at the Colonial Office at 9.00 a.m. The Canadian governor-general explained that his ministers wanted to help Britain and were 'anxiously considering the most effective means of rendering every possible aid'. The Duke requested the guidance of 'the Imperial military and naval authorities' in Britain. But, with a heavy hand, he added that the Canadian government was 'confident that a considerable force would be available for service abroad'. In this way he pushed forward the idea of an expeditionary force. His ministers, he reported, were already considering how to evade the bothersome requirement that, under Section 69 of Canada's *Militia Act*, 'the Active Militia can only be placed on active service beyond Canada for the defence of Canada'. This hitch could be got over, he speculated, by the simple expedient of enabling the Canadian regiments to 'enlist for a stated period as Imperial troops'. Then they could serve anywhere without the defence of Canada being an object. In any case, he assured London, the Canadians would cover 'all necessary financial provision for their pay, maintenance, and equipment'.[13] Here was another offer from another dominion evidently tugging at the leash and eager to be involved in any war.

The Colonial Office, of course, sent on copies of the Canadian offer to the other great offices on Whitehall and Downing Street. The reception of the Canadian offer again reveals a good deal about the expectations prevailing among those officials at work within the bureaucracies in London who were eager for rapid intervention in the European war. A great imperial struggle was dawning: imperial forces could be required anywhere to undertake a fresh partition of colonial territories. This was the spirit that animated the trustees of the empire. For example, writing to the Admiralty, Sir John Anderson at the Colonial Office interpreted the Canadian cable as a request for advice on 'the supply of a force from Canada for service in Europe' — and he then crossed out 'in Europe' and substituted 'outside the Dominion'.[14] The amendment was perfectly correct: it was indeed an offer to serve anywhere.

For its part, the Admiralty again exerted pressure in Whitehall that this fresh dominion offer should be instantly accepted. On the same day the Canadian offer was sent to London, Admiral Leveson at the Admiralty wrote to his superiors, suggesting that a Canadian force should be sent and held in Antigua. If Denmark or Holland were allied with Germany, or were forced by Germany into war, or if Germany eventually seized any other islands in the West Indies, he speculated, these would provide bases for German commerce raiders. So the 'flying force' from Canada would be a valuable addition to British forces in the Caribbean that would be strengthened and ready to retake the Dutch, Danish, or any other islands that might fall into German hands. Once again, Sturdee urged Battenberg to press that the offer should be immediately accepted, so that the 'principle' of expeditionary warfare could be endorsed. The matter of where exactly 'expeditions over the seas' might be deployed, Sturdee advised, could wait until the War Office considered the details. Churchill recorded his endorsement of the plan.[15] All of this took place within hours of the receipt of the Canadian offer.

The atmosphere was one of frantic preparation. Indeed, the publicity given the Canadian offer over several days provoked action beyond the Admiralty building. For example, the Admiralty was soon fielding inquiries from, to put it politely, interested parties. For example, on Monday 3 August the manager in chief of ocean services at the Canadian Pacific Railway Company's London office wrote to the secretary of the Admiralty, asking if it was 'contemplated' that Canadian troops would soon be sent 'over this side'. If so, he wanted advance warning, so that his cargo and mail ships could be quickly fitted out with materials that were to hand in London to enable each of the company's ships to carry between 1,000 and 1,500 troops as 'steerage passengers'.[16] An expeditionary force to England was in the wind — and so, too, were war contracts.

Back at the level of high diplomacy, it was Harcourt who once again had to react in the first instance to the Canadians' offer on behalf of Asquith's government. The Colonial Office staff drafted a reply to the Duke of Connaught on Sunday 2 August. This politely welcomed 'with great satisfaction' the Canadian telegram and promised a further reply, once the points raised by the Canadian ministers had been considered. Meanwhile, the British government sent 'their most grateful thanks and appreciation of this splendid evidence of the desire of Canada to co-operate in the defence of the Empire'.[17] There was no reference whatever to the offer of an expeditionary force. It was not until the next day that a cable was finalised and sent. This followed consultation between Harcourt and Asquith, and a referral of the matter to the Army Council.[18] In this final version of the cable, Harcourt told the duke that the British government 'prefer to postpone offering detailed observations on [the] suggestion put forward in your telegram pending further developments'. He promised another telegram 'as soon as situation appears to call for further measures'.[19] This was to say everything but the truth. In Harcourt's view, the Canadians' offer must have struck him in the same way as the New Zealanders' offer: it was simply unnecessary, and irritatingly premature.

Indeed, in political terms, the offers from New Zealand and Canada, so very suggestive of men struggling into their khaki and desperate to get at someone with a bayonet, were unwelcome complications that undermined Harcourt and his Radical allies in their efforts to stave off what they felt would be the disaster of an imperial war.

CHAPTER EIGHT

A looming love-of-Empire auction

Colac and Horsham, Friday 31 July

... whatever happens to the Empire, Australia is part of the Empire, and when the Empire is at war Australia is at war, and will have to be prepared to take her part in preserving the security of the Empire. (Loud cheers).[1]

–Prime Minister Joseph Cook, at Horsham, 31 July 1914

REPORTS OF 'PATRIOTIC OFFERS' from Canada and New Zealand began to have a direct effect in Australia from Friday 31 July. For example, on that day several reporters, brandishing cablegrams claiming that Canada was about to offer 30,000 troops to Britain, confronted Australia's minister for defence, Senator Edward Millen. He was asked 'how Australia stood in this respect'. Millen replied that Australia was not a 'fair-weather partner of the Empire'. Therefore, he explained, he had no doubt that, as in other crises, the nation would soon show ample evidence of 'Australia's loyalty and willingness to co-operate'.[2] But he did not mention specifically an expeditionary force that might be available from Australia.

The expectations raised by some in the press can be understood in the context of the range of editorial advice on the crisis that emerged across the week beginning on Monday 27 July. Some editors advised Australia's politicians that Britain's immediate entry into a European war was doubtful. The possibility of British neutrality was not ruled out: important newspapers acknowledged the power of the neutralist faction inside the British Liberal Party. Sydney's *Daily Telegraph*, for example, stressed that Britain was not bound by any treaty to assist her diplomatic partners, France and Russia. It drew attention to Asquith's many assurances in the House of Commons that Britain would not assist France in an aggressive war, but noted that she 'would support France to the utmost if Germany attacked that power'. The *Daily Telegraph* conceded that 'a considerable body of Liberals and Labor representatives in Great Britain would strongly oppose participation in a Continental war, and would urge a policy of neutrality'. If fighting broke out, however, it was 'extremely doubtful' that Britain could remain neutral for long.[3] In a feature article, the *Daily Telegraph* argued that if war erupted, Australians were not in peril, for there was 'no immediate danger of getting a whiff of powder in our nostrils'. However, the same newspaper conceded that a major war in Europe would be 'a staggering blow to our commerce and industry'.[4]

The Age was generally more moderate. The editor was, in fact, a German-born but fiercely patriotic Australian, Gottlieb Schuler — whose son would soon fight in Australian uniform and be devoured by the war. Schuler began the week with an editorial condemning 'the frenzied rush of warlike preparation' that all the European nations had indulged in over recent years. The arms race was a 'senseless riot', a 'Bedlamite extravagance', and a 'tremendous waste of brawn and brain and capital'.[5] On Thursday 30 July, *The Age* counselled that war was not imminent, and announced its confidence that Europe's sensible leaders would head off the danger. It was full of contempt for the Austrian emperor, Francis Joseph, the 'octogenarian monarch', and his truculent advisers who were exhibiting 'Austria's appalling selfishness' in their determination to wage war against Serbia. 'The situation is serious,' conceded *The Age*, 'but European statesmanship will indeed be a poor thing if it is permitted to develop into a general war'.[6] In Schuler's editorials, *The Age* did not speculate on British action until Monday 3 August.

The *Sydney Morning Herald* editor, Thomas Heney, was also cautious during the week of diplomatic crisis. He looked forward optimistically to Britain and Germany mediating a solution or localising any conflict. The *Sydney Morning Herald* stressed Britain's 'free hand', and pointed to the powerful international commercial interest, and Australia's own interest, too, in peace. Editorials advanced the case that Sir Edward Grey and the Kaiser should be relied upon to negotiate a solution. As peace was in the interests of all the great powers, the war should be localised. Heney's editorials in the *Herald* also stressed that Britain was not formally committed to her Russian and French diplomatic partners. On this basis, argued Heney, her mediation of the crisis was more likely to be successful. Significantly, Heney pointed out that if war came, it was the Royal Navy that would play a role — leaving aside any role for her army. For example, on 29 July, the *Herald* argued: 'The first object of Great Britain is the preservation of peace, but it is impossible for her to say what part her navy might be called upon to take if this frontier quarrel should lead to a war between two or more of the Great Powers.'[7]

There was no mention anywhere of Australia's expeditionary force. But on Tuesday 28 July, the *Sydney Morning Herald* did remind its readers of the strength of the British Expeditionary Force (BEF), with its six divisions and one cavalry division. This force, reported the *Herald*, was 'complete and ready for war, the object of which is to be ready for service in any part of the world at short notice'.[8] This note serves to underscore the fact that Australians were typically inclined in this period not just to aspire to service on Britain's behalf, but also to hope that loyalty to Britain might bring back tangible benefits. One day, Britain's BEF might bail out Australia.

There were other more zealous voices. From an early date in the crisis, some of the leading pro-imperial — and, it must be said, the more stridently anti-Labor newspapers — began to lecture London. They vehemently backed the idea of prompt British intervention in a continental war. Most notably, as early as Tuesday 28 July, the

Melbourne *Argus* editorialised on Britain's responsibilities in the European crisis. The paper reverently regretted that 'anything so dreadful as a general war' might arise from the Balkan assassination, but it warned immediately that, if it did, all the great powers might be forced by 'circumstances' to intervene in order to make good their alliances. In that case, both Britain and Australia simply had to face the fact that the 'almost inconceivable' could happen, and they had to act bravely. 'But the balance of power in Europe must be maintained at any cost,' declared *The Argus*. It was certain that Britain 'could not possibly sit idly by and see her group of nations subdued by the Triple Alliance. And when Great Britain is at war the whole British Empire is at war'.[9]

Looking at the balance of editorial opinion, it cannot be said that by Friday 31 July there was any irresistible movement in the press in favour of Australia making an offer of precise material support to Britain.

Over these same days, the federal election campaign began to warm up. The leading politicians spoke at a series of well-attended and noisy rallies for the coming election. In the main, they addressed the key domestic issues — pensions, social insurance, industrial law, taxes, protection, and the vexed issue of preference for trade unionists in government employment. Only toward the end of the week did the European crisis gain coverage in the newspapers, and did the leaders begin to make reference to it.

For the federal Labor Party, proud of its commitment to compulsory military training and the significant boost to defence spending during its period of office from 1910 to 1913, the sudden speculation about a war in Europe might have provided political opportunities to play up the issue of defence. Labor's defence policies could be depicted as having been vindicated. But, even as the newspapers reported the shelling of Belgrade in the middle of the week, Fisher did not immediately promote defence as the centrepiece of his addresses. Certainly he defended compulsory military training. In Adelaide on Thursday 30 July, Fisher told a gathering of the Labor faithful organised by the Women's Social League that he supported compulsory military training, and that 'National Defence should not be a party matter'. Later, he spoke at a public meeting in the Exhibition Buildings, but confined his remarks to domestic issues.[10] The war scare was not yet turning every political head.

Next, Fisher spoke to about a thousand people packed into the Victoria Hall in the Victorian country town of Colac on the evening of Friday 31 July. 'Great enthusiasm' attended the meeting, and the crowd spilled out on to the street. An overflow meeting was hastily organised for them in the nearby Oddfellows' Hall. The first speaker at Victoria Hall was Mr Thomas Burke, the candidate for Corangamite. He spoke only on the great domestic issues, preference for trade unionists, great business combinations, and the extension of social insurance to provide pensions for widows and orphans, before introducing Fisher. When Fisher stood to speak there was much applause and 'three hearty cheers'. Fisher, too, kept a tight focus upon domestic issues. He defended his record as a financial manager in his first government, claiming a £6 million surplus, and made his plan for the expansion of pensions the great theme of his remarks. He praised the current system of old-age pensions and maternity allowances. It was time, he argued, to extend the great principle of social insurance to widows and orphans. 'It was the duty of every civilised community to protect little children,' Fisher argued.

Turning to the issue of defence spending, Fisher was very cautious. Loyal to his original policy speech in which he had flagged the need for restraint in defence spending, he even declared that 'under no circumstances would there be any borrowing of money for the defence of this country in time of peace'.[11] Borrowing should be for permanent assets, such as railways, not for defence spending. Fisher explained that 'his idea of patriotism was not to go begging to the mother country and seek to lean on her. He was proud that for the first time in [the] history of Australia they now had something like a sea and a land defence'. The next Labor government, he promised, 'would economise as much as possible with defence,' while ensuring that 'the young men try and be trained for the defence of their land'.

Only at the very end of his speech did Fisher add his first comments on the situation in Europe. Indeed, he gave the undertaking that was to become the most famous of the campaign — and destined to be repeated endlessly in Australian books on the Great War as emblematic of the nation's fundamental devotion to Britain:

> Turn your eyes to the European situation, and give the kindliest feeling towards the mother country at this time. I sincerely hope that international arbitration will avail before Europe is convulsed in the greatest war of any time. All, I am sure, will regret the critical position existing at the present time, and pray that a disastrous war may be averted. But should the worst happen after everything has been done that honour will permit, Australians will stand behind our own to help and defend her to our last man and our last shilling. (Loud applause.)[12]

These were Fisher's very last words of the evening: 'Last man … last shilling'. The phrase had a past. It was familiar in the mouths of Jingoes during the Boer War, and had attracted withering criticism from Labor at that time. For example, in June 1902, Charlie McDonald had asked prime minister Deakin whether, in view of many rich men's avowed eagerness to pledge 'our last shilling and our last man' to a 'war of aggression in South Africa,' he would raise at the coming Imperial Conference the matter of 'a tax on land and income sufficient to make up our *per capita* share to meet the cost of a war by which the Rand owners alone have benefited.'[13] That was then; this was now.

At the very least, Fisher's embracing of the phrase showed that, as the barrel of electors to be appealed to by any politician is very deep, sometimes he had to speak to those nearer the bottom of the barrel. But it was a cut-through line. Of course, as the crisis in Europe deepened across the weekend, it was this self-evidently preposterous promise to spend every last coin and to throw every last body into Britain's cause that was conveniently scissored out of the speech and pasted up in columns in scores of newspapers, in Australia and Britain, as the acme of every Australian politicians' sturdy patriotism.

Prime minister Cook addressed a large crowd at an election meeting in the Town Hall at Horsham on the same Friday evening. Allegiances in the unruly hall were divided, 'with many Labor supporters present'. Like Fisher, Cook spoke chiefly on domestic policy. But much earlier in his speech than Fisher, Cook offered a bold statement on the international crisis. He expressed the hope that peace might come by negotiation.

> But if it is to be war, if the Armageddon is to come, you and I shall be in it. (Loud applause.) It is no use to blink our obligations. If the Old Country is at war, so are we. (Loud applause.) It is not even a matter of choice, but of international law.[14]

The crisis in Europe, Cook argued, showed 'how grave is the defence question here and now in Australia'.[15] He spoke of his own personal commitment to Australia's defence, declaring that he would 'twenty times rather go out of office' than 'palter' with defence. Securing Australia, Cook stressed, ultimately meant having a larger population. But his government would do all that was necessary here and now, in this crisis.

Then Cook turned to the wider domestic themes of his campaign. He pointed to the burden of taxes in New South Wales under the Labor government of William Holman. He rejected populist attacks on 'trusts', defending them with the argument that big business combinations were inevitable in the pursuit of efficiency. He mocked Labor's proposal for widows' pensions as insufficient. He lamented the growth of 'class feeling' in Australia. The nation had to choose between socialism and Liberalism, he pleaded.

This prompted Cook to return to the European situation. Cook, who twenty years previously had been a leading NSW Labor politician representing the miners of Lithgow, appeared to gloat over the practical powerlessness of European socialists to stave off the disaster of war. Working-class solidarity was crumbling, Cook told his audience:

You have the spectacle to-day of the Austrian Socialist fighting the Serbian Socialist, of the Russian Socialist preparing to fight the Austrian. I tell you that feeling of nationhood there is today. It is proof against all your brotherhood of man principle. Hadn't you better look these facts in the face? Socialist feeling is within the State, but there is something stronger — that is the feeling of nationalism that is behind all the principles that have come down to us. If it is a good thing to close up our ranks against outsiders, isn't it a good thing to close up our ranks, and try to help each other here?[16]

Cook had spoken at much greater length on the danger of war than had Fisher. But both Australia's political leaders had conceded that, if Britain was to be engaged in war, Australia could not be neutral and had no desire to be neutral. At this stage, these assertions of generous loyalty to Britain from the election platforms on both sides of the political divide were still expressed in the most general terms. Neither leader had mentioned the possibility of an expeditionary force.

Labor's expedient hyperbole

Of the two competing political leaders' first remarks on the European crisis at their respective election meetings of Friday 31 July, it was the wild hyperbole of Fisher's 'last man and last shilling' that was especially memorable — and politically lucrative.

Why had he made these remarks? Of course, it was perfectly true that Australians would wish to help Britons defend their island home, if that became an issue. But nothing of the kind was remotely in prospect on the evening of 31 July. Fisher's boast of a readiness to supply unlimited assistance — stealing the clothes of the most rabid of the imperial loyalists in Australia — was a calculated political tactic. Behind it lay a number of considerations, but the most pressing was the recent renewal in the long-simmering tension in Australian politics over Ireland. For Fisher's promise was designed to repel the expected charge that might wreck Labor's campaign: the charge that the forces of Labor, still so reliant on their many Catholic supporters, were tepid on the subject of the British Empire.

The Home Rule crisis in Britain in 1914 had only very recently reawakened sensitivities to a significant Australian political reality — that the important Catholic minority inclined mainly to the Labor side of politics. For example, the Labor-controlled Senate had passed a resolution supporting Irish Home Rule just before the proroguing of the federal parliament in late-June 1914. All twenty-four Labor senators present had supported it, while only one Liberal did so. Key Liberal senators, such as Millen and McColl, had voted against it, and prime minister Cook had refused to express a view in the House of Representatives.[17] The Senate's resolution, in turn, had been denounced at big street processions and public meetings of loyal Orangemen and Protestant clergymen called to oppose Home Rule in July 1914.[18]

This foretold political trouble for Labor: if Europe exploded into war, there was every danger that the election campaign in Australia would instantly develop into a love-of-empire auction. In war, the charge of 'disloyalty' directed against recently vocal supporters of Home Rule for Ireland could knock paint off the Labor campaign. The federal Labor Party was already at a significant disadvantage in the election as it battled, as always, against the steadfast opposition of all the big-city newspapers. This was the stark truth. As Lord Denman, the retiring governor-general, had advised Munro Ferguson in May 1914, Australia's Labor parties, state and federal, had 'practically no press behind them, so cannot well voice their opinion'.[19] In this sense, Fisher's hyperbole was an effort to counter his party's vulnerability. At Colac, therefore, Fisher had chosen to make a headline-grabbing commitment on behalf of Labor in order to gain a measure of political safety — an extravagant first bid, before any auction began. Fisher wished to protect himself from the 'Union Jackals' who had bellowed 'disloyalty!' at him in 1909 over his reluctance to fund the gift of a Dreadnought to Britain, and in 1911 over his notorious interview with W. T. Stead.[20] Fisher, understandably, wanted to take a big wide turn around that haunted corner this time.

But it should not be thought that all political speechmaking at this moment was suddenly overtaken by the prospect of war. A major political figure could ignore the crisis completely when campaigning. For example, on Friday 31 July, when the prominent Labor senator Joseph Turley, who had been president of the Senate during the Fisher government (and was famous for refusing formal dress), spoke at the town hall in Warwick, in rural Queensland, he made not a single reference to the threat of war in Europe.[21] This demonstrates both how early were the party leaders' references to the international crisis, and how rapidly the issue would rise to hypnotise the nation in the days ahead.

But pressures in this direction multiplied quickly. Over the weekend that followed, the publicity given to the offers from New Zealand and Canada did a great deal to provoke a similar offer on the part of Australia.

The promises of troops to serve in expeditionary forces from both nations were widely reported in the Australian press from Saturday 1 August. The New Zealand offer was the more real, but the 30,000 troops supposedly put forward by Canada caught the attention of dozens of newspapers, too. It was a big, round number, eclipsing that planned for Australia's expeditionary force — as very few people, but an influential few, knew only too well. For example, the *Sydney Morning Herald* of Saturday 1 August printed reports from Ottawa, dated as early as 30 July, noting that the Canadian minister of defence, Colonel Sam Hughes, was preparing an offer of military assistance to Britain. 'The military council is reported to be ready to despatch 30,000 troops to the front if Great Britain requires them,' reported the *Herald*.[22] The *Herald* of Saturday 1 August also described the heady mixture of emotions at play in the New Zealand parliament on Friday 31 July, and the rapturous reception given to prime minister Massey's offer to Britain of an expeditionary force.[23]

If Ottawa and Wellington already had their running spikes on, surely Australia's politicians could not let the nation be seen to be shuffling toward a mere bronze medal in the dominion stakes? Who would gain the glory of being first in the field? Could the New Zealanders be permitted to get away with the claim that they were always first?[24]

CHAPTER NINE

The view from 'Yaralla'

Sydney, Friday 31 July

The scene outside the palatial Yaralla throughout the afternoon was a most animated one … The Governor-General and Lady Munro Ferguson stood just below the steps at the front of the house, and shook hands with every guest, in attendance being Captain Anstruther, A. D. C., and Captain Curwen, A. D. C. Her Excellency wore a gown of draped black satin charmeuse, with a short tunic of black ninon, embroidered in iris blue silk, the bodice having a vest of cream net and lace. Her black hat had a small posy of flowers at one side, and was encircled with black ostrich plumes.

– 'Vice-Regal Garden Party', *Sydney Morning Herald*, 1 August 1914

GOVERNOR-GENERAL MUNRO FERGUSON arrived on his first-ever visit to Sydney in early July for a month of vice-regal engagements. He felt some trepidation about the visit: 'neither the Governor nor the Government of New South Wales are likely to welcome me with both hands,' he confessed in a private letter to Harcourt. Munro Ferguson had already decided that the NSW governor, Sir Gerald Strickland, was 'a very thorny kind of person,' and complicit in the wicked plot to keep the governor-general homeless in the harbour city.[1]

As mentioned earlier, Munro Ferguson had decided to resolve his homelessness in Sydney by staying at the grand mansion 'Yaralla', on the banks of the Parramatta River, west of the city of Sydney. This was the splendid home of Miss Eadith Walker, an immensely wealthy heiress, philanthropist, socialite, and Liberal Party supporter. Prompted by prime minister Cook, Miss Walker had lent her magnificent house and gardens to the new governor-general. 'Yaralla' was 'a most charming house,' he told Harcourt. Cook was happily pressing for 'the Restoration of the Dynasty', Munro Ferguson quipped, a reference to Cook's continuing efforts to restore the governor-general to some fitting pile in Sydney.[2] Naturally, Cook was among the first to be greeted as a dinner guest at 'Yaralla' by Munro Ferguson. He dined there on 19 July before resuming his election campaign in Victoria.[3]

It was at 'Yaralla' that Munro Ferguson mulled over the warning telegram that he had received on Thursday 30 July. He soon had the second cable from Harcourt to consider. This was the cable that Harcourt had been more than a little reluctant to send. It was received in Sydney on the Friday, and urged that Australian naval ships 'should take up their preliminary stations' — their war stations.[4] According to the documents, Munro Ferguson replied to London that same afternoon that he had sent on these messages to both Cook and Millen, and that Millen had assured him the movement of the ships was under way.[5]

With answers to these cables just sent on the afternoon of Friday 31 July, Munro Ferguson must have been intensely distracted. For, that same afternoon, he and Lady Helen were hosting a garden party in the extensive grounds of 'Yaralla' for some two thousand guests. It was their first large function in Sydney. Fortunately, it was a clear, sunny afternoon. The *Sydney Morning Herald*, the voice of loyal sons and daughters of the empire in Sydney, found the scene quite bewitching:

> The flowerbeds were gay with blossoms. Here and there were bright patches of colour, decidedly pleasing to the eye, while the smooth-cropped lawns, showing little signs of winter, stretched down towards the river, which was slightly ruffled by the light south-

western breeze. Weather, so fine and pleasant, assisted in crowning
the afternoon with success.[6]

Refreshments were provided from two large marquees on the
lawns, and the Royal Artillery Band struck up appropriate musical
entertainment.

'All classes of society were there,' wrote the *Sydney Morning Herald*,
improbably, ' — members of the State Ministry, of the two Houses of
Parliament, and Government officials, with their wives and families,
were present, and the Church, the Army, and the University'. Some
arrived by boat on the river from Fort Macquarie (now the location
of the Sydney Opera House). Others motored out, braving the
'fearsome' state of the Parramatta road linking Concord to the city.
Among the most prominent guests were representatives of both sides
of politics — the state Labor premier, the despised William Holman
and Mrs Holman (whom the new governor-general blamed for his
continuing exclusion from old Government House), and Mrs Mary
Cook, the wife of the Liberal prime minister, for Joseph Cook was
regrettably absent. The *Herald*'s reporter was struck by the 'sombre
order' of the dressing, and the large number of military uniforms.
'Beautiful wraps and furs were well in evidence, some being much
admired,' added the reporter.

The main event took place near the front of the house. With
Lady Helen Munro Ferguson at his side, and flanked by two military
attendants in cocked hats, Munro Ferguson stood patiently in a tall
silk hat in front of 'Yaralla'. Here the vice-regal couple shook hands
with hundreds of Sydney's social elite who stepped forward to greet
the King-Emperor's new man. The governor, Sir Gerald Strickland,
arrived at 3.00 p.m. and was 'escorted up the grounds to the strains of
the National Anthem'. Then the official party repaired for afternoon
tea to 'a large marquee on the upper lawn'. Held in 'almost spring-like
weather,' the garden party was judged a triumph.[7]

Later that day, the governor-general's patience was exhausted. He
decided he had to do something to encourage prime minister Cook
to gather his ministers together and consider the European crisis.

It was, by any sober assessment, still an early moment in the crisis. Certainly, a Balkan war was a reality: Austria–Hungary's war upon Serbia was three days old. But no other great power had yet been drawn into any declaration of war; nor had any actual combat commenced beyond the shelling of Belgrade on Wednesday 29 July. Russia's partial mobilisation was known in London by this date, but had only been reported by Grey in the House of Commons on Thursday 30 July.[8] The next step, Russia's disastrous upgrading of her partial mobilisation to a general mobilisation, was not confirmed in London until the late afternoon of Friday 31 July.[9] Russia was, of course, the first of the great powers to move to that most dangerous stage of preparation. There was no knowledge of this Russian development in Australia until Saturday 1 August.[10] So far as Australia knew on the Friday, this was still a Balkan war, and one in its earliest stages.

Nonetheless, on the Friday evening following the garden party, Munro Ferguson sent two messages to the prime minister. Cook was still electioneering in the Victorian towns of Horsham and Ballarat.[11] Munro Ferguson first pencilled the draft of a telegram to be sent in cipher:

> To the Prime Minister,
> Personal and Confidential.
>
> Would it not be well, in view of latest news from Europe, that Ministers should meet in order that [the] Imperial Government may know the attitude of Australia in case of war.
>
> R.M. Ferguson
> Sydney.

Then, evidently suspecting that this was not composed in sufficiently strong language to steer Cook toward the outcome he really desired, Munro Ferguson amended his draft. After all, he did not want the cabinet simply to meet and consider its 'attitude'. He wanted the cabinet to send an offer of assistance to Britain. So, in an amended version, the governor-general did not mask his intentions. He used difficult-to-misconstrue phrases in a revised text:

> Would it not be well, in view of latest news from Europe, that Ministers should meet in order that [the] Imperial Government may know what support to expect from Australia?[12]

Major Steward, the official secretary, sent the message in Cipher 'R' to the prime minister at Ballarat.

For the governor-general to prompt a cabinet meeting in this way was, to put it mildly, not 'strictly proper'.[13] Perhaps for this reason Munro Ferguson followed up his wire with a letter of explanation to Cook. He had suggested the cabinet meeting, he explained, because there was 'more definite news of imminent War'. He gave neither details nor source in support of this claim. It was, he wrote, 'urgent' that the Cook government 'should decide its line of action'. He pleaded that he needed to report to the 'Home Government' in London 'what support it may expect from Australia in the event of the Empire becoming involved in the European War'. His choice of words was telling. There was, of course, no questioning the obvious: if London decided for war, the empire as a whole, including Australia, would be immersed in that 'European War'. But Munro Ferguson was not above prodding the Cook cabinet: 'I notice that according to one report Canada has acted already, and generally I believe that such timely demonstrations of homogeneity have their effect on the European situation'. This flaunting of the Canadian offer was deftly done. With one eye on the staunchest empire loyalists in the Cook cabinet, the governor-general hinted that Australia surely would not wish to be eclipsed by another dominion. With another eye on anyone in the cabinet who might hope Australia could add to London's deterrence and fortify peace in Europe, he offered the rather hazier suggestion that 'such timely demonstrations of homogeneity' — that is, declarations of readiness to assist Britain from all the dominions — might 'have their effect', perhaps in deterring war. Showing his own determination to cut a patriotic figure, he also told Cook that he was always ready to 'leave for Melbourne by the first train if you have need of me'.[14]

The wire, sent in cipher, could not be read at first, because Cook 'had not the key to the cipher with him'.[15] Therefore, from Ballarat on Saturday morning, Cook's staff despatched an 'urgent telegram' back to Steward, asking him to repeat Munro Ferguson's message and asking in what cipher it had been sent.[16] Late on Saturday afternoon, Cook's staff telephoned Steward in Sydney asking for messages to be sent again in Cipher 'R'. The message was sent again to Ballarat.[17] The governor-general was irritated by the delays in contacting Cook. According to Munro Ferguson's narrative, sent on later to Harcourt, the telegram to Cook in cipher 'took two days to reach him on his electoral tour, and my letter a week'.[18] But Cook evidently did not require Munro Ferguson's letter giving the case for summoning his cabinet. He immediately accepted Munro Ferguson's suggestion, and scheduled an emergency cabinet meeting in Melbourne for Monday 3 August.

CHAPTER TEN

The view from the Customs House

Sydney, Friday 31 July to Sunday 2 August

The Gov[ernmen]t is full of zeal, and so I gather is the Opposition. There is a cheerful disposition to discharge obligations and expedite preparations. While the general attitude of the whole people is admirable.[1]

– Munro Ferguson to Harcourt, 2 August 1914

THERE WAS FRANTIC ACTIVITY in Sydney on Friday 31 July, and then over the weekend of Saturday 1 and Sunday 2 August, among the small group of senior decision-makers who gathered in the harbour city. Senator Edward Millen, the defence minister, handled the crisis from his room in the Commonwealth Offices at the Customs House. Here, since 1910, federal members of parliament had been given access to a handful of rooms when in Sydney. Millen had one of the two larger rooms reserved for ministers on the upper floors, overlooking the ships, the ferries, and the oblivious crowds of weekend holidaymakers at Sydney's famous Circular Quay. It was a location calculated to keep political factors near to the centre of Millen's mind, for the Commonwealth Electoral Office was also located there, thronged with callers checking the electoral rolls for the coming poll and making applications for their last-minute enrolments.[2]

Matters both big and small pressed upon Millen. On Friday 31 July, arrangements for Cockatoo Island naval dockyard workers to share a holiday on the coming Bank Holiday Monday were cancelled — 'with double wages' as consolation.[3] Much more significantly, on Friday 31 July, Millen wired for Major Brudenell White, acting chief of the general staff, to come up by train from Melbourne to Sydney for consultations as soon as possible. The rush of events can be illustrated by noting that Major White had jotted in his diary on Thursday 30 July that there was 'a slight war scare'. The next day, after receiving his summons to Sydney, he wrote 'Every appearance of war.'[4] Millen would soon have Major White and Admiral Creswell, and the governor-general himself, leaning over his desk.

White's status and background is worth recalling. He had been an *aide-de-camp* to General Hutton, and they enjoyed a close friendship. During his two stints in Britain, White had been in close touch with several key military figures at the Staff College, including General Wilson, promoting plans for a British BEF to be deployed on the Continent at the outbreak of war. White was steeped in the dogma of the Staff College, and had been deeply immersed in planning for mobilisation in Australia since 1912. He believed in the necessity for prompt offensive action, and in the rapid despatch of an expeditionary force. He believed also that Britain was obliged to honour her 'continental commitment'.[5] White's faith, as he expressed it, was built on 'a firmer rock' than mere Australian patriotism, for he looked instead to 'an Imperial patriotism'.[6] As luck would have it, at this historic moment for the empire, White was the acting head of the Commonwealth of Australia's army. He was relieving Brigadier-General Gordon, who had left Fremantle on 26 July bound for holidays in England.[7]

White arrived in Sydney on Saturday 1 August, bringing with him a copy of the latest version of the 'General Scheme of Defence' upon which he had worked so hard over the previous two years. He visited Millen at the Customs House. White later recalled that he had left Melbourne without having seen the warning telegram himself. But a copy was shown to him as he met with Millen. As the man most familiar with the famous Preface to the Defence Scheme — a summary of Australia's own 'War Book' — White explained the significance of the telegram to Millen. The first button had been pushed in London. White urged Millen to respond immediately by pushing Australia's first button: he should order the implementation of all the first military steps listed under the heading 'Warning Telegram' in the 'Preface' of White's copy of the Defence Scheme, which he held in his hand. Most definitely, he advised, what Britain required of Australia was to institute the 'precautionary stage'. As noted above, in essence this meant that the local military authorities in Australia's major ports should adopt the measures listed in their local 'Defended Port Defence Scheme': guards were to be mounted on wharves, fuel, ships, naval installations, gun emplacements, and other defence buildings, and preparations made in case of other telegrams from London.[8] 'Outlook black,' the major wrote in his normal cryptic fashion in his diary for the Saturday.[9]

White was not alone in seeking a rapid response. Munro Ferguson earnestly believed that his position under Australia's constitution as commander-in-chief of Australia's military forces required him to be active, far beyond any ceremonial role. He threw himself into the task. He was determined to advance Australia's military preparations, as more telegrams from London arrived in Sydney requesting action. Munro Ferguson spent the weekend locked in conferences with Major White, Admiral Patey, and Senator Millen at the Customs House. In addition, on the Sunday morning, he made a visit to Sydney's naval base at Garden Island, dressed for action — 'attired in a lounge suit, with soft shirt and no tie'. Here he met with Patey, and inspected the naval ships being prepared there, including HMAS *Australia*.[10] During conferences on the Sunday, the tieless Munro Ferguson supported White. The two men advised Senator Millen that Australia should immediately initiate all the first military measures as outlined in the Defence Scheme.

The defence minister triggers the 'precautionary stage'

Millen was initially inclined to wait — preferring not to act, as he explained, without the prime minister's consent. But White soon found an ally. Sir William Irvine, the attorney-general, a senior politician and former Victorian premier, arrived in Sydney on the Saturday to attend an election meeting. He was summoned to join the decision-makers at the Customs House, where White argued that the case was urgent. It was Millen's cabinet colleague Irvine who eventually persuaded Millen to act.[11]

On the afternoon of Sunday 2 August, Millen finally telegraphed Cook. He informed the prime minister of the decision he had made, as defence minister: he had empowered White to issue all the appropriate orders. Thus, Australia's military forces adopted the 'precautionary stage'.[12] In fact, Millen made the decision for action in Sydney *before* the prime minister had decided. As Ernest Scott put it politely later in his volume of the *Official History of Australia in the War of 1914–1918*, Millen came to 'his provisional decision' and 'agreed to give the necessary orders, and rely upon the Prime Minister's afterwards confirming what had been done'.[13]

By way of these complicated discussions at the Customs House and at Garden Island in Sydney, in the mid-afternoon of Sunday 2 August, Australia had moved toward 'the first stage of an ordinary mobilisation'.[14] From one perspective, this decision was unremarkable. The preparations were in accord with the 'General Scheme of Defence' of 1913, and they were prompted, of course, by requests from London. From another perspective, it reflected a democratic deficit. The decision was made by a handful of men in Sydney, with the governor-general's encouragement, before the prime minister had made his choice, and before any cabinet meeting had taken place. But it scarcely mattered. According to one military officer, the senior army staff officers in Melbourne around midday on Sunday were already initiating various mobilisation measures, fully confident that official orders from the defence minister in Sydney were on their way.[15] All this would soon be endorsed anyway, they must have thought, and the same men — the politicians and officers — would soon move even more rapidly toward a historic offer of Australian forces for the imperial war.

Munro Ferguson was proud of his activity in Sydney. He described his role in a 'Personal' letter composed at 'Yaralla' on Sunday 2 August, a letter that he also summarised in a cable, both of which he then despatched to the Colonial Office in London. The cable went just before he departed for Melbourne on the Sunday evening.

The Australian federal election campaign had complicated matters, the governor-general explained to Harcourt. Most ministers were unfortunately dispersed across the round belly of the continent, with lists of election meetings to attend. 'At last a few ministers are recalled from their campaign in the Bush,' he wrote. Even prime minister Cook had been elusive. 'I have had difficulty getting at the P.M.,' he complained, 'who is rushing hither & thither all over the Continent. I have located him now and join him tomorrow in Melbourne'. This meant, of course, that Cook had immediately accepted his suggestion of a cabinet meeting in Melbourne. Miss Walker's 'Yaralla' in Concord, 'this inaccessible place' as he put it, was also a problem. He complained to Harcourt that the mansion did not provide the means of communication with ministers, such as he might have enjoyed at the old Government House in Sydney — another dig at the NSW Laborites. He bemoaned the 'confusion and delays' occasioned by being marooned in such a distant suburb as Concord, reliant upon the 'worst roads and telephones in the world,' as he put it. 'I have felt for the last three days that I could not remain longer.'[16]

So, determined to be in Melbourne to endorse instantly any decisions taken by the Cook cabinet, he told Harcourt that he had decided upon another initiative of his own: he was taking the express train to Melbourne that very night. To help form a credible cabinet meeting for Cook, he planned to take with him in the vice-regal railway car the two ministers he had been working with in Sydney — Irvine and Millen.[17] He also invited his top military advisers, Major White and Admiral Creswell, to accompany him on the train as well.[18]

These two military men had been among those working most closely with Munro Ferguson over the weekend in Sydney. White's determination to lend assistance to Britain as rapidly as possible was never in doubt. So, too, in Creswell's mind, the priority of London in decision-making was a fixed idea. As we have seen, only twelve months previously, Creswell had rammed home to his brother officers the incontestable truth that London would decide upon peace, war, and all the big issues concerned with the defence of Australia.[19] Neither man was likely to counsel caution.

In this same letter to Harcourt, Munro Ferguson also described his hands-on experience of military decision-making over the weekend in Sydney with the politicians and military advisers. He felt that the Australians were solid. The government, he wrote reassuringly, was keen to assist Britain as quickly as possible. Millen had 'certain deficiencies', he admitted, but was 'extremely business-like and helpful in these anxious days, when in the absence of the prime minister a good deal of responsibility rested on us two'. Significantly, he added that he doubted 'whether Senator Millen has the confidence of the Services, who are devoted like everyone else to ex-minister Pearce', the Labor senator and former minister of defence. This was a significant tribute to Pearce — his popularity with the military men following, no doubt, from his activism in the Defence portfolio, and perhaps also his role in authorising preparations for the expeditionary force in 1912.

Munro Ferguson also proudly included details showing his own involvement in precise naval decisions. For example, he reported that he and his advisers had decided to hold up for a day a German message in cipher to a small German warship cruising off Queensland, because Patey was keen to keep the ship under close scrutiny. Similarly, he foreshadowed for Harcourt a possible strategic change. There were 'a couple of heavy German ships not far from New Guinea', Munro Ferguson explained. He and his advisers were debating whether HMAS *Australia* should 'go after them' rather than setting course immediately for Albany, as was specified in the naval war plans prepared for Australia.[20]

Most significantly, Munro Ferguson also shored up London's faith in his big achievement of recent days — the 'unofficial' assurance that there would be no delay in the transfer of all of Australia's naval ships to Britain. Highlighting his own role in this, he assured Harcourt that the most critical decision facing the cabinet in Melbourne on Monday was most likely to go Britain's way: the RAN would almost certainly be placed under the British Admiralty's control. He explained the situation fully in his letter:

> The cabinet meets tomorrow, with an Executive Council to follow, when no doubt a formal transfer of the R[oyal] A[ustralian] ships will be made. I conveyed your thanks to the Minister for Defence from whom I had unofficial assurances that this Fleet would be handed over to the Admiralty instantly.[21]

By this means — a second personal indication to the colonial secretary himself that the deal was as good as done — Munro Ferguson probably hoped to bolster these 'unofficial assurances' from Australia. For Munro Ferguson had already sent his private cable to Harcourt noting Millen's informal promise on Thursday 30 July. This second mention strengthened expectations on all sides. After all, the Cook cabinet, so anxious to be loyal and to be seen to be loyal at every point, was most unlikely to renege on an assurance twice conveyed to London, and for which London had already sent its thanks. Thus, two days before Britain declared war on Germany, the governor-general had come one step nearer to confirming the long-standing naval priority for Britain: the transfer of the entire Royal Australian Navy to London's control. He believed that this would happen the very next day.

CHAPTER ELEVEN

'A good war-cry'

Sydney, Friday 31 July to Saturday 1 August

If I might suggest the European situation affords Liberals in Australia
excellent material for a good war-cry during the current campaign.[1]
– Senate candidate T. D. Chataway to E. D. Millen, 31 July 1914

AUSTRALIA'S LEAP INTO the Great War was to be accomplished
amid the din of politics. After all, a bitter federal election campaign
was in full swing — yet another moment when, according to some,
Australia stood at a crossroads between Liberalism and socialism.
Most politicians could scarcely unfasten their eyes from that domestic
battle. Certainly the first critical decisions endorsing preparation for
war, those taken in Sydney over the weekend 1–2 August 1914, did
not happen in a political vacuum. The very same politicians who were
engaged during the day in deciding upon Australia's mobilisation
were engaged during the evening at election rallies. The temptation
to play up to the ultra-patriotic gallery was strong. The temptation
to go even lower — and frighten the electorate — was too strong to
resist. Some could adopt that familiar 'gather-round-children-while-
I-tell-you-a-ghost-story' pose, to bone-chilling effect.

Certainly, in the light of the developing European crisis, some
Liberal politicians were preparing to play the poisonous politics of
loyalty and disloyalty. For example, on Friday 31 July, Thomas D.

Chataway, who had been a Queensland Liberal senator until his defeat at the election of May 1913, and who was standing again in the coming election, sent advice along these very lines to his colleague Senator Millen.[2] Chataway was a vehement anti-socialist, and incidentally had been one of the most zealous of inquisitors, who had delighted in portraying Labor as disloyal at the time of Fisher's controversial Stead interview in 1911. He was hoping here, in the middle of the federal campaign, to put some wind beneath his wings in his push for re-election. He wrote to Cook that the crisis in Europe presented a political opportunity too good to miss, a chance to raise a 'good war-cry' at the centre of the campaign. In this spirit, Liberals should condemn 'Labor's pandering to the anti-compulsory training people, [and] Labor's neglect to establish big gun and big ammunition factories'. Liberal candidates, Chataway advised, should attack:

> generally Labor's utter disregard of the necessity of filling up Australia with people in order not only to defend her shores but also to supply ships and men for the general defence of the Empire. It might be said we are trying to have a Kahki [sic] election, but in my view the war question is swamping all political questions and our candidates should recognise this fact.[3]

Clearly, in circles typified by Chataway, the prospect of a khaki election was a gift from Mars — a chance to smear the Labor Party as traitorous, a friend of Germany, and a nest of Irishmen disloyal to the empire.

Millen was already moving in this direction. On the evening of the same Friday, he addressed a political meeting at Mosman Town Hall, focussing on defence policy. The big theme stood out plainly: only the Liberals could be trusted to keep the nation secure. He accused the Labor Party of 'a critical hostility' to defence. There was a 'marked change' in Labor, he alleged, and he dredged back into history to illustrate the point. He reminded his audience that the first Labor prime minister, Watson, a decade earlier, had absurdly sought to limit defence spending to just half a million pounds. Since then Labor had swung around and become 'almost jingoistic', rediscovering defence as a nationalist cause and adopting it 'with almost hysterical fervour'. But, more recently, Millen asserted, Fisher's party had shown 'open hostility', or, still more dangerous, 'lukewarmness' on defence. In the grip of a cynical 'opportunism', Labor in this election was 'bartering national safety for a few votes'.

Only the Liberal Party, continued Millen, was enthusiastically committed to the plans of the two British advisers on Australia's defence, Kitchener and Henderson. Labor had gone soft on defence, charged Millen. Fisher had put forward the 'almost puerile proposal to limit [defence] expenditure to such amounts as can be spared from the year's revenue'. A new Fisher government would not build the ships the Australian navy required: Labor would 'shrink from that steady effort which is essential, if Admiral Henderson's scheme is to be adhered to'.

Millen then sought to point-score on the unfolding European crisis. The question of defence was 'not only big, but urgent' because 'events are moving so rapidly that Australia is being drawn more and more towards the treacherous vortex of international complications'. There was a conspiracy afoot: 'Today, and it is idle to shut our eyes to the fact, an organised effort is being made to destroy your defence schemes'. Labor's destructive chopping and changing in defence policy was 'demoralising' the forces. If war erupted, Australia itself 'might even be imperilled'. Labor was 'a grave national danger'.[4] Millen's message, crudely crafted to spook his audience, was shrill: if Labor was elected, Australia stood in jeopardy.

While closeted away in Millen's office at the Customs House over the weekend contemplating mobilisation, members of the government had certainly found time to think political thoughts. They had been 'working day and night', as the *Daily Telegraph* assured its readers, coolly reacting to the telegrams from London and soberly assessing the advice of their military experts.[5] But there was a domestic political contest on, with federal power the prize — and political pressures were very near at hand. Political manoeuvring and posturing for the coming federal election must inevitably have had an impact upon the decisions made with regard to Australia's mobilisation. In Millen's case, he had spent Friday evening on the hustings depicting Labor as too cautious and his own Liberal Party as the only true friend of imperial defence. He must have felt keenly the pressure to match his rhetoric of Friday with action on the Saturday and Sunday.

Sir William Irvine was similarly engaged in electioneering duties over that same weekend. On Saturday evening, he spoke at a Liberal election rally at the Protestant Hall, in Crows Nest, North Sydney. The very name of the hall pointed to the sectarian tensions that cast a shadow over politics in Australia on the eve of the war. The hall was proudly the creation of local Orangemen, and the meeting place for their lodges.

The back-story to this rally was a Labor election meeting that had been held at Marrickville on the previous evening. There, the Labor premier of New South Wales, William Holman, a man with a reputation as an ardent anti-militarist, had spoken in support of the Labor senate team.[6] His speech had attracted some critical comment in the press. The great bulk of Holman's speech had been devoted to domestic political issues, but he had included a few remarks about the 'dire threat of a general European war'. Holman had observed that if Europe drifted into war it would be tragic. He had contrasted Europe's situation with Australia's. 'In Australia we cannot be plunged into calamities of that kind merely at the bidding of some irresponsible ruler,' he had told the crowd, 'because we have won the right of self-government, and by that we mean the right of the humblest member of society to be consulted as to the course the government of the country is to take'. Labor, declared Holman, stood for 'the supremacy of the people themselves over their own affairs'.[7]

At the Protestant Hall, Sir William Irvine (known as 'Iceberg Irvine' in Labor circles for his superior manner and marked hostility to the trade unions) was the chief speaker.[8] Irvine had spent the day consulting on Australia's mobilisation with Senator Millen, the governor-general, Major White, and the military elite. This was not mentioned in his address. He also devoted the great bulk of his speech to domestic issues, arguing in particular that Labor's proposals for social insurance were 'degrading to the people of Australia'. Only the Liberals would respect 'Australian self-reliance, self-respect, and character'. No surprises there. But Irvine's remarks on the European crisis were much more provocative. He attacked premier Holman's reported speech. He criticised his suggestion that Australia might be thrown into war at the whim of 'some irresponsible ruler'. He was not certain, Irvine charitably conceded, if the premier had meant the noble rulers of the British Empire. But if he had, it was a slur. 'The statesmen who have control of the affairs of the Empire,' said Irvine, could be certain 'that whatever course they may adopt in the present grave crisis they will have behind them our patriotic and loyal support. (Cheers.) They may be assured of this, the Australian people will unite to place their resources, both of men and money, at the disposal of the men of the mother country.' He summed up his own attitude to the crisis:

> What I say is that when England is at war we are at war. (Applause.) There is no half-way house. The destinies of our country, so far as foreign relations are concerned, are entrusted to statesmen who are immediately responsible to Parliament. We must take the matter as we find it. The statesmen of England are now charged with the terrible responsibility of determining the issues of peace and war for the good of the whole of the people, and we are not only bound by their decision, but to give them every assistance that lies in our power.[9]

Colonel Granville Ryrie, the local federal MP and a fiery veteran of the Boer War, then joined Irvine on the platform. He was much more provocative, smearing his Labor opponents as potentially traitorous in this crisis. He began by delivering a 'hot attack' on Holman, who he said was notorious for having disloyally opposed the Boer War. He was a treacherous man, Ryrie alleged, who had 'desired that the British should be defeated in the unfortunate war in South Africa'. This allegation provoked some dissent, and then 'a bout of fisticuffs' broke out in the hall. Ryrie warned the audience against electing

Labor men like Holman, men who cared nothing for imperial duty or their oaths of loyalty to the King: 'At such a time as this, we as a nation need men at the head of affairs who have some sentiments of Imperialism. (Cheers.) I say at this juncture we need a party in power that will ring true on a question like this. (Cheers.)'

Ryrie then turned on the 'young men' groaning and hooting at the back of the Protestant Hall. They were, shouted Ryrie, samples of 'the tyranny of the trade unions'. He taunted them. 'You would as soon be ruled by Germans as by anybody else,' Ryrie bellowed at those interjecting. 'Do you call us traitors?' someone shouted back. Ryrie replied that his anti-war critics knew nothing about the horrors of war. They should give up their 'petty political quarrels' and help Australia present a 'united front to an enemy common to all'.[10] Colonel Ryrie's contribution provided a snapshot of the facile politics into which war — or even rumours of war — usually drags nations, great and small. The accusation of preferring the enemy had already been flung in the face of dissenters, even before a shot had been fired. It is true that Ryrie had not descended to the slogan 'Vote Labor — Get a German for a Neighbour'. But he had pointed the way.

The speeches at Mosman Town Hall and the Protestant Hall in Crows Nest underscored the political backdrop to the decisions of Australia's government in this crisis. The two leading politicians of the Cook cabinet, Millen and Irvine, who were in Sydney over the crucial weekend when military decisions were made, had committed themselves in public addresses to unstinting and speedy support for Britain. Irvine had assured his audience that he was willing to follow Britain in 'whatever course' London chose. Each had sought to frighten their audiences with the claim that Labor was untrustworthy on the most critical issue of the moment — defence. This was the spirit of the men who sat with Munro Ferguson during the weekend of 1–2 August in Sydney and together cranked into action Australia's first measures of mobilisation in response to the crisis in Europe. War was being embarked upon — and cheap politics unleashed — simultaneously. A good war-cry was rising.

CHAPTER TWELVE

'There'll be no war'

London, Saturday 1 August

I fear that the foolish coquetting with the French to which some of us so strongly objected has raised expectations in that quarter which it would be criminal for us to satisfy. And there will be no doubt recriminations and charges of perfidy if the thing comes to a point and France goes to war without our aid. But I cannot bring myself to believe that any government will be capable of entering upon this war, especially on the side of Frenchmen and Russians who are wholly untrustworthy allies.[1]

– Earl Loreburn to Lewis Harcourt, 1 August 1914

WHILE AUSTRALIA'S LIBERAL POLITICIANS were making hay with their 'good war-cry' on Saturday 1 August, events in London were moving in the other direction. Decisions in the Asquith cabinet demonstrated that the choice for or against war in Britain was still balanced on a knife's edge — and that the majority was opposed to the despatch of a British Expeditionary Force (BEF) to the Continent. Britain appeared to rule out throwing her own troops into a land war.

As Asquith sat down with his cabinet on Saturday morning 1 August, he could scarcely have banished from his thoughts his intense discomfort at the news of Russian general mobilisation confirmed in London on the afternoon of the previous day. After all, he had spent some time in the early hours of the morning with the bleary-eyed King George V, in his dressing-gown, composing a last vain plea to Tsar Nicholas to keep the lines of communication with Germany open.[2] Of course, widespread apprehension created by the Russian action provided an unfavourable setting for Grey, Churchill, and other interventionists at the cabinet. It made it doubly difficult for them to gain their objective — a pledge of assistance to France, and a commitment to Belgian neutrality that would provide, either singly or jointly, a trigger for Britain to join any European war. In fact, it was probably due to the jarring news of Russian general mobilisation that the ministers making up the neutralist majority in the cabinet exerted themselves so strongly on this day. It appears to have hardened their resolve. Thus, Saturday 1 August was to mark the high tide of hope for the neutralists.

The fractious cabinet met at 11.00 a.m. at Downing Street. Grey began by focussing the attention of the ministers once again on the Belgian issue. Grey had prepared late on the Friday afternoon precisely for this debate when he had despatched two astonishingly brief telegrams to Paris and to Berlin seeking instant pledges on Belgian neutrality. Replies had arrived in the small hours of Saturday morning at the Foreign Office, and these were now on the cabinet table. The French had replied positively, agreeing to respect Belgian neutrality; the Germans had replied evasively, pleading that no commitment could be given in advance for reasons of Germany's military safety, faced as she was by two potential antagonists, in the east and the west.[3]

The immediate question was how the cabinet should react to these varying replies — one so accommodating and the other so ambiguous. The precarious balance prevailing in the cabinet was clear from the reactions around the table. Grey and Churchill regarded the German reply as proof positive of German nefariousness, and the French reply as proof positive that France was behaving faultlessly. According to Harcourt's notes, Haldane led off with a 'long essay' reviewing war preparations. Haldane may have encouraged all those still hoping that the hard facts of Germany's dangerously exposed strategic situation might serve to pacify Berlin. For Haldane noted that Germany must be acutely conscious of a shortage of 30–40 per cent in her wheat supply if a major war developed, food imports which Britain planned to cut off. Harcourt also recorded Haldane's opinion on the Belgian issue: Grey should tell Prince Karl Max Lichnowsky, the German ambassador, of Britain's 'feeling about Belgium [as the] "deciding factor", but promise our neutrality if France [was] not invaded'. If Haldane said exactly this, it would have surprised many, because to 'promise our neutrality' to either side was, of course, decidedly not the policy of Grey. The refusal to use Britain's neutrality as a bargaining piece was an essential element in Grey's stance of 'ambiguity'.

In any case, Harcourt scribbled down the fundamental point so far as the Radicals were concerned: 'Grey not committed to Cambon' — that is, Paul Cambon, the French ambassador in London.[4] On the other hand, Churchill then swung the conversation back to Belgium. He produced a letter from F. E. Smith, a leading and flamboyant Conservative MP and personal friend, boldly promising the unanimous support of the Conservative opposition for British intervention on the Continent on the basis of the indispensability of Belgium's independence. The letter, which Churchill had engineered, served no doubt to heighten the pressure on those Radicals toying with resignation as a device to stave off war. If they left the cabinet, Churchill had already earmarked some Tories to replace them in a coalition cabinet.[5]

It is important to recall the mounting political stakes being calculated by both factions in the cabinet at this point. For, according to Asquith, Grey declared once again in the course of the debate that he would resign if the cabinet embraced an 'out-and-out and uncompromising policy of non-intervention'. Asquith, in his turn, warned that if Grey were to resign he would go, too. But the interventionists were not the only ones to threaten to walk — to intimidate their opponents. Two could play at that game. At some point in the debate, Harcourt sent a note around the table to Beauchamp: 'I must resign today if there *is any decision* to take part automatically under certain circ[umstance]s without previous reference to the cabinet.' 'There will be nothing of the kind,' Beauchamp shot back to comfort his ally.[6] Once again, resignation letters were being planned, and firm intentions voiced, while the cabinet wrestled with major issues of peace and war. Small wonder that Asquith told Venetia Stanley that, in the course of this cabinet meeting, 'We came, every now and again, near to the parting of the ways.'[7]

In the context of these threats of resignation, eventually the cabinet agreed that Germany had to be warned emphatically that her reply to Grey on the matter of Belgian neutrality was unsatisfactory. According to Harcourt's description, the ministers made the decision to warn Berlin, through Lichnowsky, that Belgium could indeed prove to be the 'deciding factor' for British public opinion.[8] They fixed on an exact form of words for Grey to read to Lichnowsky that afternoon — words which the Prince, of course, was expected to send on immediately to Berlin.[9]

Having disposed of the matters raised by the replies of Paris and Berlin to Grey's telegrams, the cabinet turned to the more specific issues of Britain's preparation for conflict. Here the majority of neutralists prevailed. Harcourt's men proved to be most suspicious of the attempts of Grey and Churchill to lead the discussion back, again and again, to Belgium, and away from what they saw as the more central issues. From the Radical perspective, Britain had come suddenly face to face with the provocative Russian action of Friday, and the stiff-necked loyalty of the French toward Russia. This was the setting. Now the British interventionists were putting forward premature demands for a full British mobilisation of her armed forces, on the basis that this would show the kind of 'solidarity' that the Entente partners needed. In Radical eyes, by contrast, this was hardly likely to help restrain France and Russia. And restraint ought to be part of Britain's diplomacy. Churchill had already twice jumped ahead of the cabinet, in the opinion of the Radicals — first to achieve the concentration of the fleet on the previous Sunday 26 July, and second to secure the movement of the fleet to its war stations in the early hours of Wednesday 29 July.

So the cabinet considered carefully Churchill's case for the calling out of the fleet reserves, effectively completing full mobilisation. A tense and prolonged debate followed, during which Churchill indulged his taste for dramatic outrage. 'Churchill wants to mobilise the whole Navy: very violent,' Harcourt complained in his notes. Significantly, 'Grey supports Churchill,' Harcourt added.[10] But on this occasion Asquith backed away from his impetuous First Lord. He clearly found Churchill irritating, and he privately confessed to Venetia that Churchill had taken 'at least half the time' of the cabinet.[11] In the end, Asquith recommended that, with regard to the naval reserve, there should be 'no proclamation before Monday'.[12] Thus, the cabinet rejected Churchill's demands. As Churchill put it coyly in his memoirs, his colleagues judged full mobilisation at this stage to be 'not necessary to our safety'.[13]

Next, the cabinet surveyed the possibilities of land-battles on the Continent. Should Britain begin the process of embarking her expeditionary force? The cabinet endured a 'long speech on tactics' from Churchill and then a reply from Lloyd George, who again appeared to be in a moderate frame of mind.[14] Here was the most critically important debate of the day — perhaps of the whole diplomatic crisis, as some imagined. It provided a crucial indicator of the balance of forces between the neutralists and interventionists in the cabinet. On the vexed issue of the BEF, it was the neutralists who emerged victorious: cabinet resolved that, in the event of war, Britain should *not* send an expeditionary force to France.[15]

This decision seemed to be of tremendous significance. The cabinet's choice was to go well beyond a reassertion of the policy of ambiguity. It was the clearest indication given yet during the crisis that Asquith's Liberal cabinet was likely to cling to a neutral stance, even if actual conflict erupted on the Continent. With respect to the plan for the embarkation of the BEF, of course, the interventionists in the cabinet were on difficult political terrain. The issue reminded all at the cabinet table of the serious disputes that had rocked Asquith's cabinet in 1911 — the accusations that Grey had deceived the cabinet over a long period on the matter of military conversations;

the accusation that the interventionists had stacked the Committee of Imperial Defence to favour General Wilson's plans for the BEF at its famous meeting in August; and the accusation that McKenna had been ejected from his post as First Lord of the Admiralty because he had resisted plans for the despatch of a BEF.[16] In the wake of the shocking revelation of Russian general mobilisation, and inspired perhaps by Churchill's defeat on full naval mobilisation, the neutralists had the numbers, and chose to stand firm.

Thus, when Grey saw Paul Cambon, the French ambassador, that afternoon, he told him the grim news:

> I said that we had come to a decision: that we could not propose to Parliament at this moment to send an expeditionary military force to the Continent. Such a step had always been regarded here as very dangerous and doubtful. It was one that we could not propose, and Parliament would not authorise unless our interests and obligations were deeply and desperately involved.[17]

For the Radicals, on the other hand, the news of the decision was a joy, and gave an unexpected boost to their hopes. Walter Runciman had informed Charles Trevelyan earlier in the crisis 'that the great thing was to refuse to send an expeditionary force onto the Continent'. Naturally, he was 'very proud' when he told Trevelyan on the Saturday that he and his like-minded neutralists had 'secured a decision against it'.[18] Trevelyan certainly was elated, concluding that it was now absolutely clear that 'we are not going to war at once'.[19] Next morning, encountering his fellow Radical MP Francis Neilson in Whitehall, Trevelyan reassured him. 'There'll be no war,' he said. 'There'll be no war.'[20]

The victory of the Radicals was reported in British newspapers on Monday 3 August. The *Daily Chronicle*'s parliamentary correspondent, Harry Jones, who was known to be close to men in the cabinet, reported that the cabinet ministers had 'definitely decided not to send the expeditionary force abroad. Every honourable effort will be made to prevent Britain being drawn into the war'.[21] On Monday 3

August, in a friendly editorial that softened the paper's opposition to intervention, the *Daily Chronicle* carried to the Liberal faithful the beguiling idea that Britain's war, if it came to intervention, would only be a naval war in any case.[22]

For the moment, the wrangling Radicals in the cabinet believed they had achieved a concrete gain. Repelling the plan for the BEF was a moment to savour; it was a win to be banked. The chances of Britain maintaining neutrality had been boosted — or so the neutralists believed.

Grey's interview with the French ambassador, Paul Cambon, that afternoon turned out to be very tense. For Cambon faced, as he characterised it, a huge disappointment. Grey was required to stick with the cabinet policy of deliberate ambiguity, and to honour its rejection of plans both for naval mobilisation and the despatch of the BEF. Therefore, no promise of aid to France could be given. Grey explained to Cambon the hard fact: France must 'take her own decision at this moment without reckoning on an assistance that we were not now in a position to promise'.[23]

Those pressing Grey to achieve solidarity with France and Russia found the cabinet decisions of Saturday 1 August devastating. They considered Grey's position, as outlined in his interview with Cambon, as much too cautious. The atmosphere among Grey's advisers at the Foreign Office, and his still sterner critics at the War Office, was poisonous. For example, General Wilson recorded in his diary on that day the details of yet another visit he made to the French embassy to see Cambon. Here he had found Cambon 'very bitter, though personally charming'. In the evening, Wilson visited Eyre Crowe, the assistant under-secretary at the Foreign Office: 'Saw Crowe 7 p.m. — very pessimistic, all countries mobilizing except us'.[24] The very idea that Britain might not fight from the very first moment of war was, for some, a tormenting sore.

The men of war were right to be worried. On Saturday 1 August, the chance for Britain to remain neutral had flitted spectrally across the stage of history. On the same day, Australia's politicians were publicly promising unlimited assistance to Britain to wage war.

CHAPTER THIRTEEN

The whiff of a khaki election

Melbourne, Saturday 1 August to Monday 3 August

And yet 1914 was greeted as a great release, a purgation from the vices supposed to be engendered by peace! My God! Three days of glory engender more vices and misery than all the alleged corruptors of humanity could achieve in a millennium … Let those who are curious in human imbecility consult the newspaper-files of those days.[1]

– Richard Aldington, 1929

PRIME MINISTER JOSEPH COOK, meanwhile, had been moving swiftly from one speaking engagement to another in rural Victoria as he led the Liberals in their campaign. He travelled overnight from Horsham to Ballarat, arriving for breakfast on Saturday 1 August before proceeding to Colac for another address in the afternoon. The way political speech-making developed over the weekend, it became clear that the election campaign could indeed develop into a love-of-empire auction, perhaps a full-blown khaki election, in which those willing to promise big spending on defence — and to present a precise promise of support as a token of empire devotion — might hope to scoop the votes. And frightening the electorate in the context of the European crisis was the simplest way to justify such a precise promise.

Cook spoke at Colac, not twenty-four hours after Fisher. This speech struck a new note. At Horsham on Friday, Cook's references to the European crisis had been emphatic but relatively few; domestic issues had still been at the centre of his address. At Colac, he reordered the issues of concern to the electorate. The issue of defence was suddenly promoted to the front rank. Cook was clearly positioning himself to extract whatever small political advantage he could from this moment of international danger. Labor, he would allege, was dragging its feet on defence. Only the Liberals could be trusted to sprint.

Cook told the audience of a thousand squashed into the little Victoria Hall at Colac that 'at the present time the question of the defence of Australia was the most serious, the most vital, and the most important question of all. (Cheers.)' He referred directly to the rumbles of distant thunder emanating from Europe. The crisis provided a 'lesson' for Australia, preached Cook: it demonstrated that 'war preparations were of no use unless they were effective and timely'. Pointing to the latest developments, Cook stressed that the British fleet had been mobilised in just a few days, and claimed that the Austrians had sent three army divisions across the Serbian border in just three hours. Speed was critical. The Australian people had been shown that 'they must put their house in order — (Cheers) — and have their preparations made as complete and effective as possible'.

Cook mocked Fisher's 'tarrididdles' on defence. The truth was, Cook claimed, that the federal Labor Party was dangerously reluctant to spend money on defence. Labor was 'clamouring just now for the defence scheme to be less expensive'. Compared with the last Labor government, Fisher was 'singing a different tune now on the defence question'. Cook alleged that the Labor leader, controlled by his caucus, had thrown his previous commitments to more Dreadnoughts 'overboard' in this campaign. Labor's timidity on defence meant that the Australian people could not risk a Labor government, Cook asserted.

He reached for phrases that would frighten the audience. Only a people ready for war 'ran away with the prizes', explained Cook.

He warned that an unprepared people would be 'fleeced by their enemies'; he warned that an undertrained soldier 'might as well go to the slaughter house'. 'Our defence could not wait upon the revenue,' Cook declared. Contrasting Labor's alleged reluctance with his own rock-solid commitment, he promised that a Cook government 'would not starve the effective preparations for defence'. Indeed, he vowed that he would 'rather leave office than let the defences sink into inefficiency'. Cook repeated his unequivocal commitment to assist Britain. 'If it was to be war they would all be in it.' Australia's 'obligations' would be 'placed at the disposal of the responsible authorities'. He contrasted his own readiness for 'action' to assist Britain with the palsy that he claimed now afflicted Labor.[2]

Cook was not the only leading Liberal to trade in this spookery. Millen and Irvine in Sydney had characterised Labor as a national danger in light of the Balkan crisis. Senator James McColl, campaigning in rural Victoria like his prime minister, also added the defence theme to his standard anti-socialist sermon. Speaking at Casterton on Friday 31 July, McColl made a trenchant attack on Fisher's defence policy. Like his leader, McColl complained that Labor was planning to cut its defence spending according to its revenue cloth. It was 'unfair' that 'the people of today' should be asked to fund the required costly long-term defence works, argued McColl. The Liberal policy, he explained, was to maintain current defence spending, and to fund permanent defence works from 'loan money'. Labor refused to contemplate loans for these defence works, McColl warned, but Fisher was committed instead to more spending on pensions for widows and orphans.[3] The message was plain enough: Labor was going to leave Australia dawdling in a fool's paradise of socialist pension schemes just when the world was being threatened by a militarist Moloch.

On the Labor side, Fisher was also weaving the European crisis into his stump speech. On Saturday 1 August, Fisher gave an election address at Bacchus Marsh near Melbourne. He made only one reference to the danger of war. He scolded the Liberals for stooping to criticism of the new publicly owned Commonwealth

Bank, even though it was straining that very day to save Australia from a financial panic induced by the war scare. This, claimed Fisher, showed the Liberals' 'hatred' of Labor's banking innovations. The real lesson of the crisis, argued Fisher, was that the Commonwealth Bank was essential in safeguarding Australia's financial stability.[4]

In Ballarat, on the evening of the same Saturday, Cook suddenly pulled the plug on his campaign schedule. While he had travelled to nearby Colac for his speaking engagement in the afternoon, Cook had left his staff at Craig's Hotel at Ballarat. There they had received several messages from Sydney and Melbourne, not available in decoded form until Cook returned to Ballarat at about 6.00 p.m. on the Saturday. The governor-general's message of Friday and several 'Imperial cable messages' were among the messages waiting. Then a phone call to Cook from Melbourne at 6.45 p.m. during his evening meal prompted a sudden change of plan. Cook was 'much agitated by the matters that had been brought under his notice by the cable message,' one reporter noted. Cook scrubbed his plans to take the express train to Adelaide for another election rally, and within half an hour had boarded a train bound instead for Melbourne. He arrived at his hotel late on Saturday evening, and there he met with Senator James McColl, his cabinet colleague, who had also suspended his electioneering in the bush, and was that night 'his only colleague in town'.[5]

The next day, Sunday 2 August, newspaper reporters descended upon the newly constructed Commonwealth Offices at 4 Treasury Place, opposite the Treasury Gardens in Melbourne. In his rooms there, the prime minister was bunkered down. No election meetings were scheduled for that day. Cook devoted his entire attention to the European crisis. He directed the Defence Department to set up a series of meetings in his office so that the government's military advisers could brief him.[6] The 'Defence Scheme' was on the table, but they had to wait until Cook, a devout Methodist, 'got back from church,' as one officer recalled. After church, Cook met the military men, and they 'went over the plans for the precautionary stage with him, and were instructed to enforce that stage'.[7]

Under the orders given to the officers on that day, a number of military measures were taken: batteries at defended ports were manned by the Royal Australian Artillery; guards were placed 'at vulnerable places' in these ports; and troops were prepared for a rapid move from Townsville to Thursday Island — the only movement of troops at that stage, to guard against a German occupation of the strategic island.[8] Censorship of Australia's cable traffic was imposed, a measure that would soon irritate the Australian newspapers.

Emerging from his rooms at the end of these conferences, Cook released a morsel of news: he had summoned his cabinet to meet the next day, on Monday 3 August. Cook 'firmly, but courteously' refused to give waiting reporters any more detail. He confirmed that communications had been received from London, but 'he kept their nature a profound secret'. 'I cannot talk about these things,' he told the reporters. 'They are too grave. All I can say is that we are keeping our eyes on the whole situation. We are doing everything possible to meet any emergency that may arise. It looks serious enough, in all conscience, and we are keeping in touch.'[9]

There was never a doubt about Cook's frame of mind at this moment. The prime minister was already in the grip of an anti-German fever, fuelled by religious zeal. In his view, the powers of light were girding themselves to fight the powers of darkness. In his pocket diary for the fortnight beginning Monday 20 July, he began to compose a tirade against German philosophy — or rather a fantastic parody of that philosophy. These remarks appear to have been written, and some were definitely completed, during the week that followed the outbreak of war, but they give a guide to Cook's thinking.

Cook was ready for war. He accepted it. He vented a pious rage against all things German. With implacable conviction, he asserted that Germany's atheism was fundamental to the impending conflict. He scribbled down a savage critique of the evil genius behind it all: Friedrich Nietzsche, the 'Lunatic, atheist'. It was Nietzsche, Cook complained, who had described Christ 'as Knave and Charlatan', and Nietzsche who had derided Christianity as 'the greatest of all conceivable corruptions'. Germany was under the sway of Nietzsche's philosophy glorifying force. Thus, according to Cook's soul-shaking imaginings in his diary, the outbreak of war was quite inevitable: 'A pacific agreement with England is, after all, a will o' the wisp which no serious German would trouble to follow.'

He also jotted down his conclusions about the deeper origins of the war. It did not originate in Alsace-Lorraine, or in the arms race. It originated rather in Germany's failed morality, 'a morality which was putrid. An ethic of Hell'. It lay in the Germans' decision to exploit the weaknesses of others: 'None of the Allies was prepared for war: Germany was: She had prepared for "the day"'. Germany had deliberately chosen this moment for war, because 'Russia had social troubles,' because France was enduring 'military weakness,' and because England was preoccupied with Ireland. England's leaders were completely innocent: 'Grey, Asquith, Balfour, Bonar Law. No swashbucklerism — Tried to keep out.' Citing to himself the historical parallel of England's long resistance to French ambition during the age of the Revolution and Napoleon, Cook hailed prime minister Pitt: 'Young Pitt dying said: England has saved herself by her exertion. England will, I trust, save Europe by her example.' Cook foresaw a similarly long struggle. 'Fought for 20 y[ea]rs — Let us do likewise if necessary,' he wrote.[10] Thus, in his private musings, Cook sanctified the coming struggle as a protracted religious war, with the empire's forces playing the role of the cavalry of the Lord.

More mundane considerations, however, also competed for the prime minister's attention on the last weekend of peace, 1–2 August. Labor's stance, most obviously, was a factor that Cook needed to weigh. Each side of Australian politics had been sniping over issues raised by the looming war over the weekend. In their election addresses of Friday and Saturday, Millen, Irvine, McColl, and Cook himself had all been milking political profit from the European crisis. All had characterised the Labor Party as jeopardising Australia's safety. How would Labor react?

On Sunday 2 August, while Cook toiled away at the Commonwealth Offices, signs emerged that the Labor leadership was toying with bipartisanship — at least on the issue of national defence. Fisher had returned to Melbourne from Adelaide on Saturday, in time for his speech at Bacchus Marsh. On Sunday, he was in Melbourne all day, but was not contacted by Cook — as Fisher was soon to complain.[11] Nevertheless, he decided to fly a kite: he offered a limited kind of political truce.

Fisher issued one short statement to waiting reporters on Sunday evening. He read the statement, speaking, as the newspapers reported, 'evidently with a deep sense of responsibility'. The text was released: 'In a state of affairs like this there are no parties. The safety and welfare of our country and all near and dear to us is our first consideration. Mr Cook knows my views.'[12]

This statement was widely reported. The newspaper reports were often accompanied with this interpretation: 'From what Mr Fisher said, it may be inferred that during the afternoon he had been in communication with the prime minister Mr Cook'. No Labor spokesman corrected this immediately. However, a week later Fisher made it clear that he had not spoken personally to Cook, nor had he received any message from him, on Sunday 2 August.[13] Fisher clearly intended the patriotic extravagance of his speech at Colac to signal his readiness to put the nation first, and to back away from any partisan spirit when it came to defence. Fisher's statement on the Sunday then underlined the fact. In this sense, it conveyed an offer from Labor to suspend party-political sniping on matters concerning the 'safety' of the country.

Again, Fisher was seeking political safety. With a federal election just five weeks away, he had decided on a stratagem to repel all accusations that might be levelled at him as a traitor, a white-flagger, a wrecker — he had dutifully dumped the partisan spirit on the issue of national defence. Journalists were no doubt briefed to interpret Fisher's stance as an offer of Labor support for the existing government on everything connected with the crisis of war. After promising the last man and shilling, this was a logical step for Fisher. But the timing provided an exquisite irony. On Sunday 2 August, Fisher's former friend Keir Hardie, the fervently internationalist father of the British Labour Party, stood in Trafalgar Square in London with other Labour leaders addressing a crowd estimated at between fifteen and twenty thousand, and pleading that the people must crusade for peace, and shout for Britain's neutrality.[14] On that same day, in Melbourne, Fisher issued his statement that virtually discounted the Labor Party as a factor in Australian decision-making at a key moment.

The moment was big with menace. The Cook cabinet was scheduled to meet on Monday afternoon to discuss Australia's position on the international crisis for the first time. A glance at the leading city newspapers of Monday 3 August gives the atmosphere.

The Australian press had been moderate in its commentary on the European crisis during the preceding week, but a distinct change in tone was suddenly discernible on Monday 3 August. Of course, the chief city newspapers were at one in insisting that all partisan political spirit had been put aside. Common, too, were expressions of praise for the offers of expeditionary forces already made by both New Zealand and Canada. There was some casting of jealous editorial eyes at the other dominions' offers.

The *Sydney Morning Herald*'s editorial of Monday 3 August began with the obvious. 'We know that our security and our independence depend on the victory of the British arms,' argued the editor, Thomas Heney. 'We know that if we were to stand aside we could not be certain of our existence for a year or for a day.' But suddenly the paper advocated a definite offer of assistance to Britain. In his editorial, Heney noted that New Zealand and Canada 'have already stated definitely the offers they are prepared to make'. But Australia would soon do the same: 'The Australian people will not be behind their fellow subjects in Canada and New Zealand.' Australia's politicians should immediately act in accord with the wishes of the Australian people. The politicians should place Australian naval ships 'unreservedly at the disposal of the Admiralty'. In addition, they should assure Britain that, if necessary, 'the manhood of Australia will be as eager to come forward as it was at the time of the Boer War, to face what then seemed to be a moment of grave danger.'

Then came the claim that the Australian people were already of one mind: 'The whole of the people of this continent are united in their determination to support to the utmost limit of their resources the Empire within which they have grown and prospered for so many years.'[15]

Sydney's *Daily Telegraph* was in a chest-thumping mood. It announced that war was imminent and irresistible. Germany was to blame for provoking the war, and poor Russia simply had to respond. Britain would undoubtedly 'stand by her friends of the Triple Entente'. Australians could not expect to hold 'this vast, still undeveloped continent' if the British Empire 'goes under'. So it was right to sink all political differences, and Fisher was praised for promising the last man and shilling. Australia must fight, too — although the paper did not go so far as to urge an expeditionary force. 'We cannot doubt what Britain's choice will be, nor is there any doubt about Australia's action,' growled the *Telegraph*.[16]

More moderate was *The Advertiser* in Adelaide. Its editorial of the morning of Monday 3 August made it clear that all hope of peace had not yet been lost. On the one hand, Australia and Britain had no cause to prosecute in war. Britain was 'practically destitute' of a land army, and her powerful navy was 'not aggressive but defensive'. There was 'no quarrel' with any European power, and no 'clash of material interest' with Germany. If Italy could keep her neutrality, then 'Great Britain is certainly not called upon for a precipitate decision'. She was 'mediator and peacemaker'. On the other hand, the British Radicals were wrong to urge Britain to restrain her allies 'at any cost'. The preservation of the 'balance of power' was essential; 'splendid isolation' was impossible. Australia and the empire should simply trust that Sir Edward Grey 'will not act hastily'. If Britain did choose war, then 'Britain will fight only because honour leaves no alternative'. But what should Australia do? *The Advertiser* suggested naval help. Either HMAS *Australia* or even the whole fleet could be transferred. Japan's navy could safeguard Australia, and 'we fully believe in' Japan's friendship.[17] There was no mention of an expeditionary force.

But it was in Melbourne that the most influential newspapers, *The Age* and *The Argus*, were based. They had the best contacts, and their head offices were only a stroll from Parliament House and Cook's rooms. Their opinion would guide many other newspapers. The *Sydney Morning Herald*, for instance, drew directly on the resources of *The Argus*.[18] On this crucial day, both Melbourne's leading newspapers were adventurous — they urged the Cook government to make a sweeping offer of fighting men to support Britain.

The Age's editorial of Monday 3 August, written by Schuler, expressed pride that 'the presence in Australian waters of our little navy handsomely guarantees us from the only danger that can be immediately apprehended — attack by raiding cruisers or armed privateers'. Thus, Australia was secure, 'while we have our fleet'. Canada and New Zealand, *The Age* noted, had already offered troops. 'They could do no less, seeing they have neglected to defend themselves by sea,' commented the paper. It was a point of pride that Australians 'have performed beforehand our duty to the Empire by making Australia strong'. We have 'assumed the burden of our own defence — and more especially by sea'. But this was no reason to 'rest content'. 'We have done much already, but we can do more,' argued *The Age*. In the same spirit as New Zealand and Canada, Australia then should 'offer the Motherland similar official assurances of Australian troops being available for her service, that the world may know the whole Empire is at one'.[19]

The more bombastic, pro-imperial, blue-water *Argus* of the same day was more direct and unqualified: it shouted that the patriotic offers of military assistance from New Zealand and Canada should be matched, and even bettered by Australia. *The Argus* urged Cook and Fisher to meet. 'The hour has come for Australia to make a definite offer, and it would be a wise action and a spectacle exemplary in the eyes of the Empire if Mr. Cook and Mr. Fisher at this juncture, as the leaders of the two great parties of Australia, were to confer and consider the best means for helping Great Britain.' *The Argus* pressed the case hard, flattering readers: 'We have never hung back when war has made its appeal.' The politicians, therefore, should today be 'making an offer to Great Britain that will be worthy of us'. The final lines of the editorial struck a note of urgency: 'The form of the offer need not be suggested here. It might be ships; it might be men; it might be both. But the offer should be made, and the leaders should confer, and quickly.'[20] By making such an eye-catching offer, Australia could get its nose in front of Canada and New Zealand.

Despite *The Argus*'s prompting, no Labor leader was contacted on the matter, nor invited to the cabinet meeting of Monday 3 August. The disposition of Australia's military manhood rested solely within the trust and judgement of Cook and his cabinet ministers — with the governor-general hovering helpfully at the cabinet table. Meanwhile, over these critical days, the top Labor personalities had nothing to say on an expeditionary force. The party's leaders made no recommendation for or against the idea — even though Australia's newspapers had made it clear in reporting events in London that Britain's own position on the European war was yet to be determined.[21]

Another notable feature of the editorials on this day were signs of a competitive small-nation syndrome at work. 'We have as much at stake in this matter as Canada and New Zealand, and shall be not less loyal to the old land than they,' observed Hobart's *Mercury*.[22] In these fervent circles, it was as if a people freshly in possession of their land was fearfully desperate to be noticed, to be approved of, to be given the chance to banish 'a new nation's secret self-distrust before a supercilious ancient world' — such as one observant war correspondent noticed later in the case of the United States as she entered the war.[23]

Editorials, of course, do not a public opinion make. By Monday 3 August, there was no irresistible wave of public opinion in Australia urging the Cook government to make an offer of an expeditionary force and to transfer the navy's fleet to Britain. There were no public meetings demanding it, no flood of letters, no great processions in the streets, and no public committees being formed to agitate for such an offer. There were simply pro-commitment editorials in some influential newspapers — but not all. The demand had come forth in print on only one day: Monday 3 August. This was scarcely evidence of overwhelming pressure upon Australia's politicians from the press or the public. In truth, public opinion had barely had a chance to take in the crisis.

What evidence was there of public enthusiasm for a commitment to war *before* news of the British declaration of war? There is very little such evidence, beyond what became the well-known descriptions of 'extraordinary enthusiasm' by a flag-waving crowd outside the offices of *The Age* in Melbourne on the evening of Monday 3 August. This famous knees-up showed a Collins Street crowd at its frothiest and gaudiest.[24] But the revelries of this carnival crowd, singing British and French anthems, and threatening to trash German property, are scarcely evidence that the wider Australian public was thrilled by the prospect of sending troops to the aid of Britain anywhere that Britain chose.

Moreover, reports from Sydney were quite different. The *Sydney Morning Herald* of Monday 3 August noted that, over the weekend, curious crowds had gathered in the Botanic Gardens to see HMAS *Australia* in Farm Cove. The behaviour in the streets 'was that of thoughtful earnest men intent upon duly appreciating the international position'. According to the *Herald*, foreign bands — including German bands — playing 'well known British martial airs,' had entertained the crowds. Anti-war meetings were held, too. A rally organised by the Industrial Workers of the World (IWW) on Sunday afternoon had attracted about a thousand people.[25] The next day, Monday 3 August, the United Labourers' Protective Society, meeting at the Trades Hall in Sydney, passed a resolution condemning militarism and urging the people not to be stampeded into war.[26]

The reality was that in Australia, as in Britain — and indeed in Germany — there was no such thing as a single public opinion in 1914. The crisis had come all too swiftly. In the background, there were significant minority political movements, led by socialists, liberals, radicals, feminists, and Christian internationalists, critical of war.[27] These dissenters had long advocated international arbitration of disputes and a more democratic foreign policy for the empire and Australia. A hostile reaction to compulsory military training was gaining influence inside the Labor Party.[28] In common with labour and socialist parties in many countries at the beginning of the war, some in the ranks of Australian Labor expressed conditional support for the war — as a war of defence.[29] Small dissident groups, such as the Australasian Socialist Party, condemned outright Australia's rush into combat.[30] Thus, upon the outbreak of war, 'the prevailing note in the labour movement was perhaps one of sadness'.[31]

There was no agitation against Britain shirking the war, and no wave of emotion demanding Australia's plunge into it. Bean claimed later in the *Official History* that, over the last days of peace, Australians were 'possessed of one anxiety alone — the fear that Britain might hold aloof from the war'.[32] This is not borne out by the evidence. In fact, it is striking how very few ultra-patriotic statements were made along these lines. One can be found — from a former NSW premier, Sir Joseph Carruthers, who was an indefatigable Empire Day man. At the annual bowling match, Banks and Insurance against Waverley, held at the Eastern Suburbs club on Monday 3 August, Carruthers gave the toast to the British Empire. He told the bowlers that 'I should feel ashamed to call myself a Britisher if England failed to recognise her obligations to all her allies'. If Britain remained neutral, then 'Britain and the Empire will lose cast' [*sic*]. He praised Fisher and Cook for showing 'that England can rely upon Australia to the last penny, the last man, and the last ditch'.[33] This exceptional statement from an old imperial war-horse at a bowling club in Sydney's wealthiest suburb scarcely reveals a popular storm-surge of emotion; indeed, only local and rural newspapers gave Carruthers' speech any coverage. In spite of Bean's claims, there was no great public movement urging England to meet her obligations, and no sign that Australians were being eaten up with anxiety that they might miss the war.[34]

CHAPTER FOURTEEN

Radical angst

London, Sunday 2 August

Beauchamp feels we were 'jockeyed' this morning over the German fleet; Simon agrees & thinks we ought to have resigned with Burns.[1]
– Lewis Harcourt, cabinet memorandum, 2 August 1914

ON THE AFTERNOON of Sunday 2 August, Britain veered again toward a catastrophic war. While Trafalgar Square was filling with demonstrators urging British neutrality, at Downing Street the choice for war was being made. It was indeed to be the decisive day — and exceptionally tense. A year later, Asquith would look back on this day in a private letter, in which he recalled 'the all-day cabinet, and the resignations: and the infinite kaleidoscopic chaos of opinions and characters'.[2]

Before the critical cabinet meeting, the leaders of the neutralist group met at Lloyd George's home, Number 11 Downing Street, at 10.00 a.m. to decide upon strategy. Harcourt was in a temper. When he awoke on Sunday he had learned of another incident overnight showing how the cabinet was being overridden. He heard that at 3.00 a.m. the Admiralty had directed his Colonial Office to send telegrams across the empire calling up the Naval Reserve. This placed the Royal Navy in a state of complete mobilisation — the precise proposal rejected by the cabinet on Saturday. Trumping the Colonial Office, the Admiralty had cited a 'Naval Reserve Proclamation' already signed by the King. Again, this was Churchill's doing, and justified, in his mind, by Germany's overnight declaration of war — not upon France, but upon Russia.[3]

When Harcourt appeared at Number 11 Downing Street, he found seven ministers still firm for neutrality: 'Pease, McK[innon] Wood, Beauchamp, Simon, Runciman, Ll[oyd] Geo[rge] and self'. The key decision was soon made. 'Settled we w[oul]d not go to war for [a] mere violation of Belgian territory and would hold up if possible any decision today.' Lloyd George, significantly, joined Harcourt in a two-man delegation to see Asquith next door, a few minutes before cabinet was due to meet. Here, Augustine Birrell, secretary of state for Ireland, waiting in the Ante Room, asked that his name be added to the list of dissidents. Probably in Asquith's sitting room, Lloyd George and Harcourt then told him that they 'represented 8–10 colleagues who would not go to war for Belgium'. Harcourt recorded Asquith's astonishing response: 'PM listened and s[ai]d nothing'.[4] All filed downstairs for the fateful cabinet meeting.

The morning cabinet sat from 11.00 a.m. until almost 2.00 p.m. As Walter Runciman wrote afterwards at the top of his usual printed invitation to the cabinet, this became 'The cabinet which decided that war with Germany was inevitable'.[5]

The nineteen men at the cabinet table focussed naturally upon the big news overnight: the tragic German declaration of war on Russia. The Russian jolt of Friday had been displaced by the German jolt of Saturday. In conveying news of each development in the crisis, Asquith, Grey, and Churchill were in strong positions. They occupied the key cabinet posts — the War Office, the Foreign Office, and the Admiralty — with access to the latest intelligence. Other ministers felt starved of facts. 'I have little more news than is in the papers,' Samuel had complained on Friday 31 July.[6] Grey and Churchill were able to tell the cabinet that the latest information pointed to premeditated German aggression: not only had Germany declared war upon Russia, but German troops had also occupied strategic centres in Luxembourg.[7] But Grey was not without hope, for 'German troops are moving *south* as if they did not mean to enter Belgium'. He recapitulated that he had told Cambon 'we should not send troops to France to defend the Franco–Belgian frontier'. So, at this stage, it appeared, cabinet's decision against a BEF was holding.[8]

But Grey then shifted ground. He was suddenly vehement. 'Grey is much stronger than before for joining in war and would like to promise France our help *today*', wrote Harcourt. Grey told the cabinet that 'it was *vital* to him that he should today assure [ambassador] Cambon that if the German fleet attacked [the] French coast we w[oul]d prevent it & use all our naval power and he must say this in Parl[iamen]t tomorrow'. He was willing again to say nothing to Cambon, the French ambassador, on the subject of Belgium, but he demanded a decision on naval assistance before he saw Cambon at 2.30 p.m.[9]

Other cabinet ministers heard Grey suddenly become much more emotional. He announced that Cambon had 'appealed that morning very pathetically for a decision and we must give one'. Grey demanded to know 'what we should do to help them [the French] in war'. He employed a cascade of emotive arguments: the French 'had been relying on the entente'; the French had 'kept their Northern coast undefended'; France 'might be crushed from that quarter' [the sea]; 'Cambon had twice wept over our statement that we were not committed'. Finally, Grey produced his red flag of warning: 'he could not stay in office unless we blockaded the German Navy into the Baltic'.[10] Runciman recorded Grey's direct threat to walk out: 'Either we must declare ourselves neutral, or in it. If we are to be neutral he will go'. Grey 'asks for a sharp decision'.[11]

Samuel detected a new anti-German edge of passion. Grey was 'outraged' at German and Austrian dishonesty. They had 'played with the most vital interests of civilisation, have put aside all attempts at accommodation made by himself and others, and while continuing to negotiate have marched steadily to war'.[12] Asquith supported Grey in asserting German guilt. He reported sympathetically on a breakfast meeting with Lichnowsky, but added damaging details: Lichnowsky 'thinks his Gov[ernmen]t mad'.[13]

Samuel then suggested a compromise based on his 'own conviction'. Britain must not contemplate war for 'the sake of our goodwill for France', nor for 'the balance of power'. If Britain went to war, it must be solely for British interests. Britain could wage war for two reasons only: 'for the protection of the northern coasts of France, which we could not afford to see bombarded by the German fleet and occupied by the German army, or for the maintenance of the independence of Belgium'.[14] This formula was attractive. For one thing, Samuel distinguished it from Grey's policy, which most Radicals at the table characterised as war for the sake of the Entente. In addition, German action would appear to be the trigger.

At this point, Asquith read to the cabinet a letter he had just received from the Conservative leaders, Bonar Law and Lord Lansdowne. The Tory magnates stood firmly for intervention, with no distinction between a war in the east and the west. The letter offered their 'unhesitating support' for rapid intervention in a continental war. There was no mention of Belgium.[15] Masterman claimed the letter was 'hurriedly read and laid down without comment'.[16] But others carefully recorded its arrival. In Runciman's words, the letter meant that Law and Lansdowne 'promise that they will support us in going in with France'.[17] Harcourt scribbled down the Conservatives' big line: 'fatal to the honour and security of the UK to hesitate'.[18]

What was the impact of the letter? Years later, Asquith denied it had any bearing on the Liberals' decisions.[19] But taken together with knowledge of Churchill's ongoing contacts with the Tories, and Grey's frank suggestions of his possible resignation, the letter threatened the insubordinate Radical ministers. Some were fully seized of the heightened danger — of a coalition. Many observers noticed this. Liberal journalists regarded it as 'an open secret' that a coalition had been 'seriously discussed' at the height of the crisis.[20] Tories boasted of it. For example, Valentine Chirol, a well-connected former foreign editor at *The Times*, told his friend Hardinge that, during the crisis, Asquith had been forced to 'parry' the Radicals' resignation threats with the threat of 'the formation of a coalition government'.[21] It was a fair assessment.

Quite apart from Tory pressure, the high political drama that day was underlined by Asquith's own talk of departure. In the afternoon, Asquith wrote to Venetia that the cabinet had been 'on the brink of a split'. Grey might go, he added, and 'I shall not separate myself from him'.[22] It is very likely that the ministers appreciated this. According to Samuel, Asquith told him directly after lunch that day that 'I shall stand by Grey in any event'.[23] Samuel offered the same assessment that evening: 'Had the matter come to an issue Asquith would have stood by Grey in any event, and three others would have remained. I think all the rest of us would have resigned'.[24] As Samuel tallied the numbers, this meant the solid block in favour of intervention comprised Asquith and Grey, plus the 'three others', Haldane, Churchill, and probably McKenna. Had the Radicals pressed them to the point of resignation, these five would have walked, ending the Liberal cabinet.

The interventionist ministers employed one more subtle argument. They deliberately fostered the impression that Britain's intervention in any war would be restricted to naval action. As Churchill explained to Lloyd George, 'The naval war will be cheap — not more than 25 millions a year.'[25] Such was the assurance used to drape the crudities of war. Samuel's formula for British intervention, making it dependent on German naval action on the French coast, must have added to the impression of a naval war. Samuel himself highlighted Britain's naval preparations in a letter to his wife: 'Our great fleet is in the north; a second is waiting in port on the south coast; a third is being distributed along the trade routes.'[26]

So the cabinet debated British intervention on the basis of Samuel's formula. Grey wanted more — a straightforward commitment to defend France and Belgium. As Samuel put it, 'Grey expressed a view which was unacceptable to most of us.'[27] There were moments of high emotion. The interventionists' threats to resign provoked answering threats. Churchill goaded the neutralists: 'If Germany violates Belgian neutrality I want to go to war — if you don't I must resign'. Morley interjected, 'If you *do* go to war I resign'. Morley was 'very angry' at the revelation of naval mobilisation overnight, which was 'contrary to Winston's promise to Cabinet'. Some ministers leaned one way, and then the other. For example, Harcourt thought that 'Crewe from all he said this morning seems to be with "us".[28] Perhaps ten cabinet members were still leaning toward neutrality: Harcourt, Lloyd George, Morley, Pease, McKinnon Wood, Beauchamp, Simon, Runciman, Birrell, and possibly Crewe.

On the other side of the debate, Grey, Asquith, and Churchill pushed hard for a pledge of naval assistance to the French, to make safe the Channel and the French coasts — Britain's 'doorstep'. In the final few minutes of this three-hour cabinet, the historic breakthrough came. A momentous decision was made: Grey got his pledge to France. By a slender margin, a majority was found for a form of words, suggested by either Samuel or Crewe.[29] Grey was authorised to promise the French ambassador that, if France faced a German naval attack, then 'the British fleet will give all the protection in its power'.[30] Downing Street had decided on the first trigger for war.

From this moment on — before anything was known of the German threat to Belgium — it was certain that the British government would intervene in any war in which France was embroiled with Germany. Of course, all this was deeply secret.

But the political damage was immediate. John Burns protested. He 'lent forward' and spoke 'with deep feeling'. He spoke of the pain of separating from 'a P.M. whom he loved'.[31] But he was adamant: this pledge to France was 'an act of hostility' that might provoke Germany to 'declare war on us'.[32] Burns was 'almost in tears', announcing that he 'must resign at once'.[33] Beauchamp recalled the reaction: 'Everybody joined in a chorus of dissuasion & the PM spoke forcibly on "deserting colleagues" etc. Eventually he promised to return for the evening cabinet.'[34]

Why had the majority accepted Grey's demand for a pledge of naval support to France? Both strategic and political calculations had come into play. Morley's friendly parting exchange with Burns after the cabinet meeting helps explain the strategic thinking. 'I think you are mistaken in going on this particular proposal,' he told his friend. 'The door-step argument makes a warning to Germany defensible, apart from the French Entente.' Britain, Morley conceded, could not 'acquiesce in Franco–German naval conflict in the narrow seas, on our doorstep so to say'.[35] Morley told Burns that he, too, would resign — not over the pledge to France, but rather in protest at the whole course of Grey's foreign policy.

Clearly, as Morley believed, the 'door-step argument' had won over the majority of cabinet. Most had been prepared to back a naval pledge to France, 'as a warning to Germany'. Samuel also cited the 'door-step', explaining in a private letter that the cabinet knew Britain would not be able 'to tolerate great naval conflicts at our doors'.[36] Pease similarly thought that the dispositions of the French and British fleets since 1912 had created a sense of obligation upon Britain to protect France's northern coast, whatever had been said at the time. He hoped that Germany might accept the warning to her navy.[37] In this way, the naval promise to France assuaged consciences — and still seemed less than the full and immediate commitment to war that Grey had been seeking.

Then political calculations had come into play. The stark fact was that the pledge to France had prolonged the life of this cabinet. As Samuel explained to his wife, 'The morning cabinet almost resulted in a political crisis to be superimposed on the international and financial crisis.' The concession on the French coasts had avoided it. As Samuel argued, 'the division or resignation of the Government in a moment of utmost peril for the country would have been in every way lamentable'.[38]

The Radicals' angst

As soon as cabinet was over, Grey crossed hurriedly from Downing Street to the Foreign Office. During an interview in his study at about 2.20 p.m., he passed over an *aide-mémoire* to Cambon:

> I am authorised to give an assurance that if the German fleet comes into the Channel or through the North Sea to undertake hostile operations against French coasts or shipping the British fleet will give all the protection in its power.[39]

In his explanation to Cambon, Grey stressed that the declaration 'did not bind us to go to war with Germany unless the German fleet took the action indicated'.[40] In spite of this, there was little doubt left: *neutrality* for Britain was next to impossible. Grey himself had exposed this in cabinet. When Grey's critics had urged that he should genuinely neutralise the Channel — that is, seek 'the neutrality of France in (our) home waters also' — he had refused.[41] Grey would not consider such even-handed negotiation.

Not surprisingly, a great cloud of misgiving settled upon the Radicals. As soon as the cabinet broke up, a group made its way the short distance to Halkyn House, Earl Beauchamp's grand residence at 13 Belgrave Square. Morley accepted a lift with Simon and Lloyd George, and on the way 'our talk was on the footing that we were all three for resignation'. Simon confided to Morley that 'he felt pretty sure of decisive influence over Lloyd George, and that he (Simon) looked to resignation as quite inevitable'.[42]

On arrival at Halkyn House, Beauchamp hosted a working luncheon. His guests were Morley, Simon, Samuel, Harcourt, and, significantly, Lloyd George. By telephone, three more colleagues were summoned — Pease, McKinnon Wood, and Runciman. Morley recalled a general consensus that 'Burns was right', and 'that we should not have passed Grey's proposed language to Cambon'. All resented that 'the cabinet was being rather artfully drawn on step by step to war for the benefit of France and Russia'.[43] Harcourt also recorded a short summary of the rueful talk: both Simon and Beauchamp complained that the cabinet had been manipulated and 'jockeyed' toward the decision to promise France assistance if it came into combat with the German fleet, and both favoured following Burns into resignation. But his account included an important concession: 'I differ as I think the prevention of a German fleet attack & capture of French territory on [the] shore of [the] Channel *a British interest*'.[44] This revealed the beginnings of a shift in Harcourt's position. Samuel also was impatient, privately complaining that Morley was 'so old' and his views 'inconsistent'.[45]

Nevertheless, it was Samuel who guided discussion on the next great issue — Belgium. He supplied a formula, which all agreed to adopt for the coming evening cabinet. Harcourt jotted it down:

> We agreed to refuse to go to war merely on a violation of Belgian *neutrality* by a traverse for invasion purposes of territory but to regard any permanent danger or threat to Belgian *independence* (such as occupation) as a vital British interest.[46]

Would more ministers resign? Morley, Beauchamp, and Simon favoured this as the only honourable course. Lloyd George, they believed, was with them. Indeed, Morley thought Lloyd George and Simon were 'heading the schism'.[47] Harcourt and Samuel, on the other hand, were tilting toward the safer option — to stay in office and await developments.

A second meeting of the cabinet was scheduled to begin at 6.30 p.m. Beauchamp wrote that 'we expected a great fight over Belgian neutrality wh[ich] w[ould] end in a great rupture'.[48]

But the rupture did not come. Grey was disarming, and began with news designed to mollify the Radicals: 'Cambon has taken his communication quietly & had not pressed for further assurances about Belgium and Grey does not press for a decision on this tonight.'[49] The pledge of naval support appeared to be enough.

Recriminations were then aired, against Churchill in particular. Churchill explained that he had met with the French naval attaché, the Comte de Saint-Seine, and measures for close naval co-operation had been set in train. This was too much for Morley. Another shouting match began. Morley was 'very angry', and accused Churchill of making an 'attempt to create an alliance for war'. Again, the Radicals argued that, to be logical, Grey should inform the Germans of the pledge of naval assistance to France immediately, to dissuade them from any provocative act. Grey was resolute: 'she must learn this from the statement in the H[ouse] of C[ommons] tomorrow'. This provoked questions from the neutralists, which were cut short when Asquith revealed that, in any case, he had told Lichnowsky that morning that Britain would regard any action by the German fleet in the Channel 'very seriously' — as good as demanding that the Germans not use naval forces against France. Simon interrogated Churchill. Had any orders been issued instructing the navy 'to attack [the] German fleet if they came out tonight[?]' Churchill answered with a definite 'No'. Harcourt declared for good measure that 'it would be monstrous to attack them if they were coming out not against us and without having been informed of our decision'.[50]

The cabinet then turned to the next and thorniest issue — Belgium. During the day, confirmation had arrived at the Foreign Office of German troop movements inside Luxembourg.[51] Grey offered in addition the inflammatory detail that 'the Germans have crossed the French frontier thro[ugh] Luxembourg and probably at Nancy'. Notwithstanding the 'probably', the foreign secretary, *the* source of reliable up-to-the-minute intelligence, was suggesting an imminent German invasion of France. Was Belgium the immediate target? Was this to be the second trigger for war for Britain? In the discussion, Samuel's formula, which had been nutted out at Beauchamp's luncheon table in the afternoon, found favour. Eventually, the cabinet resolved that only 'a substantial violation' of Belgian neutrality would provide the formal *casus belli* that could be used to justify Britain's intervention in the continental war.[52] Later, Churchill told Wilfrid Blunt, the veteran anti-imperialist with whom he was friendly, that this was decided by 'a single vote'.[53]

The decision was clearly a compromise. A second trigger for British entry into war had been set. Through Radical pressure, the bar had been set higher — not any German trespass upon Belgian territory, but only something 'substantial' would drive Britain to war. Samuel was relieved. As he reported, 'the situation was easier, the point of contention was not pressed, and with the exception of the two I have mentioned [Burns and Morley] we remain solid'.[54] In his account of the cabinet, Beauchamp highlighted another very human factor at work — 'we were all jaded and exhausted'.[55] Radical resistance was being slowly worn down.

In this way, the decision of the second cabinet of the Sunday complemented that of the first: it was made to appear, on sea and land, that German action would provoke British intervention. Samuel comforted himself with this. If peace foundered, he wrote, 'it will be an action of Germany's and not of ours which will cause the failure, and my conscience will be easy in embarking on the war'.[56]

At the end of this historic day, Radical consciences were restless. Burns and Morley were determined to resign on principle — so those closest to them, Simon, Beauchamp, and Harcourt, were tormented with doubt. They had sought guidance from each other during the evening cabinet. Simon slipped a note to Burns: 'Stay at any rate *for tomorrow's cabinet*: I am disposed to think that 7 or 8 of us may be with you.' Burns replied firmly on the same piece of notepaper: '*It is then too late.*'[57] At some point in the discussion, Beauchamp passed a note to Harcourt: 'I still think Burns was right this morning.' Harcourt replied 'Perhaps — but we are holding together with a good hope of keeping out of war altogether.' 'I agree or I s[houl]d join him,' shot back Beauchamp. 'We *must* keep him,' replied Harcourt.[58]

But they could not keep Burns. As the cabinet finished at about 8.00 p.m., 'Burns renewed his protest,' Beauchamp wrote. He announced that 'nothing had occurred to change his decision and he must resign tonight'. He agreed to talk with Asquith later, but 'he was immoveable'.[59] He sent a simple letter of resignation to Asquith. 'The decision of the cabinet to intervene in a European war is an act with which I profoundly disagree,' he explained.[60]

Simon sent in his resignation letter, dated 2 August, later on that same Sunday evening. It was in Asquith's hands on the Monday morning.[61] Simon objected both to the naval pledge just given to France, and to Grey's demand that this be hidden from Germany. Grey's statement, Simon wrote to Asquith, would 'be regarded as tantamount to a declaration that we take part in this quarrel with France and against Germany. I think we should not take part, and so I must resign my post'.[62]

John Morley, the lord president, was next to go. He had warned Asquith on Sunday, but had accepted his plea to 'Sleep on it.'[63] He composed his resignation letter over breakfast on Monday 3 August, explaining that the cabinet would never agree on what was meant by Britain's neutrality. 'I press you, therefore, to release me,' wrote Morley. He would make the cabinet of Monday morning his last.[64]

Earl Beauchamp passed Sunday night in a haunted state. In the morning, he penned a letter of resignation to Asquith. With his own copy of this letter, he filed a revealing private memorandum. He stressed the disabling rapidity of the crisis: 'It is very difficult to sit down calmly in the middle of a crisis & to record events as they fly by.' Then he turned to Grey's pledge to France on Sunday, the burning issue for him. He railed against the naval arrangements with France in 1912, 'those unfortunate naval conversations wh[ich] were [meant] to pledge no one to anything'.[65] Britain had been engineered into a false position. He ended with a heartfelt cry: 'I cannot but feel that our promise to France is a *casus belli* to Germany. Alas for this country'.[66] His letter to Asquith lamented the Liberal Imperialists' manipulation of the cabinet. 'By successive acts the Cabinet has passed to a position at wh[ich] war seems to me inevitable,' he complained.[67] Beauchamp would announce his resignation at the cabinet table the next morning, on Monday 3 August.

All the resignations, it is important to note, were not 'protests against Britain entering the war', as they have since been often mistakenly described. All preceded that. They were protests against Britain preparing to embark on war for the sake of Entente solidarity.

The reaction to the resignations reveals another side of the political management of this crisis: secrecy. All were told that they had to keep knowledge of the cabinet schism secret. It would strengthen the nation's hand, preserve a 'united front' — and, temptingly, perhaps preserve peace. In their private letters, cabinet members urged their families to keep silent on cabinet divisions.[68] It was part of Asquith's unspoken strategy. Similarly, he sent no acceptance of any resignation. It would appear that he appreciated how secrecy and delay might save the cabinet. This veiling of dissent inside the cabinet would be an important factor in the days ahead. Needless to say, no one in Australia would find out about any of these cabinet resignations until the immediate crisis was over.

Harcourt — whose resignation was expected — also had an especially worrying night, but marked by frenetic activity. He had fled from the cabinet to dinner at home alone — 'housemaid, chop'. But at 10.00 p.m., he received a special message from the Admiralty: a war plan was up and running. The Admiralty suggested that the South Africans should mount an attack on Walvis Bay in German South-West Africa. The plans were hatched in the Admiralty, but were probably suggested by Sir David de Villiers Graaff, a visiting senior South African politician.[69] It took Harcourt an hour to persuade Asquith and then Churchill that the proposal 'was mad'. Again, the dominions seemed to be swaggering and spoiling for a fight.[70]

Back at home at 11.00 p.m., Harcourt found he had a late-night visitor, Sir Thomas Robinson — an Australian — who was a shipping manager and the agent-general for Queensland. He suggested that Britain should immediately buy up a consignment of 2,000 tons of meat from Queensland currently en route to the USA, which Austria was attempting to purchase and divert to her food stockpile. The visit was a reminder that, throughout this crisis, the dominions' enthusiastic response to the prospect of war was an embarrassment to Harcourt. The idea of lending assistance to the Mother Country appeared to excite the imperial enthusiasts in the dominions and some of their representatives in London. That excitement had led them to a flurry of promises and, as we have seen, public offers of military assistance to Britain, including offers to mount expeditionary forces — from New Zealand on Friday 31 July, and from Canada on Sunday 2 August.[71] These were flaunted in the Conservative press, placing great pressure upon Harcourt.[72] Would Australia add to the pressure?

CHAPTER FIFTEEN

Australia jumps the gun

Melbourne, Monday 3 August

Private and Secret. We are taking every reasonable precaution. There is throughout Australia indescribable enthusiasm and entire unanimity in support of all that tends to provide for the security of the Empire in war.[1]
– Munro Ferguson to the Colonial Office, 3 August 1914

THE GOVERNOR-GENERAL made good on his offer to travel as swiftly as he could from Sydney to Melbourne in order to underwrite any decisions of Cook's cabinet. He left Central Station in Sydney in the evening of Sunday 2 August. Travelling with him, by invitation, were Millen, Irvine, Major White, and Admiral Creswell. 'A large crowd gathered at the station, but there was no demonstration, the gravity of the situation precluding any display of any kind,' reported the *Sydney Morning Herald*. Significantly, the prominent Labor politician William Morris Hughes was on the platform to see the governor-general and his entourage depart.[2]

Munro Ferguson's overnight dash to Melbourne underlined his own emphatic support for a dramatic gesture on Australia's part. Prime minister Cook greeted the train carrying Munro Ferguson and his two cabinet ministers at Spencer Street Station on Monday morning 3 August. The governor-general then withdrew to Government House.

Cook had foreshadowed in his speech at Horsham on the previous Friday evening of 31 July that, as prime minister, he might have to act very hastily in this crisis. 'The consent of Parliament is, of course, a very proper thing to have,' he had declared, but it was not sitting. The government controlled the army and navy, and might have to act 'at once'. In short, whether an election was impending or not, the executive had the power — and it would use it if need be.[3]

Thus, on Monday 3 August, prime minister Cook, after a hasty lunch at his hotel, gathered his ministers about him at the Commonwealth Offices — all three of them — Sir William Irvine, attorney-general; Senator Edward Millen, minister of defence; and Senator James McColl, the vice-president of the Executive Council. Two of these had made it to Melbourne only through the governor-general's offer of berths on his train. Cook and his colleagues then began a series of conferences with leading public servants and military men in Cook's rooms, building upon those Cook had chaired on Sunday. The relentless Major White was the chief figure among several military experts advising the politicians. White explained the plans that had been made since the Victoria Barracks conference in November 1912 to prepare in advance an expeditionary force to Britain, in co-operation with New Zealand, with Australia supplying 12,000 troops.

Cook and his ministers then held an emergency cabinet meeting at 3.00 p.m. It is important to clarify the attendance at this historic cabinet. Only four of the ten members of the Cook cabinet were assembled around the cabinet table by this time: Cook, Irvine, Millen, and McColl.[4] Why only four? Of course, very great distances would have to be traversed if ministers were to attend this cabinet meeting. But at least one who could easily have attended was sent away. McMahon Glynn, the minister for external affairs, was among the six ministers whose presence was not deemed essential. Indeed, his small role in these events is revealing. He was the only cabinet member in Melbourne from Wednesday to Friday 29–31 July, but he did not receive copies of any of the inter-state and international cables circulating between Munro Ferguson, Cook, and Millen. He typically told inquiring reporters that he had received 'no official communication' from England on the European crisis. He even hazarded this: 'Anyone who has read the inside history of the war in the Balkans will be glad enough to keep out of wars now.' So perhaps his absence from the cabinet table was a relief to his colleagues.[5] In any case, on Saturday, he had obeyed Cook's request that he set out for Adelaide by express train, to fill in for him at rallies in South Australia, and to await Cook's resumption of his election schedule there. Similarly, according to the press, two other cabinet heavyweights were not summoned: Sir John Forrest, the treasurer, from Western Australia, and Littleton Groom, the customs minister, from Queensland. Forrest was told on the Sunday that there was 'no necessity' for him to rush to Melbourne 'in the present circumstances'. Other ministers were reported simply as being 'too far from Melbourne to reach there in time'.[6]

This left a minority of Cook's cabinet to contemplate the European crisis, in company with the military experts. Apparently, no one considered inviting any leading member of the Labor opposition to observe this thinly attended cabinet meeting, or to stand with Cook afterwards, even as a gesture to underscore the claim that the Australian people were overwhelmingly in support of what was about to be done. No one from Cook's staff had contacted Fisher — not by telephone, or telegram, or letter.[7]

The climax came at 4.30 p.m., when the governor-general was summoned back to Treasury Place from Government House to preside at a meeting of the federal Executive Council. Its task was plain: to endorse the final decisions of the cabinet. This lasted an hour and ten minutes. Neither the low attendance at the cabinet meeting, nor the fact that an election day was only a month away, had prompted anyone to hesitate. The ultimate decisions were made by this scratch cabinet of four men, with Munro Ferguson looking across at them. This pocketful of politicians took it upon itself to answer emphatically the question the governor-general had cabled to Cook on the previous Friday night: was it not right that Ministers should meet 'in order that [the] Imperial Government may know what support to expect from Australia?'[8]

This was no council of caution. The decisions at the cabinet were exactly as the governor-general had hoped for, and had predicted, in his cables to London.

Cook's ministers were indeed desperate to catch up to the Canadians and the New Zealanders in the hot rush to promise military aid to the Mother Country. Canada's figure of 30,000 troops was in the newspapers. New Zealand had made its offer on Friday. Obviously, the Australian ministers did not wish to see Australia beaten into third place. Perhaps a large contingent of troops could compensate for any perceived tardiness in Australia's offer? Thus, at the federal Executive Council, Major White found that the ministers were suddenly keen to add to the numbers of troops that had been agreed in planning with New Zealand in 1912 and 1913.[9] Cook and his ministers urged more. How about 20,000 Australian troops? Was this possible? It was roughly one-third of the Australian army's total strength of 62,000 men (counting the latest intake in July 1914).[10] White explained that this was a figure in excess of his current plans, but then he boldly reassured the politicians that preparations for such an augmented force could be completed in six weeks.[11] Munro Ferguson recalled a few days later that 'originally I had heard 3 weeks mentioned as the time required to prepare the expedition.'[12] Someone — he did not say who — was dead keen to get the offer made.

After more than an hour, the governor-general withdrew, and Cook's small cabinet deliberated for another fifteen minutes — although McColl dashed away to attend an election meeting in the country, reminding all once again that an election campaign was the backdrop to these decisions.[13]

Then, at the conclusion of the meeting, some minutes before 6.00 p.m., White was given the task that he must have considered both honourable and historic: he recorded in his diary, no doubt delightedly, that he had 'worded telegram for Min[iste]r offering Expedit[ionar]y Force fr[om] Australia'.[14] The politicians tweaked White's draft, and Munro Ferguson had the satisfaction of signing the momentous cable. This was immediately despatched to Harcourt in London:

In the event of war Commonwealth of Australia [is] prepared to
place vessels of Australian Navy under control of British Admiralty
when desired. Further prepared to despatch expeditionary force [of]
20,000 men of any suggested composition to any destination desired
by the Home Government. Force to be at complete disposal of the
Home Government. Cost of despatch and maintenance would be
borne by this Government. Australian press notified accordingly.[15]

Through this extraordinary cabinet decision, Australia announced
to the world her willingness to offer her forces to the 'Home
Government', both her warships and an expeditionary force, without
qualification as to the origins or the aims of the still undeclared
war. The ships and troops were for combat anywhere, under British
direction, with Australians footing the entire bill. Clearly, there
were no requirements that this decision be kept secret. The cable
itself announced that the local journalists had been given the news
instantly. Indeed, the newspapers in Australia were trumpeting the
news by the time Harcourt himself could read the cable, in the early
evening of Monday 3 August, London time — and the Conservative
press in Britain would follow suit in lauding the loyal offer from
Australia on the Tuesday morning.

Just after 6.00 p.m., Cook summoned the political reporter of *The
Argus* to the prime minister's room in the Commonwealth Offices.
Cook read to him the terms of the cablegram to London, and told
him it had just been sent 'to the Imperial authorities'. He read also
a second announcement assuring the Australian people that all that
could be done to curb financial panic in Australia was being done.
Millen was at Cook's side. Millen told the reporter that the 20,000
troops would not be drawn from the ordinary citizen army, of course,
because the *Defence Act* prevented soldiers being directed abroad.
Volunteers would be necessary. But Millen added that the offer of
an expeditionary force was 'indicative of Australia's determination to
take her share in any demand which may be made upon the Empire'.
He was sweeping in his claim for public support, then and in the
future. It was already 'manifest', he explained, 'that the patriotic spirit

of the people will be loyally behind any action which the government has decided to take'. *Any* action.

Where would Australia's naval and land forces serve? It was 'much too early' to discuss this, replied Millen. But *The Argus* reported the next day that 'there is reason to believe, however, that any Australian force would be directed to India' — the first of many rumours concerning the destination of Australian troops. It amply illustrated the assumption that Australians would be happy to fulfil any imperial mission, in the widest sense, anywhere.[16]

The Argus's reporter had also clearly been in touch with some of the military advisers milling around the Commonwealth Offices on that day. His report subtly conveyed something of the satisfaction experienced by White and others, who had been part of the planning for an expeditionary force for some years. The reporter gave a broad hint that events had turned out just as the military planners had wished:

> It is understood that the decision of the cabinet did not come as a complete surprise to the military authorities and there is reason to believe that arrangements for the despatch of an expedition are, as regards arms, equipment, and transport details, so well advanced that departures could be taken at any moment after volunteers had been enlisted.[17]

The Australian leaders in Melbourne also sent a revealing second cablegram on that same early Monday evening. Munro Ferguson asked the colonial secretary if 'an official communication could be made stating the present position in Europe as to a state of war or peace?'[18] This plea suggests something of the anxiety arising even among the high and mighty as a result of the lack of reliable news at the furthest reaches of the empire. 'Tell us! Is it peace or war?' the Australians were asking. But this cablegram also underlines the haste of the Australian offer. The Australian cabinet had just made a bold, apparently open-ended offer of military assistance, with Australian lives to be expended anywhere London chose, before

Britain had declared war — indeed, before the Australians were even in possession of trustworthy information about the outbreak of war in Europe.

Munro Ferguson's labours that day did not end with the despatch of these two cables. Probably very late in the evening of 3 August, knowing Britain's decision was still in the balance, he sent a third telegram to London marked 'Private and Secret'. This offered Harcourt a heartening assessment of Australian public opinion. It was an assessment that the governor-general no doubt believed would encourage his British Liberal colleagues to have confidence in deciding for war. He ladled it on thickly, claiming that Australia was awash with 'indescribable enthusiasm'. Apparently, the Australian people were fused together in 'entire unanimity to defend the Empire'.[19] This was a truly remarkable assessment for a man scarcely in touch with ordinary Australians. Nonetheless, Munro Ferguson assured London that there was only one opinion on the subject of war in the faraway dominion.

The timing of the key Australian approach to London earlier that evening is worth closer analysis. The cable making the offer of an Australian expeditionary force left Melbourne at about 6.00 p.m. on Monday 3 August (AEST). This was 8.00 a.m. (GMT) in the morning of Monday, London time. Therefore, Australia made the offer some seven hours before Sir Edward Grey was to stand in the House of Commons that afternoon to outline to the nation and the empire for the first time the position of the Asquith government on the European crisis. Australia made the offer some forty hours *before* the British government itself issued the announcement of the declaration of war at the Foreign Office, soon after midnight on Tuesday 4 August (the announcement itself backdating the declaration to 11.00 p.m.).[20]

But was war so close as to be regarded as imminent, therefore justifying the offer anyway? This depends upon the state of knowledge in Australia by the early evening of Monday 3 August, when the Cook cabinet's offer was made. The Australian press on the Monday was filled with reports from London: there was knowledge of the Russian general mobilisation that had been confirmed in London on

Friday 31 July; there was knowledge of the mobilisation of France and Germany on Saturday 1 August; there was knowledge that late on that day Germany had declared war upon Russia — but upon no other power. The German note to France demanding a statement regarding her neutrality was reported. But war had not broken out in Western Europe. There were no reports in Australia of the German ultimatum to Belgium that had been delivered on the evening of Sunday 2 August, for this was not confirmed even in London until the Monday afternoon.[21] In no sense can the Cook government's offer of troops be represented as a reaction to the outbreak of war in western Europe, as a response to a call for assistance from London, or as a requirement demanded of Australia under her imperial defence plans. The Cook cabinet simply hurtled ahead of events.

Australia's politicians also must have known that London was in two minds about the position it should take. Australia's leading newspapers did not hide the fact. They reported correctly, in their editions over the weekend and on the morning of Monday 3 August, that the Asquith government had as yet made no final decision for or against war. Indeed, these reports from London included summaries of editorial opinion in the British press, showing that important Liberal newspapers — the *Manchester Guardian*, the *Daily News*, *Reynold's News*, and the *Westminster Gazette* — were adamant in advocating British neutrality.[22] For example, the editor of *The Age* noted on the morning of Monday 3 August that, 'We learn from cables that a strong Liberal Party movement is on foot in England to keep the British Empire neutral, and that the Asquith Cabinet has already felt its pressure'. This desire to stand apart from the war, the paper predicted gravely, would not long survive the British people's desire to shoulder their obligations to the Triple Entente, 'even should these obligations be merely of a moral nature'. Therefore, war was likely to suck in Britain. But, conceded *The Age*, 'It is still permissible to hope that she may not be called upon to participate in the war.'[23]

The Australian press also reported on certain letters to the editor appearing in the British press with special relevance to Australia. For example, on Friday 31 July, Lord Lamington, a former governor of

Queensland (1896–1901) and a Conservative in politics, wrote to *The Scotsman* arguing against British intervention. He noted Asquith's numerous assurances to the House of Commons that Britain was not bound to support Russia or France in any conflict. More importantly, Lamington argued that pleas that Britain had to intervene for the sake of the 'balance of power' were foolish. This 'antiquated' idea, he wrote, 'ignores the fact that our interests are primarily world-wide and not merely European [and that] the safety of India and of our oversea dominions are of far greater importance to us than a possible defeat of France'. Moreover, a Russian victory over Germany would destroy the balance of power in Europe. A critic of Pan-Slav nationalism in the Balkans, Lamington damned interventionist editorials in British newspapers, because 'by the press declaring that it is our duty to support France and Russia, Russia is thereby encouraged to make war on Austria, and a general war will necessarily follow'.[24] Key passages from Lamington's vehement letter were reproduced widely in the Australian press.[25]

Most importantly, on Monday 3 August many Australian newspapers correctly reported the assurance of the Liberal-aligned London *Daily Chronicle* that the British cabinet had decided *against* sending an expeditionary force to the Continent — a perfectly accurate report of the decision of the British cabinet on Saturday 1 August. The same newspaper's reports, stressing that the decision not to send the BEF indicated how strongly the Asquith government was dedicated to ongoing negotiation for peace, were faithfully reproduced, in summary, in the Australian press. Frequently cited was the *Daily Chronicle* editorial of Saturday 1 August, which asserted that 'there is a deep and growing feeling amongst Liberals against Britain's participation in the war'.[26]

Even on Tuesday 4 August, as the Australian press showered editorial praise on Australia's patriotic offer of an expeditionary force, the news pages still carried headlines such as that in Sydney's *Daily Telegraph* asking 'WHAT WILL BRITAIN DO?'[27] Australia's offer of Monday 3 August had been made in the full knowledge that Britain's decision was still pending. It cannot justifiably be said that the

Australian politicians made their offer because they were persuaded of the imminence of war.

The competitive appeal of an expeditionary force

Premature? Pre-emptive? Reckless? The major Australian newspapers gave no hint of any reservation along these lines. They greeted the offer of an expeditionary force with almost unqualified acclaim. Indeed, the more rabid and pro-imperial Australian press loved it. Leader writers were full of unstinting praise when the news was reported on Tuesday 4 and Wednesday 5 August. Australia was swaggering. The newspapers stated quite openly that Australia's motive included a healthy desire to compete with Canada and New Zealand in showing the world her devotion to empire. The editor of *The Argus*, for example, expressed exhilaration that Australia was at last running hard upon the heels of the other dominions: 'In making so prompt an offer to send troops to the assistance of the motherland in the emergency confronting her the Commonwealth has risen splendidly to a great occasion. Australia is now in line with Canada and New Zealand.' The shame of even a moment of caution had been averted. Moreover, to expunge any appearance of tardiness, more troops could be promised, advised *The Argus*. Thus, the editor praised the Cook cabinet's offer as 'merely an instalment, an earnest, of the efforts and the sacrifices she is prepared to make'.[28] According to such editorials, Australia would instantly send many more troops if needed.

In the same spirit, Sydney's *Daily Telegraph* hailed Cook's offers as 'an answer to duty's call' — ironic, when it is considered that no such call had been made. Placing the whole of the Australian fleet and 20,000 men at the disposal of London was audacious, and 'heartily endorsed by the patriotic sentiment of Australia'. To defend Australia, there was no choice but 'to assist in the defence of the Empire'. In a testament to the remarkable powers of self-deception summoned up by war, the editor added — brazenly or dementedly — that 'This is no foreign expedition; it is purely a movement for Commonwealth defence'.[29]

Only *The Age*, which generally supported a greater autonomy in Australia's defence policy, risked expressing a small reservation. Schuler's editorial loyally blamed Germany for the outbreak of war, discounted any chance of British neutrality as advocated by what he dubbed 'the Peace-at-Any-Price party', and called for Britain's immediate intervention. The Australian government in its turn had 'done the right thing'. The offer of troops was admirable, but the editorial dared to criticise Cook's offer to place the ships of the Royal Australian Navy under British control. The Cook government's statement of Monday 'lacks definiteness', complained *The Age*. Was it a technical transfer of the ships, purely 'for the reason that Australia is not an independent Power'? Or was Britain being empowered 'to move our ships wherever she pleases — to European waters, let us say?' 'In view of our fearfully isolated position,' explained *The Age*, it was 'to the last degree impolitic and inadvisable' to give Britain such an unfettered control of Australian naval ships:

> We can spare soldiers to assist in the defence of Empire abroad, and
> that sacrifice every patriot is willing to make; but our war ships we
> cannot spare, for without them we should be destitute of means to
> defend Australia from destructive visitations which already loom on
> the horizon.[30]

In spite of this wave of editorial applause, the Australian press continued to report the clash of opinion in the British press on the fundamental issue. For example, the views of Sir Guy Fleetwood Wilson, a high-ranking imperial official with much experience in India and in the army, appeared in *The Times* in London on Monday 3 August. In common with Lamington, Wilson's condemnation of a war for Entente solidarity was widely reproduced in the Australian newspapers on Tuesday 4 August. Wilson argued that Britain's first responsibilities were to her empire rather than to France and Russia. Britain should defend her far-flung possessions as a first priority. Wilson blamed Russia's provocation for the coming war, in that she had foolishly supported Serbia. He urged that Britain not intervene in the quarrel on the Continent: 'It is not worth the life of one single British grenadier.'[31]

Remarkably, federal Labor's leaders offered no such criticism. They made no statement even remotely critical of either the naval or the military aspect of the Cook cabinet's decisions of Monday 3 August. Fisher himself had travelled to Benalla for an election meeting on that evening. There, at the local shire hall, he again voiced his desire to rise above petty politics on defence, because 'in times of emergency, there are no parties at all. (Applause.)' War was 'a deplorable thing'; arbitration of disputes by impartial international tribunals should ensure settlements 'without war', he pleaded. Then came a fatalistic assessment, and he repeated the ultra-patriotic boast he had made at Colac:

> In these matters, however, facts are stubborn things. It is just possible that the mother country may be drawn in, and, with her, we shall be involved more or less … We stand united against the common foe, and I repeat what I said at Colac, that our last man and our last shilling will be offered and supplied to the mother country in maintaining her honour and our honour, if we should happen to come into conflict. (Applause.) This is no time for a display of what some call limelight patriotism, but we shall maintain our own laws and settle our own disputes in our own way without any interference in the dispute from any nation whatever.[32]

Probably after Fisher's address was concluded, Cook did at last contact Fisher, by telephone to Benalla late on Monday evening. By this time, the Cook cabinet's cable offering Australia's expeditionary force was already making its way to London via the 'All-Red Route'. Fisher recalled later that he was told over the phone at Benalla of 'certain action the Government proposed to take' — presumably, but not certainly, the offer of an expeditionary force. In response, Fisher gave Cook an assurance that the Labor opposition would 'stand behind the Government in all measures it thought necessary to take to assist the Mother Country and protect Australia's interest'.[33] But

Labor did not issue a statement regarding this late-night contact with Cook, and, more importantly, did not issue any statement regarding the cabinet's offer to London.

In the press on Tuesday there was still no statement from anyone in the Labor leadership team on the offer of an expeditionary force. There was no immediate response from Fisher, although he had given glimpses of an inner turmoil over the weekend. For example, he had suggested to one reporter that the tragedy erupting in Europe highlighted the fact that disputes should be settled sanely, by international arbitration.[34] On Sunday evening he had told another reporter of his sadness at the assassination of the French socialist leader Jean Jaurès in Paris on Friday night, 'a loveable man, with a burning desire for peace'. Fisher reflected sorrowfully on the day that he and Pearce had spent seeing Paris in the company of the great socialist internationalist in 1911 on their way to the Imperial Conference.[35] But the main statements to the press on Sunday had promised that the federal Labor Party was ready to embrace a spirit of bipartisanship on defence. Fisher's speech at Benalla then underlined this. The political purpose can be easily discerned: to neutralise the Cook government's recent attempts to make local political capital out of the deteriorating situation in Europe. Thus, Fisher told a reporter from *The Advertiser* on Sunday that 'Political party strife has been forgotten for the time being in a state of affairs like the present.'[36]

Significantly, on the same Sunday evening in Sydney, Hughes also had issued a long statement dismissing those who had taken the low road and attempted to play politics over the weekend with their references to the European crisis. He pleaded that, at such a moment, the defence of Australia should be a matter far above politics. For the sake of the security of the nation, the spirit of party had to be abandoned. Cook, Millen, and Irvine were not mentioned, but they were clearly the target. 'I forbear to criticise or even to comment upon recent attempts to make political capital out of the defence question,' he wrote with uncharacteristic restraint. 'None should be for party, but all be for the State,' argued Hughes. 'Whatever needs to be done to defend the interests of the Commonwealth and of the

Empire must be done.'[37] 'Whatever' — the cheque was blank.

In case Fisher and Hughes could not hear their burning boats crackling behind them, articles appeared in the press on Monday shepherding them further down the 'patriotic' path. Prominent Liberals warmly commended the Labor chieftains' offers to put aside all criticism of the Cook government on the sacred matter of imperial security. For example, Sir Alexander Peacock, the premier of Victoria, told reporters on Sunday that he and his cabinet 'approve and appreciate heartily' the Labor men's generous and patriotic offer to shun the party spirit, an offer that would serve to 'show the world that Australia is absolutely united'.[38] This immediate background — the disavowal of defence as an election issue on the Sunday and the bouquets that greeted this decision — helps to explain the silence of the Labor leadership in response to the news of the Cook cabinet's offer of an expeditionary force. Fisher and Hughes had made it very difficult for any Labor figure to make a critical response to the news from Melbourne. Some Labor speakers simply repeated Fisher's line about the last man and shilling.[39] More determined anti-militarists — such as Frank Anstey, who opened his campaign with a speech at the Northcote Town Hall on the evening of Monday 3 August — kept the focus on domestic issues. Anstey said nothing on the European crisis, but did stick rigidly to Labor's policy commitment to spend on defence only as revenue permitted.[40] Labor candidates, and the party's leaders themselves, could scarcely offer direct criticism of Cook's offer of an expeditionary force so soon after decrying the party spirit in matters of defence.

Certainly, Fisher made no reference to Cook's offer on Tuesday 4 August. He travelled during the day, and spoke to a big crowd at Her Majesty's Theatre in Wangaratta that evening. There was still no clear or certain word from London on war, and Fisher spoke first on domestic issues. He defended the Commonwealth Bank, and stuck by his decision not to borrow for defence spending. He 'deplored' talk of war, and praised the ideal of international arbitration. But Fisher repeated the offer of a truce on defence. 'In so far as this war affects the Mother Country and ourselves there are no parties. (Applause.)

Whatever the government decided was necessary to do to protect, help and support the Mother Country and protect the interests of Australia he and his whole Party will be behind them. (Applause)'. Later in his speech, Fisher noted his pride in Labor's creation of the separate Australian fleet, and he foresaw the possibility that Australian sailors might soon be mixing 'with their cousins from the old country' — hinting that the Australian fleet might well sail to Britain's assistance. Twice he invoked his pledge that Australia would stand with the Mother Country 'to the last man and to the last shilling. (Applause,)'[41] But he offered no remark about an expeditionary force.

Next day, in a letter to the *Daily Telegraph* on Wednesday 5 August, Hughes simply accepted the war as a fact: it was a terrible thing that war was 'upon us'. He put the obvious to his readers: a British victory in such a struggle was essential for Australia. He then passed to a discussion of measures to mitigate the war's effects. Like Fisher, he made no comment whatsoever on Cook's offer of an expeditionary force or the transfer of the RAN fleet.[42]

In allowing Cook's offers to pass without direct comment, Labor's leaders again chose immediate political safety. Why? On Tuesday 4 August, the nation was awaiting news of war. Why endanger the whole Labor campaign, the leaders must have reasoned, by issuing something that would instantly be misrepresented as disloyal, when the spectre of war itself — and so, too, the offer of an expeditionary force — might well melt away as swiftly as it had appeared? On the other hand, perhaps they assumed that both war and an Australian contribution were irresistible. Again, they must have reasoned, why imperil the Labor campaign with a critical response if thousands of Australians were bound to volunteer anyway? Perhaps Labor's leaders took comfort from reports in the press that Britain, and therefore Australia, might be required only to fight at sea. In any case, Fisher had already uttered to his audiences in crowded halls, and to journalists with their pencils poised, politically expedient phrases on the subject. He had spoken like an ultra-patriot at Colac, Benalla, and Wangaratta. He had offered a limited political truce on the Sunday. Thus, he had made Labor as secure as he could from attacks based on

the charge that the party of trade unionists, Catholics, and Irish —
the last elements having been so noisy in their support of Home Rule
over recent weeks — was unsafe to be entrusted with government in
wartime. Why risk it all by pointing out that Cook's offer was rash,
impulsive, and dangerously unqualified?

CHAPTER SIXTEEN

The Sir Edward Grey show

London, Monday 3 August

He concluded by saying that 'the most awful responsibility is resting on the Government in deciding what to advise the House of Commons to do'. But he had just said that the only other policy — neutrality — is one which his own action had already made impossible — 'we have made the commitment to France!' The show of placing before the House 'the cause and the choice' was a mere pretence. The issue had already been prejudged.[1]

– Francis Hirst, editor of *The Economist*, notes on Grey's speech of Monday 3 August

SOON AFTER 3.00 P.M. on Monday 3 August — or, in real time, some seven hours *after* Australia had sent its cable to London offering an expeditionary force — Sir Edward Grey rose to deliver a historic speech to the House of Commons. This speech gave to the people of Britain and the empire the first real indication of Britain's stance on the international crisis. The speech is believed to have changed the mind of the nation. Certainly, Grey amazed some with the passion of his address. His task was to reveal and explain the pledge of naval assistance that had been given to France on Sunday. But he went further. He put the case that Britain should rush to the assistance of France and Belgium — he said little about Russia — if it came to war on the Continent.

Was it already too late? Certainly, diplomacy was being outpaced in the march to war by the men of arms. Let us recall quickly the steps that had been taken. In response to the Russian general mobilisation, the German elite around the Kaiser had panicked and decided — disastrously — to send two poorly framed ultimatums to Russia and to France on the afternoon of Friday 31 July.[2] French and German general mobilisations had been ordered almost simultaneously, in the late afternoon of Saturday 1 August.[3] Then Germany had compounded the disaster, declaring war upon Russia in the evening of Saturday 1 August.[4] But this was the only declaration of war among the great powers for two days.

Therefore, when Grey spoke in the mid-afternoon of Monday 3 August, war in the east had been declared. War in the west had not. A general war was still entirely avoidable, if the decision-makers wished it. The next fatal step, the German declaration of war upon France, was not announced in Berlin until 6.45 p.m. on the evening of Monday 3 August — that is, *after* the conclusion of Grey's speech.[5] News of it came to London *after* debates in the House of Commons were concluded.

What was it like in the House of Commons on the warm afternoon of Monday 3 August? Newspaper accounts and memoirs all testify to an extraordinary atmosphere in the House. All the galleries were crammed full. In the Distinguished Strangers' Gallery sat the Russian ambassador, Count Benckendorff.[6] Representatives of the British Empire were arrayed there, too. Among the celestially seated was Sir George Reid, Australia's high commissioner.[7]

The mood was tense. In the expectation of unprecedented numbers of MPs, extra chairs had been arranged on the floor of the House itself, and in rows of four down the gangway.[8] There was also an undertone of menace — a danger that some Conservative MPs might attempt to stampede the House. Filling the opposition benches were some who had treated the House to displays of hooliganism over recent years, most notoriously in July 1911.[9] Some of those same hotheads had been caught up in General Wilson's 'pogrom' against neutrality over the previous few days — a determined effort by right-wing Tories and journalists in touch with the French and Russian embassies to push Asquith's cabinet down the path to instant intervention.[10] In a raucous House, there was the possibility of Grey being swept toward truculence, and of dissenters being howled down.

As ministers entered the chamber, there were signs of the 'pogrom' spirit in the air. 'Mr Lloyd George and Mr Winston Churchill entered together, and both were cheered from all quarters of the House,' reported *The Times*. The *Manchester Guardian* saw it differently, noting that 'the part taken in their ovation by the Opposition was particularly marked'. The hushing-up of resignations was important at this point. 'As Ministers came to their seats those whose names had been associated with rumours of resignation were greeted with general cheering,' noted the *Guardian*.[11] The schism inside the cabinet was still hidden.

The House then displayed its impatience. Questions were given up. Business was rushed through. The Commons seemed to be 'in a state of nerves not reassuring to the nation,' as the *Manchester Guardian* reported later. The atmosphere was 'neurotic'. The House 'excitedly brushed its work aside in its hurry to hear Sir Edward Grey'.[12]

In his opening words, Grey reported that the crisis, originating in the Austro–Serbian dispute, had unfortunately escalated rapidly.[13] Britain, he insisted, had tried hard to preserve peace. But, he lamented, 'it is clear that the peace of Europe cannot be preserved. Russia and Germany, at any rate, have declared war on each other'.

Then he flourished Britain's 'free hand'. He and Asquith had told the House many times that there was 'no secret engagement which we should spring upon the House,' nor any 'obligation of honour' arising from such secrecy. Similarly, he declared, Britain was not a member of an alliance system, but was merely a member of 'a Diplomatic group'. In the present crisis, Grey asserted, the distinction was important, for no promise of anything more than diplomatic support to any friendly power had been made — 'till yesterday'.

With these ominous words, Grey turned to France. Reviewing

Britain's relations with France since the first Moroccan crisis, Grey explained that in early 1906 the French had requested military conversations with Britain, so that the naval and military experts would be ready to co-operate if the need arose. 'There was force in that,' reasoned Grey. As a result, Grey explained, he had authorised military conversations, but 'on the distinct understanding that it left the hands of the government free whenever the crisis arose'.

Naturally, Grey chose not to remind his audience of the hot water into which he had fallen in 1911 when it emerged that he had hidden his authorisation of these military conversations from most of the cabinet for almost six years.[14] The scar tissue from this squabble was still too tender. Instead, Grey moved to the healing letters — the exchange of letters with the French ambassador in the autumn of 1912 that the cabinet had carefully overseen.

He read to the chamber from his unpublished letter to Paul Cambon of 22 November 1912. This acknowledged the military conversations, but reaffirmed that 'such consultation does not restrict the freedom of either Government to decide at any future time whether or not to assist the other by armed force'. The redistribution of the French and British fleets in 1912 was specifically mentioned: 'The disposition, for instance, of the French and British fleets respectively at the present moment is not based upon any engagement to co-operate in war.' The letter then explained that the two governments had agreed on action in case of 'an unprovoked attack by a third Power'. Grey read the key paragraph, promising that each nation 'should immediately discuss with the other whether both governments should act together to prevent aggression and to preserve peace, and, if so, what measures they would be prepared to take in common'. Grey's purpose was plain: the letter, revealed here for the first time, proved that Britain's 'free hand' had been preserved. He had agreed only to consult.

'I come now to what we think the situation requires of us,' said Grey. In the second half of his speech, Grey's confidence kindled as cheers punctuated his declarations of Britain's firmness. He retreated altogether from the prospect of detachment. No longer, it seemed, was Britain 'perfectly free'. Grey referred to Britain's long-standing 'friendship' with France, and he immediately sought to conflate this with the 'obligation' he had denied only minutes before. Britain was spiritually leagued with France. Then, with some theatricality, Grey declared that, to see 'how far that friendship entails obligation — it has been a friendship between the nations and ratified by the nations — let every man look into his own heart and construe the extent of the obligation for himself'. His 'own feeling' told him there was a binding obligation.[15]

Grey then turned back to the French fleet. It was in the Mediterranean, so the northern and western coasts of France were 'absolutely undefended' — a phrase he employed three times in the course of his explanation. If France had moved her fleet to the Mediterranean 'because of the feeling of confidence and friendship' between Britain and France — no deals were mentioned — then, he asked, should Britain do nothing to defend France? Grey answered his own question with an uncharacteristically passionate flourish. Britain would be appalled if 'a foreign fleet' came into the Channel and 'bombarded and battered the undefended coasts of France'. Britain 'could not stand aside and see this going on practically within sight of our eyes, with our arms folded, looking on dispassionately, doing nothing!' The desire to rise up against this 'would be a feeling which would spread with irresistible force throughout the land'.[16] This brought forth a great wave of cheering from the opposition benches. Britain had a 'free hand' — but, hey presto, 'public opinion' must see instantly that Britain had contracted moral obligations in her dealings with France.

Next, Grey promised to look at the issue 'without sentiment and from the point of view of British interests'. Indeed, from this point in Grey's rhetorical dance, moral obligations and national interest waltzed arm in arm. If Britain left the French coast 'at the mercy of a German fleet coming down the Channel to do as it pleases', then it was likely, argued Grey, that the French would withdraw their fleet from the Mediterranean. Horrors awaited if Britain were to 'stand aside in an attitude of neutrality'. It was possible that Italy might abandon her neutrality in this crisis and threaten trade routes 'vital to this country'. Indeed, Britain's navy would have an impossible task defending her empire's trade routes everywhere. If Britain insisted on her 'negative attitude' of neutrality, she might suddenly have to send ships to the Mediterranean, thus exposing Britain to 'the most appalling risk'. In any case, France was 'entitled to know — and to know at once! — whether or not in the event of attack upon her unprotected Northern and Western Coasts she could depend upon British support'. So, Britain *was* boxed in by her naval arrangements with France, which only five minutes before Grey had insisted had left Britain entirely free. Against all assurances given to the cabinet in 1912, Grey used the position of the fleets in 1914 as a lever to promote intervention.

All this frightening of the MPs was preliminary to explaining the cabinet's decision of Sunday. Because of the 'emergency' and the 'compelling circumstances', Grey explained, a decision of great importance had been taken: on the previous afternoon, Sunday 2 August, he had given the French ambassador a pledge of naval support. He then read the statement. Tellingly, Grey immediately felt moved to explain to the cheering opposition that he had read the note 'not as a declaration of war'.

Next, Grey acknowledged an inconvenient complication. The Germans, he revealed, had moved to reassure him. The German government had just notified London that Germany was willing 'if we would pledge ourselves to neutrality, to agree that its fleet would not attack the Northern coast of France'.[17] But Grey brusquely dismissed the latest German offer. It would not save the peace: 'it is far too narrow an engagement for us', he asserted.[18] Why? Because, as Grey explained, 'there is the more serious consideration — becoming more serious every hour — there is the question of the neutrality of Belgium'.

Immediately, the foreign secretary turned to the Treaty of 1839. This, he proclaimed, was the 'governing factor' in determining Britain's attitude. He did not tell the House of discussions in the cabinet on Belgium just five days before. On Wednesday 29 July, the cabinet had debated Britain's obligations to Belgium. Ministers had examined the two scrupulously even-handed British treaties of August 1870, negotiated with both France and Prussia at the beginning of the Franco–Prussian War. Under their terms, Britain had threatened war against either France or Prussia if either power invaded Belgium, and had promised to co-operate toward the limited objective of defending Belgium. Most significantly, too, the terms were limited to a period of twelve months after peace had been established. After this time, 'the independence and neutrality of Belgium,' as the treaty stipulated, would rest again on the original Treaty of 1839.[19] It is vital to note that the old treaty did *not* require Britain to undertake war against any power that might violate Belgian neutrality — only the 1870 treaties threatened such a war. Accordingly, the Asquith cabinet had decided that Britain in 1914 was not *obliged* to make war on a power violating Belgium's neutrality. She was obliged only to respect Belgium's neutrality herself. The Radicals had successfully argued that there should be no decision in advance to intervene militarily to safeguard Belgium. The cabinet had resolved that 'the matter if it arises will be rather one of policy than of legal obligation'.[20]

Now, Grey sought to suggest the opposite — namely, that Britain was obliged to fight for Belgium under the terms of the old Treaty of 1839. He produced the two political poltergeists from 1870, prime minister Gladstone and his foreign secretary, Lord Granville. Grey reviewed the former Liberal leaders' commitments to Belgium's neutrality. He borrowed selectively from their parliamentary statements of 8 and 10 August 1870. He highlighted Gladstone, who had observed that whatever the legal obligations toward Belgium, the signatory nations had to take account of the most vital consideration — namely, their 'common interests against the unmeasured aggrandisement of any Power whatsoever'.[21]

Grey then reviewed his own brief episode of diplomacy on the matter. He cited the two telegrams he had despatched to Paris and Berlin on Friday 31 July, seeking simple assurances regarding Belgian neutrality. Grey read to the House the French commitment to both respect and defend that neutrality, and the non-committal reply from Germany. Crucially, he noted the Belgians' own assurances that they would defend their country from any violation.

Then came another breathtaking surprise. Grey revealed to the House that fresh news had arrived during the day: unconfirmed reports that Germany had presented an ultimatum to Belgium, demanding that she allow the passage of German troops through the country. He next revealed the hitherto-unknown fact of a German offer to achieve Britain's neutrality. In Grey's words, Britain had been 'sounded in the course of last week as to whether if a guarantee were given that, after the war, Belgium [sic] integrity would be preserved that would content us. We replied that we could not bargain away whatever interests or obligations we had in Belgian neutrality'. This, of course, was inaccurate and incomplete. The original German offer (of 29–30 July), to respect French as well as Belgian territorial integrity after any conflict in Europe, was not mentioned.[22] A second offer on the part of Lichnowsky (on 1 August), to respect both French continental and colonial territory, was not mentioned.[23] The initiative that Grey himself had launched and pursued ever so briefly on 1 August — the possibility of Britain and France remaining neutral or at least assuming 'passivity' in the west — was also not revealed to the House.[24]

Grey then revealed the very latest twist in the drama. He read to the House a telegram that he had received within the last hour. It had been addressed to King George V from Albert, King of the Belgians, entreating Britain's 'Diplomatic intervention' to 'safeguard the integrity of Belgium'. But, Grey told the House, Britain had tried diplomatic intervention. Moreover, Belgium's 'integrity' after conflict was not enough; if Belgium chose to tolerate German troops making passage, Grey warned, 'the independence will be gone'. Britain would wage war to defend Belgium's neutrality, Grey signalled, whether or not the Belgians wanted it.

How should Britain react to the German threat to Belgium? Again, Grey conjured Gladstone to give his opinion. Betraying the rush of his preparations, he confessed he had not had time to check the context of Gladstone's speech of 1870, but he did not think it mattered. It was pure gold. Gladstone had declared that, whatever the 'literal' guarantee to Belgium, Britain could not 'quietly stand by and witness the perpetration of the direst crime that ever stained the pages of history, and thus become participators in the sin'.[25]

Grey openly advocated British military intervention. He summoned up a nightmare vision. If Belgian independence went, then 'Holland will follow'. Denmark would fall under German influence. The House had to consider 'from the point of view of British interests,' the vital issues. France might be 'beaten to her knees'. Then, asked Grey, 'would not Mr. Gladstone's words come true', and 'just opposite to us there would be a common interest against the unmeasured aggrandisement of any Power?'

Next, Grey reviewed the theoretical possibility of neutrality. Britain might 'stand aside', husbanding its strength, or perhaps intervene only at the end of the war. But if Britain were to 'run away from those obligations of honour and interest as regards the Belgian Treaty,' Britain's force would be at a discount 'in face of the respect that we should have lost'. Britain would be without a friend in Europe.

Then, introducing remarks that would linger as his most grotesquely misleading, Grey minimised the likely cost of going to war. He hinted strongly that war for Britain would be naval only — Churchill's argument. 'For us, with a powerful Fleet, which we believe able to protect our commerce, to protect our shores, and to protect our interests,' Grey argued, 'if we are engaged in war, we shall suffer but little more than we shall suffer even if we stand aside.' Moreover, Grey appeared to dismiss the prospect of a 'continental commitment' on the part of the British army. Both the fleet and the army were being mobilised, he noted, but 'we have taken no engagement yet with regard to sending an Expeditionary armed force out of the country'. Grey did his best to make this seem unlikely, alluding to Britain's 'enormous responsibilities' in guarding her empire, and other 'unknown factors' to be weighed before 'sending an Expeditionary Force out of the country'.

In his peroration, Grey recapitulated the heart of his case. Presenting the politician's favourite device, the false dilemma, he explained that the only alternative to Britain's intervention 'would be that it [the government] should immediately issue a proclamation of unconditional neutrality'. He explained in sentences that would draw the ire of Radicals: 'We cannot do that. We have made the commitment to France that I have read to the House which prevents us from doing that.' In a cruel irony, the unpublished letter addressed to Cambon in November 1912 — the letter painstakingly devised with the assistance of the Radicals and designed to preserve Britain's freedom of action in any crisis — was interpreted by Grey as imposing an obligation of honour.

Interests and honour were carefully interleaved to the last. Grey appealed to all: could Britain act as if the Belgian Treaty, the redistribution of the French and British fleets, and the prospect of French defeat 'mattered nothing, were as nothing'? And if Britain was to say 'we would stand aside, [then] we should, I believe, sacrifice our respect and good name and reputation before the world, and should not escape the most serious and grave economic consequences'. It was too ignoble to contemplate.

Three short speeches followed. First, Bonar Law, the Conservative leader, promised 'unhesitating support' for the Liberal government in 'whatever steps they think it necessary to take for the honour and security of this country'. He noted with pride that the dominions of the empire, in offering expeditionary forces, had shown already that they could be relied upon.[26] Bonar Law did not set any limits, express any words of caution, or make any mention of Belgium in his supporting speech — for Britain's war did not depend upon Belgium in the Tory assessment.

Second, John Redmond, leader of the Irish Parliamentary Party, amazed the chamber. He rallied around the flag. He assured the Commons that all the people of Ireland would respond with 'sympathy' for Great Britain if it had to face the crisis of war. The government, he said, could even 'take their troops away'. He prophesied that 'armed Nationalist Catholics in the South will be only too glad to join arms with the armed Protestant Ulstermen in the North'. Irishmen, united as one, were prepared to 'defend the coasts of our country'. Miraculously, the prospect of civil war melted away.[27]

Finally, Ramsay MacDonald rose to speak for the British Labour Party. He shattered the mood building for war, declaring that Grey was plain wrong. Honour had been invoked. But, MacDonald reminded the House, statesmen frequently appealed to honour to cover all manner of 'crime', as at the time of the Crimean War and the South African War. The safety of Belgium, he argued, could not be considered a sufficient objective justifying Britain's entry into this war, because the conflict would scarcely be confined to Belgium. MacDonald directed the attention of the House away from Belgium and back to the seat of the conflict, in eastern Europe. Grey had ignored Russia, he complained. 'We want to try and find out what is going to happen, when it is all over, to the power of Russia in Europe, and we are not going to go blindly into this conflict without having some sort of a rough idea as to what is going to happen.'[28] He reminded the House that all opponents of the South African War had 'been through this before', only to be vindicated in the long run. 'It will come again,' he prophesied. He finished on a note of defiance. Britain 'ought to have remained neutral, because in the deepest parts of our hearts we believe that that was right and that that alone was consistent with the honour of the country and the traditions of the party that are now in office'.[29]

Later that night, in a debate only grudgingly conceded by the government, the House of Commons took up the issues once again. Radical opponents of the war entirely dominated. Sixteen Radical speakers, supported by Keir Hardie of the Labour Party, attacked Grey's speech.[30] These speeches, pleading with Grey to take up the cause of negotiation and restrain Russia and France, challenged the claim already being prepared in the Conservative press that there was unanimous support among the British people in favour of instant intervention on the Continent. No matter. *The Times* carried the message of Grey's oratorical miracle to the nation the next morning, proclaiming that there was 'general unanimity' in praise of Grey.[31]

Watching the afternoon speeches from the gallery of the House of Commons was George Reid. During the crisis, did the high commissioner bring any Australian perspective before the decision-makers in London? In practice, Reid had scarcely ever been active in his diplomatic role.[32] He had only just managed to wheedle a year's extension of his appointment out of the Cook government, and was fearful that a Labor victory at the September election might end it.[33] He would risk nothing. Moreover, the Colonial Office and the Admiralty cut him out during the crisis.[34] Not surprisingly, there is no evidence that he interacted with anyone in the British elite during the crucial days of decision-making.[35] He sent no account of the debate of Monday 3 August to Australia; instead, he was content to play the role of conduit for the imperial claqueurs. Reid's only significant cable to Australia was sent the next day, reporting the garnets of praise in the London press for Australia's promises of military assistance to Britain.[36]

Even more importantly, the imposition of newspaper censorship by the Cook government in Australia from Monday 3 August severely interrupted the supply of news cables from London. Thus, full accounts of Sir Edward Grey's vital speech, presenting Britain's case for war, were delayed. Just a few passages appeared in Australian newspapers after the decision had already been made, on Wednesday 5 August.[37] Needless to say, none of the seventeen speeches against British intervention on the Continent delivered by the Radicals and Labour in the House of Commons in the evening debate of Monday 3 August were reported at any length.[38] Australia's politicians, not to mention the Australian people, had no means to weigh up the cases for or against war, as they had been presented in London — until it was all over.

CHAPTER SEVENTEEN

'Their manhood at our side'

London, Friday 31 July to Tuesday 4 August

These kinsmen [of the Dominions] have swept away the phrases of
weakness and indifference and ranged their manhood at our side.[1]
–*The Times*, 3 August 1914

IT IS IMPORTANT to grasp how early in the course of the international
crisis the dominions had offered fighting troops for Britain to use.
The New Zealand offer of Friday 31 July came before any news of
general mobilisation on the part of Britain, France, or Germany. Even
Russia's general mobilisation was not announced in London until the
late afternoon of Friday 31 July (Greenwich Mean Time), some hours
in real time after Massey made his offer to Britain on the Friday
evening (New Zealand Time). The crisis in the east was escalating
when Canada and Australia put forward their offers on Sunday
2 August and Monday 3 August. But both came *before* news of the
key development insofar as escalation in the west was concerned: the
German ultimatum to Belgium. This was not confirmed in London
until the afternoon of Monday 3 August.[2] Of course, all three offers
were made before the advent of war itself — that is, well before Britain
declared war on Germany late in the evening of Tuesday 4 August.

What was the political effect of these early offers? The pages of
the British Conservative pro-interventionist press show the impact

clearly. The drumbeats from the dominions were a signal to strike up the band. The clamour in the Conservative press for British intervention on the Continent was part of the political setting in which Grey spoke to the House of Commons on Monday 3 August. The dominions had added decibels to that clamour.

All the major Conservative newspapers celebrated the dominions' display of 'patriotism'.[3] Preparations on the part of the Canadian Militia Council were reported from Friday 31 July. Figures of '25,000 or 30,000 men' for a proposed expeditionary force adorned these reports.[4] The probability of a Canadian offer of an expeditionary force, and the New Zealand prime minister's public offer of a force in the Wellington Parliament on Friday 31 July — the offer which had provoked MPs to sing 'God Save the King' — were both reported in *The Times* on Saturday 1 August.[5] On the same day, London's *Daily Telegraph* reported proudly on the general assurances of support to Britain in speeches given by Edward Millen and Sir William Irvine in Australia, and reproduced a telegram from Harcourt received by Thomas Mackenzie, the New Zealand high commissioner, in praise of the dominion's sturdy patriotism.[6]

Australia's stance received coverage in a special, strongly pro-interventionist Sunday edition of *The Times* published on 2 August. Assurances that 'Australia will fight for the Empire to the last' were paraded. Jose, *The Times*' correspondent in Sydney, writing on Friday 31 July, reported that Australia was 'tense with strained attention'. He was perhaps too frank in one respect, writing that there was 'little comment, because it is universally understood that the causes of the war and the means of preventing its extension are outside the sphere of Australian knowledge and interest'. Jose appeared to acknowledge that Australia had no power to influence events — she could only wait upon London's decision. Nonetheless, Jose assured London that Australians had every confidence in Sir Edward Grey, and that there was only one spirit, a spirit of 'acceptance of whatever share is allotted to the Commonwealth in the joint dangers and efforts'. Jose had no actual offer of an expeditionary force to praise yet. But he was confident: 'Doubtless too, there will be a great number of volunteers for oversea service if they are called for, but no such suggestion has yet been made.' A second report from Jose captured the immemorial hyperbole of the two rival Australian political leaders. Both Cook's statement that 'All Australia's resources are for the Empire's preservation and security', and Fisher's pledge that all Australians would stand behind Britain 'to the last man and the shilling' were in print in London's premier newspaper.[7]

Loyal statements from all the dominions, and the precise offers of expeditionary forces from New Zealand and Canada, featured in the same special edition of *The Times* on Sunday 2 August.[8] Editorially, *The Times* stressed the weighty significance of these offers. The dominions could see, argued *The Times*, that if Germany was victorious over Holland she would be forced to cede colonies, and then German forces would be 'within striking distance of Australia and New Zealand'. *The Times* argued in the punch line of its special leader, 'Britain's Part in the Crisis', that the dominions were showing Britain the way:

> Our fellow citizens in Canada, Australia, and New Zealand have been quick to see the peril. "When Britain is at war we are at war" is their message to us. To them it is unthinkable that Britain should not be at war when the whole existence of her far-flung Empire is menaced. The Government of Great Britain cannot afford at this hour of peril to be less clear sighted, less resolute, than our brethren overseas.[9]

On the same Sunday, *The Observer* appeared. It sounded a great trumpet blast for war. Leo Amery, the Tory newspapers' go-to man from Milner's Round Table movement who had been active in General Wilson's 'pogrom' for some days, was in the ear of the editor, J. L. Garvin, on Saturday, 'telling him to write all he could in the *Observer* to stiffen things'.[10] In his major editorial of Sunday, Garvin, always histrionically proficient, did his very best. There was a riot of headlines: 'THE WAR OF WARS' — 'EUROPE'S ARMAGEDDON AND THE SUPREME QUESTION' — 'SHALL WE STAND BY FRANCE?' The sub-headings shouted, too: 'GERMANY'S TRIUMPH MEANS ENGLAND'S DOWNFALL' — 'THE NEMESIS OF BETRAYAL' — 'OUR NEUTRALITY IMPOSSIBLE'. The editorial argued that the German declaration of war on Russia overnight had signalled the moment for plain speaking. Peace would mean 'doom'. Neutrality was 'desertion'. If Britain chose peace, the empire was lost, for 'all the combatants in the end would compose their quarrels at the expense of the ample assets of the British Empire. He who is no friend will have no friend'.[11] Garvin included in this remarkably trenchant pro-war edition a survey of the booming 'Voice of the Empire' on the crisis. *The Observer* also gave prominence to the unimpeachable statements of 'solidarity' made by both Millen and Cook in Australia. The paper catalogued and extolled the loyalty of the press across the dominions.[12]

On Monday 3 August, the news columns of *The Times* again surveyed the flood of offers and pledges that had reached Britain from the dominions over the previous few days.[13] The declarations in Australia from both Cook and Fisher, including the famous boast of Australia's readiness to throw 'our last man and our last shilling' into any war, were reproduced across the British press by Monday morning.[14]

What was the lesson drawn editorially in the Conservative press from these various offers? The editorial of *The Times* was typical. On the morning of Monday 3 August, *The Times* supplied leaders that were perhaps the most politically significant during the crisis, because Grey was scheduled to outline the government's policy in the House of Commons that afternoon. What did *The Times* preach to Grey's audience? One special editorial, entitled 'The Empire and the War', proudly hoisted the imperial flag to the top of the national flag-mast in making the case for war. It was the work of Edward Grigg. Geoffrey Robinson, the editor, had engineered this special contribution from his friend Grigg, a fellow member of the pro-imperial Round Table group.[15] Grigg's editorial argued that the empire's supreme interest was in sea power. 'When once France is challenged by Germany,' the editorial reasoned, 'that supreme interest of the British Empire comes into play.' In a transparent effort to embarrass the Asquith government, the editorial dwelt upon the 'splendid assurances of support' that had already come from the self-governing white dominions of the empire — from Canada, South Africa, New Zealand, and Australia. The implication was plain: if lily-livered Liberal cabinet ministers could not see that war was now required as soon as France was 'challenged', then thank God these manly dominions could see it! These 'kinsmen' from the empire, boasted *The Times*, had shown an appropriate disdain for 'weakness', and were already offering to send their own virile men to fight alongside Britain. The government should emulate their spirit.

The editorial was noteworthy, too, for its plain speaking on the ultimate authority of London to decide between war and peace on behalf of the whole empire. The Asquith government's weighty responsibility, explained *The Times*, was not only to make policy for Great Britain, but also for the 'four younger Commonwealths' and for the 'nearly four hundred million subjects of different race' that made up the empire. With brutal frankness, the editorial argued that the whole empire, including the self-governing dominions, must simply wait dutifully upon London:

> When Great Britain goes to war the whole Empire is at war. Neutrality is not possible for any of these other communities except by declaring its independence and discarding its allegiance to the KING ... Even though they [the self-governing Dominions] have no voice in the policy by which peace or war is made — and this great weakness in Imperial relations we must in future study and by some means remove — they recognise to the full that, when the crisis comes, they stand or fall by the great decisions on which naval power depends.[16]

The editorial lesson from the dominions' offers was plain. According to *The Times*, the dominions had shown that they understood the vital importance of Britain, guardian of a vast empire, deciding to stand with Britain's friends, Russia and France, and against her chief naval and imperial rival, Germany. The political message was blunt: the gun-shy Asquith government had to see the vital importance of a war of Entente solidarity, and man up. The dithering Liberals should adopt the steely resolution of the dominions.

Other Conservative-aligned newspapers also paid tribute to the dominions for having so promptly offered expeditionary forces. For example, in the conclusion of its editorial on Monday morning 3 August, *The Scotsman* seized upon the stirring news from the dominions to fortify the nation's soul:

> One great source of comfort and confidence we have in this national trial. There are no bounds to the patriotic spirit of our people; and the Overseas Dominions are already giving practical proofs that they are with us to a man.[17]

The political effects of the dominions' offers

That same Monday afternoon, as we have seen, Grey had delivered his historic statement to the House of Commons. In his brief response, Bonar Law found time to stress that the dominions' devotion to empire was a 'bright spot' in the crisis. The loyal pledges and the offers of expeditionary forces demonstrated that 'every one of His Majesty's Dominions beyond the Seas will be behind us in whatever action it is necessary to take'.[18] The lesson, clearly, was that this coalition of power was going to be irresistible, and therefore war for Britain was surely still more attractive.

Australia's cable, offering her expeditionary force, arrived in the early evening of Monday. As it had been released to the press in Australia, it was also swiftly available in London during the evening. Next morning, the Conservative press lauded the offer. In the newspapers of Tuesday 4 August, the day that would end with the British government's own late-night declaration of war, Australia's offer of its entire navy and 20,000 troops provided a riot of noughts for the headline writers in *The Times* and all the major newspapers.[19]

All the dominions were praised — for adding to the case for instant intervention.

Once again, it is important to place Australia's offer more precisely in the London context. Munro Ferguson's cable conveying the Australian offer arrived at the Colonial Office in London at 6.20 p.m. (GMT) on Monday 3 August. By this time, Grey had finished his famous speech to the House of Commons, putting the case for intervention — to the joy of the Tories and to a very mixed reception from the Liberal benches.[20] Divisions in the British cabinet had come to a climax. Only two days before, on Saturday 1 August, the cabinet had decided that a British expeditionary force would *not* be sent to the Continent. Only one day before, on Sunday 2 August, the cabinet had decided to pledge naval support to France. This most controversial decision had prompted four cabinet resignations by the Monday morning, and Grey's speech had prompted another resignation, this time from the junior ministry — that of Charles Trevelyan.[21] Asquith's cabinet faced the possibility of collapse. The man who received Munro Ferguson's cable, Lewis Harcourt, had been the leader of the cabinet faction most hostile to any notion of British intervention right up to Monday 3 August, although he had not yet joined his four cabinet colleagues in resignation. The latest public offer from the dominions — Australia's offer, made with cabinet authority — could only have worked to shake his resolve. The dominions' apparently trigger-happy impulsiveness made it easier for the interventionists in London to depict Harcourt and his Radical allies as contemptible 'fainthearts'.

The offers of expeditionary forces were exploited by those interventionists in the Tory party and the Tory press determined to ramp up pressure on the Asquith cabinet. The dominions' offers undermined the credibility and effectiveness of the neutralists in Asquith's cabinet. Years afterwards, Conservatives close to the centre of power were still confident that the eagerness of the dominions during the crisis in 1914, in booming their readiness to assist in the cause of intervention, had been a very significant factor in the drive to war. For example, Aubrey Herbert was a very well-connected

Conservative MP and a noisy interventionist in 1914. Upon the outbreak of war, he was to fight in quick succession at Mons, then with the Anzacs at Gallipoli, and later at Kut in Mesopotamia. Herbert recalled the events of early August 1914 in his diary in June 1917:

> Our great victory was won when Canada and Australia and New Zealand came in with us. [O]ur greatest victory was won when the Gen[eral] Botha [South African Prime Minister] came in with us. The Germans never won a battle like that. That stands alone.[22]

Had the dominions been more cautious in July–August 1914, Herbert was suggesting, British intervention could have been that much harder to sell to the British Liberals and to the British public.

Similarly, Julian Corbett, the Royal Navy's official historian, was revealingly frank in his work *History of the Great War*, published in 1920. Corbett wrote of the 'probably inevitable' pressure on Britain's war-makers, beginning in 1914, to move from a defensive war to a war of conquest, and from the seizure of bases to the annexation of colonial territory — as 'compensations' for the dominions. In Corbett's opinion, the dominions played a big part in this. Britain had to act in this way at the commencement of the war, Corbett explained, because of 'the moral importance of responding frankly to the outburst of Imperial enthusiasm in the self-governing Dominions'. Corbett argued:

> Not only was it necessary to listen to the keen desire of the daughter states to get their troops as quickly as possible in line with those of the homeland, but our desire was also to give all possible rein and assistance to the aspirations of each of them to remove the enemy permanently from its own doors.[23]

CHAPTER EIGHTEEN

'No immediate necessity'

London, Monday 3 August and Tuesday 4 August

Discussed seizure of German colonies. I said 'No, better wait a bit.'
I told the Cab[inet] I was holding back Dominion Exped[itionary]
forces for the present and they approved.[1]
–Lewis Harcourt, cabinet memorandum, 4 August 1914

THE POLITICS OF the British choice for war can be seen also in the
responses that London made to various offers of military assistance
from the dominions. Naturally, Lewis Harcourt, who had surprised
many by clinging to his post as colonial secretary on Tuesday 4
August, was deputed to send replies on behalf of the government. His
replies indicated that he was trying to fend off these offers of military
assistance, without giving offence.

Unsurprisingly, in his formal replies, Harcourt praised the
'patriotism' displayed by the dominions — but he politely encouraged
them to undertake only formal administrative preparations in case
war erupted. Moreover, there was in Harcourt's replies to Munro
Ferguson just a hint of his increasing embarrassment at the parade of
offers coming from the dominions. In the cabinet meeting of Tuesday
morning 4 August, Harcourt sought to restrain his own colleagues
when it was proposed they should discuss the 'seizure of German
colonies' at the commencement of a war. Harcourt resisted such

speculations, and told the ministers that he was 'holding back' all the dominions' expeditionary forces. The cabinet approved his caution.[2]

Harcourt's reply to Australia's offer came after this cabinet meeting. At 1.45 p.m. on Tuesday 4 August — more than eighteen hours after receiving the Australian cable — Harcourt sent a response to the governor-general expressing the British government's appreciation of the Australians' 'prompt readiness' to place their new navy at the Admiralty's disposal, and of their 'generous offer' of an expeditionary force. 'Will telegraph later on latter point,' concluded the cable.[3]

Less than two hours later, he sent a second cable — just one sentence, acknowledging again the Australian ministers' 'generous offer', but adding the observation that 'there seems to be no immediate necessity for any request on our part for an expeditionary force from Australia'. In addition, he requested that the ministers should merely 'take the necessary administrative steps by which they would be enabled without delay, in case it should be required, to provide such a force'.[4] This was not the expression of a floodtide of gratefulness that some in Melbourne expected. London's reply was, to some Australian eyes, distinctly underwhelming. The Australian offer was simply being held in abeyance. London was biding its time. No matter — the Australian government chose not to share this message with the Australian people. It was not published until after the declaration of war.[5]

Before news of Britain's choice for war reached Australia, Munro Ferguson continued to send messages to London, the purposes of which were readily discernible: they were calculated to reassure Harcourt that he should be absolutely confident about popular support for war in Australia. The governor-general clearly wanted his old Liberal colleague, and the British cabinet as a whole, to be certain of the spirit of the Australian people. For example, from Melbourne on Tuesday 4 August, he sent a personal note to Harcourt describing an inspiring tale of class solidarity that was doing the rounds at the very heart of the establishment, at the Melbourne Club in Collins Street:

There is a story at the Melbourne Club today that the thousands
of wharfingers [the governor-general probably misunderstood the
word 'wharfies'] at Sydney who usually set an extreme value on
their services, offered to coal up [the battle-cruiser] 'Australia' free
of charge. I don't know if it is true — but at any rate it represents
exactly the sentiment which universally prevails.[6]

Similarly, the next day Munro Ferguson replied to Harcourt's
disappointing cable of Tuesday 4 August. The governor-general sent a
message obviously designed to convey a sense of Australia's eagerness
to help — and perhaps to procure an acceptance. He acknowledged
Harcourt's earlier cable (informing Australia that there was 'no
immediate necessity'), but then appeared to discount it. He pressed
for details of London's military requirements. What would London
like Australia to send? He urged Harcourt to offer information
anyway on 'the desired composition, divisional or otherwise, of
[Australia's] expeditionary force'. This, he explained, would greatly
assist Australia's preparations.[7] Again, this request for more detail on
Britain's military requirements preceded any indication that Britain
had accepted the Australian offer, and similarly preceded news of
Britain's choice for war. There was no doubt concerning the military
activism of Australia's Liberal Imperialist governor-general.

Harcourt's initial responses to the other two dominions with
respect to their offers of expeditionary forces were very similar to
the reply sent to Australia. Harcourt had telegraphed the Duke of
Connaught in Canada on the Monday evening on behalf of the
British government, assuring the Canadians that Britain appreciated
their 'patriotic readiness to render every possible aid', but announcing
that Britain preferred 'to postpone' making any military suggestions.[8]
In the afternoon of the next day, Tuesday 4 August, Harcourt sent
another cable to Canada in almost exactly the same terms as that
just sent to Australia. He noted that 'there seems to be no immediate
necessity for any request on our part for an expeditionary force
from Canada'. But, Canada's ministers could assist, he wrote, by
taking 'all legislative and other steps' so that assistance could be

supplied 'without delay' if it should become necessary.[9] New Zealand was advised in the same terms at the same moment: there was 'no immediate necessity' for an expeditionary force.[10]

None of the messages incorporating this dampening phrase reached the people. Instead, for public consumption, Harcourt procured a much more formal statement from the King. This gave no hint of the Asquith government's reluctance. Britain's gratitude — nothing more — was conveyed, and by the King himself. Harcourt sent this much more easily composed and digested message from the Colonial Office to Australia, New Zealand, and Canada at 4.30 p.m. on Tuesday 4 August — again, before the choice for war was confirmed. In the statement, the King expressed his 'appreciation and pride' at the dominion people's 'spontaneous assurances of their fullest support'. The King declared that he would be 'strengthened' in discharging his duty 'by the confident belief that in this time of trial my Empire will stand united, calm, resolute, trusting in God'.[11] God, all were assured, stood with the British King-Emperor about to make war. As a response from the King himself, this naturally gained maximum press coverage in the dominions.

This could not obscure the essential point: three of the dominions had made offers for expeditionary forces — forces which Britain had not requested and for which there was, in London's judgement, 'no immediate necessity'. Australia's offer had arrived at the Colonial Office while Harcourt was in a cabinet meeting on the evening of Monday 3 August. In his private journal recording events at that evening cabinet, Harcourt wrote that he had raised there the New Zealand offer. He reported to his cabinet colleagues that he was replying with the comment that there was 'no condition yet which renders this necessary'. He was careful to record that he was doing this, 'With PM's concurrence'.[12] Allowing for the diplomatic language, Harcourt's responses to the three dominions gave a hint of his own conviction: the offers of expeditionary forces were gratuitous and excessive.

In political terms, they were acutely inconvenient to him. With a struggle taking place inside the cabinet between Radicals and Liberal

Imperialists, they were embarrassing and disabling. In view of Harcourt's own long-standing resistance to the despatch of the BEF under the 'continental commitment', and against any presumption of absolute fidelity to the Entente powers in a European crisis, the three dominions' offers were needlessly pulling the rug out from under him.[13] As he led his faction against Churchill's hurrying of the cabinet toward war, the dominions displayed unwarranted haste. As he led his faction against the premature movement of British naval forces, Australia offered to move hers. As he led his faction against any decision to deploy an expeditionary force upon the Continent, Australia offered to send such a force wherever London desired. To put it mildly, this was all troubling and unhelpful.

The more measured response from South Africa's government during the diplomatic crisis serves to demonstrate the haste and heedlessness of Canada, New Zealand, and Australia. The ministers of South Africa's cabinet, under prime minister General Louis Botha, an ex-Boer military man, did not meet to consider the crisis until Tuesday 4 August. Of course, compared with the other dominions, the political situation inside the new Union of South Africa was much more complicated, and memories of the Boer War were still raw. Sensitive to his ministers' reluctance to appear as mere imperial agents for the British in Africa, Botha had to be more cautious. Thus, South Africa's government sent no offer of military assistance to London until the evening of Tuesday 4 August. When it came, this message, despatched by the acting governor-general, John Henry de Villiers, conveyed no offer of an expeditionary force. Rather, the South African government simply sent an assurance of its readiness to take measures 'for the defence of the Union'. It also offered to replace the 'Imperial Troops now stationed in South Africa' in defensive duties, if Britain chose to withdraw them, with troops drawn from the new defence force of the Union. Therefore, Britain could confidently avail itself of the opportunity to use her own imperial troops wherever she wished, explained de Villiers' message. Therefore, the South Africans' offer was a slightly different offer in timing — but a very different offer in substance. It is noteworthy, too, that, in contrast with Australia and New Zealand, the South Africans had made no plans for a military campaign to seize German colonies before the outbreak of war.[14]

Was the South Africans' restraint dictated solely by political factors? Or was there not a large fragment of wisdom in it? Could Australia similarly have sent every indication of loyalty to Britain, while focussing upon her naval forces, and avoided offering to immerse her manhood utterly from the word go? We shall never know.

CHAPTER NINETEEN

Choosing war

London, Tuesday 4 August

[W]e heard of the British ultimatum to Germany. After that I walked with Henry along the Embankment, and then went to Whitehall, Downing Street, Houses of Parliament, Buckingham Palace etc. watching the crowds who were gathered together at any point where they thought there was a chance of hearing news, quietly and anxiously waiting. There seemed an extraordinary silence and sense of oppression over the whole of London.[1]

– Elizabeth Cadbury, Diary, 4 August 1914

For Britain, Tuesday 4 August proved to be the last day of peace — although few knew it as the day dawned. On that morning, those urging Britain's immediate intervention in the war erupting upon the Continent must have scanned the newspapers with increasing alarm, for Grey's interventionist speech of Monday was receiving a very choppy press. In Britain, on the eve of the Great War, nothing even approaching unanimity was to be seen.

In the Conservative press on Tuesday 4 August, men of power were beating on their jungle drums. The editors extolled Grey's speech of Monday. They reconstructed their arguments for intervention in accord with his. Britain should intervene the moment Germany touched upon either of the 'triggers' to war that Grey had created —

the coasts of France or the neutrality of Belgium. *The Times* accepted that Britain was 'bound' to fight, 'by treaty, by honour, and by regard for our own safety'.[2] Other Conservative newspapers beseeched support for Grey and war. Grey had spoken for the whole nation, they assured readers. For example, *The Scotsman* accepted the argument that Britain must go to war to defend the French coastline as 'a debt of honour to France' as well as 'a plain obligation of duty to ourselves'. Refraining from war would be 'a deep stain on our honour'.[3]

But the members of Britain's Liberal government would naturally have been more interested in the views expressed by the important Liberal dailies, such as the *Manchester Guardian*, the *Daily News*, and the *Westminster Gazette*. Were they all persuaded? Not a bit of it. In fact, the two leading morning Liberal newspapers of Tuesday 4 August were implacable in their opposition. They denounced Grey's speech as dishonest. The *Manchester Guardian* had an angry swing at Grey. The speech was 'not fair': 'It showed that for years he has been keeping back the whole truth and telling just enough to lull [us] into a false sense of security'. True Liberals should 'refuse to give up hope that we shall yet succeed in maintaining our neutrality'.[4] The *Guardian* was also especially critical of Grey's attempt to minimise the 'appalling catastrophe' of war by claiming that Britain would suffer but little more in war than in peace. It revealed his desperate wrong-headedness.[5] Similarly, A. G. Gardiner's editorial in the *Daily News* announced that the paper was 'unconvinced'.[6] Of the important Liberal papers, only J. A. Spender's *Westminster Gazette*, an afternoon paper, suddenly swung behind intervention.[7] Wilfrid Blunt, the veteran diplomat and anti-imperialist aristocrat, was not far from the mark when he declared in the privacy of his diary on 5 August: 'Nothing is more remarkable than the entire disregard paid by the Cabinet to the Liberal press which was solid for neutrality'.[8]

On the morning of Tuesday 4 August, Grey and Asquith took a momentous decision — just the two of them, in a few wild minutes. Meeting at Downing Street before the cabinet assembled, they composed the first 'ultimatum' to Germany, although it was not yet called that.

This first telegram was sent to Berlin at 9.30 a.m. It was addressed to the British ambassador in Berlin, Sir Edward Goschen, but it was of course prepared for official delivery to the German foreign minister, Gottlieb von Jagow. The telegram noted the King of the Belgians' appeal for Britain's 'diplomatic intervention' and the Belgians' refusal of the German ultimatum on the preceding day. The telegram registered Britain's 'protest against this violation of a treaty', and requested 'an assurance that the demand made upon Belgium will not be proceeded with'. Goschen was directed to 'ask for an immediate reply'. There was no time limit mentioned — and in that sense it was not an ultimatum.[9]

It is important to stress also that this first telegram was not a response to the German invasion of Belgium. German armed forces had crossed the border into Belgium at about 8.00 a.m. that morning, eventually advancing on a forty-kilometre front between Gemmenich and Malmédy during the day. Certainly, this advance was the prelude to what would become an escalating humanitarian disaster in Belgium over the next month, as civilians fell victim to military excesses.[10] But the British cabinet did not learn even of the first sketchy reports of the German invasion until about noon, well after the first telegram was on its way.[11]

The last peacetime cabinet began its deliberations at 11.30 a.m. Naturally, there was intense interest in the fact that Simon and Beauchamp appeared at the cabinet table. This told of significant events behind the scenes overnight: Asquith had split the Radicals. Two of the four resigning ministers had decided to return to cabinet, responding to pleas from Asquith. He had implored them to consider loyalty to the party and to colleagues, and he gave assurances that their objections in principle to the war would be respected while they continued to serve.[12] Belgium immediately became the focus of the cabinet's discussion. At first, the cabinet discussed the latest German diplomatic note to Belgium of Tuesday morning, threatening military action. The cabinet responded: 'We are sending an ultimatum to Germany & [are] to have the answer by midnight,' Harcourt recorded. What ultimatum? Harcourt recorded later in the discussion that 'Grey read us his telegram to Goschen.' It demanded an answer 'similar to that from France last week — as to the neutrality of Belgium', by midnight. This makes it clear that the telegram discussed in cabinet was a proposed *second* telegram. This would add to the pressure, by nominating a time limit.[13]

But the cabinet was not of one mind on a resort to force. The Radical ministers still acted as a brake on those looking for a rapid transformation of Britain's 'continental commitment' into a war of imperial conquest across the world. Even though war had still not been declared, the cabinet turned to a discussion of the seizure of various German colonies. Harcourt advised delay, noting that he was still, with some difficulty, restraining all the dominions that had already offered expeditionary forces. Indeed, he explained how, overnight, he had fended off de Villiers Graaff's suggestion that South Africa should grab German South-West Africa — if Harcourt wished it. 'Will you *not* if I ask for it?' Harcourt had scoldingly replied.[14] The cabinet approved Harcourt's caution. With these decisions made, the cabinet rose.

Did the ministers accept that war with Germany was imminent? Harcourt's notes suggest they did. But if it was to be war, the Royal Navy was in the limelight. There had been no discussion of the BEF. Saturday's startling decision against sending the BEF was being respected, so ministers believed. For instance, Samuel made mention only of coming naval action: 'The first engagement is likely to be in the Mediterranean.'[15]

But had the *cabinet* decided upon war? Had the cabinet chosen a declaration of war immediately upon expiration of the ultimatum, at midnight? Samuel thought so: 'We had another cabinet this morning. Unless Germany alters her whole course, which is now impossible, we shall certainly be at war by tonight.'[16] But Churchill insisted in his memoirs that *all* the 'supreme decisions' — to send an ultimatum, to declare war on Germany, and to send the BEF to the Continent — 'were never taken at any cabinet'. These decisions 'were compelled by the force of events, and rest on the authority of the Prime Minister'.[17] The records leave this fundamental point unclear. Asquith 'curiously' failed to send his usual letter to the King summarising cabinet proceedings, which might have resolved this. As Spender noted, 'the recollection of the survivors is that the drafting of the ultimatum was left to Asquith and Grey'.[18] There is no incontestable evidence that the cabinet as a whole was asked to vote for a declaration of war against Germany at midnight. George Trevelyan, Grey's biographer, was correct: 'Apparently there never was a formal decision taken in the cabinet to go to war or to send an ultimatum to Germany.'[19]

A brief second telegram, sent at 2.00 p.m., written in the form of instructions from Grey to Goschen, directed him to repeat his request for a German assurance regarding Belgian neutrality. Then Grey added a crucial instruction, giving this second telegram the character of an ultimatum. Goschen was told to 'ask that a satisfactory reply' to the two telegrams of that day 'be received here by 12 o'clock tonight … If not, you are instructed to ask for your passports and to say that His Majesty's Government feel bound to take all steps in their power to uphold the neutrality of Belgium and the observance of a Treaty to which Germany is as much a party as ourselves.'[20] The phrase 'all steps' meant war, of course.

Or was there a chance that Britain might simply break diplomatic relations? The British government certainly did not want to eliminate the possibility that Germany might act first. A German declaration of war was still preferable, in political terms. It would be much more palatable for a Liberal government and its supporters. Far better that Britain should be seen to be reacting to both a German invasion and a declaration of war.

Embracing Belgium

From mid-morning on Tuesday 4 August, the fact of the German invasion of neutral Belgium naturally began to dominate over all others. The fact was horrible — but it was also an event delivering enormous political gains to Asquith's government. No longer was war being contemplated as a war of solidarity with the Entente, a war to save 'the balance of power' in Europe, or a war to save France

— such as it had been depicted in the Tory press all week, and in the Conservative leaders' letter to Asquith. Now, miraculously, it was being transformed into a war of moral imperatives, to save Belgium and the sanctity of treaties. This was a war the Liberals could swallow.

Asquith coolly explained to Venetia Stanley that the German action in Belgium 'simplifies matters'.[21] In fact, it was a blessed turn of events. Or, as Frances Stevenson, Lloyd George's lover, put it, it was 'a heaven-sent excuse for supporting a declaration of war'.[22] In a sense, the 'heaven-sent excuse' became an essential shield. Any errors that the government had made in its diplomacy — for example, in its failure to restrain either Russia or France — could be forgiven in the outpouring of rage against the German action. The *faits accomplis* in naval preparations presented to cabinet could now be forgiven as necessary 'safety-first' measures taken against an unscrupulous aggressor. In the plight of Belgium, the Asquith government had an issue of such candlepower in its hands that people would be dazzled. They would certainly be distracted from the most obvious truth: Germany's passage through Belgium was merely the occasion, not the cause, of the declaration of war. As Jerome K. Jerome expressed it later, 'Had she gone round the Cape of Good Hope the result would have been the same.'[23]

If, politically, the German invasion of Belgium was the icing on the cake, the cake itself could now be made to fit the icing — that is, the story of the diplomatic crisis could now be retold to fit the tragic denouement. The government's willingness to exploit the tragedy in Belgium was on display when the House of Commons met at 2.45 p.m. on the afternoon of Tuesday 4 August. It was pure Victorian music hall: heroes, villains — with big moustaches — and the innocent maiden in distress.

The cabinet had come straight from Downing Street, where Asquith and Grey had lingered behind to compose the second telegram to Berlin. Belgium was kept front and centre. Asquith, who was greeted with cheers, told the Commons of the decisive diplomatic steps. He read to the House the text of the first 'telegram' to Germany on Belgium. This, according to *The Times*, 'called forth an answering roll of cheers from every quarter of the chamber'.[24] Then Asquith read from British and Belgian diplomatic notes attesting that Belgian territory had been violated that very morning.[25] He added the official German explanation, pleading for British understanding of the German attack, because it was 'a question of life or death to prevent [a] French advance'. The German note renewed the promise that no Belgian territory would be annexed. This provoked 'an outburst of incredulous laughter,' reported *The Times*. Asquith dismissed the German note.[26]

Asquith then explained that the government had just sent a second 'telegram' to Berlin, but he did *not* give its text. Summarising it, he explained that it repeated the request for 'the same assurance in regard to Belgian neutrality' that France had given last week. This telegram requested 'a satisfactory answer' on the Belgian issue 'before midnight'. Immediately, Asquith walked up to the Speaker and presented him with a message from the King, which was in turn read to the House. It was a message calling out the Army Reserve on permanent service.[27] This completed the army's mobilisation.

The drama of this scene bewitched many. An 'ultimatum', it seemed, had been presented to Germany. Even *Hansard* headlined the word the following day. So, too, did *The Times*.[28] But, in fact, Asquith never used the term 'ultimatum', and never announced that war would be declared at midnight. He described each communication to Berlin as a 'telegram'.[29] The reaction of the House of Commons testified to the political advantage flowing toward the men with the power to make war. No one replied. The House passed meekly to Orders of the Day. After just ninety minutes, the House adjourned.[30] *The Times* buoyantly observed that the session passed 'without the raising of a single note of controversy'.[31]

If the Radicals simply lost their courage and chose silence on Tuesday 4 August, so too did the cabinet ministers. Only one Liberal frontbencher, Grey, had been on his feet in the Commons defending intervention, on the previous day. The ornaments of British Liberalism — Asquith himself, Lloyd George, Samuel, Churchill, and McKenna — had all said next to nothing on British policy. Britain prepared to go to war, without her prime minister even arguing the case for it.

'There is a cabinet meeting at midnight to consider the German reply to our ultimatum, and it is morally certain that we shall declare war,' Hankey proudly told his wife that night.[32] Not so. There was no cabinet meeting at midnight. Characteristically for the Asquith government, the ultimate step was not taken by cabinet, but rather by a small clique bunkered down in the cabinet room. A mere coffee-table's worth of the cabinet gathered there on the night of Tuesday 4 August: Asquith, Grey, and Haldane, joined later by Lloyd George and McKenna. This little assembly made the final choice for war. In this sense, as Keith Wilson argues, 'the cabinet, as such, never did make a decision for war'.[33]

How then was the final decision made? Just after 9.00 p.m., the five men who were gathered in the cabinet room learned from an intercepted phone message from Berlin to the German embassy in London that, according to the German account, soon after 7.00 p.m. in Berlin, Goschen had indeed demanded his passports — 'declaring war'. The ministers at Downing Street interpreted this to mean that, as the Germans understood it, Goschen's demand for his passports was tantamount to a declaration of war upon Germany in the name of the British government. On the strength of this intercepted message, the five men considered the choice before them: peace or war? Sometime around 10.00 p.m., they made their decision: Britain must formally declare war upon Germany, and do so immediately upon the expiration of the 'midnight' deadline. Then the ministers suddenly chose to advance this to 11.00 p.m., London time, just in case the Germans should launch a great raid on British shipping or coasts.[34]

While all this was happening, just one mile away at the Kingsway Hall in Holborn, a protest meeting against war, called by the International Women's Suffrage Association, had begun at 8.00 p.m. The new hall, which seated two thousand people, was crammed to overflowing. International and local advocates of women's suffrage denounced war and pleaded for a negotiated settlement. The international speakers, with their accents, brought an emotional punch to the proceedings. Madame Gellrich of Germany, Rosika Schwimmer of Hungary, Madame Malmberg of Finland, and Lucy Thoumaian of Switzerland all received great receptions. On the platform, too, was Dr Marion Phillips, a young Australian, representing the Women's Labour League. Her speech was prophetic. Phillips 'ended on a note of hope that from the common privation and suffering would arise a real sisterhood, working for common needs, which no government and no wars could ever break again'.[35]

Over those same two hours, the men choosing war considered the means. How exactly was Great Britain to declare war? British constitutional procedures and international law had to be respected.

But there was no requirement for anything so transparent as a cabinet minute recording a choice for war — and nothing so dangerously democratic as a parliamentary decision. Of course, the Liberal leaders claimed to believe in the supremacy of the House of Commons. But they slid away from this. When it came to making war, all the respected legal authorities, from Blackstone to Dicey, declared that the Crown held the power, as a part of the Royal Prerogative.[36] So, too, Lord Halsbury's new Edwardian masterpiece, the *Laws of England*, confirmed it: 'declarations of war and peace, are intrusted solely to him [the monarch] and his ministers'.[37]

What body then could authorise war? The King's Privy Council — the instrument of the Royal Prerogative — was near at hand. No quorum was required.[38] A tiny fragment of this body was sufficient to rubber-stamp the prime minister's decision for war. Sir Almeric FitzRoy, the clerk of the Privy Council, worked hand in glove with Asquith to secure exactly this outcome. By Tuesday 4 August, he had organised a timetable of the movements of two compliant Liberal privy councillors at court, Viscount Allendale, Lord-in-Waiting, and the Earl of Granard, Master of the Horse. Both agreed to be near a telephone and to dash to a Privy Council when required.[39]

Late in the evening of Tuesday came the next dramatic summons. After Asquith's closest satellites had agreed upon war at Downing Street, the prime minister telephoned FitzRoy at 10.15 p.m., instructing him to call a Privy Council at Buckingham Palace as soon as possible. 'In a quarter of an hour I had my men on the spot,' FitzRoy recorded proudly.[40] King George V wrote in his diary that Asquith himself had telephoned Buckingham Palace at 10.30 p.m. 'to say that Goschen had been given his passports at 7.0[0] this evening [in Berlin]'.[41] War it was to be. It was Asquith's choice.

In an excruciating twist for Beauchamp — remembering how recently he had withdrawn his resignation — he was asked to represent the government at this Privy Council. Beauchamp agreed. He was the only cabinet minister present, and was listed as 'Acting for the Lord President of the Council'.[42] Seated with the King were just three men — Earl Beauchamp, Lord Allendale, and Earl Granard. This tiny Privy Council opened at 10.35 p.m.[43]

The Privy Council had one vital task: to confer formal approval upon the declaration of war. Two detailed proclamations on shipping and contraband did the trick.[44] There was no clarion call to a war for freedom, democracy, or civilisation. Rather, the proclamations simply referred to an existing state of war.[45] It took almost no time. As FitzRoy wrote, 'at a few minutes after 10.30 the order indicative of a state of war was approved'.[46] Thus, all immediate legalities were complete. The King, acting on the advice of his prime minister, and assisted by just three privy councillors, had 'declared war'. The King recorded the fact: 'I held a Council at 10.45 to declare war with Germany, it is a terrible catastrophy [*sic*], but it is not our fault'.[47] Faithfully reflecting the pre-democratic order, four men had launched Britain's war. There was not one elected man among them.

Thus, swift decisions by handfuls of men took Britain to war in a great leap. In the face of war itself, the politicians could invoke the safety of the nation, and undoubtedly gain the benefit of the doubt. By Asquith's rapid decision, both the full cabinet and the parliament were to be confronted, yet again, not with a choice but with a hugely powerful *fait accompli*. A great majority in favour of war, essential for the survival of the government itself, could be brought into being by one last rushed act — the declaration of war itself. And the empire would follow.

CHAPTER TWENTY

Fait Accompli

Melbourne, Tuesday 4 August and Wednesday 5 August

I think the decision to remain here is wise. I have been trying all
morning to get from Reuter any fuller message but there is none.
It looks as though the censor has chopped it off. The driblet is very
unsatisfying. Meantime private business messages indicate the
utmost seriousness and we can only stand by and wait. 'They also
serve who only stand and wait.'[1]
–Joseph Cook to Munro Ferguson, 4 August 1914

AT THE VERY BEGINNING, there was some confusion in Australia
about the British declaration of war. Just as in Britain, news of a
German declaration of war upon Britain would have been more
politically convenient in Australia than the reverse. If Germany had
taken the plunge, Australians would have been landed in a state of
war, automatically — and the fault could have been presented as
incontrovertibly Berlin's. This was marginally preferable in Australia,
and yet scarcely affected the outcome. But certainly the confusion
during the first days underlines the reality: war was received in
Australia, amidst the fog, as a *fait accompli*, presented by London. In
no sense did, or could, Australia choose war.

The first cable from London to Australia's governor-general
bearing the great news was sent at 12.30 a.m. (GMT) on Wednesday

5 August. It did *not* say Britain had declared war upon Germany. It seemed to preserve the possibility of the preferable solution to the crisis, so far as London and Melbourne were concerned, that Germany had resorted to war first. The cable read: 'War has broken out with Germany. Send all State Governors.' The Admiralty sent a cable, too, which arrived at the Navy Office in Lonsdale Street, Melbourne, around 11.00 a.m. (AEST) on the same Wednesday, and was decoded there by 11.45 a.m.: 'War has broken out between Great Britain and Germany.'[2] The Navy Office repeated the words in acknowledgement.[3] The same words, all using the passive voice and thereby masking who was responsible for what, were circulated among all the military authorities.[4] So, too, the prime minister and the various state governors all received the information over the next hour in this shy, mysterious form, as originally cabled. Cook relayed the information to his cabinet ministers, and to Andrew Fisher, in this form. Similarly, at 12.45 p.m. prime minister Cook spoke to assembled journalists, and repeated the fudge: 'War has broken out with Germany.'[5] There was no reference to *any* declaration of war, for no one knew the details.

Up until this moment, Andrew Fisher had still issued no statement with respect to the Cook cabinet's announcement of an expeditionary force on Monday 3 August. On receipt of his telegram from the prime minister two days later, informing him of the outbreak of war, Fisher replied by telegram. He released its exact terms to the press: 'Appreciate your wire, and again assure your government [that the] opposition will support you on all measures taken in support of [the] Mother Country and in protecting Australia's interests.'[6] Here was another sweeping commitment — 'all measures'. This nailed the Labor Party into position. Fisher could not retreat.

But still it remained for the authorities to discover who had declared war. The reality that Britain had declared war upon Germany, and not the other way round, was not clear from the official announcements on this first day of Australia's war, Wednesday 5 August. In fact, the confusion surrounding the actual declaration lasted for some days more.

Events in Sydney demonstrate the persistent fog. In the New South Wales parliament, on the afternoon of Tuesday 4 August, the premier, William Holman, told the expectant members of the Legislative Assembly that he had no more information on Britain's response to the crisis than was in the newspapers. Opinions on the subject were 'entirely speculative,' he remarked. He had just been in communication with the federal government, he explained, 'but no information was forthcoming'. Then, after the state opposition leader, Charles Wade, pledged in a short speech to sink all political differences, the politicians stood to sing the national anthem and 'Rule Britannia', followed by a hearty 'three cheers' for the King. Very soon after, Holman announced that he had just received a fresh cablegram 'from a leading newspaper' showing that Britain had mobilised her army 'presumably owing to the declaration of war by Great Britain'.[7] As it was still the *morning* of Tuesday 4 August, London time, this was wrong information. There had been no declaration of war at that time.

The next day, Wednesday 5 August, premier Holman again addressed the anxious faces in the New South Wales parliament in the early afternoon. This time, he announced gravely that the state governor had received information 'to the effect that war has definitely broken out between Great Britain and Germany'. But again he could give no detail on a declaration of war. Instead, he resorted immediately to the stock-in-trade pledges of firmness and unity of purpose. The state government, Holman vowed, would show 'resolute determination to remain united in front of the common danger and in opposition to the common enemy'.[8] But who had declared war? Evidently, no one knew for certain in Macquarie Street, Sydney.

The Australian press was indeed struggling to clarify the matter. On Wednesday 5 August, some newspapers did report the news from London, and rumours from the Canadian press — the correct version — that Britain had declared war on Germany.[9] But on the same day, other newspapers still argued that such a declaration of war was unlikely and could not be confirmed.[10] On 5 August, *The Argus*, which could scarcely contain its impatience for war, speculated editorially that Grey's speech in any case was 'in itself practically equivalent to a declaration of war'. Britain, by insisting Germany could not use the Channel, was signalling 'a deliberate intention to provoke Germany to a declaration of war'.[11] Similarly, the *Sydney Morning Herald* speculated upon the question of 'which of the two Powers will declare war?' and observed that 'a good deal may depend upon the reply to that question'.[12]

Resolving the issue finally on 6 August, the major newspapers reproduced the official British proclamation of 'war against Germany' from the *Commonwealth Gazette*.[13] But other newspapers, even major ones, still circulated older mistaken reports that Germany had declared war. For example, on Thursday 6 August, the *Sydney Morning Herald* produced the headlines: 'BRITAIN AT WAR — INVASION OF BELGIUM — DECLARATION BY GERMANY'. There in the main foreign news reports, on page seven, was a Reuter's cable, dated at 11.50 p.m. on Tuesday 4 August, asserting incorrectly that 'Germany has declared war on England'.[14]

The newspapers complained later that heavy-handed censorship — announced by the Cook cabinet on Monday 3 August — had been responsible for at least three days of delay in accurate news being published in Australia regarding the events at the climax of the crisis in Europe.[15] In fact, on Thursday 6 August, Ambrose Carmichael, the education minister in the NSW Labor government, who happened to be in London at the outbreak of war, presented a protest to Lewis Harcourt over 'the undue censorship of Press cables to Australia'. Carmichael reported later that Harcourt 'is investigating the matter'.[16] The censorship, imposed at both ends of the 'All-Red Route', certainly created a crucial gap in the information reaching Australia. Thus, incredibly, as Australia's politicians made their decisions about how best to assist Britain in the war, and the Australian people made up their minds about the justice of the war itself, something as fundamental as which nation had declared war — Britain or Germany — was muddled.

In the legal sense, as the experts gravely declared at the time, this mattered not at all.[17] A declaration of war, from either side, had the same result in Australia. Australia was at war. The essential political effect followed in either case, too. War itself, as a hard reality, would blunt debate and produce an outpouring of emotional support for those defending Australia and the empire — just as soon as war could be presented as an inescapable reality. Support for the troops, of course, could then be presented as support for war. But, in another sense, the confusion served the interests of those who had so swiftly chosen to immerse Australia in the conflict, even to the extent of offering an expeditionary force before any declaration had been made. The false reports that Germany had taken the initiative and declared war maximised the chances of achieving the very widest support for Britain's war in Australia. Haste could all the more credibly be presented as the taking of prudent precautions — vindicated by events.

For the first days of the war, Australia was without essential facts as her people faced the *fait accompli* of war. Ordinary citizens could be forgiven for getting it all wrong. For example, near the little town of Collarenebri in rural New South Wales, a governess named Ida Dawson was looking after her pastoralist employer's children, as usual, on the large Euralah Station. On the exciting Wednesday 5 August, a day of glorious weather, she decided to make sweet scones and take the children up a local creek for a picnic. In the evening, she wrote in her diary the details that she had doubtless learned from the newspapers: 'Germany has declared war against England, and our first Fleet has put to sea.'[18]

CHAPTER TWENTY-ONE

'A great and urgent Imperial service'

London and Melbourne,
Wednesday 5 August and Thursday 6 August

We had our usual Cabinet this morning, and decided with much less demur than I expected to sanction the despatch of an Expeditionary force of four divisions. We also discussed a number of smaller schemes for taking German ports & wireless stations in E & W Africa & the China Seas were discussed with some gusto: indeed I had to remark that we looked more like a gang of Elizabethan buccaneers than a meek collection of black-coated Liberal Ministers.[1]
– Asquith to Venetia Stanley, 6 August 1914

ONLY WHEN THE PEACE was lost, and war had been embraced, did Harcourt send formal acceptances on behalf of Britain of all the dominions' offers of military aid. But he did not do so immediately. For two days after the declaration of war of Tuesday 4 August, the Asquith government's leading men in the parliament continued to insist publicly that the dominions' offers were simply 'unnecessary'.

The apparent reluctance of the Asquith government to embrace the dominions' offers naturally irritated the Tories, who had been busily trumpeting them for some days. The pro-interventionist

Conservatives saw this reluctance as emblematic of the Liberals' reluctance to make war at all — or, at least, to make war in Europe. They had not forgotten the decision against sending the BEF to the Continent on Saturday 1 August.

The government's acceptances were, in the end, not produced until after the Conservatives had pressed the matter in the House of Lords on Wednesday 5 August. To understand this debate, it is important to be aware of the long-standing preference on the part of British Liberals for Britain to confine her main military efforts in any conflict to sea power. The Royal Navy was the 'senior service' — beloved by many Liberals.[2] The Tories, on the other hand, had a long-standing ambition for Britain to combine her sea power with a 'continental commitment', reinforced by conscription at home, so that she could contribute to a military campaign on the Continent whenever required.[3] In this context, the dominions' offers of expeditionary forces were seen as boosting Tory hopes. In the same way, dominion action would mean a widening of the war and its transformation into an imperial conflict. Dominion action would mean colonial conquest, rather than the limited naval role that Grey had signalled as the government's preference in the House of Commons on Monday 3 August. For all these reasons, strategic and political, the Conservatives wanted the dominions' offers embraced.

The politics of this were evident in the House of Lords on Wednesday 5 August, when Britain's own decision on a British Expeditionary Force was still, so far as was known, undecided. As the debate opened, Lord Denman, a Liberal Imperialist and the former governor-general to Australia, did good service to the Tory cause. He asked the government ministers whether they intended to accept the offers of such 'splendid contributions' from Canada, Australia, and New Zealand. 'I sincerely hope that they will be able to tell me that that is so, or that the offers will be accepted very shortly, because time is of great importance in this matter,' declared Denman. He helpfully suggested that the volunteer forces from these dominions could be employed 'to reinforce our garrisons in Egypt and India,' where, in addition, they would be conveniently 'some three or four weeks nearer to the scene of the war'. Denman, recalling his experiences in Australia, reminded the Lords that the Australian armed forces were formidable. Australia had some 90,000 men under arms, in twenty-nine light horse regiments and twenty-eight field batteries, he explained.[4]

For the government, Lord Emmott, Harcourt's under-secretary at the Colonial Office, replied. Naturally, he stressed that the government had received the dominions' offers of expeditionary forces with 'the greatest satisfaction', and felt 'deep gratitude' for them. Of course, he knew how vital it was not to 'damp the enthusiasm' of the dominions by 'any refusal'. But he maintained Harcourt's line: 'there is no immediate necessity for the acceptance of such offers'.

Even in this debate, it was plain that the political pressures on the Asquith government from the crusading, pro-interventionist Tory opposition, which had been very much in evidence across the preceding week, were still being applied. Indeed, it was the Tory leader in the Lords, Lord Lansdowne, who spoke at the end of the short debate. He seized the opportunity to rub in the message. He applauded the dominions for offering expeditionary forces. 'These offers have moved our people greatly,' said Lansdowne. 'They are a proof that the British Empire is not a paper Empire, but a great reality, and that from all parts of the Empire we may depend upon that co-operation to which we certainly look from the people of these islands.' He was 'content' to hear, he said, that the government 'will not hesitate' to take up the dominions' offers of military aid 'at the proper moment'.[5]

From defence to offence

As the Lords debated the dominions' offers, the crucial decisions about Britain's own commitments, and hence the empire's commitments, were being made. Everywhere in the official announcements, and especially in Asquith's historic speech in the House of Commons on Thursday 6 August in support of a request for a £100 million loan to fight the war, the defence of Belgium was presented as *the* reason —

the only reason — for Britain's declaration of war.[6] But within hours the much-heralded defensive war for the sake of Belgium began to escalate into a war of imperial spoils.

In the morning of Wednesday 5 August, Harcourt chaired an ad hoc 'Joint Committee' to make recommendations to cabinet regarding a series of expeditions to capture various German colonies — Dar es Salaam in German East Africa, German South-West Africa, Togoland, the Cameroons, German New Guinea, Nauru, and Samoa.[7] In the same spirit, the full cabinet that met at 11.30 a.m. discussed widening the war, including offering an inducement to neutral Italy to enter the war on the Entente side. 'Can we buy Italy?' Harcourt speculated in his notes: 'Tell them if they go in with us they can have our help on the Adriatic coast against Austria.'[8] But Radicals agonised over the critical question: would British troops be used in Europe? Still, Asquith hedged on this. He told the cabinet that he was meeting with the military men in the afternoon 'to examine use, *if any*, of troops.'[9]

The ad hoc 'War Council' gathered in the afternoon at 10 Downing Street. Only four ministers, all interventionists — Asquith, Haldane, Churchill, and Grey — sat down with the military chiefs, Lord Kitchener, Lord Roberts, John French, Douglas Haig, Henry Wilson, and others. Various sworn enemies of the government were now advising it. For example, Roberts was the long-standing president of the National Service League and a prominent opponent of Home Rule. Similarly, General Wilson's diary for the week was peppered with denunciations of Asquith's 'pestilent government', 'Squiff and his filthy Cabinet', and the 'cursed Cabinet' of pacifists.[10] Since the morning of Tuesday 4 August, Wilson had been colluding with leading Tories to twist arms and to get Asquith to 'send the "Expeditionary Force" *at once*'.[11] Wilson had his way. The 'War Council' recommended that the BEF should be sent to the Continent immediately.[12]

The next morning, Thursday 6 August, the cabinet crumpled. With Kitchener at the table as war secretary — an appointment that had been pressed hard by the Tories[13] — the cabinet doffed its cap.

The bulk of the BEF was to go to the Continent.[14] Kitchener told the Liberal ministers that Britain must 'put armies of millions in the field' and prepare for 'great battles on the Continent'. This was met with 'silent assent,' so Churchill recalled.[15] It was a complete victory for the advocates of Britain's continental commitment. Harcourt, the former Radical, warmed to his new tasks: 'German colonies: I shall take most of them.'[16]

While all this was being planned, the parliament was easily bounced. On the previous afternoon, Asquith had told the Commons nothing about the government's military plans. He had read the text of the Belgian appeal for military assistance — and clearly Belgian resistance was even more important in building support for Britain's war than the invasion of Belgium itself[17] — and explained gravely that he could tell the House nothing more.[18] On the afternoon of the next day, Thursday 6 August, Asquith introduced in the House of Commons a 'Vote of Credit' for £100 million. But again, where would British forces fight? In his speech, Asquith spoke vaguely of 'naval and military operations' and did *not* reveal the plan to send the BEF to the Continent.[19] In deciding on the war credit, MPs were left free to keep imagining that the empire's war would be largely a naval one. Neither the prime minister, nor a single speaker after him, mentioned an expeditionary force. But the deceptions mattered not. Asquith's focus upon Belgium, echoing Grey, succeeded fabulously. A half-dozen Radical speakers protested that Britain's own policies had contributed to the disaster.[20] But a majority accepted the case for war as unanswerable. The Vote of Credit passed on the voices.

When all this was decided, Harcourt eventually sent a gracious one-sentence acceptance on the evening of Thursday 6 August, on behalf of the Asquith government, of the Australian offer of 20,000 troops. This was two days after the declaration of war, and three days after Australia's offer had been cabled originally from Melbourne. As always, the communication was addressed to Munro Ferguson: 'His Majesty's Government gratefully accept offer of your Ministers to send to this Country [a] force of 20,000 men and would be glad if it could be despatched as soon as possible.'[21]

By this time, of course, Britain's decision to send her own expeditionary force to the Continent had been taken — although there was no announcement of this until mid-August.[22] From this point, therefore, Australia could be seen to be running in harmony with, and not ahead, of Britain. In Australia, meanwhile, prime minister Cook released to the press Harcourt's exact words from his cable of 6 August accepting the Australian force — in contrast to the treatment accorded to Harcourt's equivocal message of 4 August that had noted there was 'no immediate necessity' for any force.[23]

But there was more. A second paragraph of the cable, marked 'SECRET', was not released. It embodied the decision of the two ad hoc committees assembled by Harcourt and Asquith the previous day. It was an invitation to Australia to begin the conquest of the German colonies — as an 'Imperial service':

> If at the same time your Ministers desire and feel themselves able to seize German wireless stations at New Guinea, Yap in the Marshall Islands, and Nauru or Pleasant Island, we should feel that this was a great and urgent Imperial service. You will realise however that any territory now occupied must at the conclusion of the war be at the disposal of [the] Imperial Government for purposes of an ultimate settlement. Other Dominions are acting on the same understanding in similar way and in particular suggestion to New Zealand is being made with regard to Samoa.[24]

The war for the defence of Belgium, the vindication of public right, and the rights of small nations was escalating into something else — a war of brigandage, with all of Britain's allies pegging out claims to rival Britain's own. (Within months, Harcourt himself would be providing the prime minister with a grand plan entitled 'The Spoils', which outlined options for the territorial aggrandisement of the British Empire in Asia, Africa, the Middle East, and the Pacific.[25])

For a whole week, there was some confusion regarding the other half of the original Australian offer to London — that is, the offer to give Britain complete control over His Majesty's Australian ships.

Much to the embarrassment of all, the transfer did not go smoothly. Misunderstandings, born of Australia's hasty decision-making, got in the road.

On 6 August, Munro Ferguson inquired whether London wished the Cook government's telegram of Monday 3 August, offering both the expeditionary force and a transfer of the Australian fleet, 'to be regarded as [the] transfer to Admiralty control?'[26] London was apparently surprised to discover that the transfer had not been formally completed already, by a proclamation on the part of the governor-general. Harcourt sent a cable of inquiry to Munro Ferguson on Saturday 8 August. He explained that the British had believed the Australian fleet had been transferred to the Admiralty upon the outbreak of war, only to discover that it had not been done. Harcourt explained that he had understood the governor-general's telegram way back on Friday 31 July to mean that 'steps were being taken formally to transfer control'. If this had not been done, he noted, he would be 'grateful if transfer will be done now'.[27]

The governor-general, no doubt embarrassed and miffed, instantly contacted Cook and Millen. In the face of this rather painful revelation, that London was still awaiting Australian action, the politicians jumped to it like obedient gun-dogs. On Sunday 9 August, prime minister Cook directed Munro Ferguson to reply immediately that 'this will be done at once'.[28] Cook and his advisers dutifully prepared the required proclamation, and the governor-general advised London of the joyful outcome the next day. Issued on Monday 10 August, the proclamation announced that, under the Defence Act, from that date

all the vessels of the Commonwealth Naval Forces and all the officers and seamen of those vessels shall be transferred to the King's Naval Forces and that such transfer shall continue in force until a proclamation declaring that the aforementioned war no longer exists.[29]

A fortnight later, Munro Ferguson was still explaining the hiccough to London. He told London that he had hoped the transfer of the Australian fleet had taken place 'at once' — that is, when the federal Executive Council had met on Monday 3 August and had agreed to do so, 'taking, as I understood, instant effect'. But nothing had happened. 'Happy go lucky methods are typical of these people,' Munro Ferguson wrote grandly.[30] His belief that the transfer of the Royal Australian Navy had been completed on Monday 3 August is significant. It underlines the fact that the Australian offers of both the expeditionary force and the naval fleet came *before* the outbreak of war.

In the first days of the war, when young Australian men were eagerly volunteering for service, those men in authority who had helped organise the rapid mobilisation paused to congratulate themselves. Munro Ferguson was proud of the role he had played, and of the speed of Australia's rush to readiness. Four days after the declaration of war, Munro Ferguson told the King of the 'great enthusiasm' generated by a special message of thanks that the King had despatched to Australia on Tuesday 4 August.[31] He boasted that in faraway Australia, during the diplomatic crisis, everything had happened with lightning speed: 'The Admiralty's orders were carried out with great promptness. The "Australia" was recalled to Sydney from Brisbane *before* the "warning message" reached us.' Munro Ferguson bubbled over with confidence regarding the future. He told the King that 'the 20,000 men of the expeditionary force now being organised represent but a fraction of the contribution that Australian[s] would make should the necessity arise. She fully realises that her whole future is at stake, and is prepared to back the Imperial Forces to the utmost of her power'. With the federal election still a month away, Munro Ferguson offered the King a reassuring observation. 'It would matter little,' he wrote, 'to Your Majesty's Service which party was in power in this Commonwealth'.[32]

He told Harcourt the same thing: the war would be embraced eagerly 'which ever Party was in power'.[33] And so it proved to be. Andrew Fisher had confided to his wife on the eve of the poll that if Labor were defeated, 'we may not miss much' because the war would swamp domestic reform.[34] In the event, when the Australian people went to the polls on 5 September, with both major parties promising great efforts to 'defend the Empire', Labor won a handsome victory, giving it control of both the House of Representatives and the Senate. Fisher was prime minister again — of a Labor war government.

During the first days of the war, the major organs of the Australian press were predictably supportive of London's choice and of Australia's zeal to join the great crusade. This was buttressed, no doubt, by the popular illusion that 'it will not last long'.[35] Most newspapers were soon filled with virile posturing and staple banalities justifying London's choice for war. Editorially, there was even some expression of gladness that the British Radicals had failed in their quest to keep Britain neutral. The *Brisbane Courier*, for example, supported London's decision to fight 'to prevent the destruction of Belgian neutrality', and speculated that the alternative, a British choice for neutrality, would have 'evinced a spirit of opportunism'. The editorial was scathing toward those who had counselled peace. The awful prospect of 'peace sitting under her olive tree' while Europe succumbed to 'arrogant force' had been avoided. Fortunately, Britain had spurned this burning 'brand of shame':

> Throughout the British Empire today, throughout the Empire whose drum-beat goes thrilling round the world, there will be a sense of satisfaction that the statesmen who guide our great destinies have submitted to no craven call for abstention.[36]

In this spirit, during the first weeks of the war the prospect of colonial conquests quickened Australian hearts. Plans for small expeditionary forces to occupy the German possessions and to destroy wireless and telegraphy stations proceeded apace.[37] In military terms, the value of such expeditions was doubtful. The diversion of Australian and British naval forces to escort both the New Zealand expedition to Samoa and then the Australian expedition to New Guinea disrupted plans to find and destroy the German East Asia Squadron, which escaped toward South America.[38] A deeds-that-won-the-Empire spirit prevailed, but it produced strategic confusion.

By 18 August, Munro Ferguson reported that Australia's 'irregular Expeditions to deal with hostile wireless and German possessions are already on the move, the project being thoroughly congenial to the Minister for Defence.'[39] Harcourt replied that he was 'sure that the Australian people will be delighted at having the job of taking German New Guinea and other islands that have been allotted to them'.[40] The expeditions succeeded. German Samoa surrendered on 30 August, and German New Guinea on 17 September.[41] To what purpose? Munro Ferguson felt the push of *realpolitik*: he reported to London, after talking to Edmund Barton and Colonel Burns, that Australia and New Zealand should be given the task of administering the captured German colonies because, by this gesture, 'they will be encouraged to make the greatest exertion to do their share of Imperial Defence' — that is, more men would come forward, destined for the main battlefields, if Australia and New Zealand had trophies to flourish.[42]

CHAPTER TWENTY-TWO

Diversion to Gallipoli

1914–15

A beautiful sight and a fitting demonstration of Britain's greatness.[1]
–Brudenell White, describing the departure of the troop convoy from
Albany in his Diary, 1 November 1914

WHERE DID AUSTRALIANS believe their main expeditionary force
would be going? Where did the volunteers of the Australian Imperial
Force (AIF) imagine they were going? For the first three months of
war, almost everyone connected with the project believed the troops
were going to England.

The colonial secretary's cable accepting Australia's offer of an
expeditionary force was widely published in the Australian press from
Saturday 8 August. In that cable, Harcourt had announced Britain's
acceptance of the Australian offer 'to send to this Country' the force
of 20,000 soldiers. Those Australians who read it naturally believed
the troops were going straight to the Mother Country. Releasing the
cable to journalists, Cook added: 'We propose to send the force at the
earliest possible moment, and we will organise at the earliest possible
moment.'[2] Some newspapers headlined the fact: 'AUSTRALIAN TROOPS:
TWENTY THOUSAND TO GO TO ENGLAND'.[3] Australians had offered to
go anywhere, but thankfully they would soon be defending the very
hearths and homes of Australia's kinsmen in England.

On Saturday 8 August, Munro Ferguson cabled to London the details of the Australian force being assembled — one division and one light-horse brigade — and advised that the men would be ready to embark 'in five to six weeks'.[4] It was assumed at the highest levels that the destination was England. 'Arrangements being made for despatch of expeditionary force to England,' Munro Ferguson cabled to Harcourt again on 11 August.[5] Similarly, Lord Liverpool in Wellington advised London on 14 August that New Zealand's expeditionary force could be ready by 27 August. 'The destination is believed to be England,' minuted the Colonial Office.[6] Only the route was still to be decided. Thus, Munro Ferguson asked London on 18 August to clarify whether the troops would be going via Suez or the Cape 'to England'.[7]

Throughout September, the faith held firm. Messages from England strengthened it. On 7 September, the British Army Council told Australia that the army 'awaits the arrival of its Australian comrades in confident anticipation of their loyal and gallant support'. A place of honour lay at the front, in France and Belgium.[8] In his private letters to Harcourt, Munro Ferguson spoke of his expectation that the Australians would soon be fighting in Europe. On 17 September, after Labor's election victory, he told Harcourt that the departing prime minister Cook had done good work, as he fully recognised 'the fact that what is really needed for Australia, as for the rest of the Empire, is victory on the Rhine'.[9] On leaving office as defence minister in mid-September 1914, Millen formally recorded his satisfaction that Australia's force was 'practically ready to embark for Europe'.[10]

Similarly, England prepared to receive the Australians. The cables flowing back and forth between London and Melbourne touched on matters large and small. Even the small matters were revealing. For example, Munro Ferguson urged Harcourt to make sure that the Australian officers were not treated as mere colonials, but were granted honorary membership of the top English officers' clubs in London's West End 'before or after taking part in the war'.[11] In England, the high commissioners of Australia and New Zealand roped the good and the great into committees to organise official ceremonies of greeting and to provide facilities for the troops 'when the contingents land in England'.[12]

Suddenly, though, complications arose. In mid-September, concerns over the whereabouts of various German warships in the Pacific and Indian Oceans led both the New Zealand and Australian governments to insist on the deferral of the departure of the troopships.[13] Both Munro Ferguson and the newly returned Fisher Labor government were 'alive' to the blow to British prestige if the convoy carrying the expeditionary force was attacked. Fisher 'was very strong in private conversation', and urged delay.[14] The departure was postponed. On 9 October, Munro Ferguson reported that the Australian force was full of enthusiasm, but 'training in Aldershot or elsewhere will be necessary before they are ripe to take the field'.[15] The alluring prospect was still in view: a voyage to England, and combat alongside the British in France.

This undoubtedly stimulated recruiting. Proud volunteers and proud parents believed the soldiers would soon be defending the Mother Country. Of course, men enlisted for many reasons, spoken and unspoken — for adventure, for King and Empire, and for Australia. Some enlisted to escape the tedium of their dreary jobs. Some wanted to wear the uniform and be admired for it. The 'cry from Belgium' was high on the list, too.[16] Certainly, Belgium was everywhere in the Australian press.[17] But the inducement, above all others, was the conviction that the Australians were going to England.

Only they were not. A nation in leading strings goes where the parental leading strings steer her. Out of the blue, for a whole week in late October, a new destination was chosen — South Africa. Just as the troopships were gathering at Albany in Western Australia for the voyage to Europe, that destination was scrubbed. The Afrikaner rebellion in South Africa, in protest against plans to invade German South-West Africa, forced a change of plan. First, Australia received a request to send rifles and ammunition to South Africa. Then, Britain decided on 25 October that all the troops assembling at Albany should go first to the Cape — to put down the Boer rebels, or to assist in the invasion of the colony of German South-West Africa.[18]

This news prompted prime minister Fisher to visit the governor-general toward midnight on 29 October to share his worries. Later, Munro Ferguson reported to London that Fisher told him he was 'quite pleased' with the new route. He and the governor-general discussed the reputation the Australians had earned as 'robbers' during the Boer War for helping themselves to food from the Boer farms.[19] The discussion is revealing. News that the first soldiers raised for the war in Europe would be going to South Africa must have struck Fisher as a political embarrassment. It had the potential to revive quarrels in Labor's ranks over the divisive Boer War, and over imperial expeditions in general. Major-General Sir William Bridges, the commander of the force, also disliked the change. He told Munro Ferguson that there might be an 'Imperial disaster' if the Australian troops were not deployed alongside the English at the seat of the war. The soldiers' 'attachment to Britain,' he warned, might be weakened.[20]

Fortunately for Fisher, the rebellion in South Africa began to weaken when, on 30 October, an amnesty was offered to those rebels who chose to surrender. Soon it was clear that Australians would not be required, after all, to snuff out grass fires on the periphery of empire. On the very eve of the convoy's departure from Albany, the British authorities decided it would *not* be going to the Cape.[21] London's decisions — but no explanations — were given to Fisher's cabinet.[22] There was relief all round. 'We were all pleased to learn that our transports resume the original route via Suez, but there will probably be a meeting if our heroes are turned out to fight the Arabs instead of the Germans,' Munro Ferguson reported privately to Harcourt.[23]

Thus, the first convoy of thirty-six transports carrying the Anzacs steamed away from Albany in West Australia on 1 November. Brudenell White was with them. He had been appointed chief of staff to Bridges by the time the troops left Melbourne on 21 October 1914. White was on board the Orient Line steamer RMS *Orvieto* on the morning of 1 November 1914 when it led the troopships, with three protecting cruisers, out of King George's Sound. The convoy turned north, bound for England, via Colombo, Aden, and Egypt. Committing a tender tribute to his diary, White was in no doubt that the spectacular sight of the grand convoy forging its way into the Indian Ocean was a testament — to 'Britain's greatness'.[24]

It was chastening for Australia, in light of the long record of anti-Japanese prejudice, that the convoy was joined on 3 November by two more transports from Fremantle, escorted by the Japanese battle-cruiser HJIMS *Ibuki*. She then took up her duties escorting the whole convoy, along with HMAS *Sydney*, HMAS *Melbourne*, and HMS *Minotaur*. For Japan had been encouraged by Britain to enter the war in the first days of the conflict. With an eye on the seizure of German possessions in China (especially Tsingtao) and the Pacific, Japan had declared war on Germany on 23 August. Japan then behaved as a loyal ally to Britain, providing valuable naval assistance in the Pacific. For example, *Ibuki* had also escorted ten New Zealand troopships from Wellington to Albany. While the Australian cruisers were busy covering various expeditions to seize German colonies, Japanese cruisers began patrolling the east coast of Australia. The Japanese navy secured Australian trade.[25] Yet, even at this time, the British had to plan for Australian racial sensitivities. On 13 November, Admiral Sir Thomas Jerram, the British commander of the China Station, consulted the Admiralty on the cruiser escorts to be allocated to the convoy on the next leg of the journey, from Colombo to Aden. He recommended that it was 'undesirable' that *Ibuki* be the sole escort, 'not so much from [the] point of view of safety as of Australian sentiment'. Churchill, a staunch defender of the Anglo–Japanese Alliance, minuted: 'Yes. But I entirely disagree.'[26] HMS *Hampshire* joined *Ibuki* — for safety, and sentiment.

But the convoy's final destination was still being determined — in London. The Anzacs crossing the Indian Ocean were still getting their sea legs when a huge escalation of the war got under way. In late October, Germany had bumped Turkey into the war, when her two warships that had fled to Constantinople in the opening days of hostilities were used to mount a naval attack on Russian forces at

Odessa. Russia responded with a declaration of war upon Turkey on 2 November. On 5 November, Britain and France followed Russia in declaring war upon the Ottoman Empire. On the same day, Britain announced the annexation of Cyprus from Turkey. At the same time, a British expedition at the Gulf began to move up the Tigris toward Basra in Mesopotamia.[27]

Suddenly, the war into which the Anzacs were sailing was widening, with enormous consequences to follow for them. In mid-November, more than a fortnight after the troops had left Albany, the British at last decided to stop the Anzacs — in Egypt — for training. Kitchener summoned Reid to explain the decision: accommodation was short in England, and the troops needed training. He mentioned nothing about the diplomacy that had diverted the Anzacs to Egypt. Reid supported Kitchener's arguments, noting medical experts' views that it would be 'criminal' to expose the Anzacs so soon after their tropical sea-voyage to a winter in England when it was doubtful that even canvas huts would be ready for them to face the icy blasts of Salisbury Plain. To soften the disappointment, Reid added that Kitchener 'Pledges himself [to] send them to Europe to fight beside British troops when they have completed their training.'[28]

Harcourt also realised that this would disappoint the colonials: 'The Australians and New Zealanders are to be stopped in Egypt for its defence and their training — but they will be told definitely that they will be fighting with us in Europe later.' The immediate purpose was plain to Harcourt: 'Our people in Egypt now seem to prefer a protectorate to outright annexation at present. We agree — but regretfully.'[29] The British government had indeed imposed martial law in Egypt in early November, deposing the pro-Turkish Khedive Abbas II. Then, in December, signalling a determination to liquidate the last vestiges of Ottoman rule in Egypt, the British proclaimed a protectorate over the country and installed a new puppet sultan, Hussein Kamel. Clearly, the Anzac troops were to be deployed in Egypt to enforce the new authoritarian regime in Cairo, and to defend the Suez Canal, if need be, from Turkish attack.

Of course, the romantic Australian vision of military endeavour under the gaze of the Mother Country — sailing to England, drilling in Aldershot, fighting alongside the British in France, and turning out the German invader — was disintegrating. The Anzacs found themselves training in the sands of Egypt at the end of 1914, under the gaze of the Sphinx. They were being made ready to quash a nationalist or pan-Islamic uprising in Egypt, or elsewhere. One Anzac may speak for thousands. George Horan wrote to his father on 13 December that the soldiers had 'four days notice' before arriving in Egypt: 'We were all convinced we were going straight to England but as they are expecting an invasion of the Turks into Egypt we were landed here.'[30]

While the Anzacs journeyed to Egypt, their destiny was being decided at Chesham House, the Russian embassy in Belgravia; at Albert Gate House, the French embassy in Knightsbridge; at the Foreign Office, in Whitehall; and in Paris, Rome, and Petrograd, as St Petersburg was renamed in late August 1914. Grey and his colleagues recognised that the best way to induce Russia to keep fighting on the eastern front was for Britain and France to promise her the realisation of her most cherished war aim — control of Constantinople and the Straits. Soon after the outbreak of war with Turkey, Grey told Count Benckendorff on 9 November that the Straits question would be resolved in Russia's interest. On 13 November, King George V recklessly promised Benckendorff that his dear cousin Tsar Nicholas had to be compensated for all Russia's sufferings on the eastern front: 'In regard to Constantinople, it is clear that it must be yours.'[31]

For a host of reasons, stated and unstated, Britain began to plan an attack on the Dardanelles from late 1914: to sustain faith in Russia's war effort; to forestall a peace between Russia and Germany; to open supply lines to Russia; to assist the Russian forces bogged down in the Caucasus; to provoke the Balkan states into entering the war on the side of the Entente; to find an alternative to the costly assaults against Germany on the Western Front; and, sustained by a racial sense of absolute superiority over the Turks, to achieve a rapid military victory over the Turkish forces, thus inciting a revolution in Turkey and a rupture with Germany.[32]

For the imperially minded decision-makers in London, another motive captivated them. The safety of the British Empire was, of course, their first priority. The conviction took hold that a quick triumph over Turkey was essential to dampen Islamic unrest within Britain's Empire — in Egypt, India, and beyond. For example, in March 1915, Lord Hardinge, viceroy in India, told Lieutenant-General Sir William Birdwood, commander of the Anzacs, that he was 'very anxious' for success at the Dardanelles because 'there is a good deal of uncomfortable unrest among the Mahomedan [*sic*] population of India, and more particularly in Persia and Afghanistan'.[33] King George V was even more direct. He wrote to Hardinge two days before the Gallipoli landings that 'our position in the Moslem world is being severely tested ... If we can get through and take possession of Constantinople, British prestige will again be paramount in the East'.[34]

Also prominent in the mixture of motives for London was a military triumph to ensure alliance solidarity. The seizure of Constantinople was the paramount goal, but it was a means to an end. The chief objective of the campaign being planned for the Dardanelles was to capture the city and the Straits on behalf of Russia, in order to keep her loyally in the war, and away from central Asia. The Russians — led by foreign minister Sazonov in Petrograd, Nikolai Bazili at Russian general headquarters, Alexander Krivoshein, minister of agriculture, and ambassador Alexander Izvolsky in Paris — also began to push the issue of Constantinople very hard from November 1914. It was an historic Russian goal, with much religious resonance.[35] Its possession would compensate for Russian defeats on the Eastern Front, at Tannenberg and the Masurian Lakes, in 1914.

Weeks of tense negotiations followed in early 1915. 'We are a set of buccaneers sitting round a table,' quipped Asquith — again.[36] These climaxed in formal diplomatic exchanges between Britain, France, and Russia in March and April 1915, known to history as the 'Straits Agreement'. Under the agreement, British and imperial forces would seize the Straits and the city of Constantinople — for

Russia.[37] The British drove a hard bargain: as compensation, they would receive the 'neutral zone' in Persia, the zone between the two 'spheres of influence' that had been carved out of Persia when Russia and Britain had signed the Anglo–Russian Convention in 1907. This would ensure the safety of supplies of oil for the Royal Navy — resources that had prompted the large British government investment in Anglo–Persian Oil on the very eve of the war.[38]

The campaign was to be undertaken, above all, for Russia. As Grey told Buchanan in Petrograd in March, the 'direct fruits of these operations will, if the war is successful, be gathered entirely by Russia'.[39] In the weeks before the Anzac landings, the exultant Russians made their plans to rule the city of Constantinople, once the British and their allies had conquered it for them. The city, the symbolic heart of Russian Orthodoxy (because it had been the historic capital of the Eastern Roman Empire), would be renamed 'Tsargrad'.[40] On 12 April, the Russians selected their high commissioner who would dominate over a proposed Allied High Commission that was to administer the captured city: Prince Gregory Trubetskoi, a religious zealot, a confidante of Sazonov, and Russian ambassador to Belgrade.[41]

The deals underpinning the Gallipoli campaign were all in place.

Well, almost. On the day after the Gallipoli landings, another motive was revealed, but to only a very few, in London. Behind the scenes, the campaign to lure the Italians into entering the war ended in diplomatic victory. Indeed, the first British attacks on the Dardanelles forts by sea, in February and March 1915, had inspired the Italian foreign minister, Sidney Sonnino, to instruct Italy's ambassador in London, the Marquis Guglielmo Imperiali, to expedite negotiations on Italian intervention. The timing was no mystery. The salvoes at the Dardanelles ports signalled that Britain was about to break into the Turkish orchard and shake every tree. A whole empire would soon be falling into the laps of the conquerors. Did Italy want to be there to spread her apron or not?

The cabinet in London knew all about these secret negotiations, of course. But on 26 April 1915, no Australian had the remotest idea that the bloody landings at Gallipoli were being used as the clinching argument in London to get signatures on the secret 'Pact of London'. (The negotiators preferred the word 'pact', lest 'treaty' suggest a need for parliamentary ratification — which they all ruled out. But it soon gained the name 'Treaty of London' anyway.) The Russians finally dropped their opposition to promises to Italy of big territorial gains along the Adriatic coast as the price of her entry into the war — territories coveted by Serbia. Similarly, the landings were used as a final lever to pressure the Italian negotiators into signing. The Italians had to realise, beamed the Foreign Office men, that the partition of Turkey was just a matter of weeks away. Thus, the Italian government committed itself to turn around opinion in the neutralist Italian parliament, to defy the neutralist Pope Benedict XV, and to enter the war within a month — for the sake of the promised annexations at the expense of Austria and Turkey.

The Australians landed at Anzac Cove on 25 April, and on 26 April, in London, the secret document later dubbed the 'Treaty of London' was signed by Grey for Britain, by Cambon for France, by Benckendorff for Russia, and by Imperiali for Italy. Grey conveyed news of both the struggle ashore at Gallipoli ('successful but heavily opposed') and the signing of the treaty at the Foreign Office at the same cabinet meeting, on the afternoon of 26 April 1915. The Australians had helped make it happen.[42]

Over the next seven months, the Australians suffered 7,825 battle casualties at Gallipoli, with more dying of wounds and disease.[43] They died there, with the New Zealanders, the British, the Indians, and the French, for many reasons — for Russian war aims, for Italian ambition, for the empire's safety from Islamic unrest, and for all the resources of the Middle East. They died for many people, most of whom they had never heard of — for Sazonov, for Benckendorff, for Trubetskoi, for Izvolski, for Cambon, for Paléologue, for Imperiali, for Salandra, and for Sidney Sonnino. The Australians had been given a role in a gigantic struggle to force a breathtaking slicing-up of the whole Turkish Empire — with great chunks of territory going to the Entente powers.

The crucial deals underpinning the Gallipoli campaign were not shared with Australia's government. During the critical weeks in which these deals were being stitched up, Australia's leaders remained fixated on a much less pressing issue — the long-term fate of the German possessions in the Pacific seized by Japan.[44] So, too, the cables flowing between London and Melbourne buzzed with protests and emollient replies upon this matter, above all others. No one in authority in London appeared to believe that the ultimate purposes of the Gallipoli campaign should be discussed with Melbourne.

In early March, Harcourt pleaded with Asquith to 'realise that Dominion Contingents even though (and properly) under War Office control, cannot be treated so exclusively as a "chattel", as if they were one of our own new armies'.[45] It made no difference. Even Munro Ferguson was told very little. On 24 March, Harcourt revealed only that the Australians were 'ready for landing at the Dardanelles'. 'I rather hope that they will not have to be used for the storming of the Dardanelles forts as this would lead to very heavy losses,' wrote Harcourt. He held out the hope it could be done by ships alone. 'What, if any, fighting there will be when we get up to Constantinople I cannot at present say.' He did confide to Munro Ferguson that among the objectives of the campaign was to induce the Balkan states 'to come in on our side in order to share the spoils'. He added his personal view that Italy, too, 'will be in on our side by the end of April'.[46]

But there is no evidence that Australia's political leaders were told any of this. They groped forward in a gathering gloom. And yet, on the other hand, they had not asked for more light. Certainly, Australia had no real voice in the making of the empire's foreign policy — in war, as in peace. But Australia was not just a victim here of a British deception. It was not all about imperial subservience. Australian swagger was part of the story, too. Before the outbreak of war, and at its outbreak, some Australians were simply desperate that the youth of the new nation should cut a figure in an imperial tableau. The purposes of the great adventure were beyond Australia's knowledge, or control. Even as they planned the campaign, those in command of Australia's military manhood still pleaded for a share in the combat of the Western Front. When General Bridges told Munro Ferguson of the Anzacs' objective — Constantinople — he boasted that 'not even the hoisting of the Southern Cross on S. Sophia ['Sancta Sophia', at that time a mosque in Constantinople] would compensate his men for being longer kept out of the trenches in Flanders!' Naturally, the governor-general reported this latest instance of Australia's craving for battle on the Western Front to London.[47]

In official circles, Australia paraded an apparently inexhaustible loyalty. For example, soon after war broke out, the British government decided that it would not hold the next scheduled Imperial Conference in 1915. As Harcourt explained, it would not suit 'the convenience of any parties'. He added that, on this point, 'no communications passed between us and the Dominion Governments' — meaning that they were not consulted before the decision was taken in London. A slender chance for the dominions to contribute to the high diplomacy of war was to be withdrawn. At exactly this time, Munro Ferguson — unbeknown to the Fisher government — secretly cabled London, giving his own estimate that Australia could send another 85,000 men by June 1915.[48]

In December 1914, Fisher showed a spasm of rebellion. He told Munro Ferguson he was 'strongly of opinion' that the Imperial Conference *should* meet. In response, Harcourt privately telegraphed to the other dominion governors, and decided that Fisher was the odd man out.[49] When Fisher was told again in early 1915 that there would be no such conference, he surrendered. He indicated that 'he had no wish to press the matter'. Munro Ferguson was delighted. He told Harcourt that Fisher's 'loyal acquiescence in your decision was a good example of his sterling worth as a man'.[50]

Fisher's acquiescence was publicised in a statement in *The Times* on 3 April 1915: 'What the British Government considers to be the correct thing is good enough for my Government. That is all I have to say.'[51] This was not mere fodder for journalists, because in February Fisher had already sent a very rare private letter to Harcourt in very similar terms:

I cheerfully fall in with the decision not to hold the Imperial Conference this year, though I have not been able to convince myself that the reasons given for postponement were sufficient. However, we have a policy for this trouble that gets over all difficulties. When the King's business will not fit in with our ideas, we do not press them.[52]

Harcourt was so impressed by Fisher's low bow that he asked Munro Ferguson if he could quote it publicly. Evidently, he got permission, for Harcourt proceeded to quote Fisher in the House of Commons on 14 April 1915 in the course of an explanation of the decision to cancel the Imperial Conference. Fisher's letter, glowed Harcourt, was an 'admirable example of the spirit in which the dominions deal with Imperial affairs during the war'.[53] Thus, at Westminster, just eleven days before Australians began to die at Gallipoli, the Australian prime minister's willingness to give way to 'the King's business' was hailed with 'loud cheers' by the House of Commons.[54]

With such samples of Australian pliability abounding, it was scarcely surprising that Australia's politicians found that they exerted little significant influence over the higher direction of the empire's war. Sidelined, and contentedly indicating their willingness to be sidelined, Australian politicians could do nothing to prevent the disastrous course taken at the heart of power during this hideous war — especially the incremental and chaotic enlargement of war aims, as Britain sought to shore up her alliances with Russia, France, Japan, Italy, Rumania, and other allied nations. In this way, Australia was committed to the Entente powers' sweeping, contradictory, and often annexationist war aims that did so much to stifle opportunities for a negotiated peace in 1916 and 1917, and to prolong the bloody struggle. As a result of such imperial hubris — and not just as a result of German intransigence — Australians were still dying in a fourth year of war on the Western Front in 1918.

At Gallipoli, fortified by the knowledge that Australia would always be compliant, Britain had simply decided to expend some colonial shillings (alongside British, French, and Indian army troops) in the hope of winning some impressive imperial pounds. The campaign was underprepared and under-resourced, and a disaster unfolded. The diplomatic deal-making that absolutely underwrote the campaign — scarcely mentioned in Australian histories of Gallipoli — was simply typical of the rapid enlargement of Britain's war aims as the conflict unfolded. In this, Australia was, from the beginning, an uninformed but loyally uncomplaining partner.

Conclusion

Australia's leap into the Great War

Yet they are all honourable men ... They give us a ruined earth — honour demanded it. They are treacherous — it is a national obligation. An agreement with one party means they must betray another party. They guarantee something, and that turns another guaranty into a fraud. They have a concordance, and because of it, duty compels them to murder a population of black people, and they call that pacification. Our national responsibility may mean anything, any brutality whatever: robbery, lies, massacre, any rascality can be an obligation, when it is national. The last shilling and the last man! It is lunacy.[1]
– H. M. Tomlinson, 1930

ON MONDAY 3 AUGUST, the crucial day when the Cook cabinet decided to offer an expeditionary force to the Mother Country, the prime minister preserved in his diary a little vision of the good things that the war would bring to Australia. It was a vision mostly brightly lit: 'The good to come [,] moral tonic. Luxury, frivolity, & class selfishness will be less. A memory for our children, bitter & bracing for many.'[2] Australia would soon be renewed, it seemed, by the salutary shock of a great war.

Later, having lost office to Labor in September 1914, Cook jotted down in his personal diary plans for public addresses, offering his heroic interpretation of Australia's role in the crisis of July–August 1914 — the preferred interpretation that survives to this day. Plucky Australia had not dawdled in 1914. Australia had shown the world. Australia had 'sprung at a bound' into war. She had gained in the 'spirit of patriotism', in 'courage and fortitude', and in 'faith'.[3] But the one leap was not sufficient. Cook was soon proclaiming in public halls the need to send 100,000 men into the fray, five times the numbers despatched in the expeditionary force. 'I fear that, we as a race, are not sufficiently imbued with the idea that we are engaged in a war of extinction (Hear, hear.)', Cook told a cheering crowd at Mosman Town Hall in November 1914.[4]

British representatives of imperial authority in Australia, such as the state governors, also enthused over enlistment, preached imperial duty, and prophesied that good things would come from the war. Sometimes the reactionary political impulse driving this was privately revealed. For instance, Sir Henry Galway, governor of South Australia, told Harcourt in October 1914, after Labor's election victory, that he was disturbed that 'the wave of Socialism, ever present in Australia, is gathering strength each year'. The labouring class was overpaid, improvident, 'indulges in many luxuries', and lives 'on a lavish scale', he wrote. Some 'even go to and from their work on bicycles'. But war would change all this, he predicted, so that 'good may yet come out of evil'. The Australian working people might become 'less irresponsible and more self-sacrificing when days of trial have to be faced'. Galway speculated that 'a bad year or two would be an excellent tonic for the people, and so allow them the opportunity of practising self-denial and of learning what adversity really was'.[5]

Certainly, Australia had jumped into war at the service of empire. Her politicians had rushed ahead of events, acutely conscious of what other dominions were doing, and rather pathetically haunted by the thought that Australia might be outshone. But was this — is this — really a matter of pride? From another perspective, Australia's government had ridden pell-mell toward war, desperate to stand taller in the estimation of others. Cook's government had exercised no influence in London for caution or moderation. There had been no suggestion that Australia's offer was limited to defensive objectives. As events had balanced on the edge of Armageddon, Australia's public offer had added to the strength of those in London aiming to bulldoze events toward war.

Such people, thrilled by the prospect of war, could be found in every capital – not only in Berlin. In London, there were those who saw August 1914 as a fortuitous moment — an opportunity to eliminate Germany as an imperial, naval, and commercial rival. On Saturday 1 August, H. A. Gwynne, the editor of the Tory *Morning Post*, argued that, 'There is only one thing that can be imagined worse than a war, and that is a European war in which England did not play the game.'[6] On the same day, St Loe Strachey, editor of the Tory *Spectator*, argued that 'the moment is favourable'. A chance to crush Germany was in prospect. It would be 'madness not to make that chance a certainty by fighting on the side which we not only want to see victorious, but which must win if we are to be safe'.[7] On the night that war was declared, Amery and General Wilson telephoned Milner with the happy news. 'Germany has declared war on us', wrote Milner in his diary, incorrectly of course, and then added, 'It is *better* to have *an end* to the uncertainty.'[8] There were many in these circles who greeted the war with glee. Just after the outbreak of war, Lord Hardinge was honest enough to admit that missing the opportunity to fight Germany, with Russia and France as firm allies, would have been a tragedy. 'It would have been an universal misfortune,' he wrote, 'if we had been unable to profit by the miscalculation of Germany and had allowed her to choose a more favourable moment.'[9] These remarks typified the 'now-or-never' spirit animating many in the Tory Party and the Foreign Office during the crisis. This was the spirit braced by Australia's impetuosity in 1914.

Nor is it a satisfactory explanation to argue that the German threat was real, and that this forgave everything. Of course it was real. But this scarcely vindicates everything that Australia and the empire had done, and would do, to counter that threat. This would be to argue backwards. Indeed, it imitates the German argument that, because Russia did invade East Prussia and Austrian Galicia in 1914, and because the British Empire did seize every colony and strangle all German seaborne commerce, the German militarist advocates of endless preparedness were absolutely correct, and the invasion of Belgium was a justified act of self-defence. The stress on German perfidy hides the larger realities: the war was the work of the New Imperialism and the Old Diplomacy, springing from systemic evils in which all the great nations shared. The plague was on all their houses. To understand the huge catastrophe, we have to analyse it in that spirit.

It is easy to argue that once the fire takes hold, there is no alternative to courageous fire-fighting. But the irritating people who ask why there is so much combustible material around are truly useful. This book has sought to get at some of the useful truths about Australia in 1914. Her role in the larger tragedy was very small. Nonetheless, Australia's tumble into the Great War was impulsive, recklessly unlimited, and driven by low political calculation. It was not a moment of pride. Australia's promotion of itself as eager to participate in war, both on land and sea, could only have undermined the efforts of those seeking to preserve Britain's neutrality — and peace itself.

None of the foregoing is meant to imply that Australia ought to have remained neutral in 1914. She simply could not do so. But the rather make-believe and overheated contemporary debate about 'other people's wars' has spawned unreal exaggerations on every side. Truths, half-truths, and fictions jostle under the banner of 'Australia's war'.

The simplest truth of all is easily stated. It was 'Australia's war' in that she had no power to evade it; apart from any other consideration, Britain's enemies considered Australia their enemy. But it would be a fiction to present the war as 'Australia's war' in the sense that she coolly chose to fight it in her own interest. The matter was out of the hands of Australians.

The truth of Australia's economic interest is obvious, too. Australia had a stake in the war. From the outset, she faced potential threats from the German navy. She faced danger if British forces were defeated. In the titanic struggle to decide on a repartition of the colonial world, Australia hoped for a British victory. It was a rational hope, given Australia's economic links, and given the receding belief in free trade and the rising faith in economic nationalism across the world. But the British imperial victory helped that reactionary economic vision take hold in the post-war world. The 'New Protection', as it was called, had been stimulated by the economic blockades that were imposed during the long war.[10] It would do much to prolong economic stagnation after 1918.

It would be a fiction, however, to present a narrative of 'Australia's war' as if that phrase suggests Australia had a role in forging the diplomatic deals that drove the war. She did not. As Arthur Ponsonby, one of the most passionate of Radical dissenters on the left of the British Liberal Party, argued in 1915, greater transparency and publicity were needed to democratise foreign policy in every nation. He did not forget the dominions. 'Greater publicity would be as advantageous to the people in the Dominions as to our people at home,' he wrote. 'For the Dominions have been kept in the dark and deceived in matters of foreign policy to an even greater extent.'[11]

Ponsonby was right. In diplomatic terms, 'Australia's war' is a very limited truth. When Britain decided to commit to the 'Pact of London' at Russian insistence on 5 September 1914, promising to make no separate peace, the news appeared in *The Times* — but Australia was not consulted.[12] When London bumped Japan into the war in mid-August 1914, Australia was not consulted.[13] When London negotiated the Straits Agreement with Russia and France in March 1915 — the essential prelude to the battles at Gallipoli — Australia was not consulted.[14] When London decided to bribe Italy into entering the war, under the secret Treaty of London of 26 April 1915, Australia was not consulted.

Does it matter, some might ask? Let us contemplate facts. On 26 April 1915, Australian troops, with many Catholics among them, were frantically digging in at Anzac Cove. Under Article 15 of the Treaty of London signed that very day, the four Entente Powers pledged to cut out the Catholic Pope, Benedict XV, from any role in the diplomacy of peace. No one in Australia had any inkling of this. Similarly, Australia was not consulted on the wider diplomacy of the war. The secret Sykes–Picot negotiations of 1915–16, under which plans were made for the partition of the Middle East, where Australians fought from 1916 to 1918, were never shared with Australia. Under those plans, enlarged at the St-Jean-de-Maurienne conference of April 1917, vast tracts of the Middle East and Asia Minor itself, and their populations, were to be parcelled out between Britain, France, Russia, and Italy.[15] Does it matter that those who asserted the spotlessness of the Allied cause mired it in schemes of conquest on a vast scale? Tens of thousands of Australians continued to fight and die in a war prolonged by such commitments.

Nor did Australia play any significant role in Britain's crucial decisions to reject, again and again, opportunities for a negotiated end to the war — in, for example, the decisions to spurn both the German and American peace notes in December 1916; the Russian invitation for an inter-allied conference to revise war aims in May 1917; and the Papal Peace Note of August 1917.[16] When Lloyd George at last defined moderate war aims for the British Empire in a major speech at the Caxton Hall in London in January 1918, Australia played no role in determining those war aims.[17]

The sprawling conflict to defend the British Empire was indeed 'Australia's war' — like a disease. But, of course, Australians would learn — or would not learn — that a great deal could be smuggled into the compelling phrase 'the defence of the Empire' by those determined to aggrandise that empire. Australia did *not* have a true life-and-death interest in that aggrandisement. The rapid expansion of Britain's war aims exposed Australia to a huge cost.[18] Australians fought on, while their leaders knew very little about the expanding list of war aims to which they had been committed.[19]

The cry that 'Australia's war' was a fight for 'our' empire, therefore, does not really advance our understanding of the tragedy and reactionary impulses at the heart of the war. It was a return to medievalism. Australia fought for the empire, and all it stood for — class distinction, reservoirs of cheap labour, double standards in law, protectionism (dressed up as 'imperial preference'), captured markets and resources, hundreds of millions of colonised people locked up in an inferior economic status, and, as the Radical economist Henry Brailsford put it in 1914, the reality that investment in this empire was driven not so much by Kipling's alluring thought that there were no ten commandments east of Suez, but rather by the economic calculation that there are 'no Factory Acts east of Suez'.[20]

Australia's true long-term economic interest lay elsewhere, in the future struggling to be born. It lay in the dismantling of all the great European empires — which would prove to be the most profound historical change across the globe in the course of the twentieth century. It lay in Asian economic development beyond the pattern of the imperial masters' plantations. It lay in an economic future beyond empire. That future has created for Australia access to the huge markets in the region, as they exist today. In fighting for 'our' empire in the Great War, Australia was fighting for her present — but, in a sense, for the past and against the future.

Australia's role in the slide to disaster

What, then, does the evidence reveal of Australia's own small role in the tragic events on the eve of the Great War? Australia's dive into war in 1914 was, from one perspective, unremarkable. It was entirely predictable that the 'new Britannia in another world' would rush to the assistance of the old. Moreover, in the decade before 1914, Australian politicians had made no sustained attempt to gain greater access to decision-making in foreign policy at the heart of empire. Nor had they pursued with any great success the objective of greater autonomy in decision-making in defence policy.

Australia had settled for nationalist gestures. The form rather than the substance of autonomy proved more easily obtainable, and it could be flaunted. The separate fleet unit was real — the 'Royal *Australian* Navy', with the national flag flying from the jackstaffs as the ships entered Sydney Harbour to great acclaim on 4 October 1913. But only a minority of the sailors lining the decks on that day were Australian.[21] Most importantly, the agreement for the Australian fleet's immediate transfer to the British Admiralty in wartime was firmly in place.[22]

When war came in 1914, some Australians felt a wailing ache of desire to get involved in the great combat. Again, Australians would settle for nationalist packaging — the '*Australian* Imperial Force' was the name that Major-General Bridges gave the expeditionary force in August 1914, rather than 'Imperial Australian Force', the name planned by Major-General Hutton as long before as 1902.[23] The reality was embodied in Bridges himself, a man whose 'loyalty to his country of adoption was accompanied by an extended loyalty to the Empire, which was considerably stronger'.[24] Whatever its name, the AIF would go wherever the imperial authorities decreed.

But what of the manner of Australia's leap into the cauldron? The traditional accounts play down altogether the most obvious and troubling fact: Australia did not wait for Britain's call. Australia offered an expeditionary force *before* she was called upon. Australia certainly reacted to Britain's requests, as agreed, in readying her navy and army to defend Australia, from Thursday 30 July. But then — and in the context of an election — her politicians went further. Australia's decision-makers were intimidated by publicity given to offers of expeditionary forces already made by New Zealand and Canada from Friday 31 July. Thus, when the rump of the Cook cabinet gathered in Melbourne, assisted by the governor-general and Major Brudenell White, Australia's decision-makers leapt forward, on the afternoon of Monday 3 August, and offered Australian manhood for battle, anywhere.

The impact of events in Australia upon London in July–August 1914 is difficult to measure. Had Australia been more circumspect — had she made no offer of an expeditionary force or the transfer of her fleet until after the British declaration of war — it may have made no difference whatsoever. We cannot judge the impact of events that did not happen. Australia's strutting, her suggestion that she was craving combat, burning to provide brothers in arms, was but one small factor among many being weighed in London. But the reaction of the British colonial secretary, Lewis Harcourt, is known. He assured Australia that there was 'no immediate necessity' for such a force.

This was not a mere polite response while he waited upon events. Men of principle were struggling in London to avert disaster, to strengthen Britain's neutral diplomacy, and to limit the empire's war to a naval war, if war came. In the last days of the crisis, on Saturday 1 August, the neutralists in the British cabinet had secured a decision *against* the sending of the British Expeditionary Force to Europe. On Sunday 2 August, by a narrow margin, the cabinet had agreed on a pledge of *naval* support to France. Even this prompted the resignation of four cabinet ministers, and Harcourt was widely tipped to join them. He did not, but the government came close to being toppled. That is how close the contest was between peace and war in London — at the time when Australia offered military assistance, both soldiers and ships, for any objective.

Australia's offer set the pattern for what would follow. The Australian government committed itself without a single reservation — other than the outbreak of actual war. In doing so, it forfeited the chance to weigh up costs and benefits, to assess objectives, or to preserve Australian manhood and treasure for genuinely defensive war aims into the future. It presented itself as gallantly refusing even to contemplate the cost in blood and money. From this point onward, the Australian political elite was in a weak position when it did come to demand a voice in decision-making in the context of an escalating war.

Was the offer of an expeditionary force 'premature'? Certainly, it was not required of Australia on Monday 3 August. Australia's defence plan of 1913 had foreshadowed expeditionary forces: first, for the seizure of colonies; next, for wider imperial missions. But, according to the document, these forces were to be made available only after the declaration of the 'War Stage'.[25] No such declaration had been made when Australia made its offer.

The offer was premature in another respect. There was no necessity, no requirement in Australia's defence plans, and no implied moral obligation upon her to offer forces for a *land* war at all on Monday

3 August. Certainly, both sides of Australian politics had publicly agreed upon the transfer of the Royal Australian Navy in wartime. But no such public agreement had been reached on the matter of an expeditionary force departing Australia at the beginning of a war. Quite to the contrary, as we have seen, no less a person than General Sir Ian Hamilton believed that Australians were firmly against such a commitment.

During the July–August crisis, the British decision-makers themselves were toying with the prospect of limiting Britain's own contribution to war to a *naval* commitment only. This had long been the conviction of half the cabinet ministers. Reginald McKenna, the former First Lord, had spoken for them when he suggested at the cabinet meeting of Wednesday 29 July that Britain should limit her contribution in any war to blockade warfare.[26] Churchill had encouraged that hope.[27] Even at the climax of the crisis, during the period from Saturday 1 August to Wednesday 5 August, most ministers in Asquith's cabinet, and most members of the House of Commons, were led to believe that Britain's war would be a naval war. The newspaper closest to the government, the *Westminster Gazette*, assumed it and, behind the scenes, high-ranking British diplomats endorsed it.[28] The decision on Sunday 2 August to offer a pledge of naval support to France bolstered faith in this notion.[29] Similarly, Sir Edward Grey, in his famous speech to the House of Commons on Monday 3 August, indicated it was most unlikely that Britain could spare troops for combat on the Continent.[30] But, into this pattern of restraint, the New Zealanders, Canadians, and Australians lobbed their spectacular offers of troops for a *land* war. It was only on Thursday 6 August that Asquith's cabinet accepted the recommendation that the British Expeditionary Force should be despatched to Europe as soon as possible.[31] Australia's offer to participate in the boundless havoc of a land war had come three days earlier than Britain's own decision to throw her soldiers into such a war.

In falling upon the prospect of war so ravenously, Australian politicians were setting the nation up to be taken for granted. The spirit was certainly one of unqualified support for Britain; in fact, it would be heart-shrinking to review all the fawning and gushing on the part of the Australian 'Union Jackals' when war broke out. George Reid illustrated it: he wrote to *The Times* in late 1914 depicting the ties between Australia and Britain as those of 'enraptured lovers'.[32] The Australians' boasting was terribly tiresome, too, for British journalists in Australia, such as Henry Stead. He wrote to Harcourt in January 1915 that he was 'heartily sick' of all the crowing, the suggestions that the Australians had won the Boer War, and the endless stories of the sinking of the *Emden*. 'There is an entire lack of proportion here which is at times very trying,' he confessed.[33]

One hundred years have passed since the events of July–August 1914. How should they be remembered? We now know that, had politicians, diplomats, and military strategists made different decisions, at a dozen different points, peace was achievable. The war was avoidable, but the worst instincts of Europe overwhelmed the best, ushering in a European tragedy.

And Australia's role? As Europe's frock-coated and gorgeously uniformed decision-makers of the old order capered on the cusp of war, seeking to dare and bluff and frighten each other, occasionally putting one foot over the edge while clinging ever tighter to their trusted diplomatic partners, what did Australia do? During those last days of peace, Australia leapt well beyond offers to defend its own territorial integrity, or its surrounding seas, or even Great Britain itself, against German attack. Australia stepped forward with an apparently open-ended offer. She offered to go anywhere, and to pay any price, and to accept imperial command — before the British cabinet had made up its mind on whether to go to war at all. Australia's political leaders were willingly subservient to London. They uttered few words of caution. They exercised no brake on events.

Did Australia help or hinder in the rush to war in 1914? Probably she did neither, as she counted for so little. After all, in August 1914 Australia was offering to send one division into a conflict in which

Russia was mobilising 114 divisions, France 82, Germany 96, Austria 48, Serbia and Montenegro 21, and Britain six.[34] But what did happen is clear enough. Australia's public offer of assistance to Britain, in common with New Zealand's and Canada's, fortified those in London determined to close off opportunities for a peaceful outcome to the crisis — lest the never-to-be-equalled chance to crush Germany should be lost. We cannot quantify the impact of Australia's offer, but it is clear that Australia threw its weight, small as it was, into the oscillating scales in favour of war.

Whatever cult of the fallen was invented afterwards to invoke the Australian people's perpetual care for the Anzacs in death, their neglect of them in life was starkly revealed in the plunge into war in July–August 1914. Constantly confronted, as Australians may be, with a pantheon of heroes, it is loyalty to those in the pantheon that should inspire them to think critically about the nation's descent into war — in the past, in the present, and in the future. Certainly, the offer of an expeditionary force in 1914 was a dangerous precedent for this war, and for others to come. Australians went, freefalling, into a protracted horror, a common calamity. They leapt for the sake of the British Empire, the ruling light of the galaxy that was to be a dead star inside fifty years.

They were hell-bent — and they got there.

Notes

Introduction

1 C. E. W. Bean, Diary, entry for 26 September 1915, in 'Official History, 1914–18 War: records of C. E. W. Bean, official historian papers', AWM38, 3DRL 606/17/1 (Australian War Memorial).

2 Charles Bean, *Official History of Australia in the War of 1914–1918. Vol. I: the story of Anzac* (Sydney, 1941), 11, 15–18, 27.

3 Ernest Scott, *The Official History of Australia in the War of 1914–18. Vol XI: Australia during the war* (Sydney, 1941), 12–13.

4 Scott, *Australia during the War*, 11.

5 Bean, *Anzac to Amiens*, (Canberra, 1983, first published 1946), 22.

6 C. E. W. Bean, *Anzac to Amiens*, 21. Among other minor errors, Bean told his readers that Austria declared war on Serbia on Thursday 30 July; in fact, it was on Tuesday 28 July. Bean wrote that New Zealand offered an expeditionary force on Thursday 30 July; in fact, the offer was made in Parliament on Friday 31 July. Bean wrote that Canada 'promised the fullest aid' on Friday 31 July; in fact, the Canadian offer of 'every possible aid' and a force for service abroad was made on Sunday 2 August. Bean told his readers that Germany declared war upon Russia on Sunday 2 August; in fact, it was on the evening of Saturday 1 August. See Bean, *Anzac to Amiens*, 21–23.

7 Bean, *Anzac to Amiens*, 22.

8 Popular history is often the best guide to popular memory. For example, the three-volume *Paul Hamlyn's Complete History of Australia*, an essential reference book on library and family bookshelves since the 1970s, gets it wrong. The chapter on the Great War opens by describing Britain's declaration of war on Tuesday 4 August 1914. 'Across the other side of

the world,' the narrative then continues, 'Australia, on hearing the news of Britain's declaration of war, immediately offered troops and other aid to the Mother Country'. *Paul Hamlyn's Complete History of Australia*, Part 3 (Sydney, 1978), 1007. A page later the same book records that the offer was actually sent on 3 August, but the inconsistency is not noticed.

9 For representative examples of works in this tradition, see John Robertson, *ANZAC and Empire: the tragedy and glory of Gallipoli* (Richmond, 1990), Jeffrey Grey, *A Military History of Australia* (Cambridge, 1999), Robin Prior and Trevor Wilson, *Passchendaele: the untold story* (Melbourne, 2003). For examples of critical histories within this tradition, accepting the necessity of war but sharp in their assessment of it, see Robin Prior, *Gallipoli: the end of the myth* (Sydney, 2009), and the two valuable collections of essays, Craig Stockings, ed., *Zombie Myths of Australian Military History* (Sydney, 2010), and Craig Stockings, ed., *Anzac's Dirty Dozen: 12 myths of Australian military history* (Sydney, 2012).

10 For representative examples of this school, see Ian F. W. Beckett, *The Great War, 1914–1918* (Harlow, 2001), Gary Sheffield, *Forgotten Victory: the first world war: myths and realities* (London, 2002), Brian Bond, *The Unquiet Western Front: Britain's role in literature and history* (Cambridge, 2002), Gordon Corrigan, *Mud, Blood and Poppycock: Britain and the First World War* (London, 2003), and William Philpott, *Bloody Victory: the sacrifice on the Somme and the making of the twentieth century* (London, 2009).

11 Peter Pedersen, *The Anzacs: Gallipoli to the Western Front* (Camberwell, 2007), 411.

12 For examples of works in the tragic tradition, see Bill Gammage, *The Broken Years: Australian soldiers in the great war* (Canberra, 1974), Eric Andrews, *The ANZAC Illusion: Anglo–Australian relations during World War I* (Melbourne, 1993), Alastair Thomson, *Anzac Memories: living with the legend* (OUP, 1994), William L. Gammage, 'Was the Great War Australia's War?', in Craig Wilcox, ed., assisted by Janice Aldridge, *The Great War: gains and losses — Anzac and Empire* (Canberra, 1995), 5–15, Stephen Garton, *The Cost of War: Australians return* (Melbourne, 1996), Joy Damousi, *Living With The Aftermath: trauma, nostalgia and grief in post-war Australia* (New York, 2001), Melanie Oppenheimer, *Oceans of Love: Narelle — an Australian nurse in World War I* (Sydney, 2006), Bruce Scates, *Return to Gallipoli: walking the battlefields of the Great War* (Cambridge, 2006), Peter Stanley, *Men of Mont St Quentin* (Melbourne, 2009), Ross McMullin, *Farewell Dear People: biographies of Australia's lost generation* (Melbourne, 2012), John Hamilton, *The Price of Valour: the triumph and tragedy of a Gallipoli hero, Hugo Throssell, VC* (Sydney 2012), Bruce Scates, *On Dangerous Ground: a Gallipoli story* (Perth, 2012), Robert Bollard, *In the Shadow of Gallipoli:*

the hidden history of Australia in World War I (Sydney, 2013), and Joan Beaumont, *Broken Nation: Australians in the Great War* (Crows Nest, 2013). For a discussion of the historiography from this perspective, see Marilyn Lake and Henry Reynolds, eds, *What's Wrong with Anzac? The militarisation of Australian history* (Sydney, 2010).

13 Neville Meaney, *The Search for Security in the Pacific, 1901–14. a history of Australian defence and foreign policy, 1901–1923: Vol. 1* (Sydney, 1976), and Neville Meaney, *Australia and World Crisis 1914–1923: a history of Australian defence and foreign policy, 1901–1923: Vol. 2* (Sydney, 2010).

14 Meaney, *Search for Security*, 266.

15 Meaney, *Australia and World Crisis*, Ch. 2, 'The Imperial Cause and Aid for the Mother Country'.

16 Meaney, *Australia and World Crisis*, 44.

17 John Mordike, *An Army for a Nation: a history of Australian military developments, 1880–1914* (North Sydney, 1992), and John Mordike, *'We Should Do This Thing Quietly': Japan and the great deception in Australian defence policy, 1911–1914* (Canberra, 2002). There is a useful summary of Mordike's controversial interpretation in his 'Australia's Preparations for World War I: a new perspective', in Kevin Livingston, Richard Jordan, and Gay Sweely, eds, *Becoming Australians: the movement towards Federation in Ballarat and the nation* (Kent Town, 2001), 84–91.

18 For a critical review, see Craig Wilcox, 'Relinquishing the Past: John Mordike's *An Army for a Nation*', *Australian Journal of Politics and History*, 40, 1 (April, 1994), 52–65. For other criticism, see Jeffrey Grey, 'Defending the Dominion, 1901–18', in Carl Bridge and Bernard Attard, eds, *Between Empire and Nation: Australia's external relations from Federation to the Second World War* (Kew, 2000), 20–30. For Mordike's reply to his critics, see Part IV, 'Dealing with the Myth', in *'We Should Do This Thing Quietly'*.

19 Carl Bridge, 'Anglo–Australian Defence Relationship', Joan Beaumont, ed., *Australian Defence: sources and statistics* (Melbourne, 2001), 83–86. See also the defence of George Pearce and the denial of his partaking in any deception in John Connor, 'Coronation Conversations: the dominions and military planning talks at the 1911 Imperial Conference', in Peter Dennis and Jeffrey Grey, eds, *1911: Preliminary Moves: the 2011 Chief of Army History Conference* (Canberra, 2011), 41–55, and John Connor, *Anzac and Empire: George Foster Pearce and the foundations of Australian defence* (Cambridge, 2011), 34, 37. However, Craig Stockings writes that the theme of Mordike's book is of 'manipulation by imperial officers, working within the Commonwealth military framework, to shape the Army into a trained manpower reserve for the mother country. There is a wealth of evidence that supports this contention'. See Craig Stockings,

The Making and Breaking of the Post-Federation Australian Army,
1901–09 (Canberra, 2007), 16. The conflict in the historiography, and
the reluctance on the part of Australian military historians to embrace
Mordike's interpretation, is analysed in Greg Lockhart, "We're So Alone",
Two Versions of the Void in Australian Military History', *Australian*
Historical Studies, 120 (October, 2002), 389–97, and Greg Lockhart, 'Race
Fear, Dangerous Denial: Japan and the great deception in Australian
history', *Griffith Review,* 32 (2011).

20 For example, Neville Meaney, 'The Problem of Greater Britain and
Australia's Strategic Crisis 1905–1914' in Dennis and Grey, eds, *1911:*
Preliminary Moves, 73–74, and Craig Stockings, *Making and Breaking,* 3.

21 Bean, *Story of Anzac,* 27–28.

22 For example, Mordike drew scholars' attention to Hamilton to Asquith,
14 April 1914, Hamilton Papers 5/1/87 (Liddell Hart Centre for Military
Archives, King's College London), quoted in John Mordike, *'We Should Do*
This Thing Quietly', 90, and 138.

23 On this debate, compare John Hirst, 'Other People's Wars? Anzac and
Empire', *Quadrant,* 34, 10 (October, 1990), 15–20, and John A. Moses,
'Gallipoli or Other People's Wars Revisited: sundry reflections on ANZAC:
a review article', *Australian Journal of Politics and History,* 57, 3 (September
2011), 434–42. For a critical review, see Frank Bongiorno and Grant
Mansfield, 'Whose War Was It Anyway? Some Australian historians and the
Great War', *History Compass,* 6, 1 (2008), 62–90. For a review of the wider
historiography on the debate, see Craig Stockings, 'Other People's Wars', in
Stockings, ed., *Anzac's Dirty Dozen,* 73–99.

24 See John A. Moses, *Prussian-German Militarism, 1914–18 in Australian*
Perspective: the thought of George Arnold Wood (New York, 1991), and John
A. Moses, with Gregory Munro, *Australia and the "Kaiser's War", 1914–1918*
(St Lucia, 1993). In this vein, see the collection of essays in John Moses and
Chris Pugsley, eds, *The German Empire and Britain's Pacific Dominions,*
1871–1919 (Claremont, 2000).

25 For research on German naval planning, see especially Peter Overlack,
'German Interest in Australian Defence, 1901–1914: new insights into a
precarious position on the eve of war', *Australian Journal of Politics and*
History, 40, 1 (April, 1994), 36–51, Peter Overlack, 'German Commerce
Warfare Planning for the Australian Station', *War and Society,* 14, 1 (May,
1996), 17–48, Peter Overlack, 'The Force of Circumstance: Graf Spee's
options for the East Asian cruiser squadron in 1914', *Journal of Military*
History, 60, 4 (October, 1996), 657–82, Peter Overlack, 'The Function of
Commerce Warfare in an Anglo–German Conflict to 1914', *Journal of*
Strategic Studies, 20, 4 (December, 1997), 94–114, Jürgen Tampke, 'Imperial

Germany's Military Strategy in the South Pacific', *Australian Journal of Politics and History*, 40, 1 (1994), 98–102, and, for further documents, see Jürgen Tampke, ed., *Ruthless Warfare: German military planning and surveillance in the Australia-New Zealand region before The Great War* (Canberra, 1998). On the wider issue, see Matthew S. Seligmann, *The Royal Navy and the German Threat 1901–1914: admiralty plans to protect British trade in a war against Germany* (Oxford, 2012).

26 The classic works are V. R. Berghahn, *Germany and the Approach of War in 1914* (London, 1973), Fritz Fischer, *War of Illusions: German policies from 1911 to 1914* (London, 1975), Roger Chickering, *We Men Who Feel Most German: a cultural study of the Pan-German League, 1886–1914* (London, 1984), Hans-Ulrich Wehler, *The German Empire, 1871–1918* (Leamington Spa, 1985), and a recent study is Patrick J. Kelly, *Tirpitz and the Imperial German Navy* (Bloomington, 2011). The latest re-evaluations are James Retallack, ed., *Imperial Germany, 1871–1918* (Oxford, 2008), and Matthew Jefferies, *Contesting the German Empire* (Oxford, 2008).

27 For example, compare A. Harding Ganz, 'Colonial Policy and the Imperial German Navy', *Militärgeschichtliche Mitteilungen*, 21, 1 (1977), 35–52, W. Mark Hamilton, 'The "New Navalism" and the British Navy League', *Mariner's Mirror*, 64, 1 (February, 1978), 37–44, and Matthew Johnson, 'The Liberal Party and the Navy League in Britain before the Great War', *Twentieth Century British History*, 22, 2 (June, 2011), 137–63.

28 See Nicholas A. Lambert, *Planning Armageddon: British economic warfare and the First World War* (Harvard, 2012), especially, 'Part I: The Pre-War, 1901–1914', and Eric W. Osborne, *Britain's Economic Blockade of Germany, 1914–1919* (London, 2004), especially Ch. 3, 'Blockade Preparations in the Final Years of Peace, 1911–14.'

29 'Notes by Second Naval Member', and 'Notes and Comments on War Orders', both commenting on Admiralty Letter of 15 May 1913 conveying War Orders for H. M. Australian Ships, NAA: MP1049/1, 1914/0157.

30 Roger C. Thompson, 'First Steps in Diplomacy', in Bridge and Attard, eds, *Between Empire and Nation*, 5–18.

31 Ian Nish, 'Australia and the Anglo–Japanese Alliance, 1901–1911', *Australian Journal of Politics and History*, 9, 2 (1963), 201–12. Nish writes, 'Australia cannot be accused of sabotaging the alliance [in 1901–02] because she was unaware that negotiations were in train'. Nish also notes that Australia was 'outside the negotiations' over the renewal of the alliance in 1905.

32 Meaney, *Search for Security*, 99.

33 Nish, 'Australia and the Anglo–Japanese Alliance', 210–12. Nish writes that in 1911 'Australia was for the first time consulted over its renewal and

unexpectedly gave its approval'. She was permitted to make a 'decision'
about it, only when Britain was confident of the outcome.

34 Ruth Leger Sivard, *World Military and Social Expenditures 1987/88*
(Washington, 1987), 29–31.

Chapter 1 Cabinet crisis

1 The governor-general [of Australia] to the secretary of state [Harcourt]
(received 6.20 p.m., 3 August 1914), in The Parliament of the
Commonwealth of Australia, *European War: correspondence regarding
the naval and military assistance afforded to His Majesty's government by
His Majesty's oversea dominions*, No. 10 (printed 11 November 1914), in
The Parliament of the Commonwealth of Australia, *Papers Presented to
Parliament, Vol. V, Session 1914–17*, 1434.

2 That is, 6.00 p.m. AEST (Australian Eastern Standard Time).

3 The governor-general [of Australia] to the secretary of state [Harcourt]
(received 6.20 p.m., 3 August 1914), in The Parliament of the
Commonwealth of Australia, *European War: correspondence regarding
the naval and military assistance afforded to His Majesty's government by
His Majesty's oversea dominions*, No. 10 (printed 11 November 1914), in
The Parliament of the Commonwealth of Australia, *Papers Presented to
Parliament, Vol. V, Session 1914–17*, 1434. There is a copy of the telegram
in the Admiralty files, TNA: ADM 137/1/20 (The National Archives, UK),
confirming the arrival time of the telegram at the Colonial Office as 6.20
p.m., Monday 3 August 1914, and a note records that 'the original telegram
received by the Admiralty has not been traced'.

4 That is, 8.00 a.m. GMT (Greenwich Mean Time).

5 Naomi B. Levine, *Politics, Religion and Love: the story of H. H. Asquith,
Venetia Stanley and Edwin Montagu, based on the life and letters of Edwin
Samuel Montagu* (New York, 1991), and Michael and Eleanor Brock, eds, *H.
H. Asquith Letters to Venetia Stanley* (Oxford, 1985).

6 Cabinet Memorandum, 3 August 1914, Harcourt Papers (Bodleian Library).

7 Charles Hobhouse Diary, August [undated] 1914, in Charles Hobhouse,
Inside Asquith's Cabinet: from the diaries of Charles Hobhouse, edited by
Edward David (London 1977), 180.

8 Lucy Masterman, *C. F. G. Masterman: a biography* (London, 1968), 265.

9 Cabinet Memorandum, 3 August 1914, Harcourt Papers. These journals, a
new source, were allocated to the Bodleian Library only in 2008; see Mike
Webb, 'The Harcourt Papers', *Bodleian Library Friends' Newsletter* (Summer
2008 and Winter 2008–09), 3.

10 Herbert Samuel to Beatrice Samuel, 2 [but should be 3] August 1914,

Herbert Samuel Papers, SAM/A/157 (Parliamentary Archives).

11 Cabinet Memorandum, 3 August 1914, Harcourt Papers.

12 See Charles Trevelyan, 'C. P. T's personal record of the days that led up to the War of 1914 and to his resignation', and Charles Trevelyan to Asquith, 3 August 1914 (Draft), Charles Trevelyan Papers, CPT 59 (University of Newcastle).

13 Burns to Asquith, 2 August 1914 [handwritten copy], Burns Papers, 46282/158 (British Library).

14 Simon to Asquith, 2 August 1914, in a journal marked 'Diary #5', MS. Simon 2, Simon Papers (Bodleian Library).

15 Morley to Asquith, 3 August 1914, in John Viscount Morley, *Memorandum on Resignation, August 1914* (London, 1928), 22.

16 Beauchamp to Asquith, 3 August 1914, Beauchamp Papers (private family archive). It is noteworthy that this letter referred to Beauchamp's desire to 'confirm' his resignation, and so, in common with Morley, Beauchamp must have given Asquith some indication of his intention to resign on the Sunday.

17 Untitled, undated private memorandum (3 August 1914), Beauchamp Papers.

18 For example, one recent popular account, David Fromkin's *Europe's Last Summer*, mentions not one of the five dissenting ministers from Asquith's government who submitted resignation letters by Monday 3 August (Burns, Simon, Morley, Beauchamp, and Trevelyan). Describing the cabinet meeting of Monday 3 August, Fromkin writes quite mistakenly that 'Opinion in the Cabinet was practically unanimous'. See David Fromkin, *Europe's Last Summer: who started the Great War in 1914?* (New York, 2004), 248. Similarly, Hew Strachan, in his magisterial history of the outbreak of war, *To Arms*, seems impatient to remove these troublesome men from the British scene. 'By the morning of 3 August the Cabinet and the country were at last effectively united', remarks Strachan. See Hew Strachan, *The First World War. Vol. I: to arms* (Oxford, 2001), 97.

Chapter 2 Premonitions

1 *Commonwealth Parliamentary Debates*, Senate, Vol. 7, 9015 (22 January 1902).

2 Until Labor secured the passage of the Statute of Westminster Adoption Act in Australia in October 1942 (to cat-calls of 'anti-British' from the opposition benches), most experts regarded it as very doubtful that Australia had the power to enter into treaties, to declare war, or to declare neutrality and exempt itself from any declaration of war on the part of

the United Kingdom. See Anne Twomey, 'Sue v Hill — The Evolution of Australian Independence', in Adrienne Stone and George Williams, eds, *The High Court at the Crossroads: essays in constitutional law* (Sydney, 2000), 95, and *Commonwealth Parliamentary Debates*, House of Representatives, Vol. 172 (7 October 1942), 1455, 1462–63, 1467. See also George Winterton, 'The Acquisition of Independence' in Robert French, Geoffrey Lindell and Cheryl Saunders, eds, *Reflections on the Australian Constitution* (Melbourne, 2003), and W. J. Hudson and M. P. Sharp, *Australian Independence: colony to reluctant kingdom* (Melbourne, 1988).

3   On the long 'versatile nightmare' of Asian invasion, fostered by politicians, publicists, and cultural warriors keen to exploit racial fears in Australia, see David Walker, *Anxious Nation: Australia and the rise of Asia, 1850–1939* (St Lucia, 1999), and David Day, 'The "White Australia" Policy', in Bridge and Attard, eds, *Between Empire and Nation*, 35–54. For a stimulating account of the 'barrier mentality' in Australia and the reluctance of historians to acknowledge the power of racial fears, see Greg Lockhart, 'Absenting Asia', in David Walker and Agnieszka Sobocinska, eds, *Australia's Asia: from yellow peril to Asian century* (Perth, 2012), 269–97. On the Japanese reaction to the race frenzy in Australia, see Henry P. Frei, *Japan's Southward Advance and Australia: from the sixteenth century to World War II* (Melbourne, 1991), Ch. 6, 'White Australia, and a Shield Forged'.

4   For example, see Geoffrey Partington, *The Australian Nation: its British and Irish roots* (New Brunswick, 1997), 94–95, Henry L. Hall, *Australia and England: a study in imperial relations* (London, 1934), 103–06, and C. D. Allin, 'Proposals for the Neutrality of British Colonies', *Political Science Quarterly*, 37, 3 (1922), 415–39.

5   See Patrick O'Farrell, *The Irish in Australia: 1788 to the present* (Kensington, 2000), especially 250–52. O'Farrell calculates that 'by 1914, under 2 percent of the Australian population was Irish-born' and thus 'at most two in ten Catholics had been born in Ireland'. The census of 1911 revealed that of a total Australian population (excluding Aboriginal Australians) of 4,274,414, the number of Roman Catholics was 921,425, or 21.5 per cent. See *Official Year Book of the Commonwealth of Australia, No. 6. 1913* (Melbourne, 1913), 159.

6   In the 1880s and 1890s British forces fought in significant conflicts in Bhutan, Burma, Lake Nyasa, Bechuanaland, the North-West Frontier, Zululand, Sierra Leone, Mashonaland, Malakand, Somaliland, Manipur, Gambia, Uganda, Matabeleland, Waziristan, Chitral, the Gold Coast, Zanzibar, the Sudan, Nigeria, Crete, China, Borneo, and Aden. For a comprehensive list of British imperial conflicts, see the Appendix of Stephen Manning, *Soldiers of the Queen: Victorian colonial conflict in the words of*

those who fought (Stroud, 2009), 210–15.

7 Craig Wilcox, *Australia's Boer War: the war in South Africa, 1899–1902* (Melbourne, 2002), xiii.

8 *Commonwealth Parliamentary Debates,* House of Representatives, Vol. 7, 8749 (14 January 1902).

9 *Commonwealth Parliamentary Debates,* House of Representatives, Vol. 7, 8771–75 (14 January 1902).

10 *Commonwealth Parliamentary Debates,* Senate, Vol. 7, 9015 (22 January 1902).

11 *Commonwealth Parliamentary Debates,* House of Representatives, Vol. 7, 8754 (14 January 1902). Later, Higgins would take the post of attorney-general in Australia's first federal Labor-led cabinet under prime minister Chris Watson in April 1904.

12 For very different interpretations of the history of the new army that was built up from the former colonial militia, and the rivalry between staff officers, see the essays on Major-General Sir William Bridges, General Sir Brudenell White, and Vice-Admiral Sir William Creswell, in D. M. Horner, ed., *The Commanders: Australian military leadership in the twentieth century* (Sydney, 1984), Chris Coulthard-Clark, 'Formation of the Australian Armed Services 1901–14', in M. McKernan and M. Browne, eds, *Australia: two centuries of war and peace* (Canberra, 1988), Craig Wilcox, *For Hearths and Homes: citizen soldiering in Australia, 1854–1945* (Sydney, 1998), Craig Wilcox, 'Edwardian Transformation', in Craig Stockings and John Connor, eds, *Before the Anzac Dawn: a military history of Australia to 1915* (Sydney, 2013), 255–81, and the critical account of Mordike, *An Army for a Nation.*

13 *Commonwealth Parliamentary Debates,* House of Representatives, Vol. 3, 2990–91 (24 July 1901). See also 'House of Representatives', *The Argus,* 25 July 1901. Higgins's speech is reproduced in J. M. Main, ed., *Conscription: the Australian debate, 1901–1970* (Melbourne, 1970), 8.

14 The most detailed account is Richard J. R. Lehane, 'Lieutenant-General Edward Hutton and "Greater Britain": late-Victorian imperialism, imperial defence and the self-governing colonies', Unpublished PhD thesis (University of Sydney, 2005).

15 Lehane, 'Edward Hutton', 242–51, and compare Meaney, *Australia and World Crisis,* 32, Jeffrey Grey, *A Military History of Australia* (Cambridge, 2008), 70, and Mordike, *An Army for a Nation,* 90–92.

16 Chris Coulthard-Clark, 'Formation of the Australian Armed Services 1901–14', 125.

17 See the original Clause 45a (later Clause 49) of the Defence Bill: 'Members of the Defence Forces who are members of the Military Forces shall not be required, unless they voluntarily agree to do so, to serve beyond the limits

of the Commonwealth and those of any Territory under the authority of the Commonwealth.' Higgins endeavoured to have this tightened still further by proposing the deletion of the reference to Commonwealth Territory. This failed twenty-seven votes to ten. See Parliament of the Commonwealth, House of Representatives, *No. 6. Weekly Report of Divisions in Committee, Week Ended 7th August 1903*, 14, Lehane, 'Edward Hutton', 253–55, and Meaney, *Australia and World Crisis*, 31.

18 He borrowed the great bulk of it from an earlier paper he had prepared for Sir John Forrest, minister of defence in 1902. See 'Military Forces of the Commonwealth — Minute upon the Defence of Australia, by Major-General Hutton', 7 April 1902, in 'Colonial Conference, 1902: papers relating to a conference between the secretary of state for the colonies and the prime ministers of self-governing colonies' (Melbourne, 1903) 45–54, and a copy in 'Major-Gen. Sir Edward Hutton's scheme for the reorganisation of the military forces', NAA: B168, 1902/2688.

19 'Defence Scheme for the Commonwealth of Australia', marked '2nd Proof', in 'Cover 1: Commonwealth Defence Schemes', NAA: MP826/1, 3(A) (National Archives of Australia).

20 'Chapter 1: Strategical Considerations', in 'Defence Scheme for the Commonwealth of Australia', marked '2nd Proof', in 'Cover 1: Commonwealth Defence Schemes', NAA: MP826/1, 3(A). Emphasis added.

21 See J. A. La Nauze, *Alfred Deakin: a biography* (Sydney, 1979), Ch. 22, 'London, 1907', and Meaney, *Search for Security*, 147–50, and see Mordike, *An Army for a Nation*, 180–84.

22 *Commonwealth Parliamentary Debates*, House of Representatives, Vol. 42, 7509–36 (13 December 1907). Deakin proposed that Australia should acquire her own naval defences to protect harbours and coasts, with nine submarines and six torpedo boat destroyers. See also Meaney, *Search for Security*, 157, and Mordike, *An Army for a Nation*, 186–87.

23 *Commonwealth Parliamentary Debates*, House of Representatives, Vol. 42, 7517, 7518, 7536 (13 December 1907). For details on the scheme, see Grey, *A Military History of Australia*, 80, and John Barrett, *Falling In: Australians and 'Boy Conscription', 1911–1915* (Sydney, 1979), 65–66.

24 *Commonwealth Parliamentary Debates*, House of Representatives, Vol. 42, 7527 (13 December 1907). Emphasis added.

25 *Commonwealth Parliamentary Debates*, House of Representatives, Vol. 42, 7536 (13 December 1907).

26 Pearce complained that the IGS scheme might lead to 'the formation and provision of expeditionary forces not designed for local defence', while Fisher specified there must be no binding commitment to any such

expeditionary force. See Mordike, *Army for a Nation*, 205–06.

27 Peter Bastian, *Andrew Fisher: an underestimated man* (Sydney, 2009), 193.

28 For accounts of this episode in Britain, see Gerald H. S. Jordan, 'Pensions not Dreadnoughts: the radicals and naval retrenchment', in A. J. A. Morris, ed., *Edwardian Radicalism, 1900–1914* (London, 1974), A. J. A. Morris, *Radicalism Against War, 1906–1914* (London, 1972), Ch. 4, 'The Naval Crisis, 1908–10', A. J. A. Morris, *The Scaremongers: the advocacy of war and rearmament 1896–1914* (London, 1984), Ch. 13, 'Hysteria Navalis', and Phillips Payson O'Brien, *British and American Naval Power: politics and policy, 1900–1936* (Westport, 1998), Ch. 4, 'The 1909 Naval Estimates Crisis'. For an entertaining contemporary account, see Francis Hirst, *The Six Panics* (London, 1913), 59–102.

29 On the Dreadnought agitation, see Meaney, *The Search for Security*, 175–81, and David Day, *Andrew Fisher: prime minister of Australia* (Sydney: Harper Collins, 2008), 168–76. Fisher had finally sought refuge in assurances to the governor-general that Australia would offer Britain her 'whole resources' in a crisis. See 'Mr Fisher at Newcastle', *Sydney Morning Herald*, 23 April 1909.

30 La Nauze, *Deakin*, Ch. 24, 'Fusion'.

31 La Nauze, *Deakin*, 582. See also 'Notes of the Proceedings of a Conference at the Admiralty on Tuesday 10 August 1909', and 'Captain Creswell's views on result of Imperial Conference, 16 November 1909', reproduced in N. Lambert, ed., *Australia's Naval Inheritance: imperial maritime strategy and the Australia station, 1880–1909* (Canberra, 1999), 180–87.

32 Admiral Fisher to Lord Esher, 13 September 1909, quoted by La Nauze, *Deakin*, 582.

33 According to the papers of the Imperial Defence Conference of 1909, at a meeting held on 29 July 1909, 'The representatives of the self-governing Dominions were understood to signify their general concurrence in the proposition "that each part of the Empire is willing to make its preparations on such lines as will enable it, should it so desire, to take its share in the general defence of the Empire." See *Military and Naval Defence of the Empire (Conference with Representatives of the Self-Governing Dominions on the)* (Wellington, 1909), 32. Emphasis added.

34 Asquith, *Parliamentary Debates*, Commons, 5th series, vol. 9, 2311 (26 August 1909), and see Mordike.

35 *Commonwealth Parliamentary Debates*, House of Representatives, Vol. 51, 3624 (21 September 1909).

36 *Commonwealth Parliamentary Debates*, House of Representatives, Vol. 51, 3624 (21 September 1909).

37 Kitchener was widely known in Australia from the Khartoum connection — perhaps above all from the pages of G. A. Henty's *With Kitchener in the*

Soudan: a story of Atbara and Omdurman, the best-known title in that popular brand of deeds-of-derring-do stories. G. A. Henty, *With Kitchener in the Soudan: a story of Atbara and Omdurman* (London, 1903).

38 See 'Introductory Remarks', Points IV, V, IX, X, XII, XIII, XIV, XVI, in Kitchener, 'Memorandum on the Defence of Australia', NAA: A463, 1957/1059.

39 See 'Part I — Recommendations. Strategical Considerations', Points 1–4, Kitchener, 'Memorandum on the Defence of Australia', NAA: A463, 1957/1059.

40 See 'Part I — Recommendations. Strategical Considerations', Points 4 and 5, Kitchener, 'Memorandum on the Defence of Australia', NAA: A463, 1957/1059.

41 See Mordike, *An Army for a Nation*, 205, 228–29, and *We Should Do This Thing Quietly*, 62–63, for the argument that the structure of the forces suggested by Kitchener favoured their seaborne transportation and incorporation in British forces.

42 *Official Report of the Fourth Commonwealth Political Conference, opened at Trades Hall, Brisbane, Monday July 6, 1908* (1908), 16–20.

43 Meaney, *Search for Security*, Appendix IV, 277, shows that in 1913–14 defence spending reached £4.7 million, more than 30% of Commonwealth outlays.

44 *Commonwealth Parliamentary Debates*, Senate, Vol. 56, 1671–72 (18 August 1910).

45 *Commonwealth Parliamentary Debates*, Senate, Vol. 58, 4490 (13 October 1910).

46 *Commonwealth Parliamentary Debates*, Senate, Vol. 58, 4495 (13 October 1910), and John Connor, *Anzac and Empire: George Foster Pearce and the foundations of Australian defence* (Melbourne, 2011), 34.

47 La Nauze, *Deakin*, 583.

48 Bastian, *Fisher*, 193, and Kathryn Spurling, 'A strategy for the lower deck of the early Royal Australian Navy', in David Stevens and John Reeve, eds, *Southern Trident: strategy, history, and the rise of Australian naval power* (Sydney, 2001), 269.

49 'Memorandum Prepared by the Secretary to the Committee of Imperial Defence at the request of the Secretary of State for the Colonies', [Rear Admiral Sir Charles Ottley] 28 Febuary 1911, CID Paper 70-C, TNA: CAB 38/17/12. Emphasis added.

50 The best account of Fisher's time in Britain in 1911 is that given in Malcolm Shepherd, 'Memoirs of Malcolm Shepherd', Papers of Malcolm Lindsay Shepherd, NAA: A1632, (National Archives of Australia). For secondary accounts, see Day, *Fisher*, Ch. 9 'April–August 1911' and Bastian, *Fisher*, 205–14.

51 See 'Fisher in London' in Shepherd, 'Memoirs', NAA: A1632.

52 *Kilmarnock Standard*, 20 May 1911, quoted by Day, *Fisher*, 225. For typical criticism, see 'How far is the Australian Government Socialist?' in the Independent Labour Party newspaper *Labour Leader*, 28 April 1911. For other commentary on Australian Labor in the *Labour Leader*, sometimes critical, see for example the front-page interview with Andrew Fisher, *Labour Leader*, 2 June 1911, and other interviews with ALP personalities, for example 9 June 1911 (interview with J. S. T. McGowen), 23 June 1911 (interview with Bowman), and 14 July 1911 (interview with J. P. Jones).

53 *Minutes of Proceedings of the Imperial Conference, 1911* (London, 1911), 69, 71 (25 May 1911).

54 *Minutes of Proceedings of the Imperial Conference, 1911*, 117 (1 June 1911). See also Dawson, *Development of Dominion Status*, 11, and on Laurier's position see Patrice Dutil and David MacKenzie, *Canada 1911: the decisive election that shaped the country* (Toronto, 2011), 143.

55 Milner's protégé, Philip Kerr, put the matter to bed in his review of the conference in the *Round Table* journal, concluding sagely that 'the advocates of neutrality are attempting the impossible'. [Philip Kerr], 'Colonial Neutrality: the doctrine of colonial neutrality', *The Round Table*, 1, 4 (August, 1911), 435–42.

56 'Statement prepared by Mr Fisher for issue to press at Fremantle', in Malcolm Shepherd, 'Memoirs of Malcolm Shepherd', Papers of Malcolm Lindsay Shepherd, NAA: A1632.

57 For example, compare Meaney, *Search for Security*, 196–224, Neville Meaney, 'The Problem of Great Britain and Australia's Strategic Crisis 1905–1914', in Peter Dennis and Jeffrey Grey, eds, *1911: preliminary moves*, 56–89, and the critical account in Part II of Mordike, *'We Should Do This Thing Quietly'*, 33–80.

58 Committee of Imperial Defence, *Minutes of the 111th Meeting*, 26 May 1911, 9–20, TNA: CAB 38/18/40, and Ian Nish, *Alliance in Decline: a study in Anglo–Japanese relations, 1908–23* (London, 1972), 63.

59 Committee of Imperial Defence, *Minutes of the 112th Meeting*, 29 May 1911, 12, 16–17, 25, 27, TNA: CAB 38/18/41.

60 Committee of Imperial Defence, *Minutes of the 113th Meeting*, 30 May 1911, 8–9, TNA: CAB 38/18/42. See also 'Co-operation Between the Naval Forces of the United Kingdom and Dominions. (Principles agreed to at the 113th meeting of the Committee of Imperial Defence, held on May 30, 1911)', June 1911, CID Paper 89–C, TNA: CAB 38/18/44. See also the final agreement: 'Memorandum of Conferences Between the British Admiralty and Representatives of the Dominion of Canada and the Commonwealth of Australia', July 1911, in *Papers Laid Before the Imperial Conference,*

1911, Dealing with Naval and Military Defence (Wellington, 1912). The Memorandum declared, at Article 1, that the naval forces of Canada and Australia 'will be exclusively under the control of their respective Governments'. Article 3 declared that the white ensign, the symbol of the Crown, would be flown from the stern and the flag of the Dominion from the jack-staff. Article 16 established that: 'In time of war, when the Naval Service of a Dominion, or any part there of, has been put at the disposal of the Imperial Government by the Dominion authorities, the ships will form an integral part of the British fleet, and will remain under the control of the British Admiralty during the continuance of the war'.

61 Committee of Imperial Defence, *Minutes of the 113th Meeting*, 30 May 1911, 21, 24, TNA: CAB 38/18/42.

62 'Lord Haldane on Imperial Defence', *The Times*, 31 May 1911, and see 'Lord Haldane's Statement', *Sydney Morning Herald*, 1 June 1911.

63 John Mordike provided the path-breaking research on this point. See Mordike, *'We Should Do This Thing Quietly'*, 71–79. For a supporting discussion on the 'fudge' that was accepted at these meetings, and placing them in a wider context, see Keith Jeffery, 'The Imperial Conference, the Committee of Imperial Defence and the Continental Commitment', in Peter Dennis and Jeffrey Grey, eds, *1911: preliminary moves*, 20–40. For a defence of Pearce, see John Connor, 'Coronation Conversations: the Dominions and Military Planning Talks at the 1911 Imperial Conference', in Dennis and Grey, *1911: preliminary moves*, 41–55.

64 C. B. B. White Diary, 14 June 1911, Cyril Brudenell White Papers, MS 5172 (National Library of Australia), and John Bentley, 'Champion of Anzac: General Sir Brudenell White, the first Australian imperial force and the emergence of the Australian military culture 1914–18' (Unpublished PhD Thesis, University of Wollongong, 2003), 132. For a portrait of White, see Guy Verney, 'General Sir Brudenell White: the staff officer as commander', in Horner, ed., *The Commanders*, 26–43, and Cameron Hazlehurst, *Ten Journeys to Cameron's Farm: Australian tragedy* (Canberra, 2013) Ch. 8, 'The General: Brudenell White'. At this time, White was in Britain on the second of two military appointments. He was attached to the Staff College at Camberley from January 1906 to December 1907. After less than a year back in Australia, he returned to England to take up a position on the Directorate of Military Operations at the War Office in October 1908. He was appointed Director of Military Operations on his return to Australia in January 1912. On White's controversial post-war links with far-right politics, see Michael Cathcart, *Defending the National Tuckshop: Australia's secret army intrigue of 1931* (Melbourne, 1988), 80, and Andrew Moore, *Francis de Groot: Irish fascist, Australian legend* (Annandale, 2005), 192–93.

65 Wilson to Nicholson, 10 April 1911, quoted in Mordike, 'We Should Do This Thing Quietly', 67–68.

66 See CID Paper 76–C, 'Australia: scale of attack under existing conditions', 24 February 1911 (printed May 1911), TNA: CAB 38/17/9, and CID Paper 78–C, 'Australia and New Zealand: strategic situation in the event of the Anglo–Japanese alliance being determined', May 1911, TNA: CAB 38/18/27. Mordike demonstrates that, in order to encourage the move to Compulsory Military Training in Australia, initial versions of War Office papers on Australia's strategic situation, downplaying the scale of the Japanese threat to that of a mere 'raid', were amended. New versions highlighted the possibility of Japanese aggression against Australia in the long-term, if the Anglo–Japanese Treaty lapsed. For a discussion, see Mordike, 'We Should Do This Thing Quietly', 33–53.

67 Mordike was the first historian to stress the significance of this in Australian military historiography. See 'Operations of Defence (Military) — 2nd Day, 17 June 1911', TNA: WO 106/43, quoted in Mordike, 'We Should Do This Thing Quietly', 53–79. Emphasis added. True to this requirement for secrecy, the official report of the conference was cryptic, recording only a general discussion on 'The Co-operation of the Military Forces of the Empire'. Under this heading, the report reiterated each Dominion's commitment in 1909 to 'take its share in the general defence of the Empire'. It then recorded that 'the arrangements required to facilitate the co-operation of the Military Forces of the Empire fall within the scope of the duties of the local sections of the Imperial General Staff working under the orders of their respective Governments and in communication with the central section at the War Office, on which the Dominions will be represented'. See 'Report of a Committee of the Imperial Conference Convened to Discuss Defence (Military) at the War Office, 14th and 17th June, 1911', in *Papers Laid Before the Imperial Conference, 1911, Dealing with Naval and Military Defence* (Wellington, 1912), 4–5.

68 'The Imperial Conference', dated 'London, June 9', from 'Our Special Commissioner', in *Sydney Morning Herald,* 5 July 1911. Fletcher was coy about any further developments in London. 'I don't suggest for a moment that the possible expeditions from Australia have been discussed at any length in the conference of the Imperial Defence Committee, because I don't know,' he wrote. 'Mr Fisher told us no secrets and gave no hints'. But Pearce had a 'broad and satisfactory' view. See also C. Brunsdon Fletcher, *The Great Wheel: an editor's adventures* (Sydney, 1940).

69 The interview was reproduced as 'The Future of the British Empire: an interview with Mr Andrew Fisher', *The Review of Reviews for Australasia,* September 1911, 25–26.

70 For example, 'Imperial Outlook: Mr Fisher speaks', *The Advertiser* [Adelaide], 24 July 1911.

71 Shepherd, 'Memoirs', Shepherd Papers, NAA: A1632. For a secondary account, see David Day, *Fisher*, 243.

72 Long extracts from *Labor Call* praising Fisher's sentiments were read to the Senate by Senator Chataway. See *Commonwealth Parliamentary Debates*, Senate, Vol. 60, 433 (14 September 1911).

73 Shepherd, 'Memoirs', Shepherd Papers, NAA: A1632. Emphasis in original.

74 *Commonwealth Parliamentary Debates*, House of Representatives, Vol. 60, 129 (6 September 1911).

75 *Commonwealth Parliamentary Debates*, House of Representatives, Vol. 60, 131 (6 September 1911).

76 Most prominently, Chris Watson, the federal leader until 1907, and William Holman, a future premier of New South Wales, joined the ANDL. See John Barrett, *Falling In*, 46–56, and H. V. Evatt, *William Holman: Australian Labour leader* (Sydney, 1979), 280.

77 Among these were the following pressure groups: in Britain, the Navy League (founded 1894), the National Service League (1902), and the far-reaching Round Table movement (1909); in Canada, the Canadian Defence League (1909); in the United States, the Round Table Dining Club (founded in the nineteenth century), the Navy League (1902), and the National Security League (1914); and, in Australia, the Australian National Defence League (1905). For a general history of these movements in Britain, see R. J. Scally, *The Origins of the Lloyd George Coalition: the politics of social imperialism, 1900–1918* (Princeton, 1975), A. J. A. Morris, *The Scaremongers: the advocacy of war and rearmament 1896–1914* (London, 1984), and R. J. Q. Adams and Philip P. Poirier, *The Conscription Controversy in Great Britain, 1900–18* (London, 1987). On the role of right-wing protectionists and newspapermen, see R. P. T. Davenport-Hines, *Dudley Docker: the life and times of a trade warrior* (Cambridge, 1984). On the American connections see Carroll Quigley, *The Anglo–American Establishment: from Rhodes to Cliveden* (New York, 1981). On Hughes's role, see L. F. Fitzhardinge, *William Morris Hughes: a political biography. Vol. 1: that fiery particle, 1862–1914* (Sydney, 1964), 221.

78 Kathleen Burk, *Morgan Grenfell 1838–1988: the biography of a merchant bank* (Oxford, 1989), 58, 111–25, David Kynaston, *The City of London, Vol. II: golden years 1890–1914* (London, 1995), 190–91, 211, 215, 222–24, 234, 235–36, Jean Strouse, *Morgan: American financier* (New York, 1999), 187, 441–42. For the wider context of the 'preparedness' movement and its international links, I am indebted to Tom Reifer for sharing with me sections of his forthcoming book *Lawyers, Guns and Money: wall street and the American century*.

79 Foster, *High Hopes*, 17–18, 22, 25, 34–35, 119.

80 Hughes, 'The Case for Labor', *Daily Telegraph*, 27 May 1911.

81 Hughes, 'The Case for Labor', *Daily Telegraph*, 14 October 1911

Chapter 3 Nightmares

1 Pearce to Pethebridge, Minute, 'Co-operation for Military Defence between New Zealand and Australia', 30 December 1912, in NAA: MP84/1, 1856/1/33.

2 See Janet Hunter, 'The Anglo–Japanese Alliance and the Development of the International Economy', in *Studies in the Anglo–Japanese Alliance 1902–1923*, The Suntory Centre, Discussion Paper No. IS/03/443 (January, 2003), 20–21.

3 Ian Nish, *Japanese Foreign Policy 1869–1942* (London, 1977), Chs. 4 and 5, and Nish, *Alliance in Decline*, Chs. IV and V.

4 See Keith Neilson, 'The Anglo–Japanese Alliance and British Strategic Foreign Policy, 1902–1914', in Phillips Payson O'Brien, ed., *The Anglo–Japanese Alliance, 1902–1922* (New York, 2002), 59. On the Japanese threat, see especially D. M. Horner, 'Australian estimates of the Japanese Threat, 1905–1941', 139–150, and P. A. Towle, 'British Estimates of Japanese Military Power, 1900–1914', in P. A. Towle, ed., *Estimating Foreign Military Power, 1900–1914* (London, 1982).

5 See David Day, 'The "White Australia" Policy', in Bridge and Attard, eds, *Between Empire and Nation*, 31–46, Walker, *Anxious Nation*, 68–76, Ayako Hotta-Lister, *The Japan-British Exhibition of 1910* (Folkestone, 1999), and Ian Nish, *Meiji Japan's Ascent Towards World Power*, The Suntory Centre, Discussion Paper No. IS/11/559 (July, 2011), 15.

6 As noted in the Introduction to this book, see Mordike, *An Army for a Nation*, Mordike, *'We Should Do This Thing Quietly'*, and for a recent criticism see Connor, 'Coronation Conversations', in Dennis and Grey, eds, *1911: preliminary moves*, 41–55.

7 For a secondary account, see Geoffrey Barraclough, *From Agadir to Armageddon: anatomy of a crisis* (New York, 1982), and for an analysis see Jonathan Mercer, *Reputation and International Politics* (Ithaca, 1996), Ch. 5, 'The Agadir Crisis'.

8 Douglas Newton, *British Labour, European Socialism and the Struggle for Peace, 1889–1914* (Oxford, 1985), 246.

9 Denman to Harcourt, 17 October 1911, MS Harcourt 478, Harcourt Papers.

10 Denman to Harcourt, 14 August 1912, included in Appendix to 'Australia. Preparation of Defence Schemes — Memorandum by the Oversea Sub-Committee of the Committee of Imperial Defence', approved by the CID 11

April 1913 and issued as CID Paper 99–C, in NAA: A5954, 1719/7.

11 Denman to Harcourt, 19 December 1912, MS Harcourt 478.

12 Denman to Harcourt, 19 December 1912, MS Harcourt 478. Fisher was
loyal even to the point of insisting that only the proper imperial channels
be used for all communication with London. Fisher told Denman he
heartily disapproved of High Commissioner George Reid's initiative in
contacting the Admiralty himself to facilitate Australian assistance. In
conversation, Fisher told Denman that he was 'strongly of opinion' that a
cable he had received from Reid, giving the Admiralty's view of the loan
of the cruiser HMAS *Melbourne*, should have come from the governor-
general. This encouraged Harcourt to insist on the same channels, and he
told Denman that 'I have put my foot down rather heavily' with regard to
Reid's presumption in taking it upon himself to contact the Admiralty; see
Harcourt to Denman, 3 March 1913, MS Harcourt 478.

13 Denman to Harcourt, 20–25 June 1913, MS Harcourt 478.

14 Denman to Churchill, 19 September 1912, CHAR 13/10/64–65, Churchill
Papers. On Churchill's opposition to Dominion navies, see Churchill to
Harcourt, 29 January 1912, CHAR 13/8/37–44, Churchill Papers (Churchill
Archives Centre).

15 See the file of correspondence on the procedures for transfer and the issuing
of War Orders, especially King-Hall to Denman, 24 July 1912; Harcourt to
Denman, 16 August 1912; Admiral King-Hall to the Governor-General, 13
September 1912; Notes by Creswell entitled 'Re Sir G. K. H.'; confidential
untitled memorandum by George Pearce, 24 September 1912; Denman
to Harcourt, 22 February 1913; Pethebridge to Secretary Prime Minister's
Department, 10 February 1913, in NAA: MP1049/1, 1914/0157.

16 Denman to Harcourt, 20–25 June 1913, enclosing report to Churchill, MS
Harcourt 478.

17 Connor, *Anzac and Empire*, 34.

18 Gordon to Pethebridge, 4 October 1912, in NAA: MP84/1, 1856/1/33.

19 Fisher to Massey, 24 October 1912, in NAA: MP84/1, 1856/1/33.

20 Massey to Fisher, 31 October 1912, in NAA: MP84/1, 1856/1/33.

21 'Proceedings of the Conference between Major-General A. J. Godley, CB,
Commanding New Zealand Military Forces, and, Brigadier-General J. M.
Gordon, CB, Chief of the General Staff, C. M. Forces, 18 November 1912',
in the file marked 'Conference convened for the purpose of discussing
a scheme for mutual assistance and co-operation for submission to the
Governments of the Commonwealth of Australia and the Dominion of New
Zealand, 18th/20th November 1912', NAA: MP84/1, 1856/1/33, and for a
secondary account see Connor, *Anzac and Empire*, 36–37.

22 For example, White was critical of the separate fleet unit established by

Australia, which he saw as weakening the Imperial navy and the 'Imperial spirit'. See Verney, 'Brudenell White', 29.

23 Brigadier-General J. M. Gordon, *The Chronicles of a Gay Gordon* (London, 1921), 309–10.

24 For example, White lunched with General Wilson, the British Director of Military Operations, three days before he departed England. See C. B. B. White Diary, 19 December 1911, White Papers, MS 5172. Bentley records that White was 'under the influence' of General Rawlinson and General Wilson at Camberley. He also suggests that White's recall to England to join the Directorate of Military Operations in 1908 'was probably initiated by Wilson', and notes that White 'regularly socialised' with the British military elite in England, including Generals Hutton, Nicholson, Haig and Wilson; see Bentley, 'Brudenell White', 107–13, 116, 126. See also C. B. B. White Diary, 18–19 November 1912, White Papers, MS 5172.

25 Pearce was perfectly accurate. Under section 49 of Australia's *Defence Act* of 1903–1909, and under section 26 of New Zealand's *Defence Act* of 1909, only volunteer soldiers could be sent abroad.

26 'Proceedings of the Conference between Major-General A. J. Godley, CB, Commanding New Zealand Military Forces, and, Brigadier-General J. M. Gordon, CB, Chief of the General Staff, C. M. Forces, 18 November 1912', 4, in NAA: MP84/1, 1856/1/33.

27 'Proceedings of the Conference, 18 November 1912', 1, in NAA: MP84/1, 1856/1/33.

28 'Proceedings of the Conference, 18 November 1912', 3–4, in NAA: MP84/1, 1856/1/33.

29 'Proceedings of the Conference, 18 November 1912', 4–5, in NAA: MP84/1, 1856/1/33.

30 'Proceedings of the Conference, 18 November 1912', 5–6, and Appendix 3 and Appendix 4, in NAA: MP84/1, 1856/1/33. The second option required Australia to supply 6,669 men and New Zealand '1 Mounted Rifle Brigade composed of 4 Regiments of Mounted Rifles' (without a total of New Zealanders specified).

31 'Proceedings of the Conference, 18 November 1912', 6, in NAA: MP84/1, 1856/1/33. Thus, they recommended 'that Australia should be allotted the countries west of the 170th degree of longitude and that the remainder should fall to the Dominion of New Zealand'.

32 List of Recommendations, in 'Proceedings of the Conference, 18 November 1912', 7, in NAA: MP84/1, 1856/1/33.

33 Gordon to Pearce, 20 November 1912, in NAA: MP84/1, 1856/1/33.

34 'Scheme of Defence — Mobile forces of Australia — Strategical Considerations', enclosed with Denman to Harcourt, 14 August 1912,

and included in Appendix to 'Australia. Preparation of Defence Schemes — Memorandum by the Oversea Sub-Committee of the Committee of Imperial Defence', approved by the CID 11 April 1913 and issued as CID Paper 99–C, in NAA: A5954, 1719/7.

35 According to the papers of the Imperial Defence Conference of 1909, at a meeting held on 29 July 1909, 'The representatives of the self-governing Dominions were understood to signify their general concurrence in the proposition "that each part of the Empire is willing to make its preparations on such lines as will enable it, should it so desire, to take its share in the general defence of the Empire." See *Military and Naval Defence of the Empire (Conference with Representatives of the Self-Governing Dominions on the)* (Wellington, 1909), 32.

36 The list nominated not only the German ports of Simpson's Haven (Rabaul) in New Britain, Apia in German Samoa, and Kiao-Chau in the German concession in China, but also various French ports in her scattered colonies, Saigon, Noumea, and Diego Suarez (in Madagascar). So too the same document listed as possible hostile bases the Dutch ports of Batavia and Sourabaya in Java, and a total of four ports in Japan. Looking even further afield, the document listed the port of Vladivostok on Russia's Pacific coast, and naval harbours in various American ports in the Pacific, including Hawaii, Samoa and the Philippines. 'Scheme of Defence — Mobile forces of Australia — Strategical Considerations', attached as Appendix 2 to 'Proceedings of the Conference, 18 November 1912', 6, in NAA: MP84/1, 1856/1/33.

37 Pearce to Pethebridge, Minute, 'Co-operation for Military Defence between New Zealand and Australia', 30 December 1912, in NAA: MP84/1, 1856/1/33.

38 Pearce to Pethebridge, Minute, 'Co-operation for Military Defence between New Zealand and Australia', 30 December 1912, in NAA: MP84/1, 1856/1/33.

39 Minutes of the 122nd Meeting of the Committee of Imperial Defence, 6 February 1913, TNA: CAB 38/23/9, Meaney, *Search for Security*, 234.

40 Pethebridge to Shepherd, 28 January 1913, Pethebridge to Shepherd, 29 January 1913, White to Pethebridge, 30 January 1913, Fisher to Massey, 3 February 1913, and Massey to Fisher, 6 February 1913, NAA: MP84/1, 1856/1/33.

41 Pethebridge to Shepherd, dated 'January 1913', with item 'c' deleted and initialled 'G. F. P'. 22 January 1913, NAA: MP84/1, 1856/1/33.

42 Pethebridge to Shepherd, 22 January 1913, and Fisher to Massey, 23 January 1913, NAA: MP84/1, 1856/1/33.

43 Connor, *Anzac and Empire*, 37. Connor records that Pearce asked Gordon

not to inform the War Office of the plans for an expeditionary force. However, Major-General George Kirkpatrick, Inspector-General of the forces in Australia, relayed the details anyway to his friend General Sir Henry Wilson. See also Wilcox, 'Edwardian Transformation', in Stockings and Connor, eds, *Before the Anzac Dawn*, 278, who records that Kirkpatrick also agreed with Wilson that Egypt was the likely destination of an Australian expeditionary force.

44 Massey to Fisher, 27 February 1913, NAA: MP84/1, 1856/1/33.

45 Ian McGibbon, 'The Shaping of New Zealand's War Effort, August-October 1914', in John Crawford and Ian McGibbon, eds, *New Zealand's Great War: New Zealand, the Allies and the First World War* (Auckland, 2007), 59. The men would be combined at the moment of an emergency and, respecting the New Zealand *Defence Act*, volunteers would be drawn from the Territorial Force.

46 Gordon to Pethebridge, Minute Paper 'Military co-operation between the Dominion of New Zealand and the Commonwealth of Australia', 2 July 1913, NAA: MP84/1, 1856/1/33.

47 White for Gordon to Pethebridge, 14 November 1913, NAA: MP84/1, 1856/1/33. Gordon enclosed a table showing that New Zealand had already prepared a mounted brigade, an infantry brigade, artillery, a signals unit, train, and medical staff, with a total of some 7,300 men and 3,400 horses.

48 Gordon, *The Chronicles of a Gay Gordon*, 309–10. According to Gordon, the plans for the mobilisation of an expeditionary force were all completed 'some ten months before the war began', that is, in late 1913. 'All details of organisation were worked out', he wrote with satisfaction, adding that this hard work explained 'the rapidity and ease with which Australia mobilised on the receipt of the news of the outbreak of war'.

49 Lord Denman to Harcourt, 4 March 1913, in folder entitled 'Defence Schemes', NAA: MP 826/1, 3(A), and in folder entitled 'Defence Scheme for Australia', NAA: A6661, 1355, and see Mordike, *'We Should Do This Thing Quietly'*, 88.

50 'Australia. Preparation of Defence Schemes — Memorandum by the Oversea Sub-Committee of the Committee of Imperial Defence', signed by S. H. Wilson, Secretary of the Oversea Defence Committee and dated 2 April 1913, approved by the CID on 11 April 1913 and issued as CID Paper 99–C, in NAA: A5954, 1719/7.

51 CID Paper 99–C cautioned Australia's military experts that the CID did not mean to imply in its own strategic assessments that any invading Japanese force in Australia would 'necessarily be destroyed or compelled to surrender' when British command of the seas was reasserted, for such a raiding force 'might be able to withdraw even though it might have suffered

serious losses'. In Australian documents, the CID advised, suggestions that the Japanese force must inevitably be destroyed by British naval superiority 'might be omitted'.

52 Minutes of the 123rd Meeting of the Committee of Imperial Defence, 11 April 1913, TNA: CAB 38/24/19.

53 'Plans of Overseas Operations', undated, in 'Skeleton Plan of Study of Strategical Conditions in Australasia', and 'Work Prior to Assembly', undated, in folder entitled 'Defence Schemes', NAA: MP826/1, 3(A). For evidence of Major-General Kirkpatrick's support for planning for overseas operations, see 'Investigation of Preparatory Plans of the General Staff', 17 January 1913' in NAA: MP84/1, 1855/1/4. See also Chris Pugsley, *The Anzac Experience: New Zealand, Australia, and Empire in the First World War* (Auckland, 2004), 61, and Ian McGibbon, *The Path to Gallipoli: defending New Zealand, 1840–1915* (Wellington, 1991) 242.

54 See file jacket, signed by J. M. Gordon, 18 August 1913, to 'General Scheme of Defence', 1913, AWM113, MH 1/11 (Australian War Memorial). Another copy of this defence scheme, and files showing that it was used to guide mobilisation from 2 August 1914, are in NAA: MP826/1, 3(B): 'Cover 2: Commonwealth Defence Schemes — proofs of "General Scheme of Defence"/1913.'

55 Chapter I (A), 'Introductory Remarks and Strategic Considerations', in 'General Scheme of Defence', dated August 1913, 5, AWM113, MH 1/11.

56 Chapter I (A), 'Introductory Remarks and Strategic Considerations', in 'General Scheme of Defence', dated August 1913, 5, AWM113, MH 1/11.

57 Point D (2), in Chapter I (A), 'Introductory Remarks and Strategic Considerations', in 'General Scheme of Defence', dated August 1913, 5, AWM113, MH 1/11. Colonies were listed in the New Caledonia, the Bismarck Archipelago, New Guinea, and the Java and Flores Seas. Wilhelmshaven and Noumea were identified as the most likely 'hostile bases' that must be seized.

58 Point II, 'War', in Chapter II, in 'General Scheme of Defence', dated August 1913, 25, AWM113, MH 1/11.

59 Point (D), 'Modes of Meeting the Demands Likely to be Made in War Upon the Commonwealth Military Forces', in Chapter II, in 'General Scheme of Defence', dated August 1913, 21, AWM113, MH 1/11.

60 Point 25, 'War Stage', in Chapter II, in 'General Scheme of Defence', dated August 1913, 26, AWM113, MH 1/11. There was no detail in the scheme other than that those troops required for 'Imperial military undertakings' at a distance from Australia would be formed by methods that were still 'under consideration' and would eventually be outlined under 'Special Plans of Operation (A) and (B)'. Similarly, there was a note that those

troops required for the conquest of 'foreign possessions in the East Indian Archipelago' would be drawn from the 1st Military District (Queensland) under 'Special Plans of Operation (C)'.

61 John Connor, 'The capture of German New Guinea', in Stockings and Connor, eds, *Before the Anzac Dawn,* 290. See the advocacy of a plan to occupy Simpson's Haven using the National Regiments, in Kirkpatrick to Pearce, 30 Nov. 1911, in 'Review of Proposal to revise *(sic)* [revive] National Regiments' NAA: MP84/1, 1849/1/2.

62 Charles Bean, *Official History of Australia in the War of 1914–1918. Vol. I: the story of Anzac* (Sydney, 1941), 27.

63 For secondary accounts, see David Stevens, 'Defend the north: Commander Thring, Captain Hughes-Onslow, and the beginnings of Australian naval strategic thought', in Stevens and Reeve, eds, *Southern Trident,* 225–41, and Ian Cowman, '"The Vision Splendid": Australia, Naval Strategy and Empire, 1911–1923', in David Stevens, ed., *In Search of a Maritime Strategy: the maritime element in Australian defence planning since 1901* (Canberra, 1997), 43–66.

64 'Remarks by Mr. Manisty — Naval Policy of Australia', July 1913, NAA: MP1049/1, 1915/054.

65 For a secondary account, see Meaney, *Search for Security*, Ch. 9, 'Anglo–Australian Naval Conflict over Pacific Naval Defence, 1913–14', 242–66.

66 For example, see Legge to White, 25 July 1913, filed with 'Defence Scheme for the Commonwealth of Australia', in 'Cover 1: Commonwealth Defence Schemes', NAA: MP826/1, 3(A).

67 On the various strategic assessments, see Manisty to Creswell, 20 May 1914, enclosing reports from Capt. C. H. Hughes Onslow, Commander W. H. Thring, and Lt. H. M. Hardy; Thring to Manisty, 29 May 1913, enclosing his report; Pearce to Manisty, 17 June 1913; W. H. Thring, 'Report on the Naval Defence of Australasia', with appendices, 5 July 1913, NAA: MP1049/1, 1915/054.

68 See 'Meeting of the Naval Board held to discuss Australian Naval Defence and the Defence of British interests in the Pacific, 17 and 21 July 1913', NAA: MP1049/1, 1915/054.

69 Manisty, 'Defence of Australia — Remarks by Finance Member', 3 September 1913, and 'Naval Policy of Australia' (endorsed 'Remarks by Mr Manisty', dated July 1913) NAA: MP1049/1, 1915/054.

70 See Stephen D. Webster, 'Vice-Admiral Sir William Creswell: first naval member of the Australian Naval Board, 1911–1919', in Horner, ed., *The Commanders,* 44–59.

71 Creswell, 'Remarks on Commander Thring's Scheme', 27 August 1913, and edited as Creswell, 'Remarks by First Naval Member on Commander

Thring's Scheme', 21 October 1913; Manisty to Pethebridge, 25 October 1913; all in NAA: MP1049/1, 1915/054.

72 Creswell, 'Remarks by 1st NM', 1 September 1913, NAA: MP1049/1, 1915/054.

73 Creswell, 'Remarks by First Naval Member on Part II of the Second Naval Member's Report', 27 August 1913, NAA: MP1049/1, 1915/054. 'I consider strong criticism of the Admiralty is not in place in official papers,' wrote Creswell. Emphasis added.

74 Bentley notes: 'White's plans for this "special expeditionary force" were not tabled. They remained locked in his desk drawer until it was time to put them into action'. See Bentley, 'Brudenell White', 136. With regard to the expeditionary force, Meaney simply states that 'there is no record of the Australian Government ever approving of the plan'. See Meaney, *Australia and World Crisis*, 31.

75 Mordike, *We Should Do This Thing Quietly*, 85.

76 For example, on 31 January 1913, the New Zealand defence minister, James Allen, told reporters that New Zealand 'hoped to be able to place an expeditionary force at the disposal of the mother country for service in any part of the Empire'; see 'New Zealand's Patriotism', *Sydney Morning Herald*, 3 February 1913, citing the London *Pall Mall Gazette* of 31 January 1913. This was soon corrected by prime minister Massey, who explained that Mr Allen was merely expressing a hope, and adding that 'The Defence Act had not contemplated sending expeditionary forces outside the Dominion, which obviously would require Parliamentary sanction'; see 'Empire Defence', *Sydney Morning Herald*, 4 February 1913. The New Zealand Labour Party also repudiated the offer and sent a cablegram to that effect to Keir Hardie; see 'Expeditionary Force Offer', *Sydney Morning Herald*, 6 February 1913.

77 See 'Japan and Australia', editorial, *Sydney Morning Herald*, 15 May 1913.

78 'Defence: the progressive dominion', *Sydney Morning Herald*, 17 July 1913, 'Dominion Defence', *Sydney Morning Herald*, 25 July 1913, and 'Defence: co-operation with Britain', *Sydney Morning Herald*, 1 August 1913. Bean noted that, on a visit to Britain in 1913, the New Zealand defence minister discussed with the British Army Council the plans for an expeditionary force from New Zealand. Bean mistakenly dates this to August 1913. In fact, Allen returned to New Zealand, via Canada, in April 1913. See Bean, *Story of Anzac*, 28.

79 *Commonwealth Parliamentary Debates*, Senate, Vol. 72, 4586 (17 December 1913), and see Connor, *Anzac and Empire*, 35.

80 *Commonwealth Parliamentary Debates*, Senate, Vol. 72, 4589–90 (17 December 1913).

81 *Commonwealth Parliamentary Debates,* Senate, Vol. 74, 1665–69 (29 May 1914).

82 *Commonwealth Parliamentary Debates,* Senate, Vol. 74, 1674–75 (29 May 1914). On the General Staff's proposals to prepare the National Regiments as an expeditionary force, see Kirkpatrick to Pearce, 30 Nov. 1911, Gordon to Pethebridge, 27 Sept. 1912, and Kirkpatrick to Millen, 11 Oct. 1913, in 'Review of Proposal to revise *(sic)* [revive] National Regiments' NAA: MP84/1, 1849/1/2.

83 Emmott to Harcourt, 16 September 1913, MS Harcourt 480.

84 Emmott to Harcourt, 5 October 1913, MS Harcourt 480.

85 Henry Stead to Harcourt, 22 April 1914, MS Harcourt 467.

86 John Mordike has drawn this valuable letter to the attention of historians. Hamilton to Asquith, 14 April 1914, Hamilton Papers, 5/1/87, (Liddell Hart Centre for Military Archives, King's College London), quoted in Mordike, *'We Should Do This Thing Quietly'*, 89.

87 Meaney, *Search for Security,* 261. Meaney gives the figure of £4.3 million for defence appropriations in 1913–14, compared with only £1 million in 1908–09.

88 Henry Stead to Harcourt, 1 July 1914, MS Harcourt 467.

89 Hamilton to Asquith, 14 April 1914, Hamilton Papers, 5/1/87, quoted in Mordike, *'We Should Do This Thing Quietly'*, 90

Chapter 4 Double Dissolution

1 Munro Ferguson to W. M. R. Pringle, 10 July 1914, W. M. R. Pringle Papers, Mic. 76 (Parliamentary Archive, House of Lords, London).

2 Margot Asquith to Lewis Harcourt, 11 November 1910, MS Harcourt 421.

3 Thompson, 'First Steps in Diplomacy', in Bridge and Attard, eds, *Between Empire and Nation,* 13.

4 A. W. Jose to Fisher, 8 December 1912, quoted in Meaney, *Search for Security,* 246 (footnote 30).

5 King-Hall to Harcourt, 20 December 1913, MS Harcourt 467.

6 Thompson, 'First Steps in Diplomacy', in Bridge and Attard, eds, *Between Empire and Nation,* 9.

7 Thompson, 'First Steps in Diplomacy', 16.

8 Bernard Attard, 'The Australian High Commissioners', *Working Papers in Australian Studies. Working Paper No: 68,* (London, 1991), 5.

9 See Harcourt to Batterbee, 16 February 1917, MS Harcourt 479. Harcourt described a cache of such letters from Munro Ferguson delivered to his successor, Bonar Law, in 1917 as 'private and personal communications to me from the Governor-General, made under an implied obligation of great secrecy'.

10 For example, at the height of quarrels with Canada over naval matters, Asquith insisted that Churchill's correspondence too should go through the Colonial Office. See Asquith to Harcourt, 18 September 1912, MS Harcourt, 421.

11 Hardinge to Chirol, 20 March 1917, MS Hardinge 30, Hardinge Papers (Cambridge University Library).

12 Lord Liverpool to Harcourt, 3 November 1918, MS Harcourt 448.

13 Chris Cunneen, *King's Men: Australia's governors-general from Hopetoun to Isaacs* (North Sydney, 1983), 107–11.

14 Munro Ferguson to Harcourt, 20 May 1914, MS Harcourt 479.

15 Munro Ferguson to Harcourt, 28 May 1914, MS Harcourt 479.

16 Munro Ferguson to Harcourt, 28 June 1914, MS Harcourt 479.

17 Munro Ferguson to Harcourt, 6 July 1914, MS Harcourt 479.

18 Munro Ferguson to Harcourt, 28 May 1914, MS Harcourt 479.

19 Denman to Harcourt, 24 September 1912, MS Harcourt 478.

20 Denman to Harcourt, 16 April 1913, MS Harcourt 478.

21 Denman to Harcourt, no date but listed as '8 Jan. 1913', MS Harcourt 478.

22 For a summary of the furore, see Cunneen, *King's Men*, 99.

23 Harcourt to Denman, 20 August 1913, MS Harcourt 478.

24 Emmott to Harcourt, 21 September 1913, MS Harcourt 480.

25 Harcourt to Munro Ferguson, 2 July 1914, MS Harcourt 479.

26 See Patrick O'Farrell, *The Irish in Australia: 1788 to the present* (Kensington, 2000), especially 250–52. Mass meetings against Home Rule for Ireland were held in the Exhibition Building in Adelaide on 12 and 16 July 1914; see 'Home Rule: denounced by Orangemen', *The Advertiser* [Adelaide], 13 July 1914, and 'No Surrender!', *The Advertiser* [Adelaide], 17 July 1914. For indications of tension, see the reports on the Loyal Ulster League of South Australia's raising of £300 for the Ulster fund in late July 1914; 'Contribution from Adelaide', *The Advertiser* [Adelaide], 25 July 1914. On the Home Rule side, in July 1914 a Major McInerney was feted by the Irish National Societies in Melbourne, and a number of prominent Labor politicians spoke at a 'smoke social' in his favour, following his expulsion from the Naval and Military Club for expressing views in support of Irish Home Rule; see 'Major McInerney', *The Argus*, 4 July 1914.

27 Munro Ferguson to Harcourt, 28 May 1914 and 1 June 1914, MS Harcourt 479.

28 Munro Ferguson to Harcourt, 28 May 1914 and 1 June 1914, MS Harcourt 479.

29 Munro Ferguson to Harcourt, 28 May 1914 and 1 June 1914, MS Harcourt 479.

30 J. R. Nethercote 'Liberalism, Nationalism and Coalition', in J. R. Nethercote,

ed., *Liberalism and the Australian Federation* (Leichardt, 2001), 113–33.

31 Munro Ferguson to Harcourt, 2 June 1914, MS Harcourt 479.

32 Munro Ferguson to Harcourt, 9 June 1914, MS Harcourt 479.

33 Cunneen, *King's Men*, 112–15.

34 Munro Ferguson to Harcourt, 15 June 1914, MS Harcourt 479.

35 For the policy speeches of the leaders, see Fisher in 'Labour Aims', *Sydney Morning Herald*, 7 July 1914, and Cook in 'Policy Points: Liberal leader's speech', *Sydney Morning Herald*, 16 July 1914.

36 In Australia, the modern 'caretaker conventions', specifying that a government should not make major decisions or seek to bind the hands of its successor in a period when parliament was dissolved and an election imminent, arose only after World War II. See Anne Tiernan and Jennifer Menzies, *Caretaker Conventions in Australasia* (Canberra, 2007), 16.

Chapter 5 Slip-sliding to war

1 Cabinet Memorandum, 26 July 1914, Harcourt Papers.

2 Grey to de Bunsen, 23 July 1914, G. P. Gooch and Harold Temperley, eds, *British Documents on the Origins of the War, 1898–1914: Vol. XI: the outbreak of war: foreign office documents June 28th–August 4th, 1914* (London, 1926), (hereafter *BD*, Vol. XI), Document 91.

3 Compare the different assessments of the leanings of the ministers in the Cabinet made by historians who have studied these events most closely. See 'Parties in the Cabinet', a document drawn up by H. W. Temperley in 1928, when, with the assistance of J. A. Spender, he investigated the position of the surviving Cabinet ministers. See Temperley to Spender, 1 January 1928, Spender Papers, Add. MSS. 46386. See also varying judgements made by James Edwin Lindsay, 'The Failure of Liberal Opposition to British Entry into World War I', Unpublished PhD. thesis, Columbia University, 1969, 61, fn. 4 and 5; Cameron Hazlehurst, *Politicians at War, July 1914 to May 1915: a prologue to the triumph of Lloyd George* (London, 1971), Ch. 5.; Michael Brock, 'Britain Enters the War', in R. J. W. Evans and Hartmut Pogge von Strandmann, eds, *The Coming of the First World War* (Oxford, 1995), 145–78; Keith Wilson, 'Britain' in Keith Wilson, ed., *Decisions for War, 1914* (New York, 1990), 175–208; and J. Paul Harris, 'Britain', in Richard F. Hamilton and Holger H. Herwig, eds, *The Origins of World War I* (Cambridge, 2003), 282.

4 Churchill, *The World Crisis*, 1911–1918 (London, 1938), Vol. I, 161.

5 Grey, *Twenty-Five Years*, I, 334.

6 Cabinet Memorandum, 27 July 1914, Harcourt Papers.

7 F. W. Wiemann, 'Lloyd George and the Struggle for the Navy Estimates

of 1914', in A. J. P. Taylor, ed., *Lloyd George: twelve essays* (London, 1971), 71–91.

8 Bentley B. Gilbert, 'Pacifist to Interventionist: David Lloyd George in 1911 and 1914. Was Belgium an issue?', *Historical Journal*, 28, 4 (1985), 863–85.

9 Masterman in the *Daily Chronicle*, [undated] 1915, quoted in Masterman, *Masterman*, 266.

10 Masterman, *Masterman*, 265.

11 Asquith to Venetia Stanley, 24 July 1914, in Brock, eds, *Letters to Venetia Stanley*, 122–23.

12 Grey to Bertie, 26 July 1914, and repeated to Vienna, St Petersburg, Nish, Berlin and Rome, *BD*, Vol. XI, Document 140.

13 Ottoline Morrell Journal, reporting upon 25 July 1914, reproduced in Robert Gathorne-Hardy, ed., *The Early Memoirs of Lady Ottoline Morrell* (London, 1963), 258.

14 *Early Memoirs of Lady Ottoline Morrell*, 258.

15 'Policy of Great Britain: speeches by Sir J. Simon and Mr. Acland', *The Times*, 27 July 1914.

16 Harcourt Memorandum, 26 July 1914, Harcourt Papers.

17 Julian S. Corbett, *History of the Great War, Based on Official Documents: naval operations, Vol. 1. To the Battle of the Falkland Islands, December 1914* (London, 1920), 22–23.

18 Admiralty to C. in C. Home Fleets, 26 July 1914, Churchill Papers, CHAR 13/36/33, 'Admiralty note on the significant dates of the mobilisation of the Fleet in July–August 1914', Churchill Papers, CHAR 13/27B/2-3, Martin Gilbert, *Winston S. Churchill, Vol. III: 1914–1916* (London, 1971), 6 and Corbett, *Naval Operations*, 24–25. According to Corbett, 'Quietly, too, the Admiralty proceeded to take other precautionary actions which had been left open to it'.

19 Churchill, *World Crisis*, I, 160.

20 'British Naval Measures', *The Times*, 27 July 1914.

21 Grey to Buchanan, 27 July 1914, *BD*, Vol. XI, Document 177, marked as 'Repeated to Paris' and Grey to Bertie, 28 July 1914, *BD*, Vol. XI, Document 238.

22 'Sea Forces of the Powers', *The Times*, 28 July 1914.

23 Poincaré Diary, 27 July 1914, quoted in Gerd Krumeich, *Armaments and Politics in France on the Eve of the First World War* (Leamington Spa, 1984), 221. The cable in question was probably based on Cambon's report of his first interview with Grey on the ultimatum on Friday 24 July. See Grey to Bertie, 24 July 1914, summarising the Cambon interview, *BD*, Vol. XI, Document 98.

24 Poincaré Diary, 27 July 1914, quoted in J. F. V. Keiger, *Raymond Poincaré*

(Cambridge, 1997), 170, and Krumeich, *Armaments and Politics*, 221.

25 Quoted in Krumeich, *Armaments and Politics*, 221. Emphasis added.

26 *Parliamentary Debates*, Commons, 5th series, Vol. 65, 936–38 (27 July 1914).

27 Herbert Samuel to Beatrice Samuel, 27 July 1914, Samuel Papers, SAM/A/157.

28 Cabinet Memorandum, 27 July 1914, Harcourt Papers.

29 Grey, *Twenty-Five Years*, I, 334, 338.

30 Keith Wilson, 'The Cabinet Diary of J. A. Pease, 24 July–5 August 1914', *Leeds Philosophical and Literary Society*, XIX, III, [43], 5.

31 Charles Hobhouse Diary, 27 July 1914, in Hobhouse, *Inside Asquith's Cabinet*, 177.

32 Minute on Buchanan to Grey, 27 July 1914, *BD*, Vol. XI, Document 179.

33 Goschen to Grey, 27 July 1914, *BD*, Vol. XI, Document 185.

34 Grey to Goschen, 28 July 1914, *BD*, Vol. XI, Document 218.

35 Admiralty to all Cs in C. abroad, 27 July 1914, Churchill Papers, CHAR 13/37/59, and 'Admiralty to S. N. O. Gibraltar, S. N. O. New Zealand', 27 July 1914, TNA: ADM 137/7/11 and see Churchill, *World Crisis*, I, 166.

36 Churchill, *World Crisis*, I, 171.

37 Admiralty to C. in C. Home Fleets, 28 July 1914, Churchill Papers, CHAR 13/36/35.

38 Churchill, *World Crisis*, I, 171.

39 Corbett, *Naval Operations*, 26.

40 Corbett, *Naval Operations*, 26–27.

41 Churchill, *World Crisis*, I, 171.

42 The tsar and his ministerial council in fact decided upon partial mobilisation, under the guise of 'preparatory measures', on Saturday 25 July. See David Allan Rich, 'Russia', in Hamilton and Herwig, eds, *The Origins of World War I*, 221. This was known about at the Foreign Office in London late in the evening of 25 July, when Buchanan's cable arrived; see Buchanan to Grey, 25 July 1914, *BD*, Vol. XI, Document 125. See also L. C. F. Turner, 'The Russian Mobilization in 1914', *Journal of Contemporary History*, III (1968), 65–88.

43 Minute from Churchill to Asquith and Grey, 23 August 1912, CHAR 13/10/40–42, Churchill Papers.

44 Corbett, *Naval Operations*, 31.

45 Lord Hankey, *The Supreme Command, 1914–1918*, Vol. I (London, 1961), 154–55.

46 Asquith to the King, 30 July 1914, reproduced in J. A. Spender and C. Asquith, *Life of H. H. Asquith, Lord Oxford and Asquith* (London, 1932), II, 81.

47 Cabinet Memorandum, 29 July 1914, Harcourt Papers.

48 Cabinet Memorandum, 29 July 1914, Harcourt Papers.

49 Harcourt to Munro Ferguson, 29 July 1914, in file entitled 'War 1914. Notifications (Outbreak)', NAA: A11803, 1914/89/1, Part 1.

Chapter 6 The 'Warning Telegram'

1 Henry Wilson Diary, 29 July 1914, reproduced in C. E. Callwell, ed., *Field-Marshal Sir Henry Wilson* (London, 1927), I, 151–52.

2 The cable was still circulated with these two possible renderings of the deciphered words the next day. For example, see Acting Secretary of the Department of Defence to the Naval Secretary, 31 July 1914, in 'Outbreak of War August 1914 — Placing of H. M. A. Ships at Disposal of Admiralty', NAA: MP1049/1, 1914/0276.

3 'Council of War', *Daily Telegraph*, 3 August 1914.

4 Endorsements as to circulation on the copy, Harcourt to Munro Ferguson, 29 July 1914, in file entitled 'War 1914. Notifications (Outbreak)', NAA: A11803, 1914/89/1, Part 1. The typed version is dated 30 July, and pencilled in is '3.00 p.m', presumably the time of the cable's arrival.

5 Preface, 'General Scheme of Defence' (1913), AWM113 MH1/11 (Australian War Memorial).

6 Preface, 'General Scheme of Defence' (1913), AWM113 MH1/11. Emphasis in original.

7 Point 24, 'Precautionary Stage', in Chapter II, Preface, 'General Scheme of Defence' (1913), AWM113 MH1/11.

8 Scott, *Australia during the war*, 6–7, Meaney, *Australia and World Crisis*, 29, and John Murdoch, *Sir Joe: a political biography of Sir Joseph Cook* (London, 1996), 105. Because he was travelling in rural Victoria, prime minister Cook initially did not have the key to decipher the message.

9 On the war orders, see Grahame Greene, Secretary of the Admiralty, to Secretary Naval Board, 15 May 1913, enclosing War Orders for H. M. Australian Ships, 15 May 1913, NAA: MP1049/1, 1914/0157. These War Orders for the fleet did suggest that, 'during the period of international tension' and before the transfer of the Australian Fleet to the Admiralty, Melbourne would have to decide on the earliest movements: 'My Lords can only suggest to the Naval Board the great importance of secretly moving them as near to their war stations as possible when relations with a foreign power are strained'.

10 Creswell to Naval Secretary, 28 July 1914, in NAA: MP1049/1, 1914/0299. (George Macandie had been appointed Naval Secretary to the Naval Board in April 1914, replacing Eldon Manisty, but the Secretary was no longer a member of the Board.)

11 Secretary of Naval Board to Secretary of Admiralty, 21 April 1914, NAA: MP1049/1, 1914/0157.

12 Naval Secretary to Secretary Department of Defence, 4 September 1914, reporting that on 7 July 1914 the Admiralty had acknowledged the Australian request for a warning always to be sent 'in the event of war being imminent with a First Class Power or any Pacific Power'.

13 Creswell to Naval Secretary, 28 July 1914, in NAA: MP1049/1, 1914/0299. For examples of the press reports, see 'Britain's Navy', *Sydney Morning Herald*, 28 July 1914, 'The British Fleet: readiness for emergencies', *The West Australian*, 28 July 1914, and 'War Declared', *The Advertiser*, 28 July 1914.

14 See the narrative history prepared as White to A. W. Bazeley, 20 April 1934, in the file entitled 'Adoption of the Precautionary Stage of the Australian Defence Scheme — prepared for Major-General Sir C. B. B. White', AWM224, MSS636, and Arthur Jose, *Official History of Australia in the War of 1914–1918, Vol. XI, The Royal Australian Navy, 1914–1918* (Sydney, 1941), 3.

15 Creswell to Macandie, 28 July 1914, in NAA: MP1049/1, 1914/0299.

16 'Decode of telegram received from the Navy Office, Melbourne, dated 28 July 1914', in NAA: MP1049/1, 1914/0299.

17 Minister to Navy Office, 29 July 1914, NAA: MP1049/1, 1914/0299. An order for 3,500 tons of coal was confirmed on 30 July. In addition, the Acting Naval Secretary in Melbourne organised for the Post Master General's Department to confer with the Navy 'as to steps which can be taken immediately to establish a censorship of Wireless Telegraphy'; see Acting Naval Secretary to Secretary, PMG, 29 July 1914. 'Outbreak of War August 1914 — placing of H. M. A. Ships at Disposal of Admiralty', NAA: MP1049/1, 1914/0276.

18 The reference to the Federal Executive Council is mentioned in Memorandum and Minute from Captain A. Gordon Smith, dated 30 July 1914, recording phone calls and wires exchanged with Macandie in Sydney, in 'Outbreak of War August 1914 — placing of H. M. A. Ships at Disposal of Admiralty', NAA: MP1049/1, 1914/0276.

19 See Patey's own account of these events, Vice-Admiral Commanding Australian Fleet to Admiralty, enclosing 'War Between Great Britain, France, Russia, and Japan Against Germany and Austria, 1914: Participation by Australian Seagoing Fleet in the Operations', received in Colonial Office, 26 December 1914, TNA: ADM 137/1/257. On the arrangement of Naval Stations at this time, see Circular Letter, 'Limits of Naval Stations', 14 April 1913, TNA: ADM 137/7. Compare the later account prepared in White to A. W. Bazeley, 20 April 1934, in the file entitled 'Adoption of the Precautionary Stage of the Australian Defence Scheme', AWM224, MSS636,

and Scott, *Australia During the War*, 6–7.

20 'Vice-Regal' and 'The Elections: writs issued', *Sydney Morning Herald*, 31 July 1914.

21 See Memorandum and Minute from Captain A. Gordon Smith, dated 30 July 1914, in 'Outbreak of War August 1914 — placing of H. M. A. Ships at Disposal of Admiralty', NAA: MP1049/1, 1914/0276.

22 Munro Ferguson to Harcourt, 8 August 1914, TNA: CO 418/123.

23 Manisty to Millen, 29 December 1913, Millen to Manisty, 8 January 1913, and Manisty to Millen, 12 January 1914, with Millen's annotations on the 'fallacies' within. NAA MP1049/1, 1914/0157.

24 Patey, 'War Between Great Britain, France, Russia, and Japan Against Germany and Austria, 1914: participation by Australian seagoing fleet in the operations', received in Colonial Office, 26 December 1914, TNA: ADM 137/1/257.

25 Commonwealth Naval Board, Secret and Personal, to Minister, 1 August 1914, NAA: MP1049/1, 1914/0299.

26 'Liberal Campaign', *Sydney Morning Herald*, 25 July 1914.

27 Governor-general of the Commonwealth of Australia to the Secretary of State for the Colonies (sent from Sydney.) (Received at the Colonial Office 10.45 a.m. 30 July 1914). TNA: ADM 137/7/17. There is a paraphrase of the telegram in Harcourt's papers, with the date 29 July crossed out and 30 July substituted; see 'Telegram from Gov. Genl. Of Australia, 30 July 1914', MS Harcourt 479, f. 75. Emphasis added.

28 Munro Ferguson to Harcourt, 1 June 1914, MS Harcourt 479.

29 Henry Stead to Harcourt, 22 October 1913, MS Harcourt 467.

30 Cabinet Memorandum, 29 July 1914, Harcourt Papers.

31 'To Commanders-in-Chief and Senior Officers abroad', 30 July 1914, TNA: ADM 137/7/14. The file entitled 'Adoption of the Precautionary Stage of the Australian Defence Scheme', AWM224, MSS636, lists this as received on 31 July. See also Bean, *Story of Anzac*, 23.

32 Cabinet Memorandum, 30 July 1914, Harcourt Papers.

33 Cabinet Memorandum, 30 July 1914, Harcourt Papers. As noted, the copy of the telegram from Munro Ferguson to Harcourt at the Colonial Office is shown as received at 10.45 a.m. on 30 July 1914, but in Harcourt's account he did not see it until 5.00 p.m. See Governor-General of the Commonwealth of Australia to the Secretary of State for the Colonies, 30 July 1914, TNA: ADM 137/7/17.

34 'Colonial Office for Governor-General Australia', 30 July 1914, and various drafts, TNA: ADM 137/7/18, and A. C. C. Parkinson to Resident Clerk, 30 July 1914, TNA: ADM 137/7/22, and a copy listed in NAA: MP1049/1, 1914/0299. There is a copy also in NAA: MP1049/1, 1914/0276, showing

that it was sent from London on 30 July, at 8.00 p.m. See also Telegram, Admiralty to Colonial Office, for Governor-General of Australia, 30 July 1914, Churchill Papers, CHAR 13/35/60. This was in accord with 'Amendment to War Orders Issued by the Admiralty 15 May 1913 for HMAS Australia', 21 April 1914, in NAA: MP1049/1, 1914/0157.

35 Julian S. Corbett, *History of the Great War, Based on Official Documents: naval operations, Vol. 1. To the Battle of the Falkland Islands, December 1914* (London, 1920), 22–23.

36 Cabinet Memorandum, 30 July 1914, Harcourt Papers. The cablegram, listed as 'from Admiralty', dated London, 8.00 p.m. 30 July 1914, is given in the narrative history prepared as White to A. W. Bazeley, 20 April 1934, in the file entitled 'Adoption of the Precautionary Stage of the Australian Defence Scheme', AWM224, MSS636.

37 Telegram from the governor-general of the Commonwealth of Australia (at Sydney) to the Secretary of State for the Colonies (Received Colonial Office 11.01. a.m. 31 July 1914), TNA: ADM 137/7/29, and Munro Ferguson to Harcourt, 31 July 1914 (marked as 'sent 2 p.m.'), in White to A. W. Bazeley, 20 April 1934, in the file entitled 'Adoption of the Precautionary Stage of the Australian Defence Scheme', AWM224, MSS636.

38 Admiralty to Emmott, 31 July 1914, enclosing 'Draft Telegram to the Governor-General of Australia', TNA: ADM 137/7/24–6. See also Harcourt to Munro Ferguson, 31 July 1914: 'Pray express to your Ministers His Majesty's Government's warm appreciation of their prompt action with regard to the Australian Fleet'. This is in NAA: MP1049/1, 1914/0299.

39 Harcourt to Munro Ferguson, 1 August 1914, listed in NAA: MP1049/1/, 1914/0299.

40 Cabinet Memorandum, 30 July 1914, Harcourt Papers.

Chapter 7 *Champing at the bit*

1 Massey in the New Zealand Parliament, 31 July 1914, quoted in Telegram of The Governor of New Zealand to the Secretary of State for the Colonies (Received Colonial Office 4.24 p.m., 1 August 1914), TNA: ADM 137/1/12, and see *Papers Presented to Parliament, Vol. V, Session 1914–17*, 1437.

2 'The Governor [of New Zealand] to the Secretary of State (received 9.40 a.m. 31 July 1914)' in *Papers Presented to Parliament, Vol. V, Session 1914–17*, 1437. See also 'Naval Defence Act, 1913', *Appendix to the Journals of the House of Representatives*, 1914 Session, Vol. 3, H-I (New Zealand) AtoJsOnline, http://atojs.natlib.govt.nz (accessed 13 December 2013).

3 'The Governor of New Zealand to the Secretary of State of the Colonies (Received Colonial Office 4.40 p.m. 31 July 1914)', TNA: ADM 137/1. There is

a copy also in *Papers Presented to Parliament, Vol. V, Session 1914–17*, 1437.

4   Admiralty to Colonial Office, and Emmott to Liverpool, 1 August 1914, TNA: ADM 137/1/8d, 8e, 8g, and O. Murray to Emmott, 1 August 1914, TNA: ADM 137/7/32.

5   The Secretary of State for the Colonies to the Governor of New Zealand (sent 2.25 p.m., 1 August 1914), TNA: ADM 137/1/10. See also *Papers Presented to Parliament, Vol. V, Session 1914–17*, 1437.

6   Telegram. The Governor of New Zealand to the Secretary of State for the Colonies (Received Colonial Office 4.24 p.m., 1 August 1914), TNA: ADM 137/1/12, and see *Papers Presented to Parliament, Vol. V, Session 1914–17*, 1437. See also New Zealand, *Parliamentary Debates (Hansard)*, Vol. 169, 175 (31 July 1914), quoted in *The Times Documentary History of the War, Vol. X, Overseas — Part 2* (London, 1919), 190.

7   Telegram. The Governor of New Zealand to the Secretary of State for the Colonies (Received Colonial Office 2.30 p.m. 2 August 1914), TNA: ADM 137/1/13.

8   J. R. W. Robinson, Resident Clerk, Colonial Office, to Resident Clerk, Admiralty [2 August 1914], TNA: ADM 137/1/13.

9   Telegram. The Secretary of State for the Colonies to the Governor of New Zealand (Sent 7.55 p.m. 2 August 1914), TNA: ADM 137/1/15.

10 A. C. Leveson to C. O. S. [F. D. Sturdee], 2 August 1914, TNA: ADM 137/1/13.

11 Battenberg note, dated 2 August 1914 and Sturdee to Battenberg, 2 August 1914, TNA: ADM 137/1/14. For his part, Churchill was cautious. He asked three of his trusted advisers, Sir Henry Jackson, Colonel Aston, and Major Ollivant to investigate and 'report further as possible,' adding that the War Office 'must be consulted'. Churchill note, TNA: ADM 137/1/14. Emphasis added.

12 Ronald Haycock, *Sam Hughes: the public career of a controversial Canadian, 1885–1916* (Canadian War Museum, 1986), 177–80.

13 Paraphrase of Telegram from Gov. General Canada (Received 9.00 a.m., 2 August 1914), TNA: ADM 137/3/8 and 11d, also in *Papers Presented to Parliament, Vol. V, Session 1914–17*, 1431.

14 John Anderson to the Secretary, the Admiralty, 2 August 1914, TNA: ADM 137/3/11c.

15 A. C. Leveson to C. O. S., 2 August 1914, and Sturdee to Battenberg, 2 August 1914, marked 'First Lord concurs', TNA: ADM 137/3/10.

16 H. Maitland Kersey to The Secretary, Admiralty, 3 August 1914, TNA: ADM 137/3/15.

17 Draft telegram 'from S[ecretary] of S[tate], undated, TNA: ADM 137/3/11e.

18 Sir John Anderson to Secretary, War Office, 4 August 1914, TNA: ADM 137/3/114.

19 Telegram. The Secretary of State for the Colonies to the Governor-General of the Dominion of Canada. (Sent 7.35 p.m. 3 August 1914), TNA: ADM 137/3/13.

Chapter 8 *A looming love-of-Empire auction*

1 *Horsham Times*, 4 August 1914.

2 'Senator Millen's Views', *Sydney Morning Herald*, 1 August 1914.

3 'The European Crisis', editorial, *Daily Telegraph*, 27 July 1914.

4 'How War Would Affect Australia', *Daily Telegraph*, 27 July 1914.

5 Editorial, *The Age*, 27 July 1914.

6 Editorial, *The Age*, 30 July 1914.

7 See the editorials of the week, 'Is It War?', 'Austria and Servia', 'Great Britain and the Powers', 'Effects of War', 'War and State Finance', 'Slav and Teuton', *Sydney Morning Herald*, 27, 28, 29, 30, 31 July and 1 August 1914 respectively.

8 'Great Powers', *Sydney Morning Herald*, 28 July 1914.

9 'Tuesday, July 28, 1914', *The Argus*, 28 July 1914.

10 In Adelaide on Thursday 30 July, Fisher told a gathering of the Labor faithful organised by the Women's Social League that he supported Compulsory Military Training and that 'National Defence should not be a party matter'. Later he spoke in the Exhibition Buildings, but confined his remarks to domestic issues. See *Townsville Daily Bulletin*, 5 August 1914.

11 'Mr Fisher at Colac', *The Age*, 1 August 1914 and 'Federal Elections', *The Colac Herald*, 3 August 1914.

12 'Australia's Patriotism', *The Argus*, 1 August 1914, 'Crisis of Our Fate', *The Argus*, 3 August 1914, and 'Federal Elections', *The Colac Herald*, 3 August 1914. This last report noted that Fisher said he 'prayed that Sir Edward Grey would be able to induce the European powers to come together and discuss the matter before it went too far. If after everything had been done that human effort could do and to which honor would approve, he could say for himself and his party that if the honor of the mother country was involved, its national existence endangered, they would be by her side in time of stress and in time of danger. (Applause). War was deplorable. He hoped it would be limited, but if war followed they would stand by their own and help the mother land to their last man, and their last shilling. (Loud applause.)' See also the version given in Bean, *Official History. Vol. I: the story of Anzac*, 16. Significantly, Bean changes 'stand behind *our own*' to 'stand behind *the mother country*'.

13 See *Commonwealth Parliamentary Debates,* House of Representatives, Vol. 10, 13516 (11 June 1902). Deakin replied that the issue was not on the agenda of the coming conference.

14 'Position in Australia', *Brisbane Courier,* 3 August 1914, and 'Mr Cook and the War', *Daily Telegraph,* 1 August 1914. See also Bean, *Story of Anzac,* 16–17.

15 'The Federal Campaign: Mr Cook at Horsham', *The Age,* 1 August 1914.

16 'The Federal Campaign: Mr Cook at Horsham', *The Age,* 1 August 1914.

17 'The Australian National Parliament', *The Worker* (Brisbane), 2 July 1914.

18 'Great Citizen Anti-Home Rule Rally', *The Advertiser* [Adelaide], 11 July 1914, and 'No Surrender!', *The Advertiser* [Adelaide], 17 July 1914, and see 'Ulster's Protest: local petition', *Sydney Morning Herald,* 3 July 1914.

19 Denman to Munro Ferguson, 11 May 1914, quoted in Cunneen, *King's Men,* 112.

20 See Day, *Fisher,* 168–76, 243–44, 290.

21 'The Labour Standpoint', *Warwick Examiner,* 3 August 1914.

22 'The Dominions: anxiety in Canada: to assist Great Britain', *Sydney Morning Herald,* 1 August 1914. For other examples, see 'Suggested Offer of Force' and 'Canadian Loyalty', *The Argus,* 1 August 1914, and 'New Zealand's Decision: offers an expeditionary force', *Mercury,* 1 August 1914.

23 'New Zealand Enthusiasm: proposed expeditionary force', *Sydney Morning Herald,* 1 August 1914. Significantly, King George's thanks to Canada and New Zealand, conveyed by the Colonial Secretary, was also reported in the Australian press, but not until Tuesday 4 August. See 'King's Appreciation', *Sydney Morning Herald,* 4 August 1914.

24 'New Zealand Always First', *Auckland Star,* 3 August 1914.

Chapter 9 *The view from 'Yaralla'*

1 Munro Ferguson to Harcourt, 6 July 1914, MS Harcourt 479.

2 Munro Ferguson to Harcourt, 21 June 1914, MS Harcourt 479.

3 'Personal: Vice-Regal', *Sydney Morning Herald,* 20 July 1914.

4 See the narrative history prepared in White to A. W. Bazeley, 20 April 1934, in the file entitled 'Adoption of the Precautionary Stage of the Australian Defence Scheme', AWM224, MSS636, and Scott, *Australia During the War,* 7.

5 Telegram from the Governor-General of the Commonwealth of Australia (at Sydney) to the Secretary of State for the Colonies (Received Colonial Office 11.01. a.m. 31 July 1914), TNA: ADM 137/7/29, and Munro Ferguson to Harcourt, 31 July 1914 (marked as 'sent 2.00 p.m.'), in White to A. W. Bazeley, 20 April 1934, in the file entitled 'Adoption of the Precautionary Stage of the Australian Defence Scheme', AWM224, MSS636.

6 'Vice-Regal Garden Party', *Sydney Morning Herald*, 1 August 1914.

7 'Vice-Regal Garden Party', *Sydney Morning Herald*, 1 August 1914, and 'Vice-Regal Garden Party at "Yaralla"' and accompanying photograph, *Daily Telegraph*, 1 August 1914.

8 *Parliamentary Debates*, Commons, 5th series, Vol. 65, 1574 (30 July 1914).

9 *Parliamentary Debates*, Commons, 5th series, Vol. 65, 1787 (31 July 1914).

10 For example, 'The War Fever: Russia's determination', *Sydney Morning Herald*, 1 August 1914.

11 'Prime Minister in Ballarat', *Ballarat Courier*, 31 July 1914.

12 See original draft, with amendments, Munro Ferguson to Cook, 31 July 1914, handwritten copy in Ferguson's handwriting, in file entitled 'War 1914. Notifications (Outbreak)', NAA: A11803, 1914/89/1, Part 1. Emphasis added.

13 Cunneen, *King's Men*, 117.

14 Munro Ferguson to Joseph Cook, 31 July 1914, Novar Papers, MS 696/4003 (National Library, Canberra).

15 Scott, *Australia During the War*, 9.

16 Cook to Steward, 1 August 1914, in file entitled 'War 1914. Notifications (Outbreak)', NAA: A11803, 1914/89/1, Part 1.

17 'Telephone message received from Mr Cook, Ballarat, 5.15 p.m. 1 August 1914' and replies from Steward, one copy endorsed 6.10 p.m. and another 6.20 p.m., sending again the governor-general's request for a Cabinet meeting. Another note shows that Steward sent copies on to Shepherd in Melbourne. All in file entitled 'War 1914. Notifications (Outbreak)', NAA: A11803, 1914/89/1, Part 1.

18 Munro Ferguson to Harcourt, 25 August 1914, TNA: CO 418/123.

Chapter 10 *The view from the Customs House*

1 Munro Ferguson to Harcourt, 2 August 1914, MS Harcourt 479. There is a slightly different version, omitting the reference to 'the Opposition', in Munro Ferguson to Harcourt, 2 August 1914, Novar Papers, MS 696/589.

2 'Election Notes', *Sydney Morning Herald*, 31 July 1914.

3 'Decode of telegram received from General Manager, Cockatoo, 31 July 1914', in 'Outbreak of War August 1914 — Placing of H. M. A. Ships at Disposal of Admiralty', NAA: MP1049/1, 1914/0276.

4 C. B. B. White Diary, 30 and 31 July 1914, White Papers, MS 5172.

5 Bentley, 'Brudenell White', 134, and Bean, *Story of Anzac*, 22–23.

6 Quoted in Guy Verney, 'General Sir Brudenell White: the staff officer as commander', in Horner, ed., *The Commanders*, 29.

7 Gordon, *The Chronicles of a Gay Gordon*, 312.

8 See the measures listed as required under 'the precautionary stage' to be
   prompted by the 'Warning Telegram' (in essence, the application of the
   'Defended Ports Defence Schemes') as outlined in the 'Preface', and 'Chapter
   II', points 23 and 24, and 'Chapter IV', points 40 and 41, of the 'General
   Scheme of Defence' (1913), AWM113, MH 1/11.

9 C. B. B. White Diary, 1 August 1914, White Papers, MS 5172, and C. E.
   W. Bean to J. Treloar, 2 May 1934, and Treloar to Bean, 10 May 1934,
   AWM224, MSS636 (Australian War Memorial).

10 Munro Ferguson to Harcourt, 4 August 1914, Novar Papers, MS 696/591,
   and 'Australia's Navy: where will the vessels go?', The Advertiser, 3 August
   1914.

11 See C. E. W. Bean to J. Treloar, 2 May 1934, and Treloar to Bean, 10 May
   1934, AWM224, MSS636 and Bentley, 'Brudenell White', 143.

12 C. B. B. White Diary, 2 August 1914, White Papers, MS 5172.

13 Scott, Australia During the War, 8, 10, and Meaney, Australia and World
   Crisis, 29.

14 See 'Note by Sellheim, 2 August 1914, item 3, Series MP826/1', National
   Archives of Australia, cited by Craig Wilcox, 'Defending Australia 1914–
   1918: the other Australian army', in Peter Dennis and Jeffrey Grey, eds,
   1918: Defining Victory (Canberra, 1988) f. n. 5, and Bean, Story of Anzac, 25.

15 J. Treloar to Bean, 10 May 1934, AWM224, MSS636.

16 Munro Ferguson to Harcourt, 2 August 1914, Novar Papers, MS 696/589,
   and for a slightly different version see the letter Munro Ferguson to
   Harcourt, 2 August 1914, MS Harcourt 479.

17 C. B. B. White Diary, 2 August 1914, White Papers, MS 5172.

18 Munro Ferguson to Harcourt, 2 August 1914, Novar Papers, MS 696/589,
   and Munro Ferguson to Harcourt, 2 August 1914, MS Harcourt 479.

19 Creswell, 'Remarks by First Naval Member on Part II of the Second Naval
   Member's Report', 27 August 1913, NAA: MP1049/1, 1915/054.

20 Munro Ferguson to Harcourt, 2 August 1914, Novar Papers, MS 696/589.

21 Munro Ferguson to Harcourt, 2 August 1914, MS Harcourt 479. In Munro
   Ferguson to Harcourt, 2 August 1914, Novar Papers, MS 696/589, the key
   passage reads: 'The Cabinet meets on Monday (tomorrow) and will then
   no doubt formally transfer the "Australia" and other units of the Fleet.
   I conveyed your thanks to the Minister of Defence, from whom I had
   unofficial assurances'.

Chapter 11 'A good war-cry'

1 T. D. Chataway to E. D. Millen, 31 July 1914, NAA: B173, 1906/58 PART 2.
   I owe the reference to this document to Neville Meaney, who quotes from it

in his *Australia and the World Crisis*, 25.

2 Jennifer Ross, 'Chataway, Thomas Drinkwater (1864–1925)' in Ann Millar, Derek Drinkwater, Ann Pyle and Judy Poulos, eds, *The Biographical Dictionary of the Australian Senate, Vol. I, 1901–1929* (Melbourne, 2000), 112–14.

3 T. D. Chataway to E. D. Millen, 31 July 1914, NAA: B173, 1906/58 PART 2. W. Farmer Whyte was soon busy in this same direction. On Monday 3 August, he wrote: 'But it is quite conceivable, with the election coming on, that untold harm may be done to Labour's prospects at the poll with Mr King O'Malley and some others going about airing their views on the brotherhood of nations and crying peace where is no peace'; see 'The Election', *Sydney Morning Herald*, 3 August 1914.

4 'Defence: government policy: Labour's attitude', *Sydney Morning Herald*, 1 August 1914, and 'National Defence: Kitchener and Henderson schemes: Labor Party's destructive efforts' and 'Federal Campaign: the defence policy', *Daily Telegraph,* 1 August 1914.

5 'Council of War', *Daily Telegraph*, 3 August 1914.

6 Holman had been a prominent critic of the Boer War, but had reconciled himself to Compulsory Military Training when this became Labor policy in 1908. See H. V. Evatt, *William Holman: Australian labour leader* (Sydney, 1979), Ch. XV.

7 'State Premier's View', *Sydney Morning Herald*, 1 August 1914.

8 See John Rickard, 'Iceberg Irvine and the politics of anti-Labor', in Paul Strangio and Brian Costar, eds, *The Victorian Premiers 1856–2006* (Annandale, 2006), 119–26.

9 'Premier Attacked' and 'North Sydney Rally', *Sydney Morning Herald*, 3 August 1914.

10 'Premier Attacked' and 'North Sydney Rally', *Sydney Morning Herald*, 3 August 1914. See also Holman's dismissive rejection of the attacks on him from Ryrie and Irvine, in 'Reply to Attack', *Sydney Morning Herald*, 4 August 1914.

Chapter 12 'There'll be no war'

1 Loreburn to Harcourt, 1 August 1914, MS. Harcourt 444.

2 Catrine Clay, *King, Kaiser, Tsar: three royal cousins who led the world to war* (New York, 2006), 309; King George V Diary, 1 August 1914, quoted in Robert Lacey, '1914 — The Diary of King George V', BBC Radio 4, July 2004, also available at Imperial War Museum, Audio Recording, 20866; Grey to Buchanan, 1 August 1914, *BD*, Vol. XI, Document 384; Asquith to Venetia Stanley, 1 August 1914, in Brock, eds, *Letters to Venetia Stanley*, 140.

3 Bertie to Grey, 31 July 1914, and Goschen to Grey, 31 July 1914, *BD*, Vol. XI, Documents 382 and 383.

4 Cabinet Memorandum 1 Aug 1914, Harcourt Papers.

5 F. E. Smith to Churchill, 31 July 1914, Churchill Papers, CHAR 13/26/148, and Churchill to F. E. Smith, 1 August 1914, in Second Earl of Birkenhead, *F. E.: the life of F. E. Smith, first Earl of Birkenhead* (London, 1960), 241.

6 Harcourt to Beauchamp and Beauchamp to Harcourt, 1 August 1914, on 10 Downing Street notepaper, filed with Cabinet Memorandum 1 Aug 1914, Harcourt Papers. Emphasis in original.

7 Asquith to Venetia Stanley, 1 August 1914, in Brock, eds, *Letters to Venetia Stanley*, 140, and see Wilson, 'Britain', *Decisions for War*, 192.

8 Cabinet Memorandum 1 Aug 1914, Harcourt Papers.

9 Lichnowsky to Foreign Office [Berlin], 1 August 1914, Prince Lichnowsky, *Heading for the Abyss: reminiscences (London, 1928),* 415, and see Wilson, 'Britain', *Decisions for War*, 191–92.

10 Cabinet Memorandum 1 Aug 1914, Harcourt Papers.

11 Asquith to Venetia Stanley, 1 August 1914, in Brock, eds, *Letters to Venetia Stanley*, 140.

12 Cabinet Memorandum 1 Aug 1914, Harcourt Papers.

13 Churchill, *World Crisis*, I, 174–75.

14 Cabinet Memorandum 1 Aug 1914, Harcourt Papers.

15 See the discussion on the significance of this decision in Hazlehurst, *Politicians at War*, 86–91 and Wilson, *Policy of the Entente*, 137.

16 Howard Weinroth, 'British Radicals and the Agadir Crisis', *European Studies Review*, 3, 1 (January 1973), 39–61, John W. Coogan and Peter F. Coogan, 'The Anglo French Staff Talks, 1905–1914: who knew what and when did he know it?', *Journal of British Studies*, 24, 1 (1985), 110–31, and Martin Farr, *Reginald McKenna: financier among statesmen, 1863–1916* (New York, 2008), 207–22.

17 Grey to Bertie, 1 August 1914, *BD*, Vol. XI, Document 426.

18 Charles Trevelyan, 'C. P. T's personal record', Charles Trevelyan Papers, CPT 59.

19 Charles Trevelyan to Molly Trevelyan, 2 August 1914, Trevelyan Papers, CPT EX 106.

20 Francis Neilson, *My Life in Two Worlds* (Appleton, 1952), Vol. I, 331–32.

21 *Daily Chronicle*, reported in 'Special Morning Express', *Manchester Guardian*, 3 August 1914 and 'England's Day of Suspense', *New York Times*, 3 August 1914.

22 Editorial, *Daily Chronicle*, 3 August 1914.

23 Grey to Bertie, 1 August 1914, *BD*, Vol. XI, Document 426, but on Cambon's version of the interview see also Wilson, 'Britain', *Decisions for War*, 192–93.

24 Henry Wilson Diary, 1 August 1914, in Callwell, *Wilson*, I, 154.

Chapter 13 *The whiff of a khaki election*

1 Richard Aldington, *Death of a Hero* (London, 1929), 225–26.

2 'Prime Minister at Colac', *The Colac Herald*, 3 August 1914, 'Mr Cook at
   Colac' and 'All In It', *Daily Telegraph*, 3 August 1914, 'The Federal Campaign:
   prime minister at Colac', *The Age*, 3 August 1914, and Murdoch, *Sir Joe*, 105.

3 'Senate Elections', *Casterton News and the Merino and Sandford Record*,
   3 August 1914.

4 'Mr Fisher's Tour', *The Argus*, 3 August 1914.

5 'Mr Cook Agitated — A Disquieting Cable Message', and 'Commonwealth's
   Attitude: prime minister returns to Melbourne', *The Age*, 3 August 1914, and
   'Mr Cook Reticent: cabinet meeting', *The Advertiser*, 3 August 1914, and
   Murdoch, *Sir Joe*, 105.

6 Scott, *Australia During the War*, 8.

7 Unnamed officer's diary entries, quoted in Scott, *Australia During the
   War*, 201–2. On Cook's religious affiliation, it is noteworthy that he gave
   the address at celebrations in Sydney Town Hall to mark the thirtieth
   anniversary of Sydney's Central Methodist Mission in May 1914; see
   'Central Methodist Mission', *Sydney Morning Herald*, 12 May 1914.

8 Wilcox, *Hearths and Homes*, 75–77.

9 'Mr Cook Reticent: cabinet meeting', *The Advertiser*, 3 August 1914. A
   slightly different quotation appears in Scott, *Australia During the War*, 9,
   and see Bean, *Story of Anzac*, 26.

10 Cook, Pocket Diary for 1914, 20 July to 2 August 1914, Cook Papers, NAA:
   M3580, 6 (National Archives of Australia). Judging from the references to
   German atrocities in Belgium, it is probable that Cook filled in some of the
   latter entries retrospectively, that is, during the first days and weeks after the
   outbreak of the war, rather than during the days of crisis.

11 See Fisher's statement giving his itinerary, in 'Federal Position', *Sydney
   Morning Herald*, 10 August 1914.

12 '"No Parties": Labour consults with ministry', 'Mr Fisher Definite', *Sydney
   Morning Herald*, 3 August 1914. The *Sydney Morning Herald* interpreted the
   announcement to mean that the Federal Labor Party would 'co-operate with
   the Ministry in every possible way in the event of war occurring. They will
   facilitate supply, and assist the Government to take any measures that might
   be deemed necessary'. See also 'There Are No Parties', *Daily Telegraph*,
   3 August 1914 and 'Statement by Mr Fisher', *The Age*, 3 August 1914.

13 For example, 'Position in Australia', *Brisbane Courier*, 3 August 1914, 'Mr
   Fisher Definite', *Sydney Morning Herald*, 3 August 1914, 'Statement by

Mr Fisher', *The West Australian*, 3 August 1914, 'Statement by Mr Fisher', *Launceston Examiner*, 3 August 1914. But for Fisher's confirming that he received no communication from Fisher, see 'Federal Position', *Sydney Morning Herald*, 10 August 1914.

14 'Labour's War on War', *Labour Leader*, 6 August 1914, and 'The Workers' War on the War', *Daily Herald*, 3 August 1914. The *Manchester Guardian* reported that the Trafalgar Square demonstration was 'a vast gathering' which was larger and more impressive than the rallies mounted by the suffragettes at the height of their campaign. See 'Anti-War Demonstration in London' and 'Our London Correspondence', *Manchester Guardian*, 3 August 1914, and also 'Britain Must Be Neutral', *Daily Citizen*, 3 August 1914.

15 'A United Empire', *Sydney Morning Herald*, 3 August 1914.

16 'The Hour of Trial', editorial, *Daily Telegraph*, 3 August 1914.

17 'War in Europe', editorial, *The Advertiser* [Adelaide], 3 August 1914.

18 C. J. Lloyd, *Parliament and the Press* (Melbourne, 1988), 41.

19 Editorial, *The Age*, 3 August 1914.

20 'Russia and Germany', and 'Crisis of our Fate: Australia's call: appeal to Mr Cook and Mr Fisher', *The Argus*, 3 August 1914.

21 For example, even *The Argus* noted in its pro-interventionist editorial of 3 August that Britain's position was still undecided, and noted too the 'comparative absence of news from the United Kingdom'. Editorial, *The Argus*, 3 August 1914.

22 'The Die Cast', editorial, *The Mercury* (Hobart), 3 August 1914.

23 C. E. Montague, *Disenchantment* (London, 1922), 170.

24 'Outside "The Age" Office: enormous crowds: wild cheering and patriotic songs', *The Age*, 4 August 1914.

25 'Excitement in Sydney', and 'Socialists' Protest', *Sydney Morning Herald*, 3 August 1914. On the IWW's response to the war, see Bollard, *Shadow of Gallipoli*, 32–36.

26 See 'Anti-War Resolution', *Sydney Morning Herald*, 5 August 1914.

27 M. Saunders and R. Summy, *The Australian Peace Movement: a short history* (Canberra, 1986), Ann-Mari Jordens, 'Against the Tide: the growth and decline of a liberal anti-war movement in Australia', 1905–1918', *Historical Studies*, 22, 88 (April 1987), 373–94, Ann-Mari Jordens, 'Anti-War Organisations in a Society at War, 1914–1918', *Journal of Australian Studies*, 14, 26 (1990), 78–93, and A. Gilbert and Ann-Mari Jordens, 'Traditions of Dissent', in M. McKernan and M. Browne, eds, *Australia: two centuries of war and peace* (Canberra,1988).

28 Barrett, *Falling In*, Chs. 3–5, and J. M. Main, *Conscription: the Australian debate, 1901–1970* (Melbourne, 1970).

29 For example, 'War and Politics', editorial, *Worker* [Brisbane], 6 August 1914.

The editor, Charles Seymour, noted that 'our army and navy are primarily for defence, and not for aggressive purposes.'

30 See editorial 'War – What For', *International Socialist* [Sydney] 8 August 1914.

31 See the review of reactions in the socialist parties and trade unions in Ian Turner, *Industrial Labour and Politics: the dynamics of the Labour movement in eastern Australia, 1900–1921* (Sydney, 1979), 69–70.

32 Bean, *Story of Anzac*, 15–17.

33 The *Sydney Morning Herald* reported on the bowling match and gave none of Carruthers' address. See 'Bowling: the season's laurels', *Sydney Morning Herald*, 5 August 1914. See also 'War News', *Forbes Advocate*, 4 August 1914, 'Sir J. Carruthers' Noble Sentiments', *Northern Star*, 5 August 1914, and 'To the Last Ditch', *Clarence and Richmond Examiner*, 6 August 1914.

34 See the more general critique of the conventional view that the Australian people greeted war enthusiastically in 1914, in Grant Mansfield, '"Unbounded Enthusiasm": Australian historians and the outbreak of war', *Australian Journal of Politics and History*, 53, 3 (2007), 360–74.

Chapter 14 Radical angst

1 Cabinet Memorandum, 2 August 1914, Harcourt Papers.

2 Asquith to Pamela McKenna, 1 August 1915, McKenna Papers, MCKN 9/3 (Churchill Archives Centre).

3 O. H. L. Baynes to Harcourt, 2 August 1914, filed with Cabinet Memorandum, 2 August 1914, Harcourt Papers.

4 Cabinet Memorandum, 2 August 1914, Harcourt Papers.

5 Note by Runciman on his official summons (dated Saturday 1 August) to the cabinet of Sunday morning 2 August 1914, Runciman Papers, WR 135/92 (University of Newcastle).

6 Herbert Samuel to Beatrice Samuel, 31 July 1914, Samuel Papers, SAM/A/157.

7 News that a German force had entered Luxembourg was first received in London at 11.45 a.m. on Sunday. See F. Villiers to Grey, 2 August 1914, *BD*, Vol. XI, Document 465.

8 Cabinet Memorandum, 2 August 1914, Harcourt Papers. Emphasis in original.

9 Cabinet Memorandum, 2 August 1914, Harcourt Papers. Emphasis in original.

10 J. A. Pease Diary, 2 August 1914, in Wilson, 'The cabinet Diary of J. A. Pease', [46] 8–[47] 9, and Asquith to Venetia Stanley, 2 August 1914, in Brock, eds, *Letters to Venetia Stanley*, 146.

11 Runciman's Cabinet Memorandum, 2 August 1914, Runciman Papers, WR 135.

12 Herbert Samuel to Beatrice Samuel, 2 August 1914, Samuel Papers, SAM/A/157.

13 Cabinet Memorandum, 2 August 1914, Harcourt Papers.

14 Herbert Samuel to Beatrice Samuel, 2 August 1914, Samuel Papers, SAM/A/157.

15 Bonar Law to Asquith, 2. August 1914, signed, on Bonar Law's personal notepaper of 'Pembroke Lodge, Edwardes Square', LG/C/6/11/20, Lloyd George Papers (Parliamentary Archives).

16 Lucy Masterman, *Masterman*, 265.

17 Runciman's Cabinet Memorandum, 2 August 1914, Runciman Papers, WR 135. Grey also says that the letter was read out at the morning cabinet. See Grey, *Twenty-Five Years*, II, 11. Lindsay argues, on the strength of Leo Maxse's testimony, that the Conservatives' letter reached Asquith 'shortly after midday' on 2 August. See Lindsay, 'Failure of Liberal Opposition', 118–19, and fn. 10.

18 Cabinet Memorandum, 2 August 1914, Harcourt Papers.

19 In Leo Maxse, 'Retrospect and Reminiscence', *National Review* (August, 1918), 726–52, Maxse argued that the Conservatives' pressure had made all the difference. Asquith claimed not to remember the details of the Conservatives' letter, nor whether he read had it to the cabinet. See Asquith to Crewe, 11 August 1918, MS. Asquith 46 (Bodleian Library) and Asquith to Lewis Harcourt, 4 July 1919, MS. Harcourt 421.

20 J. O. P. Bland, 'British Liberalism and the War', *The Atlantic Monthly*, 114, 5 (November 1914), 673.

21 Chirol to Hardinge, 4 August 1914, Hardinge Papers, 93 Part I.

22 Asquith to Venetia Stanley, 2 August 1914, in Brock, eds, *Letters to Venetia Stanley*, 146.

23 Samuel, answer to question 6, in untitled document, in reply to Harold Temperley's questionnaire, 1928, Spender Papers, Add. MS. 46386.

24 Herbert Samuel to Beatrice Samuel, 2 August 1914, Samuel Papers, SAM/A/157.

25 Churchill to Lloyd George, undated cabinet note, in Randolph. S. Churchill, *Winston S. Churchill: companion volume II, Part 3, 1911–1914* (Boston, 1969), 1997.

26 Herbert Samuel to Beatrice Samuel, 2 August 1914, Samuel Papers, SAM/A/157.

27 Herbert Samuel to Beatrice Samuel, 2 August 1914, Samuel Papers, SAM/A/157.

28 Cabinet Memorandum, 2 August 1914, Harcourt Papers. Emphasis in original.

29 See Samuel, untitled document in reply to Temperley, 1928, Spender Papers, Add. MS. 46386. Crewe suggests that he proposed it. See Crewe, 'Replies to Questions', 8 May 1929, in Spender Papers, Add. MS. 46386.

30 Reproduced in Grey to Bertie, 2 August 1914, *BD*, Vol. XI, Document 487.

31 Hobhouse Diary, August [undated] 1914, in Hobhouse, *Inside Asquith's Cabinet*, 180.

32 Herbert Samuel to Beatrice Samuel, 2 August 1914, Samuel Papers, SAM/A/157.

33 Cabinet Memorandum, 2 August 1914, Harcourt Papers.

34 Untitled, undated (but from internal evidence 3 August 1914) private memorandum, on 13 Belgrave Square notepaper, filed with Beauchamp's resignation letter to Asquith 3 August 1914, Beauchamp Papers.

35 Morley, *Memorandum*, 12.

36 Herbert Samuel to Beatrice Samuel, 2 August 1914, Samuel Papers, SAM/A/157.

37 Pease to J. B. Hodgkin, 4 August 1914, copy, with Pease to Trevelyan, 5 August 1914, Trevelyan Papers, CPT 59.

38 Herbert Samuel to Beatrice Samuel, 2 August 1914, Samuel Papers, SAM/A/157.

39 Reproduced in Grey to Bertie, 2 August 1914, *BD*, Vol. XI, Document 487.

40 Grey to Bertie, 2 August 1914, *BD*, Vol. XI, Document 487.

41 Pease Diary, 2 August 1914, in Wilson, 'The cabinet Diary of J. A. Pease', [46] 8–[47] 9.

42 Morley, *Memorandum*, 14–15.

43 Morley, *Memorandum*, 15.

44 Cabinet Memorandum, 2 August 1914, Harcourt Papers. Emphasis in original.

45 Herbert Samuel to Beatrice Samuel, 2 August 1914, Samuel Papers, SAM/A/157.

46 Cabinet Memorandum, 2 August 1914, Harcourt Papers. Emphasis in original.

47 Morley, *Memorandum*, 15.

48 Untitled, undated (but from internal evidence 3 August 1914) private memorandum, on 13 Belgrave Square notepaper, filed with Beauchamp's resignation letter to Asquith 3 August 1914, Beauchamp Papers.

49 Cabinet Memorandum, 2 August 1914, Harcourt Papers.

50 Cabinet Memorandum, 2 August 1914, Harcourt Papers.

51 See documents unfortunately not stamped with the time of receipt, Consul Le Gallais to Grey, 2 August 1914, *BD*, Vol. XI, Document 468, and an undated 'Communication from German Embassy', received 2 August 1914, Document 472.

52 Cabinet Memorandum, 2 August 1914, Harcourt Papers.

53 See the notation at Blunt Diary, 5 August 1914, Wilfrid Scawen Blunt Papers, MS 13-1975 (Fitzwilliam Museum, Cambridge).

54 Herbert Samuel to Beatrice Samuel, 2 August 1914, Samuel Papers, SAM/A/157.

55 Untitled, undated (but from internal evidence 3 August 1914) private memorandum, on 13 Belgrave Square notepaper, filed with Beauchamp's resignation letter to Asquith 3 August 1914, Beauchamp Papers.

56 Herbert Samuel to Beatrice Samuel, 2 August 1914, Samuel Papers, SAM/A/157.

57 Simon to Burns, and Burns to Simon, 2 August 1914, MS. Simon 50, Simon Papers, emphasis in original, and see David Dutton, *Simon: a political biography of Sir John Simon* (London, 1992), 29.

58 Untitled notes on 10 Downing Street card, Beauchamp Papers. Emphasis in original.

59 Cabinet Memorandum, 2 August 1914, Harcourt Papers, and Untitled, undated (but from internal evidence 3 August 1914) private memorandum, on 13 Belgrave Square notepaper, filed with Beauchamp's resignation letter to Asquith 3 August 1914, Beauchamp Papers.

60 Burns to Asquith, 2 August 1914 [handwritten copy], Burns Papers, Add. MSS. 46282/158.

61 Asquith to Venetia Stanley, 3 August 1914, Brock, eds, *Letters to Venetia Stanley*, 148.

62 Simon to Asquith, 2 August 1914, in a journal marked 'Diary #5', MS. Simon 2, Simon Papers, and see Dutton, *Simon*, 30.

63 Morley, *Memorandum*, 21.

64 Morley to Asquith, 3 August 1914, in Morley, *Memorandum*, 22.

65 Untitled, undated (but from internal evidence 3 August 1914) private memorandum, on 13 Belgrave Square notepaper, filed with Beauchamp's resignation letter to Asquith 3 August 1914, Beauchamp Papers.

66 Untitled, undated private memorandum (3 August 1914), Beauchamp Papers.

67 Beauchamp to Asquith, 3 August 1914, Beauchamp Papers. It is noteworthy that this letter referred to Beauchamp's desire to 'confirm' his resignation, so, in common with Morley, Beauchamp must have given Asquith some indication of his intention to resign on the Sunday.

68 Herbert Samuel to Beatrice Samuel, 2 August 1914, Samuel Papers, SAM/A/157.

69 Cabinet Memorandum, 3 August 1914, Harcourt Papers. Sir David de Villiers Graaff was appointed High Commissioner for South Africa in early August 1914.

70 Cabinet Memorandum, 2 August 1914, Harcourt Papers.

71 See Prime Minister Massey in the New Zealand Parliament, 31 July 1914, quoted in Telegram of The Governor of New Zealand to the Secretary of State for the Colonies (Received Colonial Office 4.24 p.m., 1 August 1914); 'Paraphrase of Telegram from Gov. General Canada (Received 9.00 a.m., 2 August 1914), TNA: ADM 137/3/8.

72 For example, 'Dominion Rally', and 'On the Brink of War', *The Times*, 31 July 1914, 'Awaiting Britain's Call', *The Scotsman*, 1 August 1914, 'The Empire Ready: Canadian expeditionary force', and 'Offer of Men from New Zealand', *The Times*, 1 August 1914, 'Australia: help for the motherland: to our last man and our last shilling', *The Scotsman*, 3 August 1914, and 'The Empire and the War', editorial, *The Times*, 3 August 1914.

Chapter 15 Australia jumps the gun

1 Munro-Ferguson to Harcourt, 3 August 1914 (marked 'Paraphrase', and received at Colonial Office 11.28 a.m. on 4 August 1914.), TNA: CO 418/123/143. When exactly the telegram was sent is not clear. The telegram is also quoted twice in Scott, *Australia During the War*, 13 and 207, as proof of the enthusiasm of the people. Scott says the original cable was directed to the King.

2 'The Governor-General Leaves for Melbourne', *Sydney Morning Herald*, 3 August 1914.

3 'Australia's Position', *Brisbane Courier*, 3 August 1914.

4 The sources disagree on the ministers who attended this all-important cabinet meeting. The reporter for *The Argus*, who was at the Commonwealth Offices in Melbourne, listed only four ministers as attending, Cook, Millen, Irvine and McColl. See 'Governor-General Arrives: defence minister accompanies: meeting of cabinet', *The Argus*, 4 August 1914. *The Advertiser* [Adelaide] also reported quite precisely that only four ministers attended: 'Several of the ministers, however, are in other states, and the result was that only the two who had come from Sydney with the Prime Minister and Mr McColl constituted the meeting'. See 'Australia's Navy to be under British Control: cabinet decision', *The Advertiser* [Adelaide], 4 August 1914. In contrast, Ernest Scott listed five ministers, adding J. S. Clemons; see Scott, *Australia During the War*, 10. But the *Launceston Examiner* listed Clemons as addressing election meetings in Tasmania throughout the week, including Monday 3 August. See 'Today's Meetings', 'Campaign Notes', and 'Electoral' advertisement, *Launceston Examiner*, 3, 4 and 6 August 1914. Meaney also lists five ministers, but nominates Cook, Millen, Irvine, Clemons and Littleton Groom as attending, while omitting McColl. See Meaney, *Australia and World*

Crisis, 30. Meaney would appear to be mistaken. The *Brisbane Courier* confirms that Littleton Groom spoke at an election meeting at Wynnum in Queensland on the evening of 3 August. See 'Interesting Address by Hon. L. E. Groom,' *Brisbane Courier*, 4 August 1914. In any case, it serves as an unremarkable reminder of the nature of Australian society at the time to note that none of the four ministers who attended this cabinet, Cook, Millen, Irvine and McColl, was born in Australia. All were born in Britain or Ireland.

5 'Federal Affairs', *The Advertiser* [Adelaide], 30 July 1914, 'Keep Out Of Wars', *The Advertiser* [Adelaide], 1 August 1914. Glynn told reporters on Friday 31 July: 'We in Australia with the rest of the world, will, I am sure, give expression to the hope that the great nations concerned will not go to war and that the historic British calmness and temperateness which has been displayed will triumph. One feels that in this case all the strength and diplomacy of the Imperial Government are necessary and that the nations concerned will be actuated by the highest sense recently displayed, which was not possible in former years. Anyone who has read the inside history of the war in the Balkans will be glad enough to keep out of wars now'.

6 'Cabinet Meeting Called', and 'Australia: full precautions', *Sydney Morning Herald*, 3 August 1914, 'Prime Minister's Visit Postponed', *The Register* (Adelaide), 3 August 1914.

7 For Fisher's statement affirming this, see 'Federal Position', *Sydney Morning Herald*, 10 August 1914. Only after the cable was sent to London was Fisher contacted by telephone at Benalla. Bipartisan gestures were possible at a state level. Two days later, the state Labor Government of Western Australia did exactly that, as an indication of bipartisanship, shared responsibility, and the united front to be adopted in wartime; see *West Australian*, 6 August 1914, cited by Meaney, *Australia and World Crisis*, 25, f.n. 17.

8 Munro Ferguson to Joseph Cook, 31 July 1914, in 'War 1914. Notifications (Outbreak)', NAA: A11803, 1914/89/1, Part 1.

9 See Bean's typescript based on recollections, NAA: A6006, 1914/8/3, and C. B. B. White Diary, 3 August 1914, White Papers, MS 5172. 'Federal Preparations. Council Meeting', *Sydney Morning Herald*, 4 August 1914, and 'Australia Joins', *The Argus*, 4 August 1914. There were three military experts present, Major White, Colonel Victor Sellheim, the adjutant-general, and George L. Macandie, Secretary to the Naval Board (who had been appointed to the position in April 1914).

10 Wilcox, 'Edwardian Transformation', 273.

11 See 'Origin of AIF', NAA: A6006, 1914/8/23.

12 Munro Ferguson to Harcourt, 8 August 1914, TNA: CO 418/123.

13 'Governor-General Arrives', *The Argus*, 4 August 1914.

14 C. B. B. White Diary, 3 August 1914, White Papers, MS 5172.

15 This is the version given in the official record. The governor-general [of Australia] to the secretary of state [Harcourt] (received 6.20 p.m., 3 August 1914), in The Parliament of the Commonwealth of Australia, *European War: correspondence regarding the naval and military assistance afforded to His Majesty's government by His Majesty's oversea dominions*, No. 10 (printed 11 November 1914), in The Parliament of the Commonwealth of Australia, *Papers Presented to Parliament, Vol. V, Session 1914–17*, 1434. The official histories give slightly different versions; see Bean, *Story of Anzac*, 28–29, and Scott, *Official History. Vol XI: Australia during the war*, 11. Scott omits the phrase 'when desired'.

16 'Australia Joins', and 'Governor-General Arrives', *The Argus*, 4 August 1914.

17 'Australia Joins', *The Argus*, 4 August 1914.

18 Quoted by Scott, *Australia During the War*, 11.

19 Munro-Ferguson to Harcourt, 4 August 1914 (marked as received at Colonial Office 11.28 a.m. on 4 August 1914.), TNA: CO 418/123/143. When exactly the telegram was sent is not clear. The telegram is also quoted in Scott, *Australia During the War*, 13.

20 Foreign Office Statement, issued 12.15 a.m., 5 August 1914, reproduced in 'War Declared', *The Times*, 5 August 1914 and 'Why There is War', *Daily Mirror*, 5 August 1914. See also 'A State of War', in Supplement to *The London Gazette*, 4 August 1914 (No. 28861).

21 Villiers to Grey, 3 August 1914, reporting information from the French Embassy in Brussels, *BD.*, Vol. XI, Document 521 (received at 10.55 a.m.). In response to this Grey made a request that 'full facts' be sought from the Belgian government itself. See Grey to Villiers, 3 August 1914 (despatched at 12.45 p.m.), *BD.*, Vol. XI, Document 525. Two earlier documents in the series, reporting the German ultimatum to Belgium, Documents 514 and 515, give no time of receipt in London.

22 For example, see 'London Opinion', *Sydney Morning Herald*, 1 August 1914, giving a summary of editorial opinions from the London press of 31 July, and noting the opposition to intervention from the *Daily News* and the *Daily Graphic*. See also 'Britain's Position: peace or war', *Sydney Morning Herald*, 1 August 1914, noting letters from prominent figures against intervention in the British press.

23 Editorial, *The Age*, 3 August 1914.

24 'Lord Lamington and the European Crisis', *The Scotsman*, 31 July 1914. See also a second letter from Lamington, 'England and the Crisis: why we should not be drawn in', *Daily News*, 3 August 1914.

25 See for example summaries of this letter in 'Britain's Position: peace or war', *Sydney Morning Herald*, 1 August 1914, 'Our Treaty Obligations: discussed

in London', *The Argus*, 1 August 1914, 'What Will England Do?', *The Advertiser*, 1 August 1914, 'Cables from London', *Brisbane Courier*, 1 August 1914, 'Great Britain's Duty', *The Mercury*, 1 August 1914, 'Lord Lamington's Letter', *Kalgoorlie Miner*, 1 August 1914, and 'Workers for Peace', *Evening News*, 1 August 1914.

26 See 'Summary', *Sydney Morning Herald*, 3 August 1914, 'Russia and Germany: war declared on Saturday', *The Argus*, 3 August 1914, 'Armageddon', *The Advertiser* (Adelaide), 3 August 1914.

27 For example, 'War Spreading: what will Britain do?', and 'Newspaper Opinions', *Daily Telegraph*, 4 August 1914.

28 'Tuesday August 4, 1914', editorial, and 'Australia Joins', *The Argus*, 4 August 1914, and see 'Australia's Offer: 20,000 men. An expeditionary force', *Sydney Morning Herald*, 4 August 1914 and 'Britain's Position', editorial, *Sydney Morning Herald*, 5 August 1914, and 'Bonds of Empire', *The Advertiser* (Adelaide), 5 August 1914.

29 'Duty's Call', editorial, *Daily Telegraph*, 4 August 1914.

30 Editorial, *The Age*, 4 August 1914.

31 'Public Opinion and the Crisis', *The Times*, 3 August 1914. See the reproduction of Wilson's letter in 'Protest by British Neutrality Committee', *The Age*, 4 August 1914, and 'Newspaper Opinions', Sydney Morning Herald, 4 August 1914. It appeared in a score of other newspapers.

32 'We Stand United — Speech by Mr Fisher', *The Argus*, 4 August 1914.

33 See Fisher's statement, in 'Federal Position', *Sydney Morning Herald*, 10 August 1914.

34 'International Court', *Ballarat Courier*, 4 August 1914.

35 See 'Paris Tragedy', *Sydney Morning Herald*, 3 August 1914.

36 'Political Parties United', *The Advertiser*, 3 August 1914.

37 'United Australia: Mr Hughes and the war', *Daily Telegraph*, 3 August 1914 and 'All for the State', *Sydney Morning Herald*, 3 August 1914, and 'Statement by Mr. W. M. Hughes', *The Age*, 3 August 1914.

38 'The State Premier: expressions of loyalty', *The Age*, 3 August 1914. See also 'Party Politics and the War', editorial, *Daily Telegraph*, 5 August 1914.

39 Ex-senator J. J. Long, quoted in a speech at Launceston on Monday 3 August, in 'To the Last Man and Shilling', *The Argus*, 4 August 1914.

40 'Bourke: Mr Anstey's candidature', *The Argus*, 4 August 1914.

41 'Federal Politics: Mr A. Fisher at Wangaratta', *Wangaratta Chronicle*, 5 August 1914. Compare the account in 'Mr. Fisher on Finance', in *The Argus*, 5 August 1914. See also Meaney, *Australia and World Crisis*, 12. Meaney, misled by the report of Fisher's speech in *The Argus*, mistakenly suggests this speech was 'a far cry' from the spirit of 'last man, last shilling'; the *Wangaratta Chronicle* report shows he used that phrase twice. *The Argus*

report shows that, in the context of taking pride in the creation of the separate fleet unit, Fisher said: 'His idea of patriotism was to first provide for our own defence, and then, if there was anything to spare, offer it as a tribute to the mother country. Australians now had the opportunity for patriotism of this kind'. *The Argus*, no friend of Labor, omitted Fisher's two references to his willingness to offer Britain aid 'to the last man and to the last shilling'.

42 'To Face The War', *Daily Telegraph*, 5 August 1914.

Chapter 16 *The Sir Edward Grey show*

1 Francis Hirst, untitled notes, 3 August 1914, on notepaper of 'The Athenaeum, Pall Mall', taken in the gallery of the House of Commons during Grey's speech, Hirst Papers (Bodleian Library).

2 Schoen, the German ambassador in Paris, handed his ultimatum over to Viviani, French premier and foreign minister, at 7.00 p.m. on Friday 31 July; Pourtalès, the German ambassador in St Petersburg, handed his ultimatum over to Sazonov at about midnight on Friday 31 July. Bernadotte Schmitt, *The Coming of the War, 1914* (New York, 1966), II, 267–68, S. B. Fay, *The Origins of the World War* (Toronto, 1966), II, 528, and Frederick L. Schuman, *War and Diplomacy in the French Republic: an inquiry into political motivations and the control of foreign policy* (New York, 1969), 236–37.

3 Herwig, *The Marne, 1914: the opening of World War I and the battle that changed the world (New York, 2009),* 14, and Luigi Albertini, *The Origins of the War of 1914, Vol. III* (New York, 2005), 102–3.

4 Albertini, *Origins of the War*, III, 183.

5 Schmitt, *Coming of the War*, II, 374.

6 'A Fateful Sitting of the Commons', *Manchester Guardian*, 4 August 1914.

7 'A Memorable Day in the Commons', *The Times*, 4 August 1914.

8 'The Proceedings in Parliament', *The Times*, 5 August 1914.

9 *Parliamentary Debates*, Commons, 5th series, Vol. 28, 1467–84 (24 July 1911).

10 Leo Amery Diary, 1–4 August 1914, in John Barnes and David Nicholson, eds, *The Leo Amery Diaries: Vol. One: 1896–1929* (London, 1980), 103–7, and the editors' explanatory footnote regarding a 'pogrom'. See also Henry Wilson Diary, 31 July 1914, in Callwell, *Wilson*, I, 152–53, John Charmley, *Lord Lloyd and the Decline of the British Empire* (London, 1987), 33–34, and Chamberlain, 'Memorandum', in Austen Chamberlain, *Down the Years* (Edinburgh, 1935), 94–95.

11 'A Fateful Sitting of the Commons', *Manchester Guardian*, 4 August 1914.

12 'The Nerves of Parliament', *Manchester Guardian*, 4 August 1914.

13 Grey's speech can be found in *Parliamentary Debates*, 5th series, Commons, Vol. 65, 1809–27 (3 August 1914).

14 Coogan, 'The Anglo–French Staff Talks', 110–31.

15 *Parliamentary Debates*, Commons, 5th series, Vol. 65, 1815 (3 August 1914).

16 *Parliamentary Debates*, Commons, 5th series, Vol. 65, 1816 (3 August 1914). This was a point familiar in conversation with Grey's friend, J. A. Spender. See Spender, *Life, Journalism and Politics* (London, 1927), II, 12.

17 The German offer was made by Lichnowsky in the morning and confirmed in the afternoon by Herr von Wesendonk, Secretary at the Embassy. See Lichnowsky to the Foreign Office [Berlin], 3 August 1914, Lichnowsky, *Heading for the Abyss*, 423–24 and Communication from the German Embassy, 3 August 1914, *BD*, Vol. XI, Document 531. The German offer, noting that Britain's neutrality 'for the time being' was a condition, was formally released to the press in the morning of 3 August by Baron von Kühlmann, Councillor of the German Embassy: 'Germany would be disposed to give an undertaking that she will not attack France by sea in the North, or make any warlike use of the coast of Belgium or Holland, if it appeared that Great Britain would make this undertaking on condition of her neutrality for the time being'. See 'Germany's Offer', *Westminster Gazette* [late city extra edition], 3 August 1914.

18 *Parliamentary Debates*, Commons, 5th series, Vol. 65, 1818 (3 August 1914).

19 See the terms of the treaty, *Parliamentary Debates*, Commons, 3rd series, Vol. 203, 1776 (10 August 1870).

20 Asquith to the King, 30 July 1914, reproduced in Spender, *Life of Asquith*, II, 81.

21 The original reference is *Parliamentary Debates*, Commons, 3rd series, Vol. 203, 1787 (10 August 1870). *Parliamentary Debates*, Commons, 5th series, Vol. 65, 1819 (3 August 1914).

22 Goschen to Grey, 29 July 1914, *BD*, Vol. XI, Document 293. For varying assessments of the motives behind the German approach, see Fischer, *War of Illusions*, 492–4, Konrad Jarausch, *The Enigmatic Chancellor: Bethmann Hollweg and the hubris of Imperial Germany* (New Haven, 1973), 169–170, and Annika Mombauer, *Helmuth von Moltke and the Origins of the First World War* (New York, 2001), 203.

23 Grey to Goschen, 1 August 1914, *BD*, Vol. XI, Document 448.

24 See Lichnowsky to the Foreign Office [Berlin], 1 August 1914, Lichnowsky, *Heading for the Abyss*, 413–14. The wording is slightly different in the translation of Kautsky's collection of German Documents; see The Ambassador at London to the Foreign Office, 1 August 1914, Karl Kautsky, Walther Schücking, Max Montgelas, eds, *German Documents on the*

Outbreak of the War (New York, 1924), (hereafter *GD*), Document 562, and Grey to Bertie, 1 August 1914, *BD*, Vol. XI, Document 419. For full accounts of this controversial episode from the British perspective, see especially Keith Wilson, 'Understanding the "Misunderstanding" of 1 August 1914', *Historical Journal*, 37, 4 (1994), 885–89, which builds on Harry Young, 'The Misunderstanding of August 1, 1914' *Journal of Modern History*, XLVIII (1976), 644–65, and Stephen Valone, '"There must be some misunderstanding": Sir Edward Grey's diplomacy of August 1, 1914', *Journal of British Studies*, XXVII (1988), 405–24.

25 The original reference is *Parliamentary Debates*, Commons, 3rd series, Vol. 203, 1788 (10 August 1870).

26 *Parliamentary Debates*, Commons, 5th series, Vol. 65, 1827–28 (3 August 1914).

27 *Parliamentary Debates*, Commons, 5th series, Vol. 65, 1828–29 (3 August 1914).

28 *Parliamentary Debates*, Commons, 5th series, Vol. 65, 1829–31 (3 August 1914).

29 *Parliamentary Debates*, Commons, 5th series, Vol. 65, 1831 (3 August 1914).

30 Sixteen Radicals spoke in support of peace and non-intervention, Philip Morrell, Josiah Wedgwood, Edmund Harvey, Arthur Ponsonby, Sir Albert Spicer, Arnold Rowntree, Percy Molteno, Llewellyn Williams, Robert Outhwaite, Joseph King, Sir John Jardine, Aneurin Williams, William Byles, Annan Bryce, Richard Denman, and Ellis Davies. One socialist, Keir Hardie, supported them. Only one Conservative, Arthur Balfour, and only two Liberals, Arthur Markham and W. M. R. Pringle, spoke in defence of Grey and in favour of British intervention in a Continental war. See *Parliamentary Debates*, Commons, 5th series, Vol. 65, 1833–84 (3 August 1914).

31 'The Nation and the Government', editorial, *The Times*, 4 August 1914.

32 Meaney remarks that 'there is no evidence that Reid was ever consulted about the major defence and foreign policy issues troubling Anglo–Australian relations or that he considered it his task to inform Melbourne about British views on these matters'. See Neville Meaney, 'The First High Commissioners: George Reid and Andrew Fisher', in Carl Bridge, Frank Bongiorno and David Lee, eds, *The High Commissioners; Australia's Representatives in the United Kingdom, 1910–2010* (Canberra, 2010), 42.

33 W. G. McMinn, *George Reid* (Melbourne, 1989), 261–62.

34 See O. Murray to Emmott, 31 July 1914. The Admiralty wanted to send Reid thanks for Australia's offer to transfer its fleet. The Colonial Office decided it was better not to send a copy of the telegram to Reid for 'he will want all the prev[ious] tel[egram]s'. See Minute by G. V. Fiddes, dated 1 August 1914. TNA: CO 418/128.

35 George Houstoun Reid, *My Reminiscences* (London, 1917), 206–09.

36 Reid to Glynn, 4 August 1914, quoted in 'What Sir George Reid Says', *The Advertiser*, 7 August 1914, and 'Position in Australia', *Brisbane Courier*, 7 August 1914.

37 For example, 'Britain to Act', editorial, *Daily Telegraph*, 5 August 1914.

38 For example, 'England Firm', *Sydney Morning Herald*, 6 August 1914, and 'Scene in Commons', *The Argus*, 6 August 1914.

Chapter 17 'Their manhood at our side'

1 'The Empire and the War', editorial, *The Times*, 3 August 1914.

2 Villiers to Grey, 3 August 1914, *BD.*, Vol. XI, Document 521 (received at 10.55 a.m.) and Grey to Villiers, 3 August 1914 (despatched at 12.45 p.m.), *BD.*, Vol. XI, Document 525.

3 For example, 'Awaiting Britain's Call', *The Scotsman*, 1 August 1914.

4 'Dominion Rally', and 'On the Brink of War', *The Times*, 31 July 1914, and 'Canadian Offers to the Mother Country', *The Scotsman*, 1 August 1914.

5 'The Empire Ready: Canadian expeditionary force', and 'Offer of Men from New Zealand', *The Times*, 1 August 1914, and 'British Dominions and the Crisis', *The Scotsman*, 1 August 1914.

6 The reports in the *Daily Telegraph* of 1 August 1914 were then echoed back in the Australian and New Zealand press. For example see 'Patriotic Offers', *Evening Post*, 3 August 1914 and 'New Zealand Always First', *Auckland Star*, 3 August 1914, 'Australia's Offer: no fair-weather partner', *The Argus*, 3 August 1914, quoting the London *Daily Telegraph* of 1 August 1914.

7 'Australian Readiness to Help', and 'Australian Support', *The Times*, 2 August 1914.

8 'The Empire Ready: Canadian expeditionary force', 'A Loyal Empire', and 'Whole-Hearted Support', *The Times*, 2 August 1914.

9 'Britain's Part in the Crisis: the issues at stake', *The Times*, 2 August 1914.

10 Amery Diary, 1 August 1914, Barnes and Nicholson, *Leo Amery Diaries*, I, 104.

11 'The War of Wars', editorial, *The Observer*, 2 August 1914.

12 'Voice of the Empire', and 'An Empire War', *The Observer*, 2 August 1914.

13 'Aid from the Empire', *The Times*, 3 August 1914

14 For example, 'Australia: help for the motherland: to our last man and our last shilling', *The Scotsman*, 3 August 1914.

15 Dawson Diary, 31 July 1914, MSS Dawson 20, Geoffrey Dawson Papers.

16 'The Empire and the War', editorial, *The Times*, 3 August 1914.

17 Editorial, *The Scotsman*, 3 August 1914.

18 *Parliamentary Debates*, Commons, 5th series, Vol. 65, 1827–28 (3 August 1914).

19 'Australia's Offer: a force of 20,000 men', *The Times*, 4 August 1914, 'Loyalty of the Dominions: Australia offer: an expeditionary force of 20,000 men', *The Scotsman*, 4 August 1914, 'Oversea Dominions: Australia offers force of 20,000 Men', *Manchester Guardian*, 4 August 1914.

20 Courtenay Ilbert Diary, 3 August 1914, Courtenay Ilbert Papers, ILB/2/12 (Parliamentary Archives), Hugh Spender, 'A Dramatic Scene', *Westminster Gazette*, 4 August 1914, 'A Fateful Sitting of the Commons', *Manchester Guardian*, 4 August 1914, and Michael MacDonagh, *In London During the Great War: the diary of a journalist* (London, 1935), 5.

21 Charles Trevelyan to Asquith, 3 August 1914 (Draft), Charles Trevelyan Papers, CPT 59 and see A. J. A. Morris, *C. P. Trevelyan, 1870–1958: portrait of a radical* (New York, 1977), 99.

22 Aubrey Herbert Diary, 4 June 1917, Aubrey Herbert Papers, DD/HER/70/1 (Somerset Archive Centre, Taunton). For his war experiences, see also his memoir, Aubrey Herbert, *Mons, ANZAC, and Kut* (London, 1919), based upon the diary.

23 Corbett, *Naval Operations*, 129.

Chapter 18 'No immediate necessity'

1 Cabinet Memorandum, 4 August 1914, Harcourt Papers.

2 Cabinet Memorandum, 4 August 1914, Harcourt Papers.

3 'Copy of cablegram received from the Secretary of State for the Colonies, dated London, 4th August, 1.45 p.m.' in 'Outbreak of War August 1914 — Placing of H. M. A. Ships at Disposal of Admiralty', NAA: MP1049/1, 1914/0276.

4 The Secretary of State [Harcourt] to the Governor-General [of Australia] (sent 1.45 p.m. 4 August 1914), in *Papers Presented to Parliament, Vol. V, Session 1914–17*, 1434. There is confusion in the official printed records on these cables. The official record in the Parliamentary Papers lists this *one* cable as sent on Tuesday 4 August at 1.45 p.m., while Scott reproduces *two* cables sent from Harcourt on this day (one at 1.45 p.m. and a second at 3.05 p.m.). Scott quotes the second telegram, sent at 3.05 p.m. as that assuring Australia that there was 'no immediate necessity' for an offer of an expeditionary force. See Scott, *Australia During the War*, 12.

5 Initially, Harcourt's actual words were not reproduced in the press. Only on Thursday 6 August did the Australian press reveal that Harcourt had replied to the Australian offer from the governor-general with a reference to there being 'no immediate necessity'. The exact terms were hidden. According to these later reports Harcourt had simply 'stated that the Government was greatly appreciative, and would inform later respecting the use thereof'. For

example, see 'Australia's Offer: Britain appreciates', *Sydney Morning Herald*, 6 August 1914.

6 Munro Ferguson to Harcourt, 4 August 1914, Munro Ferguson Papers, MS 696/591.

7 The Governor-General [Munro Ferguson] to the Secretary of State [Harcourt], (Received 5.47 p.m., 5 August 1914), in *Papers Presented to Parliament, Vol. V, Session 1914–17*, 1434.

8 The Secretary of State [Harcourt] to the Governor-General [of Canada] (Sent 7.35 p.m., 3 August 1914), in *Papers Presented to Parliament, Vol. V, Session 1914–17*, 1431.

9 The Secretary of State for the Colonies to the Governor-General of Canada (Sent 1.45 p.m., 4 August 1914), TNA: ADM 137/3/16, and see *Papers Presented to Parliament, Vol. V, Session 1914–17*, 1431.

10 The Secretary of State for Colonies to the Governor of New Zealand (Sent 1.45 p.m., 4 August 1914), TNA: ADM 137/1/18, and also in *Papers Presented to Parliament, Vol. V, Session 1914–17*, 1439.

11 'Dominions' Zeal: the King's message', *Manchester Guardian*, 5 August 1914. The message was reported in the Australian press from Thursday 6 August 1914. For example, see 'Message from the King', *Brisbane Courier*, 6 August 1914.

12 Cabinet Memorandum, 3 August 1914, Harcourt Papers.

13 Harcourt had been a leading player in the two cabinet revolts, first, in the autumn of 1911, against Grey's secret authorisation of 'military conversations' from 1906, and second, in the autumn of 1912, against any presumption that Britain would come to the military assistance of France on the basis of the redistribution of the French and British naval fleets. For the dispute in 1911, see 'Decision of the cabinet, 15 November 1911', and separate notes giving consent from Loreburn and Morley to Harcourt filed with Cabinet Memorandum, 15 November 1911, Harcourt Papers. For the dispute in 1912 see Cabinet Memorandum, 30 October 1912 and 1 November 1912, Harcourt Papers.

14 'The Acting Governor-General [De Villiers] to the Secretary of State [Harcourt]' (Received 8 p.m., 4th August 1914), in *Papers Presented to Parliament, Vol. V, Session 1914–17*, 1439. See also S. B. Spies, 'The Outbreak of the First World War and the Botha Government', *South African Historical Journal*, 1, 1 (1969), 47–57.

Chapter 19 Choosing war

1 Elizabeth Cadbury Family Journal, 6 August 1914 (describing Tuesday 4 August 1914), Elizabeth Cadbury Papers, MSS 466/205/21 (Birmingham Central Library).

2 'The Nation and the Government', editorial, *The Times*, 4 August 1914.

3   Editorial, *The Scotsman*, 4 August 1914.

4   'Peace or War?', editorial, *Manchester Guardian*, 4 August 1914.

5   'Sir Edward Grey's Strange Blunder', editorial, *Manchester Guardian*, 4 August 1914.

6   'Sir Edward Grey's Statement', editorial, *Daily News*, 4 August 1914.

7   'Here We Stand', editorial, *Westminster Gazette*, 4 August 1914.

8   Blunt Diary, 5 August 1914, MS13–1975, Blunt Papers.

9   Grey to Goschen, 4 August 1914, *BD*, Vol. XI, Document 573.

10 John H. Horne and Alan Kramer, *German Atrocities, 1914: a history of denial* (New Haven, 2001), 10, and Jeff Lipkes, *The German Army in Belgium, August 1914* (Leuven, 2007), 39.

11 'In Downing Street', *The Times*, 5 August 1914. See also Asquith to Venetia Stanley, 4 August 1914, Brock, eds, *Letters to Venetia Stanley*, 150. Villiers to Grey, 4 August 1914 (Received 6.30 p.m.) *BD*, Vol. XI, Document 621.

12 Simon to Asquith, 4 August 1914, journal marked 'Diary #5', MS. Simon 2, Simon Papers, and George Cunningham to Beauchamp, 4 August 1914, Beauchamp Papers, and Herbert Samuel to Beatrice Samuel, 4 August 1914, Samuel Papers, SAM/A/157.

13 Cabinet Memorandum, 4 August 1914, Harcourt Papers.

14 Cabinet Memorandum, 3 August 1914, Harcourt Papers. Emphasis in original.

15 Herbert Samuel to Beatrice Samuel, 4 August 1914, Samuel Papers, SAM/A/157.

16 Herbert Samuel to Beatrice Samuel, 4 August 1914, Samuel Papers, SAM/A/157.

17 Churchill, *World Crisis*, I, 178.

18 Spender, *Life of Asquith*, II, 93.

19 Trevelyan, *Grey of Fallodon*, 262.

20 Grey to Goschen, 4 August 1914, *BD*, Vol. XI, Document 594.

21 Asquith to Venetia Stanley, 4 August 1914, in Brock, eds, *Letters to Venetia Stanley*, 150.

22 Frances Stevenson, *The Years That Are Past* (London, 1967), 73–74.

23 Jerome K. Jerome, *My Life and Times* (London, 1926), 265.

24 'The Commons Resolute', *The Times*, 5 August 1914.

25 The note from Brussels was Villiers to Grey, 4 August 1914, *BD*, Vol. XI, Document 584 (Received 11.20 a.m.); the note from the Belgian Legation was M. Davignon, Belgian minister for foreign affairs, to the Belgian ministers at London and Paris, 4 August 1914, *Belgian Grey Book*, Document 30.

26 The German note was Jagow to Lichnowsky, 4 August 1914, *GD*, Document 810.

27 *Parliamentary Debates*, Commons, 5th series, Vol. 65, 1925–28 (4 August 1914).

28 'The Commons Resolute', *The Times*, 5 August 1914.

29 This important point is made by Lindsay, 'Failure of Liberal Opposition', 166.

30 *Parliamentary Debates*, Commons, 5th series, Vol. 65, 1941–52 (4 August 1914).

31 'The Commons Resolute', *The Times*, 5 August 1914.

32 Hankey to Adeline, 4 August 1914, Hankey Papers, HNKY 3/19 (Churchill Archives Centre).

33 Wilson, 'Britain', *Decisions for War*, 201.

34 Lloyd George, *War Memoirs of David Lloyd George* (London, 1938), I, 45–47. A Belgian request for military assistance did not reach the Foreign Office in London until 12.50 a.m. on 5 August. See Villiers to Grey, 5 August 1914, *BD*, Vol. XI, Document 654. (Despatched at 4 p.m.)

35 'What War Means — Great Women's Meeting at Kingsway Hall', *Common Cause*, 7 August 1914, 'Women's Protest Against War', *Daily News*, 5 August 1914, and Helena Swanwick, *I Have Been Young* (London, 1935), 233–239. For secondary accounts see Jo Vellacott, 'Feminist Consciousness and the First World War', in Ruth Roach Pierson, ed., *Women and Peace: theoretical, historical and practical perspectives* (London, 1987), 121, Jo Vellacott Newberry, 'Anti-war Suffragists', *History*, 62, 206 (October, 1977), 414–15, and Beryl Haslam, *From Suffrage to Internationalism: the political evolution of three British feminists, 1908–1939* (New York, 1999), 41.

36 In Blackstone's words, the Crown held 'the sole prerogative of making war and peace'. See William Blackstone, *Commentaries on the Laws of England* (1765–69), Book 1, Chapter 7. On the Crown's prerogatives, see also Joseph Chitty, *A Treatise on the Law of the Prerogatives of the Crown* (London, 1820), 43. See especially the 'Introduction' to Walter Bagehot, *The English Constitution* (Boston, 1873), 31–32, and Alpheus Todd, *On Parliamentary Government in England* (London, 1869), Vol. I, 598. Regarding the power to declare war, Todd asserted that the Constitution had 'vested this right exclusively in the crown'. See also A. V. Dicey, *Introduction to the Study of the Law of the Constitution* (London, 1902), 369–70 and 408–12.

37 On the King's ultimate and formal responsibility to control foreign policy and to make a declaration of war, unfettered by Parliament, see Lord Halsbury, ed., *The Laws of England*, First Edition, Vol. VI (London, 1909), 375, 386, 427–28, 440–41, 442, 444, and on the Privy Council's role in giving formal approval to documents previously approved by the cabinet, see Halsbury, ed., *The Laws of England*, Vol. VI, 386, 427–28.

38 Alpheus Todd, *On Parliamentary Government in England* (London, 1869),

Vol. II, 622–23, and see Lord Halsbury, ed., *The Laws of England*, First
Edition, Vol. VII (London, 1909), 51–52. It had not been called together as
a whole since in 1839. An old requirement for a quorum of seven members
had fallen into disuse after Prince Albert's death in 1861. On the matter of a
quorum for the Privy Council, see also *Halsbury's Laws of England*, Fourth
Edition, Vol. 8 (2), para. 525, f. n. 1.

39 Sir Almeric FitzRoy, *Memoirs* (London, 1922), Vol. II, 561.

40 FitzRoy, *Memoirs*, II, 561.

41 George V Diary, 4 August 1914, quoted in the introduction to Christopher
H. D. Howard, ed., *The Diary of Edward Goschen, 1900–1914*, Camden
Fourth Series, Vol. 25 (London, 1980), 48.

42 Beauchamp was named Lord President of the Council the next day. Second
Supplement to *The London Gazette*, 4 August 1914, supplement dated 5
August 1914 (no. 28862).

43 Typescript headed 'AT THE COURT OF BUCKINGHAM PALACE,
THE 4th DAY OF AUGUST 1914 (AT 10.35 P.M.)' listing only The King,
Granard, Beauchamp, and Allendale as 'Present', appended to Almeric
FitzRoy to Beauchamp, 30 October 1918, in Beauchamp Papers. Also see
'Court Circular', *The Times*, 6 August 1914. Two more Privy Councillors
were procured to stand 'in attendance', Lieut-Colonel Sir William
Carington, a guardsman, and Sir Charles Cust, a naval officer and old
personal friend of the King, at this time his Equerry in Waiting.

44 See the typescript headed 'Business for the Council', listing the agenda,
appended to Almeric FitzRoy to Beauchamp, 30 October 1918, in
Beauchamp Papers. For the full text of the two proclamations, see
Supplement to *The London Gazette*, 4 August 1914 (No. 28861).

45 Almeric FitzRoy to Beauchamp, 30 October 1918, in Beauchamp Papers.

46 FitzRoy, *Memoirs*, II, 561.

47 George V Diary, 4 August 1914, quoted in Clay, *King, Kaiser, Tsar*, 314.

Chapter 20 Fait Accompli

1   Cook to Munro Ferguson, 4 August 1914, Novar Papers, MS 696/4007.

2   'Decode of Cablegram received from Admiralty, 5/8/14. Sent to Navy Office',
in 'Outbreak of War August 1914 — Placing of H. M. A. Ships at Disposal of
Admiralty', NAA: MP1049/1, 1914/0276. There is another version that reads
'See Preface Defence Scheme war has broken out with Germany', marked
as received at 12.30 p.m., 5 August 1914, and endorsed 'Copy sent to Prime
Minister and Minister of Defence, in file entitled 'War 1914. Notifications
(Outbreak)', NAA: A11803, 1914/89/1, Part 1.

3   'Decode of cablegram sent to Admiralty London dated 5/8/14 sent at 12.30

p.m.' in 'Outbreak of War August 1914 — Placing of H. M. A. Ships at Disposal of Admiralty', NAA: MP1049/1, 1914/0276.

4 Naval Secretary to Director of Naval Reserves, 5 August 1914, in 'Outbreak of War August 1914 — Placing of H. M. A. Ships at Disposal of Admiralty', NAA: MP1049/1, 1914/0276.

5 Scott, *Australia During the War*, 14. For example, McMahon Glynn received his telegram about 1.00 p.m. See Gerald O'Collins, *Patrick McMahon Glynn: a founder of Australian Federation* (Melbourne, 1965), 244.

6 'Will Support Prime Minister: Mr Fisher's undertaking', *Daily Telegraph*, 6 August 1914. See slightly different wording in 'Parties in Unison: Opposition supports ministry', *The Argus*, 6 August 1914.

7 *New South Wales Parliamentary Debates*, 2nd series, Vol. 55, 580–81 (4 August 1914).

8 *New South Wales Parliamentary Debates*, 2nd series, Vol. 55, 584–85 (5 August 1914).

9 For example, 'Declaration of War', *Examiner* (Launceston), 5 August 1914, 'Britain and Germany: rumoured declaration of war', *Brisbane Courier*, 5 August 1914.

10 'The War', editorial, *The West Australian*, 5 August 1914.

11 'Wednesday, August 5, 1914' editorial, and 'Notes on the Cables', *The Argus*, 5 August 1914, and 'A Great Empire', *The Argus*, 6 August 1914.

12 'Britain's Position', editorial, *Sydney Morning Herald*, 5 August 1914.

13 'Declaration of War', *The Argus*, 6 August 1914.

14 'Declaration by Germany', *Sydney Morning Herald*, 6 August 1914. 'A later cable announced that Germany had declared war on England.'

15 See John Williams, *Anzacs, the Media, and the Great War* (Sydney, 1999), 45. For complaints about the censorship, see for example, 'Censorship', editorial, *Daily Telegraph*, 5 August 1914, 'A Great Empire', *The Argus*, 6 August 1914.

16 See 'Censorship in Australia: protest against severity', *Brisbane Courier*, 7 August 1914.

17 Professor Pitt Corbett, 'Declaration of War', *Sydney Morning Herald*, 5 August 1914.

18 Ida F. Dawson Diary entry, quoted in Gavin Souter, *Lion and Kangaroo: Australia: 1901–1919. The rise of a nation* (Melbourne, 1976), 212.

Chapter 21 'A great and urgent Imperial service'

1 Asquith to Stanley, 6 August 1914, in Brock, *Letters to Venetia Stanley*, 158.

2 See Matthew Johnson, *Militarism and the British Left, 1902–1914* (London, 2013), esp. Ch. 3.

3 See Bernard Semmel, *Liberalism and Naval Strategy: ideology, interest, and sea power during the Pax Britannica* (London, 1986), Morris, *The Scaremongers*, and Adams and Poirier, *Conscription Controversy*.

4 *Parliamentary Debates*, Lords, 5th series, Vol. xvii, 398–403 (5 August 1914).

5 *Parliamentary Debates*, Lords, 5th series, Vol. xvii, 404–5 (5 August 1914).

6 Foreign Office Statement, issued 12.15 a.m., 5 August 1914, reproduced in 'War Declared', *The Times*, 5 August 1914, and Asquith's speech, *Parliamentary Debates*, Commons, 5th series, Vol. 65, 2074–83 (6 August 1914).

7 'Secret Proceedings of a sub-Committee of the Committee of Imperial Defence, assembled on the 5th of August, 1914, to consider the question of offensive operations against the German Colonies', filed with Cabinet Memorandum, 5 August 1914, Harcourt Papers. The committee decided to send an expedition from India to take Dar es Salaam in East Africa; that the fate of South-West Africa should await War Office advice; that British forces should seize Togoland; that British troops in Nigeria would move against the Cameroons, but not immediately because the defences were 'formidable'; that Australia 'should be invited to send an expedition to attack the island of Yap and German New Guinea, in order to seize the cables and radio telegraph stations'; and similarly that New Zealand 'should be invited to send an expedition to attack Samoa and Nauru'. See also Hankey, *Supreme Command*, I, 168.

8 Cabinet Memorandum, 5 August 1914, Harcourt Papers.

9 Cabinet Memorandum, 5 August 1914, Harcourt Papers. Emphasis added.

10 Henry Wilson's Diary, 23 May, 30 June, 1, 4, 10, 14, 31 July 1914, quoted in Hazlehurst, *Politicians at War*, 28, 31, and 73.

11 Milner Diary, 4 August 1914, Milner Papers, Milner dep. 85 (Bodleian Library). Emphasis in original.

12 Hankey, *Supreme Command*, I, 169–72.

13 Milner Diary, 4–6 August 1914, Milner Papers, Milner dep. 85.

14 Cabinet Memorandum, 6 August 1914, Harcourt Papers.

15 Churchill, *World Crisis*, I, 191.

16 Cabinet Memorandum, 6 August 1914, Harcourt Papers.

17 Spender, *Life, Journalism and Politics*, II, 18.

18 *Parliamentary Debates*, Commons, 5th series, Vol. 65, 1963–64 (5 August 1914).

19 *Parliamentary Debates*, Commons, 5th series, Vol. 65, 2074–83 (6 August 1914).

20 See the speeches of Ponsonby, Dickinson, Wedgwood, Lawson, Rowntree, Aneurin Williams, and Allen Baker, *Parliamentary Debates*, Commons, 5th

series, Vol. 65, 2089–2100 (6 August 1914).

21 The Secretary of State for the Colonies to the Governor-General of the Commonwealth of Australia (sent 7.30 p.m. 6 August 1914), TNA: ADM 137/5/9, and see *Papers Presented to Parliament, Vol. V, Session 1914–17*, 1434.

22 There was no publicity about a British Expeditionary Force leaving Britain until its arrival in France. See 'The Expeditionary Force', *The Times*, 18 August 1914.

23 For example, 'War News', *The Argus*, 8 August 1914, 'Australia's Offer Gratefully Accepted', *Brisbane Courier*, 8 August 1914, and 'The War', *The Advertiser* [Adelaide], 9 August 1914.

24 The Secretary of State for the Colonies to the Governor-General of the Commonwealth of Australia (sent 7.30 p.m. 6 August 1914), TNA: ADM 137/5/9. This section of the cable was not released in the version published in *Papers Presented to Parliament, Vol. V, Session 1914–17*, 1434.

25 See Lewis Harcourt's Memorandum 'The Spoils', 25 March 1915, TNA: CAB 63/3.

26 Munro Ferguson to Harcourt, 6 August 1914, listed in NAA: MP1049/1, 1914/0299.

27 Harcourt to Munro Ferguson, 8 August 1914, included in Steward to Millen, 9 August 1914, in NAA: MP1049/1, 1914/0299.

28 Secretary of Prime Minister's Department [Shepherd] to Official Secretary of the Governor-General [Major Steward], 9 August 1914, in NAA: MP1049/1, 1914/0299.

29 Shepherd to Naval Secretary [Manisty], 10 August 1914, in NAA: MP1049/1, 1914/0299, and The Governor-General [of Australia] to the Secretary of State [Harcourt] (received 11.35 a.m., 11 August 1914), in *Papers Presented to Parliament, Vol. V, Session 1914–17*, 1435.

30 Munro Ferguson to Harcourt, 25 August 1914, TNA: CO 418/123.

31 'Australia's Offer: the King's appreciation', *The Advertiser* [Adelaide], 6 August 1914.

32 Munro Ferguson to the King, 8 August 1914, Munro Ferguson Papers, 696/5. Emphasis added.

33 Munro Ferguson to Harcourt, 8 August 1914, TNA: CO 418/123.

34 Fisher to Margaret Fisher, 29 August 1914, cited by Meaney, *Australia and World Crisis*, 28.

35 'Australia in War', editorial, *Sydney Morning Herald*, 3 August 1914.

36 'Britain at War', editorial, *Brisbane Courier*, 6 August 1914.

37 Connor, 'The capture of German New Guinea', in Stockings and Connor, eds, *Before the Anzac Dawn*, 283–303.

38 Geoffrey McGinley, 'Divergent Paths: problems of command and strategy in

Anglo–Australian naval operations in the Asia-Pacific (August-November, 1914)', in Stevens and Reeve, eds, *Southern Trident*, 242–61.

39 Munro Ferguson to Harcourt, 18 August 1914, MS Harcourt 479.

40 Harcourt to Munro Ferguson, 31 August 1914, MS Harcourt 479.

41 McGibbon, 'The Shaping of New Zealand's War Effort, August-October 1914', in Crawford and McGibbon, eds, *New Zealand's Great War*, 63–65, Connor, 'The capture of German New Guinea', in Stockings and Connor, eds, *Before the Anzac Dawn*, 297.

42 Munro Ferguson, 21 October 1914, MS Harcourt 479.

Chapter 22 Diversion to Gallipoli

1 C. B. B. White Diary, 1 November 1914, White Papers, MS 5172.

2 For example, 'Australian Offer: 20,000 men. Accepted by Britain', *Sydney Morning Herald*, 8 August 1914.

3 'Australian Troops: twenty thousand to go to England', *The Register* (Adelaide), 8 August 1914.

4 Munro Ferguson to Harcourt, 8 August 1914. 1914, TNA: ADM 137/1.

5 Munro Ferguson to Harcourt, 11 August 1914. 1914, TNA: ADM 137/1.

6 Liverpool to Harcourt, 14 August 1914 and George Aston minute dated 18 August 1914, TNA: ADM 137/1.

7 Munro Ferguson to Harcourt, 18 August 1914. 1914, TNA: ADM 137/1.

8 Colonial Office to Governor-General, 7 September 1914, TNA: CO 418/131.

9 Munro Ferguson to Harcourt, 17 September 1914, TNA: CO 418/123.

10 'Memorandum by Senator the Hon. E. D. Millen on Relinquishing Office as Minister for Defence', undated [September 1914], TNA: CO 418/123.

11 Munro Ferguson to Harcourt, 18 September 1914, MS Harcourt 479.

12 Lord Islington to Lord Bryce, 20 August and 7 September 1914, MS Bryce 239, Bryce Papers (Bodleian Library).

13 McGinley, 'Divergent Paths', in Stevens and Reeve, eds, *Southern Trident*, 259.

14 Munro Ferguson to Harcourt, 25 September 1914. 1914, TNA: ADM 137/1, and Munro Ferguson to Harcourt, 29 September 1914, TNA: CO 418/123.

15 Munro Ferguson to Harcourt, 9 October 1914, TNA: CO 418/123.

16 L. L. Robson, *The First A. I. F. A Study of its Recruitment* (Melbourne, 1982), Ch. 2, Bill Gammage, *The Broken Years: Australian soldiers in the Great War* (Canberra, 1974), Ch. 1, Alistair Thomson, *Anzac Memories* (Melbourne, 1994, Ch. 1. See also J. N. I. Dawes and L. L. Robson, *Citizen to Soldier: Australia before the Great War: recollections of members of the First A. I. F.* (Melbourne, 1977), 12.

17 Souter, *Company of Heralds*, 114.

18 Admiralty to Naval Board, 26 October 1914, CHAR 13/38/40, Churchill Papers. On the 1914 rebellion, see T. R. H. Davenport, 'The South African Rebellion, 1914', *The English Historical Review*, 78, 306 (January 1963), 73–94.

19 Munro Ferguson to Harcourt, 29 October 1914, MS Harcourt 479.

20 Quoted in C. Coulthard-Clark, 'Major-General Sir William Bridges: Australia's first field commander', in Horner, ed., *The Commanders*, 19.

21 Bean, *Story of Anzac*, 97–98, and Munro Ferguson to Harcourt, 23 January 1915, MS Harcourt 479.

22 Arthur Jose, *Royal Australian Navy, 1914–1918*, 161. Jose remarks, 'It may be noted that, while the Commonwealth Government was kept fully informed of the successive changes of destination, no explanation of the reasons that dictated them ever reached the cabinet'. See also Harcourt's insistence that this was 'a dead secret here and even in South Africa', which he did not share with Australia, in Harcourt to Munro Ferguson, 11 December 1914, MS Harcourt 479.

23 Munro Ferguson to Harcourt, 3 November 1914, MS Harcourt 479.

24 C. B. B. White Diary, 1 November 1914, White Papers, MS 5172.

25 Yoichi Hirama, 'Japanese Naval Assistance and its Effect on Australian-Japanese Relations', in O'Brien, ed. *The Anglo–Japanese Alliance*, 140–58. See also C. in C. China, Singapore, to Admiralty, 14 September 1914, announcing plans for two Japanese cruisers to 'cover Australia during absence of Australian cruisers'. Churchill Papers, CHAR 13/41/72.

26 C. in C. China, Singapore, to Admiralty, 13 November 1914, Churchill Papers, CHAR 13/35/100.

27 For a narrative of these events, see David French, *British Strategy and War Aims, 1914–1916* (London, 1986), Ch. 3 'Russia, Turkey and the Balkans, September-December 1914'.

28 'Decode of cablegram from High Commissioner', 17 November 1914, recording Kitchener's explanation to Reid, marked as approved by the Fisher Cabinet, 18 November 1918, NAA: A6006, 1914/11/18.

29 Cabinet Memorandum, 18 November 1914, Harcourt Papers.

30 George Horan to Joseph W. Horan, 13 December 1914, George Horan letters to his father, 2 October 1914-22 December 1916, MLMSS 1468/ Item 1 (Mitchell Library, State Library of New South Wales, courtesy copyright holder), transcripts available online, http://acms.sl.nsw.gov.au/_transcript/2013/D20763/a6001.html (accessed 5 March 2014).

31 On the early diplomacy, see especially C. J. Smith, 'Great Britain and the Straits Agreement of 1914–1915 with Russia: the British promise of November 1914', *American Historical Review*, 70, 4 (1965), 1015–34, and A. L. MacFie, 'The Straits Question in the First World War, 1914–18', *Middle*

Eastern Studies, 19, 1 (January 1983), 50.

32 For studies of the strategic and political reasons behind the campaign, see MacFie, 'The Straits Question', 43–74, David French, 'The Origins of the Dardanelles Campaign Reconsidered', *History*, 68, 223 (June, 1983), 210–24, French, *British Strategy and War Aims*, Ch. 5, 'The Constantinople Agreement, Italy and the Collapse of the Asquith Government, February–May 1915', and Graham T. Clews, *Churchill's Dilemma: the real story behind the origins of the 1915 Dardanelles Campaign* (Santa Barbara, 2010).

33 Hardinge to Birdwood, 29 March 1915, Hardinge Papers, 93, Part II.

34 King George V to Hardinge, 23 April 1915, Hardinge Papers, 105.

35 See Ronald P. Bobroff, *Roads to Glory: late imperial Russia and the Turkish Straits* (London, 2006).

36 Harcourt Cabinet Memorandum, 10 March 1915, Harcourt Papers.

37 On the diplomatic background to the Gallipoli campaign, see the recent survey in Sean McMeekin, *The Russian Origins of the First World War* (New York, 2011), esp. Ch. 5, 'The Russians and Gallipoli'. For more detailed accounts, see R. J. Kerner, 'Russia, the Straits and Constantinople, 1914–1915', *Journal of Modern History*, 1, 3 (1929), 400–15, R. J. Kerner, 'Russia and the Straits Question, 1915–17', *The Slavonic and East European Review*, 8, 24 (March 1930), 589–60, W. A. Renzi, 'Great Britain, Russia and the Straits, 1914–1915', *Journal of Modern History*, 42, 1 (1970), 1–20, W. A. Renzi, 'Who composed "Sazonov's thirteen points"? A Re-examination of Russia's War aims of 1914', *American Historical Review*, 88, 2 (1983), 347–57, C. Jay Smith, *The Russian Struggle for Power, 1914–1917: a study of Russian foreign policy during the First World War* (New York, 1956), and Michael Eckstein, 'Russia, Constantinople and the Straits, 1914–1915', in F. H. Hinsley, *British Foreign Policy Under Sir Edward Grey* (Cambridge, 1977), 423–35.

38 Jennifer Siegel, *Endgame: Britain, Russia and the final struggle for central Asia* (London, 2002), 182–96, and for the background see Marian Kent, *Oil and Empire: British policy and Mesopotamian oil, 1900–1920* (London, 1976), and Marian Jack, 'The Purchase of the British Government's Shares in the British Petroleum Company, 1912–1914, *Past and Present*, 39 (April 1968), 139–68.

39 Grey to Buchanan, 11 March 1915, quoted in Lowe, 'Britain and Italian Intervention', 544.

40 McMeekin, *Russian Origins*, 139.

41 Smith, *The Russian Struggle for Power*, 240.

42 Cabinet Memorandum, 26 April 1915, and cabinet note, Harcourt to Grey and Grey to Harcourt, 26 April 1915, Harcourt Papers. On the diplomacy, see W. A. Renzi, 'Italy's Neutrality and Entry into the Great War: a re-

examination', *American Historical Review*, 73, 5 (1968), 1414–32, and C. J. Lowe, 'Britain and Italian Intervention, 1914–1915', *Historical Journal*, 12, 3 (1969), 533–48. On both the Straits Agreement and the Treaty of London, see also, W. W. Gottlieb, *Studies in Secret Diplomacy during the First World War* (London, 1957), especially Chs. III-VI, and XXII. For a recent narrative, see James Barr, *A Line in the Sand: Britain, France and the struggle that shaped the Middle East* (London, 2011).

43 Total Australian casualties were 25,725; total Entente casualties were probably 390,000; total Turkish casualties were probably 289,000. See Prior, *Gallipoli*, 242, and Tim Travers, *Gallipoli 1915* (Stroud, 2004), 311–12.

44 For example, Munro Ferguson to Harcourt, 24 February 1915, and 10 March 1915, 12 March 1915, 24 March 1915, 6 April 1915, and Harcourt to Munro Ferguson, 11 March 1915, 27 March 1915, MS Harcourt 479. See especially Munro Ferguson to Harcourt, 15 April 1915, TNA: CO 418/132.

45 Harcourt to Asquith, 3 March 1915, filed with Harcourt Cabinet Memoranda 1915, Harcourt Papers.

46 Harcourt to Munro Ferguson, 24 March 1915, MS Harcourt 479.

47 Munro Ferguson to Harcourt, 10 March 1915, MS Harcourt 479.

48 Munro Ferguson to Harcourt, 28 December 1914, MS Harcourt 479. He noted 'Ministers unaware of this communication'.

49 For correspondence on this issue, see Munro Ferguson to Harcourt, 10 December 1914, 28 December 1914, 23 January 1915, 13 April 1915, and Harcourt to Munro Ferguson, 24 and 27 March 1915, (referring to a letter from Fisher dated 15 February 1915), MS Harcourt 479.

50 Munro Ferguson to Harcourt, 13 April 1915, MS Harcourt 479. See also Munro Ferguson to Harcourt, 25 January 1915, in TNA: CO 418/132.

51 'News in Brief', *The Times*, 3 April 1915, citing an interview in Sydney on 2 April 1915.

52 Harcourt cited the letter (dated 15 February 1915) in *Parliamentary Debates*, Commons, 5th series, Vol. 71, 16 (14 April 1915). It is also quoted in Harcourt to Munro Ferguson, 27 March 1915, MS Harcourt 479.

53 *Parliamentary Debates*, Commons, 5th series, Vol. 71, 16–18 (14 April 1915).

54 Harcourt to Munro Ferguson, 15 April 1915, MS Harcourt 479, and 'The Dominions and Peace', *The Times*, 15 April 1915.

Conclusion

1 H. M. Tomlinson, *All Our Yesterdays* (New York, 1930), 433

2 Cook, Pocket Diary for 1914, 3 August 1914, Cook Papers, NAA: M3580, 6.

3 Cook, Pocket Diary for 1915, memoranda pages, Cook Papers, NAA: M3580, 7.

4   'Entry into Berlin', *Sydney Morning Herald*, 30 November 1914.
5   Lord Galway to Harcourt, 1 October 1914, TNA: CO 418/126. On receipt of this, a Colonial Office clerk minuted: 'I hope this comfortable rich man who grudges the labouring man's bicycles will practice some of the self-sacrifice which he unctuously preaches.'
6   'The Need for Guidance', editorial, *Morning Post*, 1 August 1914.
7   'Britain's Duty', editorial, *Spectator*, 1 August 1914.
8   Milner Diary, 4 August 1914, Milner Papers, Milner dep. 85. Emphasis in original.
9   Hardinge to Nicolson, 8 October 1914, Hardinge Papers, 93 Part II.
10 The 'Paris Resolutions', proclaimed by the inter-allied Economic Conference in Paris in June 1916, threatening a post-war economic boycott of German commerce, were the major product of the movement to protectionism stimulated by the war. See V. H. Rothwell, *British War Aims and Peace Diplomacy, 1914–1918* (Oxford, 1971), Ch. VII, 'Economic War Aims'.
11 Arthur Ponsonby, *Democracy and Diplomacy* (London, 1915), 42.
12 See 'The Declaration of the Allies', *The Times*, 8 September 1914.
13 Meaney, *Australia and World Crisis*, 59. Meaney records that Britain 'was not disposed to consult Australia about Japan's entry into the war and the role it might play in the war'.
14 Meaney, *Australia and World Crisis*, 44.
15 On the essential diplomatic background, see Jukka Nevakivi, *Britain, France and the Arab Middle East, 1914–1920* (London, 1969) and the various essays in Marian Kent, ed., *The Great Powers and the End of the Ottoman Empire* (London, 1996), especially Marian Kent, 'Great Britain and the End of the Ottoman Empire, 1900–23', 165–98.
16 On the escalation of the war, the development of the Entente's and the Central Powers' war aims, and the lost opportunities for a negotiated peace, see David Stevenson, *The First World War and International Politics* (Oxford, 1988), H. E. Goemans, *War and Punishment: the causes of war termination and the First World War* (Princeton, 2000), and the classic account by Kent Forster, *The Failures of Peace: the search for a negotiated peace during the First World War* (Washington, 1942).
17 Meaney, *Australia and World Crisis*, 247. Meaney records that Hughes 'had no part in making British policy' and that he 'had not been privy to the British Government's peace negotiations with enemies or Allies'.
18 Garton, *Cost of War*, 32, estimates that the death, injury and illnesses originating in the war affected 'nearly one-quarter of all Australian men aged from eighteen to forty-five years.'
19 On the escalation of British war aims, see Rothwell, *British War Aims and Peace Diplomacy*, Paul Guinn, *British Strategy and Politics, 1914 to 1918*

(Oxford, 1965), and J. S. Galbraith, 'British War Aims in World War I: a commentary on "Statesmanship"', *Journal of Imperial and Commonwealth History*, 13, 1 (1984), 25–45.

20 Henry Noel Brailsford, *The War of Steel and Gold: a study of the armed peace*, 3rd ed. (New York, 1918), 82.

21 Spurling, 'A strategy for the lower deck', in Stevens and Reeve, eds, *Southern Trident*, 268–69, 273–74. Spurling records that, when HMAS *Australia* departed Plymouth for Australia on 30 June 1913, 53% of the crew were on loan from the Royal Navy, and half the remainder were ex-Royal Navy, recruited in Britain. Only 25% had come from Australia.

22 See Article 16 in the final agreement, 'Memorandum of Conferences Between the British Admiralty and Representatives of the Dominion of Canada and the Commonwealth of Australia', July 1911, in *Papers Laid Before the Imperial Conference, 1911, Dealing with Naval and Military Defence* (Wellington, 1912).

23 Meaney, *Australia and World Crisis*, 32, and Bean, *Story of Anzac*, 36.

24 C. Coulthard-Clark, 'Major-General Sir William Bridges: Australia's first field commander', in Horner, ed., *The Commanders*, 17.

25 Point D (2), in Chapter I (A), 'Introductory Remarks and Strategic Considerations', in 'General Scheme of Defence', dated August 1913, 5, AWM113, MH 1/11.

26 In the cabinet on Wednesday 29 July McKenna took the lead in proposing a limited naval war as the most that Britain should contemplate. If 'German aggression on Belgium' was to be countered, argued McKenna, this could be done more effectively 'by our Fleet sealing up German ocean traffic'. A food crisis in Germany would follow, he predicted, for the impact of the blockade would be exacerbated by the fact that Germany's railways would be engulfed by troops. See Cabinet Memorandum, 29 July 1914, Harcourt Papers.

27 Churchill to Lloyd George, undated cabinet note, in R. S. Churchill, *Winston Churchill: companion volume*, II, 3, 1997.

28 See 'On the Brink', editorial, *Westminster Gazette*, 1 August 1914, and Grey to Bertie, 1 August 1914, *BD*, Vol. XI, Document 426, and Bertie to Grey, 3 August 1914, *BD*, Vol. XI, Document 566.

29 The wording of the pledge to France is reproduced in Grey to Bertie, 2 August 1914, *BD*, Vol. XI, Document 487.

30 Grey did his best to make the despatch of the BEF seem unlikely, alluding to Britain's 'enormous responsibilities' in guarding her Empire, and other 'unknown factors', all of which would have to be taken into account before any decision was made about 'sending an Expeditionary Force out of the country'. Grey's speech can be found in *Parliamentary Debates*, 5th series, Commons, Vol. 65, 1809–27 (3 August 1914).

31 Hankey, *Supreme Command*, I, 169–72, and Churchill, *World Crisis*, I, 191.

32 George Reid, 'Empire Trade', *The Times*, 7 October 1914. Reid incorporated this letter in his formal report, 'Fifth Annual Report of the High Commissioner of the Commonwealth in the United Kingdom (printed 21 July 1915)', dated 5 April 1915, in *Papers Presented to Parliament, Vol. V, Session 1914–17*, 247.

33 Henry Stead to Harcourt, 15 January 1915, MS Harcourt 467.

34 Norman Stone, *The Eastern Front, 1914–1917* (London, 1998), 40, Herwig, *Marne*, 61, and Richard F. Hamilton and Holger H. Herwig, eds, *War Planning 1914* (Cambridge, 2010), 34, 39, 147, 232, and 234.

Archival Material

The following archival institutions, personal papers, and manuscript collections have been utilised in this study. Full details of secondary material, books, and articles can be found in the endnotes.

In Australia

Australian War Memorial
AWM38, 3DRL 606/17/1: 'Official History, 1914–18 War: Records of C. E. W. Bean, Official Historian', Diary, Sepember–October 1915.
AWM113, MH 1/11: 'General Scheme of Defence' (1913).
AWM224, MSS636: 'Adoption of Precautionary Stage of the Australian Defence Scheme in 1914: by Maj-Gen Sir C B B White'.

National Archives of Australia
A463, 1957/1059: 'Report on the Defence of Australia by Field Marshal Viscount Kitchener 1910'.
A1632: Papers of Malcolm Lindsay Shepherd.
A5954, 1207/2: 'Defence Policy — Reports'.
A6006, 1914/8/3: 'Aid to Britain in Event of War'.
A6006, 1914/8/23: 'Origin of AIF (Australian Imperial Force)'.
A6006, 1914/11/18: 'Military Forces nearing Egypt to be landed there for training — Suggestion by Lord Kitchener'.

A6661, 1355: 'Defence Scheme for Australia' [1913–1914].

A11803, 1914/89/1, Part 1: 'War 1914. Notifications (Outbreak)'.

B168, 1902/2688: 'Major-Gen. Sir Edward Hutton's scheme for the reorganisation of the military forces' [1902–1905].

B173, 1906/58 PART 2: 'Personal Papers of Mr Millen, Minister of Defence'.

M3580: 'Personal Papers of Prime Minister Cook'.

MP84/1, 1849/1/2: 'Review of Proposal to revise (sic) [revive] National Regiments'.

MP84/1, 1855/1/4: 'Inspector-General's Investigation of progress of plans of organisation and concentration and defence schemes', 1912–13.

MP84/1, 1856/1/33: 'Conference on Mutual Assistance between Australia and New Zealand.' [18–20 November 1912].

MP826/1, 3(A): 'Cover 1: Commonwealth Defence Schemes'.

MP826/1, 3(B): 'Cover 2: Commonwealth Defence Schemes – proofs of "General Scheme of Defence"/1913.'

MP1049/1, 1914/0157: 'War Orders for H. M. A. Ships'.

MP1049/1, 1914/0299: 'Transfer of HMA Ships to Admiralty on outbreak of war'.

MP1049/1, 1915/054: 'Australian Naval Defence'.

MP1049/1, 1914/0276: 'Outbreak of War August 1914 — Placing of H. M. A. Ships at Disposal of Admiralty'.

National Library of Australia
Ronald Munro Ferguson (Lord Novar), Cyril Brudenell White

In the United Kingdom

Birmingham Central Library
Elizabeth Cadbury

Bodleian Library, Oxford
Herbert Henry Asquith, Margot Asquith, James Bryce, Geoffrey

Dawson, Lewis Harcourt, Francis Hirst, Alfred Milner, John Morley, John Simon

British Library
John Burns, John Alfred Spender

Cambridge University Library
Charles Hardinge (1st Baron Hardinge)

Churchill Archives Centre, Cambridge
Winston Churchill, Maurice Hankey, Reginald and Pamela McKenna

Fitzwilliam Museum, Cambridge
Wilfrid Scawen Blunt

Parliamentary Archive, House of Lords
David Lloyd George, Courtenay Ilbert, William Pringle, Herbert Samuel

Private family archive
William Lygon (7th Earl Beauchamp)

Robinson Library, Newcastle University
Charles Trevelyan, Walter Runciman

Somerset Archives Centre, Taunton
Aubrey Herbert

The National Archive, Kew
ADM 137/1: Escort of First Australasian Convoy, 31 July–30 September 1914
ADM 137/3: Escort of First Canadian Convoy, 2 August–15 October 1914
ADM 137/5: New Guinea and German Pacific Islands, 5 August–22 December 1914.

ADM 137/7: Australasia Telegrams, 27 July–29 September 1914.

CAB 38/17: Minutes and Papers of the Committee of Imperial Defence, January–May 1911

CAB 38/18: Minutes and Papers of the Committee of Imperial Defence, May-August 1911

CAB 38/23: Minutes and Papers of the Committee of Imperial Defence, January–February 1913

CAB 38/24: Minutes and Papers of the Committee of Imperial Defence, April–August 1913.

CAB 63/3: Notes, memoranda, etc. (some printed) prepared for the CID. War Cabinet and Cabinet Office: Lord Hankey: Papers. Magnum Opus files. [January–March 1915]

CO 418/123: Despatches. Governor-General's. 1 June–31 December 1914.

CO 418/124: Despatches. New South Wales, 1 January–31 October 1914.

CO 418/125: Despatches. New South Wales. 1 November–31 December 1914. Despatches. Queensland, 1914.

CO 418/126: Despatches. South Australia. Despatches. Tasmania. 1 January–15 April 1914.

CO 418/127: Despatches. Tasmania. Despatches. 16 April–31 December 1914. Victoria and Western Australia, 1914.

CO 418/128: Offices: Admiralty, Agents, Council, 1914.

CO 418/131: Offices: War, Miscellaneous, Miscellaneous Institutions; Individuals, 1914

CO 418/132: Despatches. Governor-General's. 1 January–31 May 1915.

CO 418/133: Despatches. Governor-General's. 1 June–15 October 1915.

Acknowledgements

My love and gratitude go especially to Julie Newton for her optimism, her inspiration, and for her close reading of the manuscript, more than once. I would like to thank my family for their constant encouragement: David Newton, Juliette Warren, Pamela Mary Newton, my mother, and Michael Newton, Mary Anne Anastasiadis, Robert Newton, Richard Newton, and especially my sister Pamela Newton for steering the project toward a publisher. For their willingness to read the whole manuscript and to offer perceptive suggestions I must thank warmly Greg Bateman, Greg Lockhart, Joy Melhuish, Roderick Miller, Andrew Moore, and Alan Roberts. The following deserve thanks also for advice and constructive criticism: Frank Bongiorno, Brian Brennan, Belinda Browne, Peter Butt, Daryl Le Cornu, Peter Henderson, Bruce Hunt, Robert Lee, John Mordike, Thomas Reifer, Bruce Scates, Ken Stewart, and Dimity Torbett. For making very valuable recommendations for changes, I would like to thank sincerely Craig Wilcox and one anonymous referee, who were the initial readers at Scribe. Of course, none of the above necessarily endorse the interpretation presented here, and all the blemishes in the work are mine.

I would also like to thank sincerely the following individuals and institutions for making it possible for me to access personal papers, and for granting me permission to quote from personal papers over which they hold copyright: Robert Bell (Geoffrey Dawson); Allen Packwood at the Churchill Archives Centre (Maurice Hankey);

Christopher Arnander (Reginald and Pamela McKenna); the Bonham Carter Trustees (Herbert Henry Asquith and Margot Asquith); Christopher Osborn (for the unpublished diaries of Margot Asquith); the Parliamentary Archives (Lloyd George, Herbert Samuel, Bonar Law); Charles Simon (Viscount Simon); the Warden and Scholars of New College Oxford (Viscount Milner); the Somerset Heritage Service (Aubrey Herbert); Mr E. B. Le Couteur and Mrs A. M. Carroll (Charles Edwin Bean); Mark Derham (Cyril Brudenell White); and Ronald Munro Ferguson (Ronald Munro Ferguson, Lord Novar).

I am grateful to Helen Langley, Curator of Modern Political Papers at the Bodleian Library, for granting permission to quote from the unpublished diary of Lewis Harcourt, 1st Viscount Harcourt, on behalf of William Gascoigne, the owner of the Harcourt copyright. Quotations from the diary of Wilfrid Blunt are made by permission of the Syndics of the Fitzwilliam Museum. Quotations from the papers of Charles Hardinge, 1st Baron Hardinge, are reproduced by permission of the Syndics of Cambridge University Library. Quotations from the papers of Charles Trevelyan and Walter Runciman are reproduced by permission of the Librarian, Robinson Library, Newcastle University. Quotations from Sir Winston Churchill's papers are reproduced with permission of Curtis Brown, London, on behalf of the Estate of Sir Winston Churchill. © Copyright, Winston S. Churchill. Quotations from the papers of the Seventh Earl Beauchamp are reproduced by permission of the copyright owners.

I have made every effort to contact copyright owners for the quotations from private papers contained within this book. Some of my enquiries have not been answered or have been returned from old addresses. If I have inadvertently infringed the copyright of any person I do apologise sincerely.

For permission to reproduce material that has previously appeared in an extended version in several chapters in my book *The Darkest Days: the truth behind Britain's rush to war, 1914*, I would like to thank Verso.

Finally, for his faith in the project at the outset, for perceptive suggestions at every point, and for his sharp eyes in the editing process, I would like to thank warmly Henry Rosenbloom at Scribe.

Index